PARIS – CAPITAL OF IRISH CULTURE

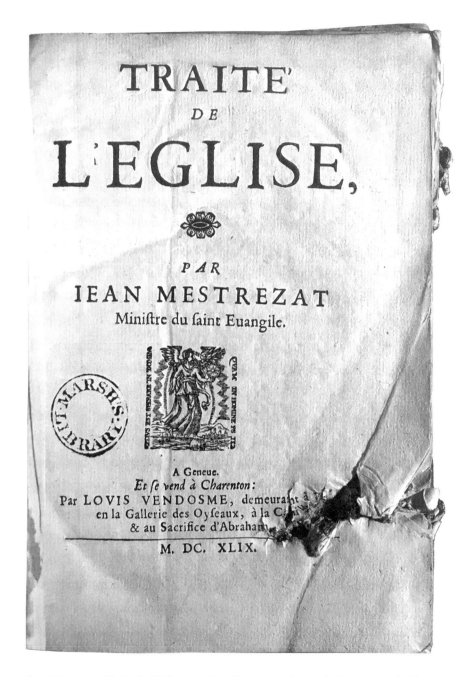

TRAITE'
DE
L'EGLISE,

PAR

IEAN MESTREZAT
Miniſtre du ſaint Euangile.

A Geneue.
Et ſe vend à Charenton:
Par LOVIS VENDOSME, demeurant à
en la Gallerie des Oyſeaux, à la C
& au Sacrifice d'Abraham.

M. DC. XLIX.

Jean Mestrezat, *Traité de l'Eglise, par Jean Mestrezat, ministre du Saint Evangile* (Geneva, 1649). Mestrezat (1592–1657), a celebrated Reformed preacher and polemicist, born in Geneva, was pastor at Charenton and died in Paris. This book, in the collection of Marsh's Library, took a stray bullet in 1916 (Marsh's Library, Dublin).

Paris – Capital of Irish Culture

France, Ireland and the Republic,
1798–1916

Pierre Joannon & Kevin Whelan

EDITORS

FOUR COURTS PRESS

Typeset in 10.5 pt on 12.5 pt EhrhardtPro by
Carrigboy Typesetting Services for
FOUR COURTS PRESS LTD
7 Malpas Street, Dublin 8, Ireland
www.fourcourtspress.ie
and in North America for
FOUR COURTS PRESS
c/o ISBS, 920 NE 58th Avenue, Suite 300, Portland, OR 97213.

A catalogue record for this title is available
from the British Library.

ISBN 978-1-84682-651-1

303.4884

SPECIAL ACKNOWLEDGMENTS

Printed in England
by CPI Antony Rowe, Chippenham, Wilts.

Contents

Acknowledgments

The genesis of this book was a set of paired conferences organised to explore Franco-Irish links, and their long-term influence on the 1916 Rising. These conferences were held at the Irish Cultural Centre in Paris on 16–17 September 2016 and in the University of Notre Dame Global Gateway in Dublin on 14–16 October 2016.

The editors gratefully acknowledge the support and assistance of the Irish Embassy in France and the French Embassy in Ireland, and the abiding commitment of the two Ambassadors, HE Mrs Geraldine Byrne Nason and HE Mr Jean-Pierre Thébault. We are especially grateful to HE Mrs Geraldine Byrne Nason, who generously hosted a reception for the conference delegates at the Embassy, Avenue Foch. The editors also wish to thank Sir Michael Smurfit and the Jefferson & Michael Smurfit Monegasque Foundation for their generous help. Other sponsors included the University of Notre Dame Gateway in Dublin and the Irish Cultural Centre in Paris.

As well as our distinguished contributors, we are very grateful to our chairs and panellists at these conferences: Lara Marlowe (France correspondent for the *Irish Times*), Wesley Hutchinson (Professor of Irish Studies at the Université Sorbonne Nouvelle-Paris 3), Joseph Cleary (Professor of English at Yale University), Joe Mulholland (former Managing Director, RTÉ Television), Thomas O'Connor (Professor of History, Maynooth University), Michael O'Dea (President, Royal Hibernian Academy) and Adrian O'Neill (Second Secretary General, Department of Foreign Affairs).

We are grateful to Bríona Nic Dhiarmada (Thomas J. & Kathleen O'Donnell Chair of Irish Language and Literature at the University of Notre Dame) for introducing and screening her multiple award-winning documentary *1916: The Irish Rebellion* in both Paris and Dublin.

The first drafts of the translations from French were created by Garrett Moran, Sylvie Kleinman and Mary Pierse.

For help with various queries, the editors are most grateful to Jack Rooney, Christopher J. Wood, Seamus Deane, Tim O'Neill and and Sinéad Mac Aodha (Director of the Irish Cultural Centre in Paris). For assistance with illustrations, the editors are indebted to Anne Brady (Vermillion Design), Matthew Stout (cartography), Rolf Loeber, Anthony J. Mourek, Adrian Frazier, Jason McElligott (Marsh's Library), Laura Conlon, Danielle Meersman and Eimear Clowry Delaney. We thank Sammie Leslie and Yvonne Kelly for authorisation to publish the photograph of Shane Leslie, courtesy of Castle Leslie Archives.

The Four Courts Press produced our book with their characteristic professionalism and ease of manners.

Introduction

PIERRE JOANNON & KEVIN WHELAN

Seamus Heaney stressed the Irish ability to live in two places at one time, and in two times at one place – to be both in Manulla and in Manhattan, in Portumna and in Paris.[1] A history of Ireland that is written only about the little island itself is too narrow. Irish culture is at once enduringly small-scale and intimate, but unusually porous and unbounded. One out of every two people born on the island since 1840 has emigrated. The Irish sense of identity needs to accommodate this porosity and dispersal. Embracing our diasporic dimension is accordingly an ethical responsibility. Ireland needs to keep open vital arteries of contact and communication, nourishing a living relationship between people of Irish descent worldwide, and transmitting into practical action the palpable but occasionally dormant affections between us.

FRANCE AND IRELAND

As early as 1322, the Irishman Simon Fitzsimons could describe Paris as 'the home and nursery of theological and philosophical knowledge, the mother of the other liberal arts, the mistress of justice, the standard of morals, and in short the mirror and lamp of all moral and theological virtues'.[2] After the Reformation split Europe into a Protestant north and a Catholic south, Paris was the most powerful and largest Catholic city in Northern Europe, matched in prestige only by Rome itself. And Paris enjoyed equal prestige as a stop on the Grand Tour, and the *arbiter elegentiae* on fashion, cuisine and architecture. In 1779, the citizens of Dublin were regaled with an eighteen-foot square model of Paris displayed in the Dublin Exhibition Rooms on South William Street.[3] In the 1780s, Arthur O'Leary encountered a performing bear at Boulogne-sur-Mer, that could mark time, count with his paw on the sand and bow gracefully. The bear grew sulky at being poked with a pole by its owner and growled out: 't'anam ón Diabhal, táim cráite go deo leis an buc seo'. The bear turned out to be a monoglot Irish speaker from Dungarvan, shipwrecked while sailing to Bilbao with dried cod. A Frenchman had subsequently sewed him up in a bearskin and

---

1 Seamus Heaney, lecture to International Fund for Ireland, 1992.   2 Colmán Ó Clabaigh, *The friars in Ireland, 1124–1540* (Dublin, 2012), p. 260.   3 *Dublin Evening Post*, 23 October 1779.

made him perform. O'Leary called the mayor, the skin was ripped and out clambered the naked Decies man![4]

In 1817, a poem called *Quadrillery* was published in Dublin, on the new craze of dancing the French quadrille. The outraged author asked whether France was to be conquered on land and sea and then be allowed to win on the ballroom floor? Were Irishmen to lose their jigs to the French reels?[5]

In the late nineteenth century, Irish nationalists drew on the Irish heritage in the French armies to act as an inspiration for the current generation. Michael Cusack, founder of the Gaelic Athletic Association, noted in 1887:

> Ireland in future times, as it has so often been in the past, may be the arena of deadly struggles. Let us hope, if such an emergency arises, that Irish manhood will display the courage which their kinsmen did at Fontenoy and Fredericksburgh, and their ancestors at the glorious triumph of Oulart.[6]

Dublin became festooned with Fontenoy GAA clubs, and Fontenoy Streets, and Fontenoy poems and tunes – notably the well-known 'An ghaoth aniar aneas'. In Irish folklore, the ghosts of the Wild Geese slain at Fontenoy came back on the south-west wind (an ghaoth aniar aduaidh): their cries (conceived as the cries of the seabirds) haunt the coast of Clare, and the tune evokes the sounds carried on the wind. This motif inspired Emily Lawless' poem sequence.[7] Paintings of Fontenoy still adorn Versailles palace. In 1903, a hurling game (Tipperary versus Cork) was played at Brussels to commemorate the Battle of Fontenoy. Cork had an easy victory – allegedly because some of the Tipperary players went missing in Brussels in the red-light district![8] When Margaret Mitchell wrote *Gone with the wind* (1936), Tara Hall was first called Fontenoy Hall.

Seán Ó Faoláin launched his modernising crusade in his new journal *The Bell*, established in 1940. *The Bell* was named after and modelled on its precursor, edited by Alexander Herzen for the Russian expatriates in Paris. The name was Ó Faoláin's way of suggesting that Irish intellectuals were internally exiled in their own country.

PARIS AND IRISH ACCESS TO EUROPE

Writing about Paris in 1878, the fastidious Henry James described it as 'the most brilliant city in the world'.[9] The Fenian Eugene Davis recorded the resonance of France for Irish patriots:

4 Davis, *Souvenirs of Irish footprints*, pp 90–1.   5 *Quadrillery* (Dublin, 1817).   6 *Celtic Times*, 19 Feb. 1887.   7 'War-dogs, hungry and grey/Gnawing a naked bone,/Fighters in every clime. Every cause but our own … The wept-for, the theme of songs./The exiled, the injured, the banned./The men of a thousand wrongs'. See the sequence of poems 'Clare Coast 1710', 'After Aughrim', 'Fontenoy 1745' in Emily Lawless, *With the Wild Geese* (London, 1902). 8 Séamas Ó Neill entry, *Beathfhaisnéis*.   9 James, *Art of travel*, p. 216.

I do not envy the Irishman who can step for the first time on France's soil without feeling his heart throb faster or without finding himself carried back in fancy to a past that speaks so eloquently on his countrymen's prowess.[10]

William Butler Yeats once observed that Ireland could only be 'freed from provincialism by an exacting criticism, a European pose'.[11] It was at Parisian theatres – Théâtre de la Gaîté and Antoine's Théâtre Libre (which staged European plays from Ibsen, Strindberg, Hauptmann and Bjørnson), watching productions of *Axel* and *Ubu Roi* – that Yeats incubated the idea of the Abbey Theatre.[12] Among the many Irish writers who resided in Paris were George Moore, Oscar Wilde, J.M. Synge, James Joyce and Samuel Beckett. They were followed by more contemporary figures – Denis Devlin, Brendan Behan, John Montague, Derek Mahon and John McGahern. It was while encountering the 'powerful, shattered sculpture' of the Celto-Ligurian sites of Roquepertuse and Entremont in 1965 that Louis Le Brocquy gained the inspiration for his magnificent obsession with the Celtic heads – 'the outer reality of the invisible interior world of consciousness'.[13]

FRANCE/PARIS NOT IRELAND

While it is easy to be seduced by the glamour, the glitter and the gloire of France and Paris, we need to keep in mind that it was a relief for many Irish exiles to escape the island – a ravaged land of emotional restraint hiding behind its dreary drapery of church and state. The Parisian shimmer on the horizon was all the more luminous because of the gloomy realities of Irish life. Starving and lonely in Paris in 1920, Arthur Power was still vehement that he 'would sooner die of loneliness and poverty in Paris than parade around the [Waterford] countryside to tea parties and horse-jumping shows'.[14] Growing up in Ireland, John Banville had a sense amid the stercorine and banossic realities of Irish life that 'life was always elsewhere'.[15] Michel Déon has noted 'the slow poison of its sluggishness'.[16] The incomprehending Bogside parents in Seamus Deane's *Reading in the dark* round on their intelligent son: 'French! What do you want to be bothered with French for? Sure who speaks French round here? Waste of time. Fit you better to be studying Irish, your own language'.[17]

10 Davis, *Souvenirs of Irish footprints*, p. 76.   11 Yeats, *Autobiographies*, pp 101–2.
12 Michael McAteer, *Yeats and European drama* (Cambridge, 2010).   13 Louis Le Brocquy, 'The human head: notes on painting and awareness', *Études Irlandaises* (Dec. 1979), pp 149–62.   14 Arthur Power, *From the old Waterford house* (Waterford, 1940). In Paris, he could discuss Irish literature with a bookseller in the Place de l'Odéon 'who knew far more about it than the majority of Irish people did'.   15 Banville, *Time pieces*, p. 57.   16 Michel Déon, *Cavalier, Passe ton chemin!* (Paris, 2005).   17 Seamus Deane, *Reading in the dark* (London,

'THE OLD HAUNTS'

There are so many ways – sometimes venomously complicated ways – of being Irish. A common one is to want to have nothing more to do with it. Home is where the hurt is. Edna O'Brien's aphorism is 'Many and terrible are the roads to home'. Derek Mahon, 'raised in a northern land of rain and murk',[18] noted in his *Paris Review* interview that 'For a large part of my life I've been *terrified* of home'.[19] For him 'Paris flamed on the defining dark' and he headed off from Trinity College to study at the Sorbonne in 1965–6.[20] Samuel Beckett's last visit to Dublin from 18 to 23 March 1968 was 'to see the whole clan' at a family funeral at Redford, outside Greystones. Staying at the La Touche Hotel in Greystones, he recalled 'the old lovely familiar through the mist. Saw the beaten silver last night' [the moonlit sheen of the Irish Sea]. But he fought to resist it: 'The sea and [Wicklow] mountains were looking marvellous. I was glad to get back here [Paris], out of their clutches'. It was 'good to get away from them'.[21] And because 'Wicklow was more beautiful than ever', I understood even better than before the need to stay, the need to return and was glad to get out'.[22] And yet Beckett never forgot Ireland. 'I sometimes go over the old Irish haunts in my mind'; insomniac, he would replay in his mind the holes of Carrickmines golf course.[23]

CONCLUSION

This volume offers an overview of the complex and shifting relationships between France and Ireland, and between Paris and Dublin, over the long nineteenth century – from the French Revolution to the 1916 Rising. It also offers a combination of different perspectives, ranging from history to politics to literature to language. The contributors come from Ireland, France and America, and they offer a fascinating set of varied perspectives on these relationships. The 'Postscript' suggests how understanding this complex history can provide relevant insights into our current situation.

1996), pp 117–80.   **18** 'Death and the sun' in Derek Mahon, *Antarctica* (Oldcastle, 1985), pp 35–7. The poem is a homage to Albert Camus. Terence Brown, 'Home and away: Derek Mahon's France' in B. Hayley & C. Murray (eds), *Ireland and France – a bountiful friendship* (Gerrards Cross, 1992), pp 144–51.   **19** 'Derek Mahon: the art of poetry Number 82. Interviewed by Eamonn Grennan', *Paris Review*, 154 (Spring 2000), pp 156–68.   **20** 'A tolerable wisdom' in Derek Mahon, *Lives* (London, 1972).   **21** See the correspondence in *The letters of Samuel Beckett, volume 4, 1966–1989*, ed. G. Craig, M. Dow Fehsenfeld, D. Gunn & L. Overbeck (Cambridge, 2016), pp 119–23.   **22** Beckett, *Letters*, iv, p. 123.   **23** The 'old haunts' is a phrase that Beckett uses frequently.

Paris: the promised land?

INTRODUCTION

Paris, that mythical beacon of freedom, culture and modernity, has never ceased to attract the Irish. For these exiles, who did not always consider themselves to be refugees, the City of Light appeared as a Promised Land where it was possible to regain their liberty – religious liberty for clergy and laity who had been persecuted for adherence to their ancient faith; political liberty for patriots whose dream was a sovereign Irish nation; or artistic freedom for those who sought liberation from insular constraints. For Irish exiles from 1700 to 1916, Paris shimmered as a beacon of liberty – religious, political and artistic – to attract the Irish.

 In seeking to understand what this privileged destination meant to Irish people, a good guide is Shane Leslie (1885–1972).[1] Half-American, as was his cousin Winston Churchill (their mothers were the famous New York Jerome sisters), this whimsical Anglo-Irish man was a product of Eton and Cambridge. Aged 23, he distanced himself from his peers as he discovered within himself an all-consuming passion for the Irish language and culture, Catholicism and Irish nationalism. He renounced his ancestral rights, changed his first name to Shane from John, and often appeared dressed in a saffron kilt, like the Irish clan leaders of former times. He supported himself by writing books, giving classes in French literature, and by undertaking unlikely diplomatic tasks. He served on the management board of St Enda's, the school founded by Patrick Pearse. Leslie viewed 1916 with mixed feelings: he felt the Rising lacked any legal basis but he considered it justified on moral grounds. This advocate of compromise still regretted not having taken any part in it.

 It was in Paris between 1903 and 1905, during the presidency of Emile Loubet and under the influence of the Belle Otero (Galician-born dancer, actress and courtesan) and Cléo de Mérode (a glamorous French dancer), that his Irish identity was revealed to Shane Leslie. In *Doomsland*, an autobiographical *bildungsroman*, published in 1923, his hero discovered this capital city where everyone spoke to him about his native island:

> He wandered about Paris in the tracks of Irish exiles. Paris cemeteries were full of Irish graves, her archives were choked with Irish plots and documents. The Irish swarmed in French history. In old Colleges and

1 Otto Rauchbauer, *Shane Leslie, sublime failure* (Dublin, 2009).

behind crumbling walls, priests, soldiers, and secret agents had conspired. Through eighteenth-century Paris passed the Wild Geese of the Irish Brigade. In Notre Dame knelt the victors of Fontenoy. From the Irish College priests passed to and fro between the two countries. It was an Irish *abbé* who remembered the right words to cry to Louis XVI at his execution, and an Irish physician accompanied Napoleon to St Helena. Here Wolfe Tone met the First Consul. Here Humbert and Hoche received orders for their invasions of Ireland. And the gorgeous sunset behind the mighty Arc de Triomphe goldenised the ashes of the anonymous myriads of Irish dead.[2]

Alongside the dead there were the living. In a restaurant on the Boulevard Montparnasse, frequented by Poles and anarchists, Leslie's *alter ego* was welcomed by a strange set of 'Irish Bohemians, living in one country and thinking in another. They were exiles from the old country who had never been exiled, poets still dreaming publication and patriots meditating execution'.[3] In their midst, an old poor, emaciated man with nicotine-stained fingers, tightly bundled in an overcoat buttoned up to his chin, cast a bleak eye over the gathering. 'The last of the Invincibles' was whispered to the new arrival, as they pointed out the sole accomplice who had escaped the gallows after the savage assassination of Cavendish (chief secretary for Ireland), and Burke (the permanent under-secretary) in Dublin's Phoenix Park on 6 May 1882. The young man intuited that Irish history could originate or terminate in this metropolis, at once strange and familiar.

Paris also offered the young Leslie attendance at a course given by the distinguished Celtic scholar Marie-Henri d'Arbois de Jubainville (1827–1910), who gave him sage advice, books and manuscripts. Swelling with wonder, the student discovered the works of this 'band of Celtic scholars working in all lands to recover this mysterious tongue'.

> John O'Donovan and Eugene O'Curry in Dublin, Whitley Stokes in Calcutta, Standish Hayes O'Grady in London became fixed lanterns shining through the dark haze of Celtic studies. Irish epic, Irish literature, Irish law, Irish poetry came upon him with successive rush. It was like entering a secret kingdom or acquiring magical powers, or learning cabalistic signs.[4]

Paris conjured up in him the ancient Irish language, d'Arbois de Jubainville, and the Táin Bó Cuailnge which he aspired to translate.[5] Paris also instilled the determination to endow Ireland with a literature as sparkling as that of the French capital:

2 Shane Leslie, *Doomsland* (London, 1923), p. 246.   3 Leslie, *Doomsland*, p. 135.   4 Leslie, *Doomsland*, p. 108.   5 Leslie, *Doomsland*, p. 198.

1.1 Shane Leslie (1885–1971). His official name was Sir John Randolph Leslie, 3rd Baronet, but he assumed the name Shane Leslie, and became a well-known writer and diplomat (Castle Leslie Archives, Glaslough, County Monaghan).

Once out of Ireland, the Irish background becomes discernible, and Irish figures surged on the canvas of his uncoloured mind. True – there was an awkward difference between imagining and writing. Every French book he read set him imagining an Irish parallel [...] Richard read Zola in long exhausting stages, and visioned an Irish Zola writing the natural history of an Anglo-Irish family of Rougon Macquarts or Roger Macquaids during the nineteenth century. What a theme! And perhaps Zola's *Trois Villes* could be matched by novels written about three Irish cities. There was Dublin and Cork and Belfast, all good titles as yet unused. What a trilogy![6]

Paris also opened his eyes to the exotic glamour of smells and bells Catholicism, and Ireland's age-old links to it. A priest with whom he became friendly showed him how much Irish history was intertwined with Catholicism:

France as the eldest daughter of the Church raised Irish Colleges throughout her demesne, and how in return Irish soldiers by the thousand and ten thousand had served in the Irish Brigade, fighting for a Louis or a Napoleon

6 Leslie, *Doomsland*, pp 106–7.

instead of the King's shilling. The whole Napoleonic era, from the Revolution down to its anti-cyclone at Sedan, had only resulted in leaving an Irish MacMahon at the head of France. There was thought in that.[7]

The priest convinced the young man that Catholicism was the national religion of Ireland: 'Irishry had soaked into his soul's recess'.[8] Intoxicated by Catholic liturgy, Leslie taught himself the catechism in French, bought rosary beads and plunged into the writings of Bossuet, Massillon and Pascal. He was most convinced by the reactionary mystics, the novelist, convert, dandy and decadent Jules-Amédée Barbey d'Aurevilly (1808–89), Joris-Karl Huysmans (1848–1907), whose 1890s trilogy track the spiritual progress of Durtal from atheism to Catholicism, and Léon Bloy (1846–1917), an angry millenarian and anti-materialist ('In Paris you have the Sainte Chapelle and the Louvre, true enough, but we in Chicago kill eighty thousand hogs a day'), another Catholic convert from atheism. At odds with the family religion, Leslie converted to Catholicism, wrote devotional books, made friends with theologians and bishops, and came to be viewed in London and Dublin as principally a Catholic *littérateur*.

Doomsland's title indicated that Leslie anticipated that condemnation would be his fate.[9] The novel tracks and registers the influence brought to bear by Paris on successive waves of Irish people who sought religious liberty and political freedom there, and with it access to artistic and literary modernity. The city of light shone all the more brightly against the tawdry grey of post-Famine Dublin.

THE IRISH COLLEGE

Heir to a tradition that dates back to 1578, the Irish College in Paris symbolises the Irish refusal to abandon Catholicism under the combined pressures of political persecution and the institutionalised discrimination of the Penal Laws. In 1677, Louis XIV conferred the College des Lombards in rue des Carmes on the Irish and this soon became the meeting and rallying point, the place of worship and the intellectual centre for the Irish who had sought refuge in the French capital. Less than a century later, it was necessary to seek more spacious premises to cope with the flood of Irish seminarians and students. This new building, called the Irish College, was situated near the Pantheon in rue du Cheval Vert. Although primarily a religious institution, the Irish College also assisted in training doctors, army officers, bankers, clerks and teachers. The college assured the preservation of precious manuscripts and a subsidy from Philippe Perrotin in 1736 promoted the teaching of the Irish language –

---

7 Leslie, *Doomsland*, pp 216–17.   8 Leslie, *Doomsland*, p. 243.   9 Rauchbauer, *Shane Leslie, sublime failure*, p. 173.

considered as an essential qualification for priests returning to the Irish mission. The college sent home a steady stream of missionary priests and provided more than fifty bishops for the Irish church. In 1734, half of the twenty-four Irish bishops had been trained in Paris. Brendan Devlin summed up the situation before the Revolution: 'Paris was the cultural capital of the Irish nation. From Dublin, there came only laws and dread'.[10]

The Anglo-Irish historian William Lecky paid a gracious tribute to these churchmen:

> They grew up at a time when Catholicism throughout Europe was unusually temperate, and they brought with them a foreign culture and a foreign grace, which did much to embellish Irish life. Their earlier prejudices were corrected and mitigated by foreign travel. They had sometimes mixed with a society far more cultivated than an Irish Protestant country clergyman was likely to meet, and they came to their ministry at a mature age, and with a real and varied knowledge of the world.[11]

The anti-clerical French Revolution, together with the progressive dismantling of the Penal Laws, prompted the establishment of a Catholic seminary at Maynooth in 1795, as Irish Catholicism and the British state faced a common foe in republican and secularising France.

The revolutionary troubles deluged Paris in suspicion, arrests, executions, property seizures and mob rule, and spelled disaster for the Irish Colleges throughout France. Most students and seminarians fled to Ireland. The College des Lombards closed permanently. In the rue du Cheval Vert (renamed rue des Irlandais on 6 February 1807), the Irish College never recovered its former glory. However it limped along with a handful of Irish and French students, among whom were Napoleon's youngest brother, Jérôme Bonaparte, the future king of Westphalia, and his stepson, Eugène de Beauharnais. A Consular decree of 1802 reopened the Irish College in 1805 under the supervision of a Bureau of Superintendence or *Fondation*, subject to the authority of the Ministère des Cultes (later Ministère de l'Education et des Cultes). Under this system of management, the college in the rue des Irlandais has weathered many vicissitudes: the Franco-Prussian War of 1870 during which it was converted into a hospital for three hundred wounded French soldiers; the Commune of 1871 which sought in vain to occupy the premises; the threat of suppression following the 1905 Law of Separation of Church and State; and the outbreak of the First World War in 1914, when the college was closed for the duration of the conflict.

10 Translated from a quotation in Tomás Ó Fiaich, *The Irish Colleges in France* (Dublin, 1990), p. 26.   11 W.E.H. Lecky, *A history of Ireland in the eighteenth century* (London, 1913), iii, pp 354–5.

TONE AND THE UNITED IRISHMEN

Following the seizure of the Bastille on 14 July 1789 and the subsequent French Revolution, several waves of Irish people were attracted to Paris by the hope of seeing their country following France into the ranks of the sovereign republican nations. In autumn 1791, the Society of United Irishmen encouraged Irish men to form societies 'for the promotion of constitutional knowledge, the abolition of bigotry in religion and politics, and the equal distribution of the rights of man through all sects and denominations of Irishmen'.[12] Enlightenment philosophy, liberalism, and particularly the glowing French ideals of liberty, equality and fraternity are clearly evident in that declaration.

As the United Irishmen evolved rapidly from being reformist into an explicitly revolutionary movement, they resolved to seek military aid from France. On 18 November 1792, one hundred individuals, the cream of the anglophone community, met for dinner at White's Hotel near the Palais Egalité (formerly the Palais Royal). They toasted the French victories at Jemmapes and Valmy, and paid homage to the rights of man and to 'universal peace, founded on universal liberty'.[13] An address to the National Convention was passed and the republican banquet concluded with the *Marseillaise*. Twenty Irishmen were among the most enthusiastic participants: foremost was the young Lord Edward FitzGerald, son of the duke of Leinster, who renounced his title to be called 'Citoyen Edouard Fitzgerald'; there too were the brothers John and Henry Sheares, Generals Arthur Dillon and Thomas Ward of the old Irish Brigade, and several defrocked priests and seminarians from the Irish College. They would regroup, in company with hundreds of their fellow countrymen, at every stage of the revolutionary process. The French and the United Irishmen were becoming 'partners in revolution'.[14]

During these turbulent years, the most influential Irish figure in Paris was Theobald Wolfe Tone, a founder of the Society of the United Irishmen, the inspiration behind the Franco-Irish military alliance, and the ambassador incognito for the republican movement in France.[15] On his arrival in Paris on 12 February 1796, he moved into the Hotel des Etrangers in the rue Vivienne, behind the Palais Egalité. In early 1797, he moved to No. 7 on Petite rue St Roch Poissonnière in Montmartre, but fled when his amorous landlady made too flagrant advances. He moved to the Hotel des Etats-Unis in the rue de Tournon, not far from the Luxembourg palace.

---

12 Quoted by Marianne Elliott in *Wolfe Tone*, 2nd ed. (Liverpool, 2012), pp 133–4.
13 Matthieu Ferradou, '"Un festin patriotique" at White's Hotel, 18 November 1792: the "secret" origins of Irish revolutionary republicanism', *History Ireland*, 24:3 (2016), pp 26–9.
14 Marianne Elliott, *Partners in revolution: the United Irishmen and France* (London, 1989).
15 Sylvie Kleinman, 'Ambassador incognito and accidental tourist: cultural perspectives on Theobald Wolfe Tone's mission to France 1796–8', *Journal of Irish and Scottish Studies*, 2:1 (2008), pp 101–22.

Tone left a sparkling account of Parisian life under the Directory and an exact report of his ambitious mission. He besieged ministers, wrote memoirs, networked furiously, forced his way to the Directors, pleaded Ireland's cause before army chiefs, talked with Bonaparte. Treated as a minister plenipotentiary, he found that idea amusing:

> When a government was formed in Ireland it would be time enough to talk of embassies, and then if my country thought me worthy, I should be the happiest and proudest man living to accept the office of ambassador from Ireland [...] I should like very well to be the first Irish ambassador, and if I succeed in my present business, I think I will have some claim to the office. 'O, Paris is a fine town and a very charming city'. If Ireland were independent I could spend three years here with my family, especially my dearest love, very happily.[16]

Contrary to expectations, Tone's mission proved a striking success. His tact, his passion and his powers of persuasion swept away countervailing arguments. The French approved a plan for a landing in Ireland and entrusted responsibility for it to General Lazare Hoche, among the most capable and popular officers in the army. What followed is well-known: the fiasco of Bantry, the premature triggering of the rebellion, the failure of the expedition led by General Humbert, the defeat of the French fleet off Donegal, the arrest and suicide of Tone.

Parisian Irishmen paid an onerous tribute to the revolutionary Moloch: General Theobald Dillon was assassinated by his soldiers in 1792; his brother, General Arthur Dillon, was guillotined two years later; Lord Edward FitzGerald died on 4 June 1798 from wounds he received while being arrested; the Sheares brothers were hanged on 14 July; in November, Tone slit his throat in a prison protest to avoid besmirching the honour of the French army by being forced to mount the gallows in its uniform. Robert Emmet, who had also tramped Paris appealing for fresh French help, was hung and decapitated on 20 September 1803.

Reeling from a deluge of blood, the United Irishmen leadership once more sought refuge in France. They were assigned to the Irish Legion formed on 30 August 1803 by the First Consul – the only foreign unit in the French army to which Napoleon granted an eagle standard. This unit, which proved notably fractious, was dissolved by King Louis XVIII on 28 September 1815.

Under the restoration of the monarchy and the reign of Louis Philippe, the Irish in Paris maintained a low profile. Survivors of the Rebellion and of the Napoleonic wars, they lived from hand to mouth, caballed in cafés, or perhaps like Miles Byrne, wrote their memoirs. Byrne was a survivor both of the 1798 Rising and the Napoleonic campaigns. The third volume of his *Mémoires d'un*

16 T.W. Moody, R.B. McDowell & C.J. Woods (eds), *The writings of Theobald Wolfe Tone, 1763–1798* (Oxford, 2001), ii, pp 59–60.

1.2 This 1848 book on Daniel O'Connell was written by Joséphine-Marie-Anne Maillot, grandmother of Charles de Gaulle. It was one of the earliest books to be read by de Gaulle. His biographer claimed that he 'would always remember this inspiring example of resistance to religious and national persecution' (David Schoenbrun, *Les trois vies de Charles de Gaulle* (Paris, 1965), p. 41). When de Gaulle visited O'Connell's house in Derrynane in 1969, he amazed his entourage with his detailed knowledge of O'Connell's life, as recalled by Admiral Flohic, his aide-de-camp (Collection Pierre Joannon).

exilé irlandais de 1798 contains more than 200 pages of 'biographical sketches of the principal exiles and Irish patriots' that he encountered in Paris.[17]

O'CONNELL AND FRANCE

France now turned its gaze towards Ireland. The success of the democratic mass movement created by Daniel O'Connell to wrest religious freedom for his co-religionists from England stirred the younger generation of French Catholics

17 Miles Byrne, *Mémoires d'un exilé irlandais de 1798* (Paris, 1864), ii, pp 151–378.

who intended to move the hitherto rigidly conservative church in the direction of liberalism. In July 1830, the first issue of *L'Avenir* appeared, a journal that became the focal point for this first manifestation of Christian democracy. One article 'Lettre sur le Catholicisme en Irlande' attracted admiring attention. It was composed by a twenty-year old aristocrat, Count de Montalembert, who had made a recent pilgrimage to Derrynane to meet the Liberator. When the dying Irish orator, en route to Rome, stopped in Paris, a delegation led by Montalembert rushed to his bedside to convey to him the fervent admiration of young Catholic liberals:

> I have come to present to you the men who in France have enrolled themselves as the first soldiers under a banner that you were the first to unfurl and that will never disappear. We are all your children or, rather, your pupils. You are our master, our model, our glorious preceptor.[18]

O'Connell's last known public utterance was his short reply delivered in his excellent French to these lavish compliments.[19]

Balzac, in *Les lettres à l'Etrangère*, compared O'Connell to Napoleon. The ultramontanist Louis Veuillot regarded him as his leader. When the Liberator died, Henri Lacordaire, the celebrated Dominican preacher, delivered his funeral eulogy at Notre Dame de Paris on 10 February 1848. Numerous books were published about the Irish leader. One, *Le libérateur de l'Irlande ou vie de Daniel O'Connell*, published in Lille in 1848, issued from the pen of Joséphine-Marie-Anne Maillot, paternal grandmother of General Charles de Gaulle, founder of the Free French and of the Fifth Republic. Did de Gaulle find inspiration in her rousing glorification of that extraordinary man? Later abandoned by his beloved France, it was on the beach at Derrynane that he sought solace.[20]

YOUNG IRELAND AND THE TRICOLOUR

The rising in Paris that overthrew Louis Philippe and proclaimed the Second French Republic revived the hopes of Young Ireland, a literary and then political movement that had emerged under the tutelage of O'Connell before breaking from him. The Irish Confederation (the most advanced faction of Young Ireland) congratulated the French people and appointed a delegation to the provisional government of the Second Republic in Paris. The delegates were

18 Pierre Joannon, 'A romantic hibernophile: Charles de Montalembert, the O'Connell of France' in *Les romantismes Irlandais/Currents in Irish romanticism* (Lille, 1991), pp 75–87. 19 Denis Gwynn, *Daniel O'Connell* (Cork, 1947), p. 250. 20 Joséphine-Marie-Anne Maillot, *Le libérateur de l'Irlande ou vie de Daniel O'Connell* (Lille, 1848).

William Smith O'Brien, Thomas Francis Meagher, Martin McDermott, Eugene O'Reilly, Richard O'Gorman and Edward Hollywood, a silk worker from the Liberties who was identified as the counterpart of 'l'ouvrier Albert' (Alexandre Martin, nicknamed 'Albert the Worker', the French socialist statesman of the French Second Republic).

The Young Ireland delegation returned empty-handed. The plenipotentiaries claimed to have brought back from revolutionary Paris a banner designed like the French tricolour. On 15 April 1848, at the Music Hall in Dublin, Meagher received an ovation when he presented 'a splendid flag surmounted by the Irish pike'. 'The material was of the richest French silk, which was most gorgeously trimmed and embroidered; the colours were orange, white and green'. Meagher spoke:

> From Paris, the gay and gallant city of the tricolour and the barricades, this flag has been proudly borne. I present it to my native land, and I trust that the old country will not refuse this symbol of a new life from one of her youngest children. I need not explain its meaning. The quick and passionate intellect of the generation now springing into arms will catch it at a glance. The white in the centre signifies a lasting truce between the 'Orange' and the 'Green' and I trust that beneath its folds the hands of the Irish Protestant and the Irish Catholic may be clasped in generous and heroic brotherhood.[21]

Meagher was vague about the provenance of his banner. The only known flag waved by the Irish in Paris in spring 1848 was the time-honoured green flag stamped with the golden harp. The tricolour is never mentioned and the provenance of this flag, which had a fine future ahead of it, remains mysterious.

THE FENIANS IN PARIS

The Young Irelanders convinced themselves that the Famine sufferings demanded a new rising. On 29 July 1848, their efforts ended in ignominious defeat. The leaders were arrested, sentenced and deported. Some escaped to America or France. Once again, Paris became the refuge for fugitive Irish revolutionaries and conspirators. The most determined, James Stephens and John O'Mahony, lived in hovels and had a hard time until matters settled somewhat for them. Stephens gave English classes to the sons of noble families in Faubourg St Germain, translated Dickens into French, and published in the *Moniteur Universel*. O'Mahony gave Irish classes to students at the Irish College

---

21 Michael Cavanagh (ed.), *Memoirs of Gen. Thomas Francis Meagher comprising the leading events of his career* (Worcester, MA, 1892), pp 163–4.

and survived on remittances from his sister in Ireland. In their free time, the two men frequented the back rooms of Paris cafés where *carbonari*, Blanquists, avant-garde republicans and revolutionary socialists brooded and plotted. From those contacts, they learned the methods that continental subversive associations used to recruit, organise and compartmentalise their divisions.

In December 1853, O'Mahony arrived in New York, determined to apply his French lessons. After seven years in Paris, Stephens returned to Ireland in 1856. In 1858, acting in concert, Stephens founded the Irish Republican Brotherhood in Dublin while O'Mahony set up the Fenian Brotherhood in New York.[22] The Fenian dream had solidified in the Latin Quarter of Paris amid pipe smoke and absinthe. Another survivor of 1848 was also pacing the streets of Paris. John Mitchel had been sentenced for 'treason and felony' due to his unabashed advocacy of violence in his newspaper *The United Irishman*. Deported, he escaped, wrote his searing *Jail Journal*, settled in Knoxville, Tennessee, and championed the South in the Civil War. He never forgot Ireland and retained his interest in Paris, the traditional incubator for Irish revolutionaries, drawn there by the prospect of possible conflict between France and England. Believing that an outbreak was imminent, Mitchel settled in Paris in August 1860 with his wife and children.

In summer 1862, Mitchel felt it preferable to return to America and support the Confederate side in the fratricidal war. An obdurate supporter of the southern cause, he saw two of his sons die, and a third lose an arm, serving under the Confederate flag. The Northern victory exposed Mitchel to reprisals. To assist him and to capitalise on his popularity, the Fenians appointed him as their financial agent in Paris. Although distrustful of secret societies, the veteran of 1848 accepted the well-paid post as a way to resume his campaigning for Irish liberty. O'Mahony revealed the names of Paris banks that held the Irish funds, the secret ways to transfer substantial subventions to the IRB, and the codes for secure correspondence with Stephens. Mitchel was also encouraged to take advantage of any political openings: 'Your diplomatic relations with the French Government, or any other public or private parties on the European continent that may be found useful to the Fenian movement, are left to your own judgement and discretion'.[23]

On 23 November 1865, Mitchel moved into rue Richer, near rue du Faubourg Poissonnière. The rent there proved too expensive so he moved to the Pension Bonnerie at 26 rue Lacépède, where Stephens had taken up residence a fortnight previously. Scrupulously carrying out the financial side of his mission but lacking political impact, Mitchel led an austere existence: in 1866, he confided 'I am as lonely as Robinson Crusoe in this great city'.[24] This was light years away

22 Desmond Ryan, *The Fenian chief: a biography of James Stephens* (Dublin, 1967), p. 45.
23 William Dillon, *Life of John Mitchel* (London, 1888), ii, p. 230.   24 Dillon, *Life of John Mitchel*, ii, p. 235.

from the feverish and lively excitement that Tone first experienced in Paris under the Directory. Mitchel informed his wife: 'I have been a martyr now for eighteen years, and it is quite a bad trade. I had rather be a farmer'.[25] He was assailed by doubt when the Fenian Brotherhood split into rancorous factions in the United States, and he detested Irish-American bombast. Mitchel questioned the motivation of the secretive and manipulative Stephens, whose lightning visit to Paris in March 1866 did not reassure him.

On 22 June, he resigned his Fenian post. At the Irish College, and contrary to his expectations, he received a rousing ovation from the professors and students who lined up to give him a guard of honour. This warm reception from Irish young people – not even born in 1848 – restored hope to the battle-weary revolutionary.[26] In October 1866, Mitchel left Paris forever: 'I looked back until the last blue lines of the French coast faded into the evening mist. Perhaps it is the last time I shall ever see that fair and pleasant land. Yet who knows? […] Anyhow, *Vive la France*'.[27] Those last three words kept cropping up in his writing right through the 1870 war between France and Prussia: 'Everybody is taking part in the grand struggle. We take part instantly, frankly and zealously for France'.[28] He judged Napoleon III harshly, vehemently asserting that the dying Empire was not France and that the legacy of the Revolution was embodied in France, and in the two great fundamental liberties of the people's right to self-determination and equality before the law. 'Since that is what is at stake', declared Mitchel in 1871, 'all our friends will unite with us in sending over words of cheer, and say with all their hearts, as we do, *Vive la France*'.[29]

PARNELL AND O'LEARY

During the Second Empire, as Paris became the playground of the cosmopolitan rich, wealthy Americans took up residence in Paris. Charles Tudor Stewart, maternal uncle of Parnell, rented a luxurious apartment at 122 Avenue des Champs Elysées, sufficiently spacious to receive all his impecunious Irish relatives. Of his sister Delia's eleven offspring, ten stayed regularly in the French capital, then the biggest marriage market in Europe. In April 1870, the American uncle pointed out to his nephew, 25-year-old Charles Stewart Parnell, heir to Avondale in County Wicklow, that the running costs of his indebted estate exceeded any possible future revenue and that he should pursue a rich transatlantic heiress to restore its prestige and guarantee his income. At a party in his Parisian home, he introduced Parnell to Mary Woods, only daughter of a

25 Dillon, *Life of John Mitchel*, ii, p. 237.   26 Patrick Pearse viewed Mitchel as one of 'the four evangelists of Irish nationalism'. Patrick Pearse, *Political writings and speeches* (Dublin, 1952), p. 91.   27 Dillon, *Life of John Mitchel*, ii, pp 250–1.   28 *Irish Citizen*, 23 July 1870. 29 *Irish Citizen*, 7 Jan. 1871.

moneyed family in Newport, Rhode Island. A romance began in Paris, continued in Rome but abruptly ended in Newport when the young woman dismissed Parnell as a nonentity: 'I could never bring myself to marry you, an obscure Irishman who has no higher ambition than to run an estate. When I marry I want a brilliant and famous man, whom I can respect as well as love'. She married an obscure lawyer in Boston.[30]

Shortly after the Commune, another exiled Irish republican came to Paris. John O'Leary, a veteran of 1848 and editor of the paper the *Irish People*, was arrested in 1865, and sentenced to twenty years hard labour (commuted to fifteen years in exile). The forty-year-old, banned from his native land, was no stranger to Paris where he had studied for a short time in 1855. Like Stephens and Mitchel, he then lived in rue Lacépède in the very house that was used by Balzac as a model for the Pension Vauquer where Old Goriot lived.[31] He shared this modest accommodation with four young people with bright futures: the American artist James Whistler, the English poet Algernon Swinburne, the English artist John Edward Poynter and the cartoonist and writer George du Maurier, grandfather of the novelist Daphne du Maurier. O'Leary made friends with all the Irish in Paris, especially John Patrick Leonard, the *de facto* Irish ambassador, a man who ardently publicised the ills of Ireland, and helped his compatriots in need. A journalist and an English literature teacher, Leonard associated with the veteran United Irishmen, the survivors of 1798; he greeted O'Connell on his Paris visit in 1847; he guided the Young Ireland delegation in 1848; he helped the Fenians to find their feet in clandestine Paris. O'Leary called him 'my most intimate friend, and my most constant companion'.[32]

O'Leary's verdict on Stephens, the Fenian leader, was harsh: he found him arrogant, dogmatic and contemptuous. Yet some years later, that did not prevent him from helping Stephens to escape the Parisian poverty in which he languished. After six months in the United States, O'Leary returned to Paris in 1872 and stayed there for the next thirteen years, living in the Hôtel Corneille, a stone's throw from Théâtre de l'Odéon. Unlike the famously book-shy Parnell, he was a voracious reader who scoured the stalls of the booksellers on the quays of the Seine. He could be seen at Café de la Paix, at the Bouillon Duval, or at the Café Voltaire, alone, accompanied by the loyal Leonard, or with IRB emissaries from New York or Dublin. He wrote for the Irish-American press, and despatched impassioned letters to the Irish daily papers. Those letters reflected a haughty Fenianism, fiercely hostile to parliamentarism, to agrarian agitation and to the futility of the 'dynamite party'. O'Leary's intransigent nationalism

---

30 Pat Power, 'The Parnells and Paris' in P. Travers & D. McCartney (eds), *Parnell reconsidered* (Dublin, 2013), pp 76–91. **31** John O'Leary, *Recollections of Fenians and Fenianism* (London, 1896), p. 60. **32** John O'Leary, *Recollections of Fenians and Fenianism* (London, 1896), p. 64; Janick Julienne, *Un Irlandais à Paris. John Patrick Leonard, au cœur des relations franco-irlandaises, 1848–1889* (Oxford & Berne, 2016).

was less concerned with practical action than with moral influence. He was more a literary than a political figure and that explains why he was so popular with writers of the Irish Literary Revival when he returned to Ireland in 1885. Yeats immortalised O'Leary in 'September 1913', in which every verse ends with the refrain: 'Romantic Ireland's dead and gone/ It's with O'Leary in the grave'.

Charles Stewart Parnell reconnected with Paris in the 1880s. Since the lease on the Champs Elysées apartment terminated on the death of his uncle, he stayed in the Hotel Brighton at 218, rue de Rivoli. His new scheme was to shelter from the English authorities the American money used to finance the Land League's agitation and the Irish Home Rule campaign. Two bank accounts were opened: 'Paris Fund Account 1', intended to finance agrarian agitation, for boycotting intransigent landlords, and for helping those evicted from their holdings; and 'Paris Fund Account 2' (the 'Special Fund'), intended to pay the salaries and expenses of penurious deputies, at a time when MPs were unsalaried. One in four Home Rule members depended on the Paris 'Special Fund' for a respectable annual income of between £200 and £300. Management of those two accounts was devolved on Patrick Egan (1841–1919), one of three treasurers of the Land League, and a veteran Fenian devoted to Parnell.

A complex system of double signatures allowed Parnell, in Paris, to orchestrate key elements of the Land War and the Home Rule campaign. Although sometimes challenged by disgruntled activists, the Irish war chest functioned smoothly until the funds evaporated soon after the death of Parnell in October 1891.

MAUD GONNE

During the last decade of the century, Paris, always susceptible to glamorous exotic women, fell under the sway of a strikingly regal young woman, who made a sensational entrance into the life of William Butler Yeats on 30 January 1889:

> She seemed a classical impersonation of the Spring, the Virgilian commendation 'She walks like a goddess' made for her alone. Her complexion was luminous, like that of apple-blossom through which the light falls, and I remember her standing that first day by a great heap of such blossoms in the window. In the next few years I saw her always when she passed to and fro between Dublin and Paris, surrounded, no matter how rapid her journey and how brief her stay at either end of it, by cages full of birds, canaries, finches of all kinds, dogs, a parrot, and once a full grown hawk from Donegal.[33]

33 William Butler Yeats, *Autobiographies* (London, 1995), p. 123.

Maud Gonne, this vernal apparition who lit an unquenchable flame in the poet's heart, was the daughter of an English colonel who had converted to Irish nationalism. Passionate, generous and reckless, this cosmopolitan bohemian aspired to be the Irish Joan of Arc; in Dublin, she would incarnate the Caitlín Ní Uallacháin of ancient legends. Gonne spent long periods in Paris between the end of the 1880s and 1917. She changed address several times, always within the fashionable areas: Avenue de Wagram, Avenue de la Grande Armée, Avenue d'Eylau, rue de Passy and finally rue de l'Annonciation. She fell into the amorous arms of Lucien Millevoye (1850–1918), a flamboyant Boulangist member of the French parliament with whom she sought an even more ambitious alliance: he would help her to free Ireland; she would support his efforts to regain Alsace and Lorraine. Millevoye and Gonne had two children: a daughter Iseult, and a son Georges Silvère, who died aged one year from meningitis, to the heart-rending grief of his mother. In Paris, Gonne moved in journalistic circles, worked (unsuccessfully) to galvanise the staidly conservative Association de la Saint Patrice, and recruited French sympathisers for the Irish cause.

In 1897, she founded the Irish Association and launched *L'Irlande Libre*, a paper whose head office at 6 rue des Martyrs harmonised with its revolutionary outlook. Yeats, James Connolly, Michael Davitt, Millevoye, the poet François Coppée (1842–1908), and many others, both French and Irish nationalists, wrote for her journal. Whether in Paris or in Dublin, Gonne was at the forefront of demonstrations against eviction; she campaigned for political prisoners; she helped organise the 1798 centenary commemoration; she marched against the Boer War; she belittled Victoria during the queen's visit to Ireland (conferring on her the stinging nickname 'the Famine Queen'), and she was President of *Inghinidhe na hÉireann* (Daughters of Ireland). Millevoye, her estranged lover and ally, doubly betrayed her: he took a mistress, and with perverse timing privileged his germanophobia over her anglophobia, at the very moment when the French government pivoted to the Entente Cordiale to retain the upper hand over Germany.

Gonne herself plunged headlong into a disastrous political/romantic entanglement: at the Church of Saint-Honoré-d'Eylau on 21 February 1903, she married Major John MacBride, former commander of the Irish Brigade fighting for the Boer republics (and later executed as a leader of the 1916 Rising). The Joan of Arc of Ireland and the hero of Southern Africa soon produced a son, Seán MacBride, who never fully shed his French accent acquired in his Parisian childhood, and who became chief of staff of the IRA in the 1930s, minister for external affairs of the Republic of Ireland in 1948, and (as co-founder of Amnesty International) Nobel Peace Prize winner in 1974. His parents, two years after their disturbing marriage, separated acrimoniously after sordid divorce proceedings.

Through her glorification of war, her sanctification of martyrdom, her self-presentation as the personification of Ireland, her anglophobia and her desire for military action, Maud Gonne embodied the 1916 spirit, and a link between the barricades of Paris and Dublin's General Post Office. After the Easter Rising, she wrote to Yeats:

> I am overwhelmed by the tragedy and the greatness of the sacrifice our countrymen and women have made. They have raised the Irish cause again to a position of tragic dignity. They will have made it impossible to ignore Ireland or to say that she is satisfied at the conference where at the end of the war, much will be heard about the right of small nationalities [...] Practically, and politically I do not think their heroic sacrifice has been in vain.[34]

SINN FÉIN DIPLOMACY IN PARIS

The secessionist deputies, members of Dáil Éireann elected in December 1918, shared her views. Once elected, they despatched a delegation to Paris with the double task of getting Ireland admitted to the negotiating table, and of seeking international recognition for the Irish Republic. Led by Seán T. O'Kelly, later joined by George Gavan Duffy, and supported by a small but capable team that included Joseph Walshe, Seán Murphy and Michael MacWhite, the Sinn Féin delegation moved into the Grand Hotel in rue Scribe, just beside the Opéra Garnier. For the Irish, it was essential that they be there. George Gavan Duffy made that clear:

> Paris is still the political capital of Europe; it is the most important international meeting ground; there is there no censorship and comparative liberty of speech and growing hostility to England and a genuine traditional sympathy for Ireland.[35]

The Sinn Féiners were quickly disillusioned: Clémenceau and Wilson had no intention of alienating the English, and Ireland was the least of their concerns. Even on the propaganda front, the Dáil deputies experienced tremendous difficulty in getting their case heard. Success came in another way. Confronting the harsh reality of international powers in Paris, the Irish, neophytes in this sphere, eventually succeeded in building up from scratch a diplomatic service that was worthy of the name. Every member of that Paris delegation went on to a brilliant career. O'Kelly was twice President of Ireland: Gavan Duffy was

34 A. MacBride White & A. Norman Jeffares (eds), *The Gonne–Yeats letters, 1893–1938* (London, 1992), pp 372–3; Anne Magny, 'Maud Gonne: réalité et mythe' (Thèse pour le Doctorat, Université de Caen, 1992); Adrian Frazier, *The adulterous muse. Maud Gonne, Lucien Millevoye and W.B. Yeats* (Dublin, 2016).   35 R. Fanning, M. Kennedy, D. Keogh & E. O'Halpin (eds), *Documents on Irish foreign policy, volume I, 1919–1922* (Dublin, 1998), p. 85.

minister for external Affairs; Walshe was secretary general of the Department of External Affairs from 1923 until 1946; Kearney was Irish ambassador to Spain between 1935 and 1946; Murphy was Irish ambassador to France from 1938 to 1950. Between 1919 and 1922, Paris was a nursery for Irish diplomacy.

GEORGE MOORE

The artistic and literary influence of Paris drew both painters and writers from Ireland, especially those who felt artistically suffocated in their native island. George Moore wrote in *Confessions of a young man*:

> France! The word rang in my ears and gleamed in my eyes. France! All my senses sprang from sleep like a crew when the man on the look-out cries 'Land ahead!' Instantly I knew I should, that I must, go to France, that I would live there, that I would become as a Frenchman.[36]

He was just twenty-one when he arrived at the Hotel Voltaire, where Richard Wagner had recently written the libretto of *The master singers of Nuremberg*. Aspiring to be a painter, Moore enrolled at the Beaux Arts. More than anything, he ached to blend into his adopted country:

> Two dominant notes in my character – an original hatred of my native country, and a brutal loathing of the religion I was brought up in […] With Frenchmen I am conscious of a sense of nearness […] when I am with them, I am alive with a keen and penetrating sense of nearness.[37]

This was especially so in the cafés frequented by art students and the literati. Moore became a regular at the Rat Mort and at La Nouvelle Athènes, on the Place Pigalle, the fashionable meeting places for impressionist painters and writers. He befriended Manet, Degas, Jacques-Emile Blanche and Pissarro, and quickly realised that his real gift was for literature not for painting. He knew the poet Mallarmé, the novelist Alphonse Daudet, the writer Edmond de Goncourt, the poet Catulle Mendès, the historian Daniel Halévy and, most notably, Emile Zola, whom Moore acknowledged as his model (that admission predated Moore's repudiation of naturalism). 'I did not go to Oxford or Cambridge, I went to the café Nouvelle Athènes'.[38]

Moore recreated himself by appropriating Parisian ideals, customs and thought: 'French wit was in my brain, French sentiment was in my heart'.[39] In 1906, Moore reflected:

36 George Moore, *Confessions of a young man* (New York, 1901), p. 6.   37 Moore, *Confessions of a young man*, p. 55.   38 Adrian Frazier, *George Moore, 1852–1933* (London, 2000), p. 162.
39 Moore, *Confessions of a young man*, p. 125.

I cannot look upon this city without emotion; it has been all my life to me.
I came here in my youth, I relinquished myself to Paris, never extending
once my adventure beyond Bas Meudon, Ville d'Avray, Fontainebleau –
and Paris has made me. How much of my mind do I owe to Paris? And by
thus acquiring a fatherland more ideal than the one birth had arrogantly
imposed, because deliberately chosen, I have doubled my span of life. Do
I not exist in two countries. Have I not furnished myself with two sets of
thoughts and sensations?[40]

WILDE, YEATS AND SYNGE

Paris was also the last refuge of Oscar Wilde whose lonely death aged 46
occurred in the Hotel d'Alsace, rue des Beaux Arts, on 30 November 1900,
followed by burial in the cemetery of Père-Lachaise. He visited the capital from
January to May of 1883, staying at the Hotel Voltaire, where his fur coat and
turquoise-inlaid ivory cane caused a stir. He was received by Victor Hugo and
exchanged words with Verlaine at the Procope. Wilde associated with the cream
of Parisian artistic and cultural life of the period, rubbing shoulders with Degas,
Pissarro, Sarah Bernhardt, the critic and novelist Paul Bourget, Edmond de
Goncourt, Jacques-Emile Blanche, the politically minded novelist Maurice
Barrès, and many others. Wilde viewed the French language as the most
appropriate one for achieving stylistic perfection. The symbolist poet Henri de
Régnier (1864–1936) praised him on that score: 'Wilde is a very good writer in
French; he is only slightly less at ease than in English'.[41] Wilde first wrote his
play *Salomé* in French in 1890–1 and it was in French that Sarah Bernhardt
intended to play the title role in London. When the English censor banned it,
Wilde threatened to seek French nationality. At the peak of his fame, Wilde was
as popular in Paris as in London and he was a frequent visitor between 1884 and
1891. The avant-garde art critic, novelist and venomous pamphleteer Octave
Mirbeau (1848–1917) considered inviting him onto the board of the new
Académie Goncourt but abandoned that idea following his scandalous trial.

   When Yeats first set foot in Paris in 1894, the city seemed to him to be
simultaneously a centre for the occult, a refuge for banished Irish nationalists,
the home of his muse Maud Gonne, and the capital of symbolist literature and
experimental theatre.[42] As a guest of the celebrated Paul Verlaine, he was treated
to coffee and cigarettes and reflections on the fin-de-siècle poet's world-
weariness, trapped in Paris 'like a fly in a pot of marmalade'.[43] He accompanied

---

40 George Moore, *Memoirs of my dead life* (London, 1906), p. 45.   41 Quoted by Jacques de
Ricaumont, 'Oscar Wilde, écrivain français' in *La Nouvelle Revue des Deux Mondes* (October
1975), p. 55.   42 R.F. Foster, *W.B. Yeats, a life. I: the apprentice mage* (Oxford, 1997), p. 138.
43 Yeats, *Autobiographies*, p. 341.

Gonne to the first night of *Axël* by Villiers de l'Isle Adam at the Théâtre de la Gaîté, and its Rosicrucian symbolism, heightened prose and allegorical personification swept him away through the play's five-and-a-half hours.[44]

In autumn 1896, Yeats was back in Paris at the Hotel Corneille where his attention was drawn to a gloomy and penniless Irishman in the garret – John Millington Synge. He was devouring the works of Ronsard, Villon and Rabelais while composing mediocre melancholy poetry. Yeats rebuked him: 'I urged him to go to the Aran Islands and find a life that had never been expressed in literature, instead of a life where all had been expressed'.[45] A year later, Synge acted on that advice: on Aran, he developed his theatrical genius and honed his evocative language. Yeats also attended the tumultuous 1896 premiere of Alfred Jarry's *Ubu Roi* at the Théâtre de l'Oeuvre in rue Ballu. Despite its mocking of everything that he revered, the admirably open-minded Irish poet still acclaimed the play and its author.

Yeats was in Paris in June 1908 at the Hotel Gavarni on rue Gavarni in the sixteenth *arrondissement*, just a few metres from Maud Gonne on the rue de Passy. In December 1908, in an encounter that still attracts prurient attention, Gonne and Yeats may or may not finally have consummated their relationship: Gonne's ability to inspire Yeats' poetry is a much more durable achievement. After one of his many stays in Paris, Yeats experienced a feeling of renewed fulfilment:

> After Stéphane Mallarmé, after Paul Verlaine, after Gustave Moreau, after Puvis de Chavannes, after our own verse, after all our subtle colour and nervous rhythm, after the faint mixed tints of Conder, what more is possible? After us, the Savage God.[46]

JOYCE

Like Moore, Joyce fled Dublin with its religious, political and intellectual turpitude, which he rejected with every fibre of his being. In early December 1902, he moved into the Hotel Corneille, as had some of the famous names in Irish literature. As a destitute and sickly medical student, he soon had to abandon his medical studies and survived by giving English lessons. He

---

44 *Axël* represented the epitome of symbolist drama for Yeats. 'Count Villiers de l'Isle-Adam swept together words behind which glimmered a spiritual and passionate mood, as the flame glimmers behind the dusky blue and red glass in an Eastern lamp'. W.B. Yeats, 'The Autumn of the body' in W. Gould & D. Toomey (eds), *The collected works of W.B. Yeats, volume IV: early essays* (London, 2005), p. 139. Paralleling his own metaphysical studies (oscillating between occultism and Catholicism), these positions were examined and rejected by his characters before the dramatic dénouement – the discovery of the highest ideal.   45 Yeats, *Autobiographies*, p. 343.   46 Yeats, *Autobiographies*, p. 349.

frequented theatres and brothels and lamented the meagre French appetite for poetry. Penniless, he returned to Dublin within a month but returned on 23 January 1903. In April, a telegram about the impending death of his mother guiltily brought him back to Dublin. Late in 1904, Joyce and Nora Barnacle, his partner and eventual wife, finally abandoned Dublin, living the rest of their life together in Paris, then Trieste and finally Zurich. When Ezra Pound dangled before Joyce the tantalising prospect of a French translation for *Portrait of the artist as a young man* and possibly *Dubliners*, they returned to Paris on 8 July 1920. Their intention was to stay only a few days, but those days stretched to twenty years. Paris, a flourishing centre for modernist experimentation, gave Joyce the stimulation to write *Finnegans wake*, the greatest experimental novel of them all.

Those two French decades were the most fruitful of his life. *Ulysses* was published in English in 1922 by Sylvia Beach of Shakespeare & Co., at 12 rue de l'Odeon, and then in French in 1929 by Adrienne Monnier, who ran La Maison des Amis du Livre on the same street. Valery Larbaud, who supervised the translation of Joyce's work, was unequivocal:

> Amongst his peers, his name is as well-known and his work is as much discussed as would be the names and theories of Freud and Einstein among the scientists. For some, he is the greatest of living writers in the English language.[47]

That opinion was endorsed by Paul Valéry, Edmond Jaloux, Louis Gillet (author of *Stèle pour James Joyce* in 1941), Léon-Paul Fargue, Jean Paulhan and many others.

Paris launched Joyce's reputation. On meeting George Moore, Joyce agreed that 'Paris has played an equal part in our lives'.[48] His Parisian experience strongly influenced maturation in the directions taken by his work, a development that Joyce himself defined: 'Hibernicise Europe and Europeanise Ireland'.[49] In *Exiles*, he had put words into the mouth of a character: 'If Ireland is to become a new Ireland she must first become European [...] Some day we shall have to choose between England and Europe'.[50]

47 Valery Larbaud, *Ce vice impuni la lecture. Domaine anglais*, in *Œuvres complètes de Valery Larbaud* (Paris, 1951), iii, p. 316. 48 Frazier, *George Moore*, p. 456. 49 Quoted by Richard Kearney, 'L'identité irlandaise ancienne et moderne' in G.F. Dumont (ed.), *Les racines de l'identité européenne* (Paris, 1999), p. 192. 50 James Joyce, *Exiles* (London, 2006), p. 30.

Paris: capital of Irish culture

KEVIN WHELAN

THE CATHOLIC DIASPORA

A significant Irish diaspora emerged from the post-Reformation crisis in late sixteenth and early seventeenth-century Ireland.[1] At this time, European states initiated systematic expulsion as a deliberate policy, detonating a cascade of expulsions across Europe and rendering the religious refugee a mass phenomenon. Between 1609 and 1614, 300,000 Muslims were forced out of Iberia, 150,000 Huguenots out of France after 1685, 20,000 Protestants fled Salzburg in 1731–2 (the last large-scale religious expulsion in pre-modern Europe), while the British forcibly relocated at least 11,000 French Catholic settlers from Acadie after 1755.[2] The word refugee first appeared in both English and French in 1685 – the year of the Revocation of the Edict of Nantes. The Irish Catholic diaspora in continental Europe, especially France and Spain, consisted of three principal components – priests, merchants and soldiers. Networks, flows and brokerage deposited nodes of students, clerics, soldiers and merchants, as well as the cultural circuits that nurtured them, along the Atlantic Catholic littoral.

Paris absorbed a ragged colony of indigent Irish, displaced in the brutal turmoil of the Elizabethan wars in Ireland, who settled on the Île de la Cité. By 1605–7, these displaced, ill-nourished Irish were becoming a public nuisance to the host French, who feared that they carried the plague. Up to two thousand Irish men, women and children lived in filthy conditions around the Pont Neuf (especially on the Place Dauphine). Pierre De l'Estoile regarded the ragged and lousy Irish under Saint-Honoré bridge as the very epitome of poverty, 'people expert in begging and excelling in the supreme science of this profession, which consists in doing nothing and living under the sign of the old man Peto d'Orléans [father of a celebrated Jesuit]: what is more, they are light-fingered, good at making children and from their ranks Paris has been overrun'.[3]

---

1 These preliminary remarks summarise material covered in detail in Kevin Whelan, 'A nation in waiting? The Irish in France in the eighteenth century' in J. Conroy (ed.), *Franco-Irish connections: essays, memoirs and poems in honour of Pierre Joannon* (Dublin, 2009), pp 304–20. 2 Nicholas Terpstra, *Religious refugees in the early modern world. An alternative history of the Reformation* (Cambridge, 2015). 3 Mary Ann Lyons, '"Vagabonds", "mendiants", "gueux": French reaction to Irish immigration in the early seventeenth century', *French History*, 14:4 (2000), pp 363–82: Éamon Ó Ciosáin, 'Hundred years of Irish migration to France, 1590–1688' in T. O'Connor (ed.), *The Irish in Europe, 1580–1815* (Dublin, 2001), pp 93–106.

PRIESTS AND THE IRISH COLLEGES

Catholic Europe offered an alternative for a displaced intellectual elite expelled from the exclusively Protestant educational world of post-Reformation Ireland – 'Ormuzd abroad, to compensate for Ahriman at home' (the good and evil spirits in Zorastrianism).[4] The Irish were drawn to the Counter-Reformation powerhouses of the new learning, notably Paris, Louvain, Douai, Prague and Salamanca.

A network of Irish Colleges provided access to the leading Catholic universities across Europe from the late sixteenth century until the French Revolution. Twelve were run by the already multi-national religious orders, plugging them into an existing institutional network. The Irish orders negotiated free admission for Irish clerical students to French universities – 'gratis cum titulo paupertatis' (free by reason of poverty) – in the eighteenth century. These were the 'spectra Hibernorum turmatin invadere portas' ('the hordes of Irish spectres bursting through the doors') of Paris.[5] They endured severe hardships to get there. In 1662, Fr James Cusack arrived in Paris bone-tired: most of his journey had been on foot.[6] Tyrone man Charles O'Donnell travelled from Strabane to Paris from 8 July to 26 July 1777. His route was from Strabane to Augher, then Castleblayney, Drogheda and Dublin, then by ship to Liverpool, by coach to Coventry, London, Canterbury and Dover, by ship to Calais and finally by coach to Paris.[7] The Irish proved to be no shrinking violets once they arrived in Paris: they gained a reputation for combative loquacity, appearing in that role in Alain-René Lesage's *Gil Blas* (1715–35) and Montesquieu dryly noted their 'undoubted talent for disputation'.[8]

While the principal purpose of the Irish Colleges was to cater for Irish priests prohibited from being educated at home, they also hosted well-connected lay Catholics preparing for the professions, notably law and medicine. Paris, the largest Catholic city in northern Europe, exerted a powerful influence on Irish culture, as marooned eighteenth-century Irish Catholics gazed longingly south to Catholic Europe. Paris proved a magnet from the closing years of the seventeenth century until the final quarter of the eighteenth, and many Irishmen

---

4 John Cornelius O'Callaghan, *History of the Irish brigades in the service of France: from the revolution in Great Britain and Ireland under James II to the revolution in France under Louis XVI* (Glasgow & London, 1870), p. vii.   **5** Cited in John Silke, 'The Irish abroad, 1534–1691' in T.W. Moody, F.X. Martin & W.E. Vaughan (eds), *A new history of Ireland*; iii, *Early modern Ireland, 1534–1691* (Cambridge, 1976), p. 605.   **6** Benignus Millett, 'Catalogue of Irish material in vols 370 and 371 of the *Scritture riferite originali nelle congregazioni generali* in Propaganda Archives', *Collectanea Hibernica*, 27/28 (1985–6), p. 76.   **7** Diarmaid Ó Doibhlin, 'Penal days' in H. Jefferies & C. Devlin (eds), *History of the diocese of Derry from earliest times* (Dublin, 2000), p. 176. O'Donnell, a future bishop of Derry, carried with him 15 linen shirts, nine pairs of stockings, eight stocks, six pairs of ruffled sleeves, two flannel waistoats, two pocket handkerchiefs, two Irish [language?] hymn books, one French grammar, and one pair of breeches.   **8** Montesquieu, *Lettres persanes*, ed. P. Verniere (Paris, 1969), p. 79.

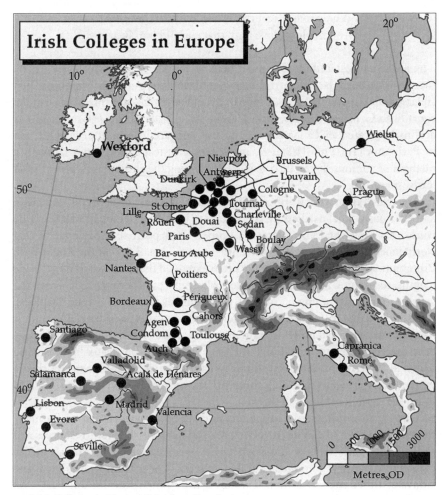

Irish Colleges in Europe

2.1 Irish Colleges in Europe (Matthew Stout).

lived there in this period. Participation in continental universities opened Irish Catholicism to fresh thinking. Unlike their Anglican counterparts, closeted in the inward-looking and intellectually undistinguished environment of Trinity College, these returning multi-lingual priests brought with them a contrastingly excellent university education.

In 1729, a Dublin-based priest Daniel Dowdall died. Dowdall, originally from Athlumney in Meath, had been educated in Paris, Venice and Rome: his funeral elegy praised his cosmopolitanism:

> who went to study not to rant,
> And learn'd to speak their languages, not cant,

Who's rich discourse, ravish'd his hearer's ear,
And made all love him, that e'er did him hear.[9]

The finest, earliest and most popular book in French by an Irish author was by the Roscrea-born Jacobite Anthony Hamilton (1646–1720). Hamilton fled Ireland with the doomed Stuart monarchy and spent his later life in exile at the court of St Germain-en-Lay. His *Mémoires de la vie du Comte de Grammont* was originally pirated in Cologne in 1713, but appeared in an approved edition in Paris in 1721. The *Mémoires*, in elegant classical French, ran through a plethora of editions. It can be considered as among the earliest examples of Irish 'exile' literature.

The exiled Irish were fortified by knowledge of other cultures and languages, and the confidence instilled by an awareness that they belonged to a Catholic world that flourished elsewhere in Europe. Their positive experience of that world inoculated them against the allure – and the hostility – of the Anglo-Irish Protestant world. The Irish students often extended their studies to improbable lengths, to prolong their stay in France. Many clergy – perhaps half – took the softer option of remaining permanently in France as pastors or private chaplains. Those who came to France as teenagers tended to stay, as their mature adult identities were formed more in France than in Ireland. 1,500 priests have already been traced, with concentrations in Paris, Nantes and Bordeaux.[10] Those who declined the Irish mission stayed put in Europe – an advantage rather than a weakness, as it meant that only those priests with real conviction returned to brave the rigours of the Irish mission.

Until 1789, continental Europe remained the primary destination for many thousands of Irish Catholics, involving a sustained flow of people, resources and skills. More than half of the Irish clergy were educated in France in the eighteenth century. The most durable colleges, Paris, Nantes, Toulouse and Louvain, functioned at a high level until the French Revolution. Paris and Toulouse educated 1,500 Irish students between 1550 and 1789. As late as 1789, almost three-quarters of Irish clerical students educated abroad were in France – 348 from a total of 478, and of these, 180 were in Paris. The closing of the colleges with the French Revolution necessitated the opening of an Irish seminary – Maynooth in 1795 – and this transition is often regarded – admittedly usually by hostile observers – as marking an inward turn in Irish Catholicism.[11]

---

9 *Reverend Father in God Sir Daniel Dowdwel, who departed this life on Sunday the 4th of this inst. May 1729. Near his chappel on Arron's Key* (Dublin, 1729). This one-page elegy survives in Trinity College library. My thanks to Penelope Woods for this reference.   **10** L.W. Brockliss & Patrick Ferté, 'Irish clerics in France in the seventeenth and eighteenth centuries: a statistical study', *Proceedings of the Royal Irish Academy*, Section C, 77 (1987), pp 527–72. **11** Patrick J. Corish, 'Les seminaires Irlandais du continent, la Révolution Française et les origines du College de Maynooth', *Études Irlandaises*, 23:2 (1998), pp 121–35.

TRADE: THE MERCANTILE LITTORAL

If Catholic clerical, legal and medical students pushed inland to the intellectual centres of Europe, Irish merchants clung limpet-like to the coastal ports. The Atlantic ports of Cork and Waterford played a crucial path-finding role in launching these expatriate merchants in the seventeenth century. Irish mercantile communities evolved from the 1640s onwards, expanding in the 1660s after the expulsion of Catholic merchants from Cromwellian Ireland. An embryonic network edged the southern Atlantic façade of continental Europe. The Irish, capable brokers, handlers and fixers, were integrated smoothly in France and Spain, as Catholic anglophones who managed the European contact with Protestant Great Britain and America.

These mercantile flows overlapped with family and financial networks, and with the diasporic Jacobite community after the 1690s. There were Irish clusters in the court cities of Paris and Brussels inland, and these tight-knit expatriate communities, often originating from the same Irish source city, were recruited from the displaced Old English mercantile elites south of a line from Galway to Dublin.

SOLDIERS: THE WILD GEESE

Eighteenth-century European armies were largely mercenary, and accordingly were disproportionately composed of recruits from the poorer peripheral regions, notably Switzerland, Scotland, Sweden, Ireland and Hesse. One-fifth of the eighteenth-century French army was composed of foreigners. Irish penetration of the officer class was helped by the genealogical obsession of the lineage-based Gaelic society – they could document their claim to aristocratic ancestry. The Irish officers tended to be effective military men because they were career soldiers rather than courtiers. Officers were then well positioned to recruit rank-and-file from their homeland. As early as the 1630s, France emerged as a destination of choice. 30,000 Irish volunteered for the French service between 1630 and 1660. Following the defeats at the Boyne and Aughrim, an additional 20,000 went to France where they formed the celebrated Irish regiments in the service of France. They gained a reputation for élan, impetuosity and stubbornness, as at Cremona (1702), Ramillies (1706), Fontenoy (1745) and Laffeldt (1747).

The term 'na géanna fiáine' first circulated in Irish in the early decades of the eighteenth century: it gradually became more specific after appearing initially as a metaphor for the dispossessed Irish forced overseas – 'dá mbocadh ó thoinn go toinn mar éanlaith' ('buffeted from wave to wave like birds') – in a 1697 poem.[12]

12 Vincent Morley, *The popular mind in eighteenth-century Ireland* (Cork, 2017), p. 65. There is a detailed section on the Wild Geese at pp 148–56.

The English version 'Wild Geese' first surfaced in the 1720s and waves of recruiting coincided with shifts in European politics and warmongering. The British state was relaxed (except at moments of military crisis) about this state of affairs, having concluded from early on that the vast majority never returned and that the French conveniently siphoned off discontented young Irishmen.

Detailed records exist for the Irish Brigade from 1716 until their disbandment in 1791. In this period 25,000 Irishmen entered the French service.[13] Rank-and-file numbers fluctuated with the rise and fall of French wars, but they held up reasonably well until the 1760s, and then plummeted. The percentage of Irish-born in the Irish Brigades declined across the eighteenth century: Irish-born soldiers composed over ninety per cent of the Irish Regiments in 1729, almost half in the late 1740s, one quarter in 1763 and only ten per cent by the late 1770s. The sharpest drop was after the 1740s, a decade when the Irish Brigades bled at Fontenoy (1745) and Laffeldt (1747). The losses inflicted in these two battles were never replenished.

The four leading counties for 'Wild Geese' recruitment were Cork, Tipperary, Limerick and Kerry, followed by Dublin, Kilkenny and Galway. The compact Munster/south Leinster nature of the source region for the Irish Brigade is striking, all the more so when contrasted with the earlier dominance of Ulster Gaelic families like the O'Neills in the officer class in Spanish military service. This southern region was the heartland of eighteenth-century Irish Catholicism. Here the 'underground gentry' survived as the submerged but effective leadership of Irish Catholicism: these men came from a solid family background, had a high sense of their own importance, and maintained intimate links with Europe, including close connections with the Jacobite officer corps in Continental armies. This region fostered the most durable contact with Catholic Europe, as shown by the location of continental-educated priests in Ireland in 1703.

AN EXPATRIATE INCUBATION OF IRISH NATIONALISM

The nation-building role of the Irish exiles reflected a precocious Europeanisation of the Irish Catholic experience, a source of fresh thinking in learning, literature, politics and religion. This world produced intellectuals of distinction, like Seatrún Céitinn (1569–1644), David Rothe (1573–1650), Luke Wadding (1588–1687), Michael Moore (1640–1726) and James Usher (1720–72).[14] Irish

13 Colm James O'Connell, 'The Irish regiments in France: an overview of the presence of Irish soldiers in French service, 1716–1791' in E. Maher & G. Neville (eds), *France-Ireland: anatomy of a relationship* (Frankfurt, 2004), pp 327–42; David Murphy, *The Irish brigades, 1685–2006: a gazetteer of Irish military service, past and present* (Dublin, 2007).   14 Bernadette Cunningham, *The world of Geoffrey Keating: history, myth and religion in seventeenth-century Ireland* (Dublin, 2000): Thomas O'Connor, 'Custom, authority and tolerance in Irish political thought: David Rothe's *Analecta Sacra et Mira* (1616)', *Irish Theological Quarterly* 65:2 (2000),

Continental migrants were overwhelmingly derived from the Old English (especially of the towns), and (to a much lesser extent) Gaelic elites, newly fused into a common Catholic identity in the religious furnace of late sixteenth-century Europe. The State Papers indicate the English point of view:

> It is the perfidious Machiavellian friars at Louvain who foster this new perspective – who seek to reconcile all their countrymen – to unite both the old descendants of the Old English race and those that are mere Irish in a league of friendship and concurrence against Your Majesty and the true religion now professed in your Kingdoms.[15]

At Douai in 1600, it was noted that the 'young gentlemen' of the Pale (Plunketts, Barnewalls, Warrens, Rochfords) had been infected with nationalism because 'they speak all Irish': 'many become in language and disposition fermented with the ancient hatred of the Irish to the English'.[16] Sir George Carew (1555–1629), President of Munster from 1600, noted that 'As a consequence of exile, the Irish have become more civilised, grown to be disciplined soldiers, scholars, politicians and much further instructed in most points of religion than they were accustomed to be'.[17]

THE IRISH LANGUAGE

The European bridgehead carried Irish-language scholarship across the chasm created by the disappearance of patronage with the brutal crushing of Gaelic Ireland in the late sixteenth century. The multi-lingual intellectual world that they encountered in Europe stimulated Irish-language scholarship in the seventeenth century. Exiled clerics and scholars quickly became aware that even educated Europeans knew next to nothing about Ireland. Only a programme of scholarship and publication could make their distinctive case better understood.[18] Irish exiles and migrants rapidly realised the acute need to explain and express themselves to their host countries, to give a voice and a cultural density to an otherwise silent and spectral 'Ireland'.

It was on the Continent, notably in Louvain, Rome and Paris, that the Irish language achieved visibility in the form of distinctive typefaces. The transition

pp 133–56: Liam Chambers, *Michael Moore, c.1639–1726: provost of Trinity, rector of Paris* (Dublin, 2005): Kevin Barry, 'James Usher (1720–1772) and the Irish Enlightenment' in *Eighteenth-century Ireland*, 3 (1988), pp 115–22. **15** Cited in C.P. Meehan, *The fate and fortunes of Hugh O'Neill, earl of Tyrone and Rory O'Donnell, earl of Tyrconnell* (Dublin, 1868), p. 328. **16** *Calendar of state papers: domestic, 1598–1601*, p. 496. **17** George Carew, 'A discourse of the present state of Ireland 1614' in *Calendar of Carew manuscripts, 1603–14*, pp 305–6. **18** John McCaffrey, 'Leuven as a centre for Irish religious, academic and political thought' in Éamonn MacAodha & A. Murray (eds), *Ireland and Belgium: past connections and*

from manuscript to typescript marked a cultural advance, given the enhanced prestige accorded to typefaces. The new European typeface displayed the specific identity of the Irish language, visible in the new fonts that evolved from the Irish script.[19] These fonts respected the visual uniqueness and the venerable cultural antecedents of the existing script – a post-classical vernacular version that had been elaborated and refined by a hybrid clerical/secular intellectual class over many centuries. The font for Maol Brighde Ó hEodhusa/Bonaventure O'Hussey, *An Teagasg Críosdaithe* (Antwerp, 1611, Louvain, 1614), was based on his own cursive handwriting.[20]

A new type (possibly cut by Jean-Claude Fournier of the distinguished Parisian typesetting family) was designed at the Irish College in Paris. In 1732, an *English-Irish dictionary*, compiled by Aodh Buí Mac Cruitín and Conchubhair Ó Beaglaíoch (parish priest of Saint Germain l'Auxerrois), was issued in Paris by Jacques Guérin: its more robust and less spidery typeface (which 'familiarized the Irish characters to those of the English as much as I durst without departing from the form of them') marked an aesthetic departure from preceding cruder designs.[21] It was also from Paris in 1742 that the Sligo man Andrew Donlevy (1694–1765), Rector of the Irish College, issued his celebrated catechism *An Teagusg Críosduidhe do réir Ceasda agus Freagartha* – one of the most widely disseminated Irish language books in eighteenth-century Ireland.[22]

In 1768, John O'Brien (1701–69) produced his *Focalóir gaoidhilge-sax-bhéarla; or; An Irish-English dictionary*, printed by Nicolas-François Valleyre in Paris. O'Brien, the Catholic bishop of Cloyne since 1748, argued that Irish priests trained in European seminaries lost fluency in the language, which hindered their ability to serve effectively once they returned to Ireland.[23] Even the most

continuing ties (Brussels, 2014), pp 27–48.   19 Mícheál McCraith, 'Printing in the vernacular: the Louvain project', *History Ireland*, 15:4 (July–Aug. 2007), pp 27–31; Seamus Heaney, 'The font of identity' in N. Nic Gabhann (ed.), *Shaping identities together: ag cruthú le cheile* (Leuven, 2013), pp 8–11. On the wider context, see Niall Ó Ciosáin, 'Print and Irish, 1570–1900: an exception among the Celtic languages?', *Radharc*, 5–8 (2004–6), pp 73–106. 20 Salvador Ryan, 'Bonaventura Ó hEoghusa's *An Teagasg Críosdaidhe* (1611/1614): a reassessment of its audience and use', *Archivium Hibernicum*, 58 (2004), pp 259–67. In the wider context, the essential guide to the manuscript tradition is Timothy O'Neill, *The Irish hand: scribes and their manuscripts from the earliest times* (Cork, 2014). Dermot McGuinne, *Irish type design: a history of printing types in the Irish character* (Dublin, 1992) is the indispensable guide on type.   21 Hugh MacCurtin, *The English-Irish dictionary. An Focloir Bearla Gaoidheilge. Ar na chur a neagar le Conchobar O Beaglaoich mar aon le congnamh Aodh Bhuidhe Mac Cuirtin, agus fós a bPairis, ar na chur acclodh le Seamus Guerin, an bhliadhain daosi an tiaghrna* M. DCC. XXXII *le haonta an Rígh* (Paris, 1732). The approbation of the French king was dropped discreetly from copies destined for Ireland.   22 Andrew Donlevy, *An Teagasg Críosduidhe do réir ceasda agus freagartha, air na tharruing go bunubhasach as bréithir hsoilléir Dé agus as toibreachaib fiorghlana oile. A bPairís air na chur a gclódh re Seumus Guerin, ag San Tomás ó Acuin, a sráid Sain-Seum[as]. M.D. CC. XLII Ré Cead an Rígh, agus re Déightheisd na nOllamhun re Diaghacht* (Paris, 1742). A nod in the direction of King James is embedded in the place of printing – 'is leor nod don eolach'.   23 F.M. Jones, 'The Congregation of Propaganda and the publication of Dr O'Brien's Irish dictionary', *Irish Ecclesiastical Record*,

cursory of treatments of the fate of the Irish language must acknowledge this critical Continental dimension.[24]

IRELAND AND THE FRENCH REVOLUTION

In December 1797, the following United Irishman catechism was reported in County Cork. The recruiter triggered a sequence of set questions and answers:

What is that in your hand?	It is a branch.
Of what?	Of the Tree of Liberty.
Where did it first grow?	In America.
Where does it bloom?	In France.
Were did the seeds fall?	In Ireland.
When will the moon be full?	When the four quarters [provinces] meet.

Gustave de Beaumont (1802–66), following his visit to Ireland in 1835 with Alexis de Tocqueville (1805–59), noted that 'When a subjugated people secretly nourishes prospects of independence, even if it is apparently inert and mute, there is a latent threat'. The American Revolution activated that latency, initially in Presbyterian Ulster and embracing the Catholic south as well: 'America instructed Protestant Ireland: that in its turn taught Catholic Ireland'.[25] Republicanism was crossing – or more accurately recrossing – the Atlantic.

If the American Revolution electrified Irish radicalism, the French Revolution energised the entire course of Irish history. The leading Catholic power in Europe had, astonishingly, produced a revolution more radical than the Glorious Revolution of 1688 or the American Revolution of 1776. France, enslaved by Popish despotism and the very antithesis of liberty, played the supreme negative role in the British imaginary of the eighteenth century. In 1778, when lower-class Protestants were urged to arms in Wexford town to resist a French invasion, their captain exhorted them in terms drawn from an entrenched rhetoric: 'we are fighting for our liberties and if we are conquered, we shall have nothing but French slavery, Popery and small beer: if we conquer, we shall have liberty, property and good Irish porter'.[26]

From an Irish perspective, the defining feature of the French Revolution was that it happened in France. Thomas Addis Emmet observed that 'A Catholic country had, by its conduct, contradicted the frequently repeated dogma, that

5th series, 77 (Jan. 1952), pp 29–37: Seán Ó Cearnaigh, 'The Irish-English dictionary of Bishop John O'Brien', *Linen Hall Review*, 10:1 (1993), pp 15–17.   **24** Thomas O'Connor, 'Religious change, 1550–1800' in R. Gillespie & A. Hadfield (eds), *The Oxford history of the Irish book, volume III: The Irish book in English, 1550–1800* (Oxford, 2006), pp 169–93. **25** Gustave de Beaumont, *Ireland, social, political, and religious*, ed. T. Garvin & A. Hess (Cambridge, MA, 2006), p. 217.   **26** *Dublin Evening Post*, 22 Aug. 1778.

Catholics are unfit for liberty'.[27] The long-standing equation between
Catholicism and despotism had been shattered overnight by the Revolution.
Once Catholics could be accepted as citizens, a transformation in Irish politics
became possible – a hitherto unthinkable alliance between Presbyterian and
Catholic radicals. Catholics could be admitted to the Irish polity without
reservation and the United Irishmen were founded simultaneously in Belfast and
Dublin in 1791 to give cohesion and momentum to this innovation in Irish
politics. It was in this sense that Tone described the French Revolution as 'the
morning star of liberty' in Ireland.[28]

The fall of the Bastille was adopted as the symbol of the revolution, and its
anniversary was vigorously celebrated at Belfast, Dublin, Kilkenny, Wexford and
elsewhere in the early 1790s. On 14 July 1791, 20,000 people attended huge
illuminations on St Stephen's Green.[29] That night, Napper Tandy paraded 200
Volunteers through Dublin, bearing an illumination: 'We do not rejoice because
we are slaves but we rejoice because of the French being free'.[30] At Kilkenny
Theatre, the main attraction that Summer was a spectacle called the 'Triumph
of liberty or the destruction of the Bastille, exhibiting one of the most grand and
interesting spectacles that ever engaged the feelings of the world'.[31] In Belfast, a
parade of Volunteer companies, Whigs and United Irishmen carried portraits of
Mirabeau and a large standard showing the fall of the Bastille, while a cheap
eight-page pamphlet for mass circulation was published in the city – *Songs on the
French Revolution. That took place at Paris, 14th July, 1789; sung at the celebration
thereof at Belfast, on Saturday 14th July, 1792* (Belfast, 1792).[32] In 1793, a model
of 'the modern beheading machine at Paris' was on display at the Dublin
Museum on Mary Street.[33]

The French Revolution had another pronounced effect in Ireland: it
appreciably quickened the pulse of political change. The lethargic Catholic leaders
of Ireland, hitherto acquiescent in the glacially slow thaw in Protestant attitudes,
were emboldened. The French Revolution 'aroused Irishmen from the sleep of
centuries. They indeed awoke but they awoke only to a sense of their misery and a
sight of their chains'.[34] After the French Revolution, Catholics high and low
surveyed the Irish political landscape anew from above the parapet of the Penal
Laws.[35] In the 1790s, to list only Wexford United Irish leaders, Edward Sweetman,
William Barker, John Hay, James Edward Devereux, John Esmonde, Edward Hay,
Mogue Kearns and William Kearney were all educated or lived in France.

27 William James MacNeven (ed.), *Pieces of Irish history illustrative of the condition of the Catholics of Ireland* (New York, 1807), p. 12.   28 Tone, *Writings*, i, p. 105.   29 *Dublin Evening Post*, 16 July 1791.   30 *Hibernian Journal*, 15 July 1791.   31 *Finns Leinster Journal*, 19–23 Feb. 1791.   32 Samuel McSkimmin, *Annals of Ulster from 1790–1798*, ed. E.J. McCrum (Belfast, 1906), p. 5.   33 *Massacre of the French King. View of the guillotine or the modern beheading machine at Paris by which the unfortunate Louis XVI (late King of France) suffered on the scaffold, January 21st 1793* (Dublin, 1793).   34 Bernard Dornin, *A sketch of the life of Samuel Neilson* (New York, 1804), p. 7.   35 Timothy Murtagh, 'Hibernian sans-culottes?

By systematically extending political participation and the rights of citizenship to the 'men of no property,' the United Irishmen were increasingly successful in 'making every man a politician', as Thomas Addis Emmet expressed it.[36] The old grievances of the poor – tithes, taxes, rents, living conditions – hitherto addressed directly only by the agrarian secret societies were now linked for the first time to a viable programme for radical reform. This rhetoric introduced the French Revolutionary vocabulary of the rights of man. Janus-headed, it spliced together an inward and backward look to a densely specific Gaelic tradition, and a forward and future look to the European revolutionary arena. The United Irishmen were therefore the crucial bridge between Jacobitism and Republicanism for the Irish poor. Once the French Revolution occurred, everything changed. Local and historically rooted grievances were now presented in national and international terms, and linked to an explicit programme for political and if necessary revolutionary regeneration.

THE IRISH NAPOLEON

In the first half of the nineteenth-century, the Irish cult of Napoleon was stimulated by widespread importation of French writings in translation.[37] Bonaparte's brooding presence – what the Irish Gothic novelist Charles Maturin called his 'appalling supernatural greatness' – transfixed Europe until 1815.[38] A Listowel schoolteacher put it crudely in 1802, 'go mbainfidh Bónaparte an các as Rí Seoirse' ('Bonaparte will beat the shit out of King George').[39]

Napoleon fascinated the Irish, dominating the Irish song tradition of this period in both Irish and English, as the Jacobite messianic mantle descended on his shoulders.[40] In 1802, the Dubliner Michael Daly of Drury Lane lost his publican's license for displaying a print of Bonaparte.[41] In 1803, the bishop of Killaloe reported the explosion of cheering among a Limerick audience when a portrait of Napoleon was shown.[42] In 1804, a pedlar was arrested in Loughrea, County Galway for selling a chapbook life of the emperor.[43]

Dublin's artisans and radical politics, 1790–1798', *La Révolution française. Cahiers de l'Institut d'histoire de la Révolution française*, 11 (2016), pp 1–36.   **36** MacNeven, *Pieces of Irish history*, p. 77.   **37** There is a detailed treatment of these materials in Michèle Milan, 'Found in translation: Franco-Irish translation relationships in nineteenth-century Ireland' (PhD, DCU, 2013), pp 125–8.   **38** David Dickson, *Dublin: the making of a capital city* (Dublin, 2014), p. 274.   **39** Morley, *Popular mind*, p. 264.   **40** Morley, *Popular mind*, pp 263–70. G.-D. Zimmerman, *Songs of Irish rebellion: political street ballads and rebel songs, 1780–1900* (Dublin, 1967), pp 186–92; Terry Moylan, *The age of revolution in the Irish song tradition, 1776–1815* (Dublin, 2000), pp 133–86; Frank Harte, *My name is Napoleon Bonaparte*, 2 CDs (Dublin, Humingbird Records, 2001) is a magnificent realisation of these English-language songs in circulation in Ireland. Harte popularised the aphorism: 'The winners write the history, the losers write the songs'.   **41** Petition of Michael Drury for restoration of his license, NARP, 620/61/78.   **42** Bishop of Killaloe to Alexander Marsden, 25 June 1803, NARP, 620/65/136. **43** Sir Eyre Coote (Loughrea) to Edward Cooke, 8 Jan. 1804, NARP, 620/50/51.

According to William Drennan, Bonaparte was 'a fashionable theme of admiration in Belfast'.[44] Drennan himself, gifted a glazed print of Napoleon, cautiously hung it out of sight in his bedroom.[45] His more forthright sister Martha judged Bonaparte to be 'Washington's equal'.[46] Drennan later reported that ordinary Belfast people believed that the Messiah would appear in the form of Bonaparte.[47] In 1809, a Meath drinking song was hopeful that 'Más go hÉirinn a thriall le coscradh gach riail/do chuid Chromail agus Liam na Bóinne' ('if he was intent on coming to Ireland, he would demolish every law of Cromwell and Billy of the Boyne').[48] The French visitor J. Joseph Prevost noted his portrait (and a wooden Madonna) in an impoverished cabin at Glendalough in 1843.[49]

Napoleon failed the Irish just as the Stuarts had failed them. Daniel O'Connell, the next broad shoulders on whom the Messianic mantle fell, concluded that Napoleon's 'great mistake was to go to Egypt not Ireland'.[50] Charles Teeling bemoaned the fact that 'The conqueror of Italy had sailed for Egypt with the finest army that Europe could boast and with the destinies of Britain in his hand, he abandoned Ireland to her fate'.[51] Bonaparte soon faded back into the elegaic misty line of lost Irish saviours: 'He preferred eventually mooning around the Pyramids and addressing high-falutin' harangues to his troops on the banks of the Nile to storming Dublin Castle'.[52] He did however deliver one very specific Irish project – the Irish Legion.

THE IRISH LEGION

The Irish Legion was raised by Napoleon in 1803, part of his grand strategy for a mass invasion of Britain.[53] Originally it was a shadow regiment, comprised of officers, almost all of United Irish background, and of outstanding reputations – the idea being that once the French landed in Ireland, locals would flock to the standards of these well known men and rapidly fill up the rank-and-file. That

44 Jean Agnew (ed.), *The Drennan–McTier letters*, 3 vols (Dublin, 1998–9), ii, p. 603. **45** *Drennan–McTier letters*, ii, p. 476. **46** *Drennan–McTier letters*, ii, p. 637. **47** *Drennan–McTier letters*, ii, p. 605. **48** Morley, *Popular mind*, p. 266. **49** J. Joseph Prevost, *L'Irelande au dix-heutieme siècle* (Paris, 1845), p. 146. The book, dedicated to de Beaumont, is notably sympathetic to Ireland. **50** Cited in Paul Bew, *Ireland: the politics of enmity* (Oxford, 2007), p. 160. **51** Charles Teeling, *History of the Irish rebellion of 1798 – a personal narrative* (Glasgow, 1876), pp 193–4. **52** Eugene Davis, *Souvenirs of Irish footprints over Europe* [1889], ed. O. McGee (Dublin, 2006), p. 120. **53** Pierre Carles, 'Le Corps Irlandais au service de la France', *Revue Historique des Armées* (1976), pp 25–54; John Gallaher, *Napoleon's Irish Legion* (Carbondale, IL, 1993): Thomas Bartlett, 'Last flight of the Wild Geese? Bonaparte's Irish Legion, 1803–1815' in O'Connor & Lyons (eds), *Irish communities*, pp 160–71: Nicholas Dunne-Lynch, 'The Irish Legion of Napoleon, 1803–1815' in N. Genet-Rouffiac & D. Murphy (eds), *Franco-Irish military connections, 1595–1945* (Dublin, 2009), pp 189–218. We await Dunne-Lynch's *The Irish Legion, 1803–1815*, which will offer the most archivally-dense

2.2 This 1821 drawing by 'L.F., Paris' is inscribed on the rear in Thomas Moore's hand 'Our residence in the Allée des Veuves, Champs Élysées, 1820'. Moore noted: 'I have been lucky enough to find a Cottage, just as you know I like, for a workshop, within fifteen minutes walk of Paris (indeed hardly out of it)'. The Allée des Veuves is the modern Avenue Montaigne. Moore lived in Paris, 1819–21, in this surprisingly bucolic setting. Moore also noted that Paris is 'a better place to pick up music in than Italy' (Collection Rolf Loeber).

aspiration wilted after the catastrophe of Trafalgar in 1805, and the skeletal regiment was subsequently filled by non-Irish conscripts. After that, sequestered in Morlaix in Brittany, waiting for an increasingly unlikely invasion, the Legion gained an unenviable reputation for desertion, fractiousness and insubordination. The usual mixture of principle, opportunism and careerism prevailed among the officer class, as well as a smouldering sullenness towards Napoleon as a betrayer of Ireland. William James MacNevin bristled that the Irish in France had been reduced to 'instruments of Bonaparte to answer his own selfish views'.[54] After Waterloo, the regiment was disbanded, despite protests from the Irish officers, who claimed that the Irish had selflessly offered a century of service to France, and regarded the country 'as a second fatherland'.[55] Their plaintive pleas fell on deaf Bourbon ears.

treatment.   **54** MacNevin to Cormick, 5 Aug. 1805 in Thomas Addis Emmet, *Memoir of Thomas Addis and Robert Emmet, with their ancestors and immediate family*, 2 vols (New York, 1915), i, p. 394.   **55** Cited in Bartlett, 'Last flight of the Wild Geese', p. 170.

THE AMERICAN ALTERNATIVE

Until 1789, continental Europe remained the primary destination for many thousand Irish Catholics, involving flows of people, resources and skills. This flow was declining from the 1780s, as Catholics turned first to America, and then to the British Empire, army and navy, once it became legally permissible for Catholics to attain high ranks in those institutions following the French Revolution. In its own desolate way, the fate of the Irish Legion represented a fading of France in the Irish imagination from 1815 to the Famine. After the French Revolution, wealthy Catholics no longer sought to move to France, with the sole exception of United Irishmen hounded out after 1798. America offered an alternative for prospective emigrants, with a consequent reorientation of the Irish Catholic diaspora from France to the United States.

THE FRENCH O'CONNELL

If Irish popular interest in France waned after Waterloo, French interest in Ireland was reinvigorated from the 1820s onwards by O'Connell and his experimental catalysis of Catholicism with democracy.[56] French intellectuals wrote extensively about him – notably Tocqueville, Beaumont, Lamennais, Lacordaire and Montalembert.[57] Both Tocqueville and Beaumont visited Ireland and Britain for four months in 1835 and Beaumont returned to Ireland in 1837. His impressive book on Ireland appeared in 1839, when the island for him merited its reputation as the most impoverished, tumultous and socially divided country in Europe. Beaumont assailed the Anglo-Irish as a malign aristocracy, 'in the grip of fear and irritation'. Aristocratic privilege needed to be abolished: 'No tears will be shed for their fate' because in the end they offered only 'their blood-stained phantom of a government'.[58] Therefore they were constantly 'at open war with the people'[59] and 'a social war' raged all the time between the rich and the poor, which equally engulfed the Protestants and the Catholics.[60] For Beaumont, it was all too easy to understand Irish secret societies: 'Misery armed the Whiteboy'.[61] The Irish Protestant state was fundamentally a state of fear, and that inevitably spawned harshness and sectarianism, which ultimately

---

56 The background context is brilliantly elucidated in Seamus Deane, 'A church destroyed, the church restored: France's Irish Catholicism', *Field Day Review*, 7 (2012), pp 203–51. **57** When Lamennais, Lacordaire and Montalembert launched *L'Avenir* in 1830 to spearhead a movement for political democracy and economic justice, it proved the catalyst for the establishment of the *Catholic Penny Magazine* in Dublin in 1834. *L'Avenir* launched an appeal to French Catholics to alleviate famine in the west of Ireland (1832–36), and raised 46,000 francs (Mary Purcell, 'Dublin Diocesan Archives: Murray Papers, file 31/3: 1831 and 1832', *Archivium Hibernicum*, 37 (1982), pp 31–3). **58** Beaumont, *Ireland*, p. 296. **59** Beaumont, *Ireland*, p. 247. **60** Beaumont, *Ireland*, p. 150. **61** Beaumont, *Ireland*, p. 78.

contaminated the law itself, by creating Catholic contempt for it: 'the strong exterminated the weak in the name of justice and the laws'.[62]

For Beaumont and Tocqueville, the imperative first step in dissolving this insolent state of fear must be to dissolve the State church: the state itself was tainted and rendered partisan and odious by the tithe system.[63] Only disestablishment – the clear separation of church and state – could deliver what Ireland needed above all – a neutral state. The defining flaw of the Protestant Ascendancy was its delusions of grandeur.[64] It made them unable to withstand the rise of democracy, which would inevitably open the Irish future only to the middle class.[65] 'The opposition is then the nation and the government a party or faction'.[66] Once the short-sighted Protestant Ascendancy allowed that democratic chasm to open between them and the people, they were doomed, as the O'Connellite party became 'the real representatives of the great body of the nation'.[67] The Catholic Association was 'a government within a government',[68] 'a disciplined army'[69] led by O'Connell and waging an incessant 'constitutional war'[70] against the 'Irish aristocracy'.[71]

This Catholicism-plus-democracy linkage in the O'Connell phenomenon fascinated French liberal intellectuals of this generation. Ireland was also an experimental test case for British institutions – so admired by Tocqueville, Beaumont and Lamennais – and in both America and Ireland these anxious men sought another future for France. They were all in quest of a vanished authority that could bind the wounds of France, and eager to seek it in a rejuvenated Catholicism rather than a renovated Bonapartism. Royal despotism of the eighteenth century had paved the way for Jacobinisn and Bonapartism by eliminating civil society: with Napoleon, 'nothing showed except the colossal figure of the emperor himself'.[72] French liberal Catholics despised centralisation as an enemy of liberty. Tocqueville's conclusion was that democracy was the only viable alternative to the dictator, and essential to the preservation of liberty.

Catholic liberals were equally fixated on France's fragility and political fluctuations, its geological propensity for volcanic episodes. For Tocqueville, that sense of dislocation was class-based; he was after all an aristocrat making his way in a determinedly post-revolutionary and bourgeois world (which he detested). That gave him the unmoored detachment but also the pessimism of a disappointed and displaced traditionalist in internal exile – an eighteenth-century man adrift in a nineteenth-century world and tossed emotionally between them.

62 Beaumont, *Ireland*, p. 158.   63 Beaumont, *Ireland*, p. 322.   64 Beaumont, *Ireland*, p. 203.
65 Beaumont, *Ireland*, p. 216.   66 Beaumont, *Ireland*, p. 218.   67 Beaumont, *Ireland*, p. 220.
68 Beaumont, *Ireland*, p. 221.   69 Beaumont, *Ireland*, p. 223.   70 Beaumont, *Ireland*, p. 226.
71 Beaumont, *Ireland*, p. 231.   72 Hugh Brogan, *Alexis de Tocqueville: a biography* (London, 2007), p. 497.

> I am weary of repeatedly mistaking treacherous fog-banks for the shore, and I often wonder if the terra firma which we have been seeking for so long actually exists or if our destiny is not rather to beat about eternally at sea.[73]

None of these intellectuals exhibited any much curiosity about the Presbyterians or the north of Ireland: Beaumont devoted a mere three pages of his lengthy book to that subject.

Thomas Macaulay in the House of Commons in 1844 was exasperated by the French fascination with O'Connell:

> Go where you will on the Continent, visit any coffee-house, dine at any table, embark upon any steamboat, enter any conveyance – from the moment your accent shows you to be an Englishman, the very first question you are asked by your companions, be they advocates, merchants, manufacturers, physicians or peasants like our yeomen, is 'What is to be done with O'Connell?' Look over any file of French journals; and you will see what a space he occupies in the eyes of the French people.[74]

Honoré de Balzac described O'Connell as 'the incarnation of a people' while Élias Regnault featured him strongly in his attack on the criminality of the English.[75]

PARIS: CAPITAL OF THE NINETEENTH CENTURY

In the second half of the nineteenth century, Paris loomed so large in the wider European imaginary that Karl Ludwig Borne (1786–1837) dubbed it the capital of the nineteenth century in 1834, a formulation later made famous by Walter Benjamin.[76] Victor Hugo claimed that 'Paris is the brain of France and the heart of the world's fashion and amusement' while Dumas fils called Paris 'the capital of the civilised world' in 1854.[77] The Irish writer Eugene Davis offered this opinion of Paris in 1889:

> Paris is the most cosmopolitan of cities. Representatives of all semi-civilised races and of mostly all civilised ones rub up their skirts against one another on the boulevards. Here the Russian prince sips his perfumed

---

73 Brogan, *Tocqueville*, p. 499.   74 Cited by Felim Ó Briain in 'Daniel O'Connell: a centenary evaluation', *Studies*, 36:143 (1947), p. 263.   75 Honoré de Balzac, *La Comédie humaine* (Paris, 1951), p. ix; Élias Regnault, *Histoire criminelle du gouvernement anglais depuis les premiers massacres de l'Irlande jusqu'à l'empoisonnement des Chinois* (Paris, 1841).   76 'The Paris of the Second Empire' in Walter Benjamin, *Selected writings*, ed. M. Jennings, 4 vols (Cambridge MA, 1996–2003), iv, pp 3–92.   77 Higonnet, *Paris, capital of the world*, p. 229.

wines in the Jockey Club, while his wife and daughters, lolling in an easy carriage and smoking dainty Turkish cigarettes, drive up the Champs Elysees, and around the lake in the Bois De Boulogne, where the wealth and fashion of Paris congregate to admire and be admired, to smirk and bow, and bandy oily platitudes to each other in a Babel of tongues.[78]

In the first half of the nineteenth century, the café Voltaire on Place de l'Odéon remained a favoured haunt for exiled European republicans. Balzac described an Irishman there amid an international group seated at 'the philosopher's table', in his story 'Les martyrs ignorés', set in 1827.

Théophile Ormond is a very Byronic Irishman with a long neck, an immaculate tie, an English complexion, excessively decorous and perfumed with copaiba balm.[79] He is elegantly dressed, with a fob watch and a petite monocle; he spends half an hour grooming his nails. He is a fanatical admirer of Ballanche,[80] then unknown; he hates England and above all the English *saints* (pronounced *seintz*) who invite you for *tea and the Bible*.[81] A young aunt belonging to this sect of saints had deprived him of his paternal inheritance, by spreading a thousand lies about him, poor gentleman, painting him as a scoundrel, just because his Tilbury[82] was often seen at the door of a French actress, despite his engagement to Miss Julia Marmaduke. He supports Repeal of the Union, worships O'Connell and [Thomas] Moore, when the latter had not yet defected to the aristocracy. He spends five francs every evening, coming in [to the restaurant] after the show, while Mademoiselle Lureuil undresses and dresses. He speaks French fluently, and has religious principles without ever entering a church. Suffering from consumption, he is besotted with Lureuil, an actress at the Odéon [rue Corneille], on whom he had bestowed an annual pension of three thousand livres in 1827. He is greeted by all the café waiters. He has a clear and gracious voice.[83]

The Irish exiles clustered in the cheaper Latin Quarter, among the students, the expatriates and the cafes.[84] Whereas in cloudy Ireland, social life gravitated indoors into the warm pub interior, sunnier Paris embraced the café, the life of the streets and the flâneur. George Moore contrasted his informal Parisian 'café

---

78 Davis, *Souvenirs of Irish footprints*, p. 101.   79 A fashionable balsam from South America.
80 Pierre-Simon Ballanche (1776–1847), a French counter-revolutionary philosopher, elaborated a tragic view of life as sanctified suffering, within a progressive version of Christianity.
81 Evangelical Methodists were disparagingly called 'saints'.   82 A Tilbury was a stylish, light, open, fast two-wheeled carriage, imported from London.   83 My translation. Honoré de Balzac, *Le curé de ville suivi des Martyrs ignorés* (Bruxelles, 1839), pp 134–5. Balzac himself famously said in 1840 'Je hais les Anglais'.   84 Lloyd Kramer, *Threshold of a new world: intellectuals and the exile experience in Paris, 1830–1848* (Ithaca, NY, 1988).

2.3 The café Voltaire at the Place de l'Odéon. Founded in 1750, it was frequented by the Encyclopedists and later by Camille and Lucile Desmoulins. Balzac described it in his novella 'Les martyrs ignorés', set in 1827, which features an exiled Irish republican. In the 1880s, le 'Grand Café-Restaurant Voltaire' attracted political and literary figures: Verlaine, Gide, Moréas, France, Vallette and Rachilde. A little later, it was a favoured haunt of symbolist poets and painters, and for Gauguin, Mallarmé ('wearing a Basque beret, decked out in an indescribable mac and shod in carved clogs'), Rodin, Bourget and Barrès. It was also a favoured rendez-vous for the 'lost generation' – Hemingway, Fitzgerald, Lewis, Eliot and Stein. This 1909 photograph is by Eugène Atget (1857–1927) (Musée Carnavalet, Paris).

education' with sterile university education, while a political apprenticeship could also be served there. Tocqueville noted in 1850 that Parisian cafes, cabarets and salons were politicised along party allegiances.[85] John Savage as a young art

85 Patrice Higonnet, *Paris, capital of the world* (Cambridge MA, 2002), p. 49.

student in Dublin in 1848 had proposed a revolutionary club modelled on the École Polytechnique of Paris. Exiled to America for his Fenian activities, he looked back on Parisian influence on the movement:

> At this period, the Continent of Europe generally, and Paris particularly, was inwoven with a network of secret political societies. As a means of inviting and combining the people for the purposes of successful revolution, they had peculiar fascinations for those whose former attempts at rebellion proved a failure, simply for want of previous organisation of the revolutionary elements. [John] O'Mahony and [James] Stephens soon conceived of the idea of entering the most powerful of these societies, and acquiring those secrets by which means an undisciplined mob can be most readily and effectually matched against an army of 'professional cut-throats'. Accordingly, they became enrolled members – and most valuable ones too – of one of those very 'dangerous brotherhoods' which some well-to-do impostors so religiously anathemise; and thus they became pupils of some of the ablest and most profound masters of revolutionary science which the nineteenth century has produced.[86]

The political glamour of Paris and France was reburnished by the 1848 Revolution. Its sequence of dramatic revolutions (1789, 1830, 1848 and 1871) generated a super-charged image of the city as a vibrant space alive with revolutionary energy – Victor Hugo called it 'this human Vesuvius'.[87] Paris was also notoriously receptive to international ideals.[88] Paris functioned as a political capital for fugitive Irish republicans from 1848, which it remained until 1916.[89] Here the Irish mingled with and learned from other displaced writers, intellectuals and republicans who also flocked there – the Poles, Greeks, Russians and Americans. Robert Fulton called Paris 'the Bohemia of literature'.[90] 'Heterdoxies overlapped' in Hobsbawm's succint formulation.[91] The encounter between different nationalities forced exiles to explain themselves to others, and to sharpen their sense of how their own project fitted into the wider European frame. The resulting mediation, émigrés and hosts explaining their cultures, encouraged a penetrating analysis of both homeland and hostland, and fostered creative hybridisation. Those encounters were cucial to deprovincialisation (affecting both sides of the encounter), ensuring, for example, that republicanism was constantly forced to develop its terms and to embrace a wide set of historical experiences.[92]

86 John Savage, *Fenian heroes and martyrs* (Boston, 1868), p. 307.   87 Higonnet, *Paris, capital of the world*, p. 60.   88 Priscilla Parkhurst Ferguson, *Paris as revolution: writing the nineteenth-century city* (Berkeley, 1994).   89 An indispensable guide is C.J. Woods, 'Notes on some Irish residents in Paris' in Conroy (ed.), *Franco-Irish connections*, pp 321–38.   90 Davis, *Souvenirs of Irish footprints*, p. 137.   91 Eric Hobsbawm, *Uncommon people: resistance, rebellion and jazz* (London, 1998), p. 172.   92 Peter Burke, *Exiles and expatriates in the history of knowledge, 1500–2000* (Lebanon NH, 2017).

Characteristic of the displaced Irish was Professor Mortimer Murphy of Cork whose many jobs included ship carpenter, hotel tout, champion vaulter in the Austrian circus, a professor of Hebrew in Hamburg, secretary to Murphy, the Irish giant, lecturer on Shakespeare in German and tutor to Charles Lever's children in Brussels. Murphy, who knew thirteen languages, eventually settled permanently in Paris, where he was an intense republican. His evening haunt was the café Cluny on the Boulevard St Michel whose clientele included Fenians, Sorbonne students, special correspondents, compositors, Notre Dame and Pantheon guides (all from Munster), and teachers of English, French and German. This 'little dapper man, white haired and bespectacled' was considered by his fellow Irish as 'a walking encyclopedia'.[93]

PARIS AND THE FENIANS

The Fenians or Irish Republican Brotherhood regarded themselves as the authentic heart of revolutionary nationalism, and proved to be the main driving force behind the 1916 Rising.[94] Founded in 1858, they were among the first diasporic nationalist organisations in the world – they were as much a product of Paris and New York as of Dublin or Cork, of the British Empire as of rural Ireland. The well-informed policeman and spy Thomas Doyle reported in 1860:

> It was when the British army stood before Delhi and Lucknow, and the affairs of India required the presence of a powerful British force, that the Phoenix Society as now organised, was initiated in New York. The idea connecting the one with the other is clear enough, it is that of the political maxim 'England's difficulty, Ireland's opportunity'.[95]

Their exposure to radical political culture in Paris convinced the Fenians – Irish nationalism was always paranoid about informers – that discipline could be enforced through oath-bound secret societies.[96]

In the 1860s, a generation of Fenians arrived in Paris, including James Stephens, John O'Mahony, John Mitchel, John O'Leary, John Walter Bourk, Thomas O'Donnell, Eugene Davis, Michael Doheny, Edmond and William O'Donovan, Sylvester O'Mahony, Thomas Clarke Luby, John Devoy and James J. O'Kelly. Stephens, who claimed proficiency in sixteen languages, had worked as a French tutor in Dublin and translated Dickens' *Martin Chuzzlewit* into French. Many, including Stephens, lived in the 1850s at the Pension Bonnery in

93 Davis, *Souvenirs of Irish footprints*, pp 138–9.   94 Owen McGee, *The IRB: the Irish Republican Brotherhood from the Land League to Sinn Féin* (Dublin, 2005).   95 Cited in Brian Sayers, 'John O'Mahony: revolutionary and scholar 1815–1877' (PhD, Maynooth University, 2005), p. 196.   96 R.V. Comerford, 'France, Fenianism and Irish nationalist strategy', *Études Irlandaises*, 7 (1982), pp 115–25.

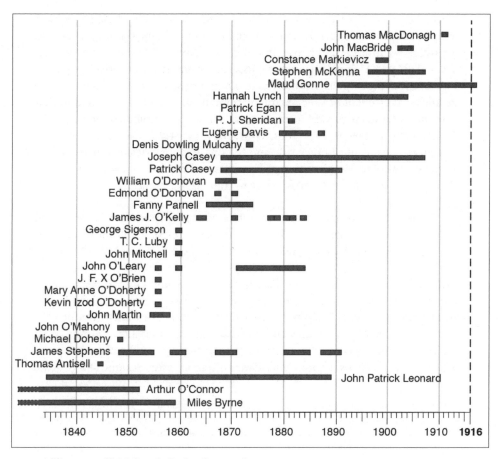

2.4 The span of Irish lives in Paris, 1840–1916.

26 rue de Lacépède, the Bohemian boarding-house described by Balzac in 1835 as the Maison Vauquer in the opening pages of *Le Père Goriot*.[97]

John O'Mahony claimed that he and Stephens had fought with the republicans on the barricades during the resistance to the *coup d'etat* in

97 'The house is of three storeys, with attic chambers. It is built of rough blocks of stone, plastered with the yellow wash that gives so contemptible a character to half the houses of Paris. The five windows of each storey of the facade have small panes and are provided with green blinds, none of which correspond in height, giving to the outside of the house an aspect of uncomfortable irregularity ... The ground-floor, necessarily the part of the house where the affairs of such an establishment are carried on, consists, first, of a parlor lighted by two windows looking upon the street ... Nothing can be more dismal than this sitting-room, furnished with chairs and armchairs covered with a species of striped horsehair ... The room has a shabby ceiling, and is wainscoted a third of the way up; the hearth, always clean, gives

December 1851.[98] O'Mahony boasted in 1856 that 'I still hold the same political faith we both pledged ourselves to so often in our eyrie in the *Quartier Latin*, and for which we proffered our lives in the bloody days of December in the *coup d'etat* 1851'.[99] O'Mahony lingered in Paris, still dreaming the old Irish dream: 'In the hope that the impulse from without, which I then deemed, and which I still deem, to be essential to success, might come from France, I remained in that country under many privations till after the fall of the Republic of February'.[100] As late as 1870, now in New York, O'Mahony was still insisting that republicanism in Ireland and France rose and fell on the same tides of global history: 'Ireland's cause no less than that of France is now at stake beneath the walls of Paris'.[101] He appealed to Irish-America to support the French republicans:

> The success of the present Republic of France is the great hope of all oppressed peoples today. It is the universal terror of all monarchs and oligarchs. It is Ireland's surest reliance for the attainment of her liberty.[102]

Francophile Fenians, like Luby, Devoy, O'Donovan and O'Kelly,[103] hankered after military training, and sought to enlist in the Légion Etrangère. John Devoy wanted 'to run away and join the Zouaves'.[104] The Franco-Prussian War of 1870 gave the waning Fenians a fillip, and they came up with the wheeze of recruiting an Irish ambulance unit to support the French. Their implausibly large 400–strong unit (to staff four ambulances) was covertly designed to provide

---

evidence that a fire is never kindled there except on great occasions … This room is pervaded by a smell for which there is no name in any language. We must call it an odour de pension, l'odeur du renfermé, the odor of the shut-in. It suggests used air, rancid grease, and mildew …; it fills the nostrils with the mingled odors of a scullery and a hospital … The dining-room, with panelled walls, was once painted of a colour no longer discernible, which now forms a background on which layers of dirt, more or less thick, have made a variety of curious patterns … In one corner is a box with pigeon-holes, in which are placed, according to number, the wine-stained and greasy napkins of the various guests. The whole room is a depository of worthless furniture, rejected elsewhere and gathered here, as the battered relics of humanity are gathered in hospitals for the incurable …; a long table covered with oilcloth, so greasy that a facetious guest has been seen to scratch his name upon it with his finger-nail; … To describe how old, how ragged, rotten, rusty, moth-eaten, maimed, shabby, and infirm these remnants are would delay too long the current of this story, and readers in haste to follow it might complain … In a word, here is poverty without relieving sentiment; hard, bitter, rasping poverty'. The (unattributed) translation is from an 1885 Cambridge edition of *Père Goriot*. **98** Cited in Sayers, 'John O'Mahony', p. 160.   **99** Quoted in Desmond Ryan, *The Fenian chief: a biography of James Stephens* (Dublin, 1967), pp 61–2.   **100** John O'Mahony, 'Fenianism as it was', *Irish People*, 14 Dec. 1867.   **101** *Irish People*, 29 Oct. 1870.   **102** *Irish People*, 5 Dec. 1870.   **103** Paul Townend, 'A cosmopolitan nationalist: James J. O'Kelly in America' in T. McMahon, M. de Nie & P. Townend (eds), *Ireland in an imperial world: citizenship, opportunism and subversion* (London, 2017), pp 223–43. James J. was the brother of Aloysius, the artist.   **104** The Igawawen or Gawawa were a confederation of Kabyle Berber tribes in Algeria. The Arabs called them Zwāwa – Zouaoua in French transliteration. The Zouaves in the French army were initially recruited solely from these tribes who were

military training and exposure for an Irish service in the future. This Irish unit proved to be surprisingly capable and resilient. The Franco-Prussian War terminated the enduring Irish tradition of French military service.[105]

There were two different factions of Irish in Paris – the Irish born, and those of Irish descent – 'anciens Irlandais' – who hosted an annual dinner at Le Grand Véfour – 'known from San Francisco to Astrakan' – since 1863. In 1877, the twenty-seven attendees included Viscount O'Neill de Tyrone and his sons, Colonel O'Brien, Colonel McDermott, the composer O'Kelly, Count Nugent, Dr O'Loughlin, John O'Leary, J.P. Leonard and his son.[106] The Irish-born used the church of the Passionist fathers in the Avenue Hoche to maintain their network.

> The Church is the Sunday rendezvous of many members of the Irish colony. Standing outside that edifice after High Mass, on any given Sabbath, one finds himself listening to the old familiar accents of the four provinces – to the hard clink of the north, and the mellifluous brogue of the south, while Leinster and Connaught are also proportionately represented in the chorus.[107]

PARIS IN THE SECOND HALF OF THE NINETEENTH CENTURY

By 1870, Paris was lit by 56,573 gas street lights, conferring its 'city of light' moniker: 'Night truly is no more because darkness has been banished'.[108] Wilkie Collins described the newly bright city: 'Paris is more magnificent than ever. The Rue de Rivoli is now in a perpetual state of illumination. In each arch of the area and on the sides towards the street is placed a brilliant gas light'.[109] For the Fenian, J.F.X. O'Brien, 'London was gloomy, dark and depressing, Paris was bright, dazzling, exhilarating'.[110] Paris became the city of sensation, sex (taking

---

celebrated for their exotic dress.   **105** James McConnell & Mairtín Ó Cathain, 'A training school for rebels: Fenians in the French Foreign Service', *History Ireland*, 16:6 (2008), pp 46–9. Alfred Duquet (1842–1916) led a French delegation (including Ferdinand de Lesseps) to Ireland to thank Irish sympathisers for their help in the Franco-Prussian War. His report is in Alfred Duquet, *Ireland and France: translated by J. De L. Smyth* (Dublin, 1916). This volume had first appeared in Baltimore in 1899.   **106** *Irish Times*, 22 Mar. 1877. 'Various works of art were scattered about in the admirable way that French people can disperse pretty or beautiful things – so that you can't have the idea that you are in a museum. O'Connell looked down on the company from an elegant encadrement of gold and greenery. The bust of Marshall MacMahon held the place of honour, for of all the anciens Irlandais certainly he is the man who makes the greatest figure in the Europe of the day. Then there were portraits of other distinguished Irishmen – orators and men of the sword and pen'.   **107** Davis, *Souvenirs of Irish footprints*, p. 139.   **108** Higonnet, *Paris, capital of the world*, p. 172.   **109** Wilkie Collins to Charles Ward, 19 Mar. 1856, in W. Baker, A. Gasson, G. Law & P. Lewis (eds), *The public face of Wilkie Collins: the collected letters*, 4 vols (London, 2005), i, p. 245.   **110** J.F.X. O'Brien, *For the liberty of Ireland at home and abroad*, ed. J. Regan-Lefebvre (Dublin, 2010),

over from Venice and Amsterdam), spectacle, commodification and consumption. The word souvenir is of French (more specifically Parisian) origin, as tourism exploded.[111] From 1870 to 1890, the number of restaurants in Paris almost doubled to 42,000, the number of prostitutes soared to 70,000 by 1925 (Kaiser Wilhelm dismissed Paris as 'the whorehouse of Europe'), Paris became the acknowledged centre for opera, ballet and art (the term avant garde first surfaced there in 1845), Leotard invented the flying trapeze there in the 1860s, Paris boasted the first specimen of starchitecture in 1889 with the Eiffel Tower, the Moulin Rouge music hall opened in 1899, 90 per cent of world conferences were based there by 1900, fin-de-siècle Paris was a centre of carnal pleasures.[112]

Paris remained the hub of European republicanism and the capital of revolution in the Victorian period and it was notably more hospitable to refugees from all nations than London. Among the artists were Mihály Munkácsy, James MacNeill Whistler[113] and Diego Rivera (from 1911 to 1920). Among the writers were Adam Mickievicz, Gabriel D'Annunzio (1910–14), Henry James, Ivan Turgenev, Gustave Strindberg (1882–3, 1885–7, 1994–8), Gertrude Stein (1903–38), Tristan Tzara (1919–63), Ezra Pound (1921–4), Djuna Barnes (1921–31), Ernest Hemingway (1922–8), Ford Madox Ford, Jean Rhys and most famously of all James Joyce. Among the politicians who lived there were Karl Marx (from 1843 to 1845), Zhou EnLai, Deng Xiaoping, Dom Pedro II (deposed emperor of Brazil), Porfirio Díaz (deposed President of Mexico, exiled in Paris 1911–15), Lenin (1901–12), Dullep Singh, the Sikh Majarah (from 1886 to 1903), and Ho Chi Minh. He was a pastry chef at the Carlton (Churchill's favoured hotel in Paris) in 1913, where Auguste Escoffier taught him how to make the Bombe Néro – a flaming ice cream dessert.

ARTISTS AND SCHOLARS

Paris dominated the global art training and market in the second half of the nineteenth century.[114] The many Irish painters who went to Paris included Nathaniel Hone in the 1850s, Aloysius O'Kelly[115] and Sarah Purser in the 1870s,

---

p. 36. His original manuscript dates from 1895–8.   **111** 'Souvenirs' in the plural retained its literary status, as in Renan's *Souvenirs d'enfance et de jeunesse* (1883).   **112** Christophe Charle, *Paris fin de siècle: culture et politique* (Paris, 1998).   **113** Whistler retained an Irish model, muse and mistress in Paris – Joanna 'Jo' Hiffernan (1843–1903?). She is the subject of his painting *Symphony in White, No. 1: The White Girl* (1862). She is also the subject of Gustave Courbet's *La belle Irlandaise (Portrait of Jo)* (1865–6) and of his notoriously frank *L'Origine du Monde* (1866). Nicholas Daly, 'The woman in white: Whistler, Hiffernan, Courbet, Du Maurier', *Modernism/Modernity*, 12:1 (2005), pp 1–25.   **114** Jean-Marie Perouse de Montclos, *Paris, city of art* (New York, 2003).   **115** In 1884, O'Kelly had his painting, *Messe dans une chaumière de Connemara* (Mass in a Connemara cabin) accepted at the Salon – 'the first painting of an Irish subject ever shown in that all-important venue'. Niamh O'Sullivan, *Aloysius O'Kelly: art, nation, empire* (Dublin, 2010), p. 23.

Musicians and dancers in Paris, 1816–1939

Antheil, George (1923–8)
Casals, Pablo (1895, 1899–1909, 1919–33, 1936)
Chopin, Frédéric (1832–49)
Copland, Aaron (1921–4)
Diaghilev, Sergey (1907–29)
Donizetti, Gaetano (1835, 1838–47)
Duncan, Isadora (1900–14)
Fuller, Loie (1892–1928)
Heine, Heinrich (1831–56)
Liszt, Franz (1823–39)
Mendelssohn, Felix (1816–17, 1825, 1831–2)
Meyerbeer, Giacomo (1822–64)
Offenbach, Jacques (1833–80)
Paderewski, Ignacy (1886, 1888–95, 1915, 1919, 1923, 1930, 1933, 1934, 1939)
Paganini, Nicolò (1831–3, 1838)
Prokofiev, Sergey (1920–35)
Rossini, Gioachino (1824–9, 1855–68)
Schoenberg, Arnold (1933)
Strauss, Richard (1897–1900, 1906–8, 1911, 1914, 1921, 1925, 1930, 1935)
Stravinsky, Igor (1934–8)
Tchaikovsky, Pyotr Ilyich (1861, 1883)
Verdi, Giuseppe (1847–9, 1851–7, 1861–2, 1865–7, 1874–6, 1878, 1880, 1882, 1894)
Weill, Kurt (1933–4)

Rose Barton and Roderic O'Conor in the 1880s, and Paul Henry (who lodged on rue de la Grande Chaumière) in the 1890s. Henry's post-impressionist canvases, with their curiously luxuriant skies and stylised mountains, responded to his stifling childhood in a non-conformist Belfast family, where he had to 'smoke in secret, drink in secret and think in secret'.[116] Henry believed that Paris allowed him 'to see his own country with new and clear eyes'.[117]

The last quarter of the nineteenth century saw the heaviest concentration of Irish artists in Paris.[118] Harry Clarke's artistic breakthrough came when he was awarded a scholarship to visit French medieval cathedrals in 1914. At Notre

116 Paul Henry, *An Irish portrait: the autobiography of Paul Henry* (London, 1952), p. 6.
117 Power, *From the old Waterford house*, p. 82.   118 Julian Campbell, *The Irish impressionists: Irish artists in France and Belgium, 1850–1914* (Dublin, 1984), p. 12.

Dame and Chartres, Clarke encountered the flaming reds and blues that the medieval masters had perfected. Back in Dublin, Clarke applied techniques (flashed glass, aciding, plating) to replicate these glowing jewel-like colours, notably his ruby and deep blues.[119] The Académie Julian accepted female students after 1880. Mainie Jellett (1897–1944) and Evie Hone (1894–1955) brought Cubism back from Paris after being trained by Albert Gleizes in their soujourn there from 1920.

Leading French thinkers like the neurologist Jean-Martin Charcot (1825–93)[120] inspired those who attended their lectures. Charcot, 'the Napoleon of the neuroses', held public lectures at La Salpêtrière hospital that attracted a stellar audience, notably Guy De Maupassant, Sigmund Freud, William James, Émile Durkheim, Henri Bergson, Sarah Bernhardt and Pierre Janet (1859–1947), who originated the theory of dissociation. George Sigerson (1836–1925), who considered Charcot 'the precursor of all modern movements dealing with the subconscious', translated Charcot into English, and hosted him when he visited Dublin to lecture.[121] Sigerson had trained as a doctor in Paris and he himself published on hysteria and epilepsy.[122] Mary Colum described him as 'very Frenchified', keeping a salon and living in a charming house 'full of French furniture and bibelots'.[123] Contact with cutting-edge French thought ensured that the Irish Revival was never insular or parochial in outlook: the Sigerson of Freud, Charcot, Janet and women's sexuality was also the Sigerson of *Bards of the Gael and Gall* (1897) and of the Sigerson Cup in the GAA.

THE FRENCH ROOTS OF IRISH CELTICISM

The Irish Revival grafted itself on the well-ventilated French idea that the Celtic people had dominated Europe before the Romans expelled them from the European core, but who now survived peripherally along the Atlantic littoral, in Brittany, the Basque country, Cornwall, Wales, Scotland and Ireland. Celticism emerged out of the French/Catholic/Breton reaction against Parisian metropolitan modernity, but it achieved a quite extraordinary potency in Ireland. In France the Félibrige, the language revival movement for the Provencal language (Occitan), was founded in 1854 by Mistral, and later included Alphonse Daudet. This movement prefigured the literary revival in Ireland by asserting a

119 Lucy Costigan and Michael Collins, *Strangest genius: the stained glass of Harry Clarke* (Dublin, 2010).   120 Christopher Goetz, Michel Bonduelle & Toby Gelfand, *Charcot: constructing neurology* (New York, 1995).   121 Mary Colum, *Life and the dream* (New York, 1947), p. 166.   122 Jean-Martin Charcot, *Lectures on the diseases of the nervous system: delivered at La Salpêtrière by J.M. Charcot, professor in the Faculty of Medicine of Paris; physician to La Salpêtrière …* First & Second Series (London, 1877–81). These were translated 'by George Sigerson, M.D., Ch.M., Licentiate of the King and Queen's College of Physicians of Ireland; Dean of the Faculty of Science, C[atholic] U[niversity [of] I [reland]'].   123 Colum, *Life and the dream*, pp 163–7.

direct line of affiliation between current tradition and ancestral religious beliefs, while presenting 'modernity' – and big city culture – as the enemy.

Celticism was an expression of cultural nationalism, a central, fundamental and persistent version of nationalism, evolving and deepening across nineteenth-century Europe. The diversity of European cultural traditions was reconfigured as 'national', elevating them to decisive diagnostics in a Europe considered as a set of nations. Theorists of nationalism have prioritised modernisation processes and political activism rather than the equally crucial realms of vernacular culture, philology and folklore.[124] The nineteenth century saw the flourishing of intellectual interest in vernacular culture, not as picturesque 'customs', but as embodying and preserving the core national identity, displaying its specificity amidst other nations. This dynamic of culture underpinned scholarly investment in language, folktales, myths, legends, place names, mythology, antiquities, artefacts, archaeological sites, material culture, dances, pastimes, sports, customs, and especially music.

These new ideas first surfaced in systematic intellectual form in Ireland with James Hardiman's *Irish minstrelsy* in 1831, which was inspired by Claude Fauriel's *Chant populaires de la Grèce moderne* (1824). Fauriel asserted the value of popular poetry as an expression of national character against the weight of the classical tradition. He was also an early champion of French regionalism with his interest in Breton and Provencal. This French thinking made it easy to align with Irish cultural nationalism. *L'Irlande Libre*, the newspaper that Maud Gonne edited in Paris, noted in its first issue in May 1897: 'In this title, an expression of our hope, we place the whole programme of our national demands; And it is to France, a country always so dear to the oppressed, that we come to issue this cry of freedom. Besides, are we not also Celts, sons of the same race, and has our blood not flowed many times over the same battlefields, under our allied flags?'

Scholarship, translation and philology fed comparative mythology, a discipline that emerged out of intellectual circles in Paris and Berlin. A significant cohort of Irish scholars studied in Paris, including Margaret Stokes (1832–1900),[125] Richard Irvine Best (1872–1959), Thomas MacGreevy (1893–1967) and Daniel Binchy (1899–1989). The lectures of Henry d'Arbois de Jubainville (1827–1910) in comparative literature were attended by Synge, Best and Sigerson. He inspired Best to develop his expertise in Old and Middle Irish and he went on to translate de Jubainville in *The Irish mythological cycle and Celtic mythology* (Dublin, 1903). This and other works allowed the Celtic Gods and fighting men to spring vividly alive in the contemporary Irish imagination. The Revival was saturated in Pagan and Celtic Gods, as a way of evading British

124 The blatant example is Benedict Anderson. For the culturalist perspective, Joop Leerssen is the main protagonist.   125 Emily Cullen, 'Margaret Stokes (1832–1900) and the study of medieval Irish art' in C. Breathnach & C. Lawless (eds), *Visual, material and print culture in nineteenth-century Ireland* (Dublin, 2010), pp 73–84.

Victorian pieties, and of establishing the pre-Christian Celtic period as a shared cultural space, beyond the debilitating labels of Catholic and Protestant.[126]

It was also from France that the Irish imported the concept that the real Ireland was rooted in the country not the city. The French myth of the country developed in the second half of the nineteenth century– a counterpoise to the sordid city. The future of France should spring from its deep rural past – *France profonde* – not its shallow urban present. The turn to the provinces could then be experienced as a return. The leading characters in nineteenth-century French fiction emanated from the provinces: Rastignac from Angoulême, Julien Sorel from Besancon. This was the era of the backlash to urbanisation. John Ruskin abhorred 'that great foul city of London – rattling, growling, smoking, stinking – a ghastly heap of fermenting brickwork, pouring out poison at every pore'.[127] Modernism in this sense was drenched in urban disenchantment, a fading aura eclipsed by an implacably bright modernity. There was no longer any home to go to, for the once tightly woven fabric of faith, family, community and place had unravelled.

SYNGE IN PARIS

The radical Irish republicans, artists and scholars in Paris were joined by the writers. Among the stream of distinguished Irish writers who resided in Paris were George Moore, Oscar Wilde, J.M. Synge, James Joyce and Samuel Beckett. The sickly Synge was famously admonished by W.B. Yeats in Paris in 1896: 'Give up Paris. You will never create anything by reading [the French dramatist] Racine, and Arthur Symonds will always be a better critic of French literature. Go to the Aran Islands, live there as if you were one of the people themselves: express a life that has never found expression'. In 1898, Synge lived on Aran, and produced his compelling *The Aran Islands*. This work could never have been conceived without his rootless restless Paris experience, nor his exposure to French thinking about Brittany, so venerated by Ernest Renan, Anatole le Braz and Pierre Loti.[128] Lavoir noted that 'I go to Brittany to replenish my personality and become entirely myself again'.[129]

Synge posited the West as an environment where humans faced a natural world so stark as to be incomprehensible to the upholstered world of twentieth-century domesticity. Like Brittany, the West of Ireland retained the authentic civilisation that rebuked modernity, an alternative to London, Paris or Dublin. Aran and the Atlantic seaboard had been enriched rather than diminished by its

---

126 Mark Williams, *Ireland's immortals: a history of the Gods of Irish myth* (Princeton, NJ, 2016).   127 John Ruskin, *The crown of wild olive: three lectures on work, traffic and war* (New York, 1866), p. 9.   128 J.M. Synge, *The Aran Islands, with drawings by J.B. Yeats* (Dublin, 1907).   129 Higonnet, *Paris, capital of the world*, p. 211.

isolation from modernity. They preserved what had been lost elsewhere – customs, beliefs, attitudes, generosity of spirit, old-world courtesy, a communal mindset. The sense of the loss is as crucial as the sense of preservation; the prestige of the country could only be elevated against the degradation of the city.[130]

Yeats and Synge argued that the Irish as a communal people were distinguished from their atomised European counterparts. Ireland was the sole enduring ancestral civilisation in Europe, because every other country had been so ravaged by industrial modernity that they had ceased to have continuous communities and they existed now only in the dishevelled state of the modern urban crowd. The Irish Revival could challenge the relentlessly arid march of modernity by opposing it to this rural culture saturated in a vivid and still living past. The bracing encounter with the country rinsed the modern soul of city grime. The Celts retained the ultimate civilisational secret that Europe had carelessly discarded – their metaphysical view of the world. These were a people who still lived both in time and in eternity.

The value of a therapeutic but vanishing Ireland exerted an enormous appeal for French people, because it was the French themselves who had first incubated the concept. Roger Chauviré described the Irish speaking communities of the west of Ireland in a 1930 essay as 'a gentle night-lamp, which burned still tenderly in the cruel night of its world'.[131] It flickered all the more poignantly by being on the brink of enforced extinction.

WHY PARIS? MODERNITY AND MODERNISM

If modernity is the period, and modernism is the style, how were they linked? The contemporary thinking ran like this. Before modernity, life had an integrated belief system which balanced past and present, faith and reason, embodied in formal ritual, seasonal rhythms and shared set pieces. People lived in coherent knowable communities, and enjoyed a settled repose no longer available to the modern person, trapped on an accelerating treadmill of splinter, fragment and meaninglessness. Urbanisation carried with it a sense of city life being too artificial, too complex, too hurried to be experienced or understood any longer as a whole. That created two novel sensations – the dislocation of family, neighbourhood, community and nature, and solitude in the crowd.[132] Alienation became the quintessentially urban sensibility. Paris after Haussmann exhibited, in Henry James' words, a 'deadly monotony', with 'its huge, blank, pompous, featureless sameness'.[133]

130 This point is well made in a different context in Mark Ford, *Thomas Hardy: half a Londoner* (Cambridge, MA, 2016).   **131** Roger Chauviré, 'Un monde quie meurt' in *Contes d'un autre monde* (Paris, 1947), p. 242.   **132** The subject of Georg Simmel's 1908 essay 'The stranger' in *The sociology of Georg Simmel*, K. Wolff (trans.) (New York, 1950), pp 402–8.   **133** Henry

This new sensibility birthed a new sociology, with the discovery of what Durkheim (elevated to a Sorbonne Professorship in 1902) termed *anomie*. The term captured the besetting urban ills of the modern world: isolation, frustration, boredom, a lack of sexual and martial energy ... This sense soon went inwards in Proust and in Freud. The experience of modernity transformed subjectivity itself, as it struggled to adopt to the cacophonous kaleidoscopic street.

With modernity, the old aesthetic practices proved to be terminally inadequate, as contemporaries sensed that history had dealt them the fatal blow. The quiet century from 1815 to 1914, with its Belle Époque and the Gilded Age, was followed by the mechanistic killing fields of the morally bereft First World War. These changes presaged the collapse of authority both political and religious, the loss of faith, the fall of empire (the Boer War), the rise of communism (the Russian Revolution 1917), even capitalism itself convulsing (Wall Street Crash and the Great Depression) ....

The First World War killed realism stone dead: it stripped large-scale historical processes like war and imperialism of glamour and weaned Europe from its long infatuation with melodrama. After the First World War, realism proved an exhausted form. Henry James conducted a now celebrated interview with the *New York Times* in 1915, where he diagnosed the literary impact of the European conflagration:

> The war has used up words; they have weakened, they have deteriorated like motor car tires; they have, like millions of other things, been more overstrained and knocked about and voided of the happy semblance during the last six months than in all the long ages before, and we are now confronted with a depreciation of all our terms, or, otherwise speaking, with a loss of expression through increase of limpness, that may well make us wonder what ghosts will be left to walk.[134]

The Paris-based Walter Benjamin noted:

> A generation that had gone to school on a horse-drawn street car now stood under the open sky in a countryside in which nothing remained unchanged but the clouds, and beneath these clouds, in a field of force of destructive torrents and explosions, was the tiny, fragile human body.[135]

Against this backdrop, Paris was represented as the quintessential modern metropolis – a city of jagged shocks. The transitional generation experienced

James, *The art of travel: scenes and journeys in America, England, France and Italy*, ed. M. Zabel (New York, 1958), p. 217. **134** *New York Times*, 21 Mar. 1915. **135** Benjamin, *Selected writings*, iii, pp 143–66; Walter Benjamin, *The Arcades project* (Cambridge, MA, 2002);

modernism as a radical historical rupture, hopelessly suspending them between a nostalgic inner life and a disenchanted external reality: human beings who once were everything were suddenly nothing, evicted from the cosy cocoon of cosmic meaning.[136] Georg Simmel's 1903 essay 'The metropolis and mental life' argued that:

> The deepest problems of modern life flow from the attempt of the individual to maintain the independence and individuality of his existence against the sovereign powers of society, against the weight of the historical heritage and the external culture and technique of life.[137]

Modernism as a style repudiated representational realism, the omniscient narration by a 'central intelligence' (Henry James) of a Balzac, a Dickens, a Zola, a Hardy or a Trollope, self-professed analysts of the new city, but still essentially old style realists. Modernism espoused a flattened language to capture the new urban reality. This first surfaced in Flaubert's bleak depiction of Paris in his *Sentimental education* (1869) – a stylistic break that dismayed the old guard – James decried reading Flaubert as like 'masticating ashes and sawdust'[138] – but one that signalled the decisive break from the unities of realism to the fragmentations of modernism. These traits of modernism were incubated in Paris, as in the shift from Cezanne to Picasso, from Zola to Proust, from Offenbach to Stravinsky, from Newton to Einstein in 1922.[139]

Modernism was forced to grapple with the extreme specialisation of the modern world: Simmel noted the existence of an 'extreme phenomenon' in Paris – the remunerative occupation of the *quatorzième*.

> These are persons who identify themselves by signs on their residences and who are ready at the dinner hour in correct attire, so that they can be quickly called upon if a dinner party should consist of thirteen persons.[140]

The modernist novel assumed reponsibility for explaining this newly fragmented world, in which accelerating scientific specialisation rendered each discipline impenetrable to other scientists, let alone ordinary citizens. As Magris wryly

Margaret Cohen, *Profane illumination: Walter Benjamin and the Paris of surrealist revolution* (Berkeley, 1995). **136** Claudio Magris, 'A cryptogram of its age', *New Left Review*, 95 (Sept.–Oct. 2015), pp 95–107. This elegant essay ponders the relationship between the novel and modernity. An earlier and still-exhilarating version is Marshall Berman, *All that is solid melts into air: the experience of modernity* (New York, 1982). **137** Georg Simmel, 'The metropolis and mental life' in *The sociology of Georg Simmel*. **138** Eric Bulson, *Novels, maps, modernity* (New York & London, 2010), p. 10. **139** Stravinsky in Paris in 1920 was intrigued by what was happening in Ireland, as he recalled in his 1963 interview with the *Irish Times* (cited in *Irish Times*, 5 Feb. 2016). On Einstein's visit to Paris in 1922, see Charles Nordmann, 'Einstein expose et discute sa théorie', *Revue des Deux Mondes*, 9 (1922), pp 129–66. **140** Simmel, 'Metropolis and modern life'. The city could drive you 'mental' in the modern

notes, 'it was left to novelists to take up the questions that the sciences could not answer and show us how to live in a disintegrated world'.[141]

FROM PARIS TO DUBLIN: JOYCE'S TRAJECTORY

How then should we make the interpretative leap from Paris to Dublin? Why did the global modernism of this period develop so pronounced a Dublin accent – Joyce, Yeats and Beckett (arguably the 'big beasts' of modernism in the novel, poetry and drama respectively), and Eileen Grey (1878–1976), an architectural pioneer of the modernism movement in her E1027 (1926–9)? One answer is that the dislocated subject of modernity and of modernism as a style resembled the colonial subject. The colonial encounter in Ireland had excavated a hollowed-out identity. Linguistically adrift between two languages, Irish writers possessed the hyper-consciousness of language-as-aftermath characteristic of modernism, that at its best encouraged experimentation, subversion and the ability to escape the gravitational field of an entrenched language. Modernism was readily intelligible to those who were already acutely aware of the instability of language. Every post-Famine Irish writer had to negotiate shifting terrain, with a stranded sense that the tide had gone out on a shared language, a shared community.[142] Joyce showed in the starkest of terms that an Irish deep past no longer existed because it had been eviscerated by a dual colonialism – 'the English tyranny and the Roman tyranny' – that curious complicity of British imperialism and Roman Catholicism which made Ireland 'the scullery maid of Christendom'.[143] In Joyce's most lacerating phrase, Ireland was now the home of 'the gratefully oppressed'.[144]

This opened an Irish space receptive to modernism. The modernist move was towards the free indirect style, at once public and private, first person thoughts expressed in third person grammar. In Joyce's *Ulysses*, the *monologue intérieur*, as the French critic Valéry Larbaud had christened it, achieved full realisation as Bloom moved through an ordinary day in Dublin. Joyce claimed to have derived the interior monologue from Édouard Dujardin's 1888 novel *Les lauriers sont coupés*, read on his first visit to Paris in 1903.[145] This fusion of the social and the personal, self-reflective interiority, displayed the uninterpreted perception of the characters through narrated monologue, rendering immediacy but also incoherence.

Dublin sense of that word.   **141** Magris, 'A cryptogram of its age', p. 106.   **142** I trace this concept in 'The memories of "The Dead"', *Yale Journal of Criticism*, 15:1 (2002), pp 59–97. **143** James Joyce, *A portrait of the artist as a young man*, ed. S. Deane (London, 1992), p. 222. **144** James Joyce, 'After the race' in James Joyce, *Dubliners*, ed. T. Brown (London, 1992), p. 35. **145** Jean-Michel Rabate, 'Joyce the Parisian' in D. Attridge (ed.), *The Cambridge companion to James Joyce* (Cambridge, 1990), pp 83–102. Mary Colum thought all of this palaver was a

For his contemporaries, the encounter with Joyce's novels resembled encountering a shattered mirror where everything reflected obliquely. *Ulysses* offered scattered shards of a jigsaw but without supplying the picture on the box – and thereby crystallised the modernist moment. Joyce mastered verbal flow rather than fixity, trying to mimic a fluid reality via narrative experiments.

Joyce also mastered montage, mosaic and collage, his texts studded with embedded quotations like shrapnel from older texts, to indicate that the heads of his characters were full of jumbled echoes, bits and pieces, floating fragments of what had once been complete and monumental. This fragmentation contextualises the notorious difficulty of modernism as a style: Proust, Stravinsky, Schoenberg, Joyce, Picasso all required explication and commentary, as opposed to the ease of reading Dickens, Hardy or Zola, the instant legibility of a painting by Jean-Léon Gérôme, or the catchy melodies of Bizet, Berlioz and Offenbach.

Joyce's achievement was his audacious reimagining of Dublin as a universal city. If Paris was the laboratory where modernism was invented, Dublin became the scene of its first explosion. Exile was critical for Joyce, liberating experience into memory, thickening time into a mille feuille of memories, 'there to be shaped and burnished to finished radiance'.[146] Joyce living in host cities – 'Trieste, Zurich, Paris, 1914–1921' are the last words of *Ulysses* – became the exile necessarily open to everybody and everything – empathetically 'married to the crowd'. The metropolis of modernity, with its endless parade of strangers, expanded the horizon of sympathy, thereby expanding the self, and that encounter encouraged Joyce to formulate his radical version of democratic citizenship.[147]

Paris in that imaginative sense launched Joyce's marvellous experiments. His stylistic innovations were even more extravagantly on display in *Finnegans wake* in 1939, the work that consumed Joyce's life in Paris after 1920. Now not only was the overall picture withheld from the reader as in *Ulysses*, but the individual pieces were blurred, phantasmagoric, and the English language suffered a meltdown as it sought to absorb hundreds of others in a maelstrom of linguistic collision. Joyce in that sense is a literary founder, a master of creative destruction who displaced the incumbent traditional narrative paradigm not through launching an incremental 'new and improved' model, but through the invention of an utterly different one. After Joyce, the realist novel lay dead beneath the Liffey water, a few stray bubbles burbling to the surface.

Paris was equally crucial to Joyce through the reality that the city also bankrolled his work. Paris was cheap with a very favourable exchange rate for the pound and dollar and it also had more relaxed obscenity laws than London or

gigantic leg-pull by Joyce (Colum, *Life and the dream*, p. 394).   **146** John Banville, *Time pieces: a Dublin memoir* (Dublin, 2016), p. 4.   **147** This is the theme of Declan Kiberd, *Ulysses and us: the art of everyday living* (New York, 2009).

New York, especially for English-language publications. Accordingly Paris incubated experimental modernist presses like Shakespeare and Company.[148] Joyce met Sylvia Beach at her Parisian bookshop in 1920. She 'worshipped' Joyce – 'tall, thin, slightly stooped, graceful' but 'always a bit shabby'. The generosity of this exceptional woman made possible the publication of *Ulysses*.[149]

JOYCE, PARIS AND THE FENIANS

Joyce visited Paris in 1903 to meet an acquaintance of his father, the veteran Fenian Joseph Casey (1845–1911), on whom he modelled his *Ulysses* character Kevin Egan (he was called Joe Egan in the first draft). He refused to look up Maud Gonne, despite his mother's urgings, perhaps because of his shabby clothing, and casually dismissed *Riders to the sea* (loaned to him by Synge) as 'dwarf drama'. Arthur Power's well-known description of Joyce was that 'there was much of the Fenian about him – his dark suiting, his wide hat, his light carriage, and his intense expression. A literary conspirator, [he] was determined to destroy the oppressive cultural structures under which we had been reared, and which were then crumbling'.[150] In *Ulysses*, Dedalus watched Egan roll 'gunpowder cigarettes through fingers smeared with printer's ink'. Egan himself is described as 'In gay Paree he hides … unsought by any save by me … Loveless, landless, wifeless … Weak wasting hand on mine. They have forgotten Kevin Egan, not he them'.[151]

    After Joseph Casey was arrested in London in 1867, his brother Patrick and other Fenians hatched a plot to spring him from Clerkenwell Prison by piercing the walls with a bomb. It failed miserably. Joseph was later released and sought exile in Paris ('Remembering thee, O Sion'), where he was employed as a printer and compositor. The brothers Patrick and Joseph both worked as typesetters for Galignani's *Messenger* on rue de Rivoli, then for Henri Rochefort's initially radical socialist *L'Instransigeant* from 1880, and later at the Paris-office of the *New York Herald*. There were four Caseys in Paris in 1870: Patrick, James and Andrew all fought in the 1870 war, and two (James and Andrew) were killed. Patrick was involved in Paris in a Grand Guignol episode with the Maharajah Duleep Singh (1838–93), the last Sikh sovereign, involving the Koh-i-Noor diamond, Fenians, fake passports, a wife who turned out to be a British spy, and a putative Russian invasion of the Punjab.[152] Patrick returned to Dublin in 1891, where he became a neighbour and friend of Joyce's father.

---

148 The publication of pornography moved in the last quarter of the nineteenth century from London to Amsterdam before concentrating in Paris.   149 Sylvia Beach, *Ulysses in Paris* (New York, 1956), p. 9. Shakespeare and Company is described as the 'quintessence of the literary bookshop' in Noel Riley Fitch, *Sylvia Beach and the lost generation: a history of literary Paris in the twenties and thirties* (London, 1985), p. 43.   150 Arthur Power, *Conversations with James Joyce*, ed. C. Hart (London, 1974).   151 Rabate, 'Joyce the Parisian'.   152 Christy

Michael Davitt described Joseph Casey as a man 'with a leaning toward dynamite and a decided taste for absinthe'.[153] Casey had joined the National Guard when he moved to Paris in 1868, and defended the capital against the Prussians in 1870. In a newspaper interview, he noted: 'When the revolt broke out in Paris with the shooting of Generals Thomas and Clement, I went to the Hotel de Ville and handed in my gun. I told them that I had volunteered to fight against the enemies of France, not to take part in a civil war'.[154]

When Joyce went to Paris in 1903, he was connected to Joseph Casey. The old man – separated, lonely, querulous, garrulous, and a 'bitter-ender' in Fenian terms – helped Joyce to settle in Paris. He frequently brought him for lunch at the Restaurant des Deux Écus near rue de Louvre, where Casey worked at the *New York Herald* office. Joyce's luminously ominous phrase 'Shattered glass and toppling masonry' summoned the Clerkenwell explosion, but also the First World War and Dublin in 1916. The spectacles-dependent Joyce had a horror of breaking glass – a prolepsis of blindness. That metaphoric cluster of eyes, blindness and broken glass recurs again and again in his work.

JOYCE: HOME AND AWAY

Joyce's close friend Con Curran described him at home in Paris.

> I once asked Joyce when was he coming back to Dublin. 'Why should I?' he said. 'Have I ever left it?' And of course he never really had. He contained Dublin. His knowledge of the town by inheritance, by observation, by memory was prodigious, and he was at pains to keep his picture of it up to date. When he challenged me to mention some new feature of Dublin to justify his return, I could only instance the new smell of petrol. If Dublin were destroyed, his words could rebuild the houses; if its population were wiped out, his books could re-people it. Joyce was many things, but he was certainly the last forty volumes of Thom's Directory thinking aloud.[155]

Even as Joyce killed realism and stretched the English language beyond its breaking point, Dublin was never not there: he told a friend that the real heroes of *Finnegans Wake* were 'time and the river and the mountain'. Joyce assured the

Campbell, *The Maharajah's box: an imperial story of conspiracy, love, and a guru's prophecy* (London, 2002). In his 1889 proclamation, he was confident that he could get 'volunteers to join him from Ireland, and that the three or four thousand Irish in the British Indian army would join the revolt' and 'freely shed their blood for your liberty'. In an ironic Irish twist, the Guinness family bought his Elveden Estate in 1894. **153** Richard Ellman, *James Joyce*, revised edition (New York, 1982), p. 125. **154** *Freeman's Journal*, 29 Mar. 1915. **155** *Irish Times*, 14 Jan. 1941.

Irish diplomat Sean Lester in Geneva in 1940 about his link to Dublin: 'I am attached to it daily and nightly like an umbilical cord',[156] while still retaining a riveting sense of its intimate spite, edge and gossip. Like so many Irish writers, Joyce liked to play both home and away.

MAUD GONNE

Maud Gonne – or Gone Mad as the Dublin wits liked to call her – modelled her distinctive self-presentation on Juliette Adam (1836–1936), the flamboyant feminist founder/editor of *Nouvelle Revue*, whom she had met in Paris in the 1890s.[157] Gonne was six foot two inches tall, conferring the advantage of visibility in an era of street politics. The Boulangist Lucien Millevoye, whom she met in Paris in 1887, clarified Gonne's hitherto vague political aspirations. His generation was rife with grievance over France's humiliating defeat in the Franco-Prussian War of 1870 and the resulting loss of Alsace-Lorraine. Gonne was also sufficently accomplished socially – and sufficiently elegant – to make it into the social pages of the French press. In 1896, the *Album Mariani* gave 'Miss Maud Gonne' – 'a woman of the world, wonderfully beautiful and sweet' – star treatment, as an 'Ibsen woman'.[158] They noted that she made political prisoners her special care, visiting them and writing letters on their behalf. A polished ebony paper knife, incised 'Miss Maud Gonne, Paris / Made by / Prisoners of War/Ceylon/1900/1901' was sold at auction in Dublin in 2016. Throughout her life Gonne remained an active supporter of prisoners of war and conscience in various countries – and inspired her son Seán, co-founder of Amnesty International.

In 1898, Maud Gonne and W.B. Yeats issued an invitation on behalf of 'Le Comité Irlandais', in a printed circular in French, to join in events celebrating the centenary of 'the effort which our ancestors made a century ago towards liberty, with generous aid from France', especially at banquets for French delegates organised by the Irish in London, Dublin, Killala, Ballina and Castlebar.[159]

Gonne lived in the city throughout her rancid marriage with John MacBride. Gonne felt that her husband had fallen in with the 'wrong crowd', especially the journalist Victor Collins, who was his' 'undoing':

---

156 Ulick O'Connor (ed.), *The Joyce we knew* (Dublin, 2004). Introduction.   **157** Davis, *Souvenirs of Irish footprints*, pp 138–9.   **158** 'Miss Maud Gonne', *Figures contemporaines tirées de l'Album Mariani*, volume two, unpaginated, Paris 1896. My thanks to the ever-generous Pierre Joannon for making this available to me.   **159** In the author's possession. The subscribers' list for the *Shan Van Vocht* in 1898 listed four Parisian subscribers: Miss Maud Gonne at 7 Avenue D'Eylau, Miss Barry Delaney at the Office of *L'Irlande Libre*, 6 rue de Martyrs, Mrs Rowley at 11 Avenue du Bois de Boulogne and Madame la Vicomtesse de Vercelli de Ranzi, 32 rue du Pont, Neuilly, Paris (in possession of the author).

John worked as Secretary to Victor Collins, who earned a large salary as correspondent to the *New York Sun* and Laffan's Bureau, a fairly important news agency. Despite my warning, John became the inseparable companion of Collins, who introduced him to a rather undesirable drinking set who usually foregathered in the American Bar. He had an unhappy life in Paris. He did not know a word of French.[160]

Gonne raised funds in Paris for the Irish pro-Boer movement and (with Mark Ryan in London) was the key funder of Irish separatist organisations between 1899 and 1903.[161] The 1890s globally was a decade of imperial wars – Britain in Africa, Spain in Cuba, America in the Philippines – and the changing international atmosphere resonated in Paris as in Ireland.[162] The Irish Pro-Boer Transvaal Committee, established in 1899, provided the nucleus for the emergence of Sinn Féin.[163] The Committee included Gonne, Connolly, Arthur Griffiths and John O'Leary; supporters included Yeats and Davitt. This new grouping advocated for an independent foreign policy for Ireland for the first time. The Committee organised street protests, civil disobedience, and riots. Gonne spearheaded opposition to recruiting in Ireland. Davitt withdrew from Westminster, inaugurating the policy of abstentionism, later a key plank of Sinn Féin policy. Divisions on the Boer War exposed the growing divide between radical separatists and conservative parliamentarians.

CATHOLIC LINKS

Parisian links remained strong in the build-up to the 1916 rising and the French exerted an influence, notably through the cultural prestige of French intellectuals who visited Ireland pre-1916, including Vicomte Florimond de Basterot (1836–1904), whose ancestors had settled on the Galway/Clare border, Guy de Maupassant, Maurice Barrés and Paul Bourget. The Irish Catholic affinity for France (despite French secularism) was strengthened by the fact that leading Irish clerics like Fr John Miley (1805–61), Archbishop T. W. Croke (who relished French wine and literature),[164] Cardinal Michael Logue (1840–1924), Fr Patrick Lavelle (1825–61), Monsignor Pádraig de Brún (1889–1960) and Fr John Hayes (1889–1957) (founder of Muintir na Tíre) were educated in Paris, that French Catholic devotional literature was widely translated in nineteenth-century Ireland, and through the astonishing influx of French orders in Irish schools.[165]

160 Maud Gonne MacBride, Witness Statement 317, Bureau of Military History. **161** McGee, *The IRB*, p. 283. **162** Benedict Anderson, *Under three flags: anarchism and the anti-colonial imagination* (London, 2006). **163** P.J. Mathews, 'Stirring up disloyalty: the Boer War, the Irish literary theatre and the emergence of a new separatism', *Irish University Review*, 33:1 (Spring 2003), pp 99–116. **164** Mark Tierney, *Croke of Cashel: the life of Archbishop Thomas William Croke, 1823–1902* (Dublin, 1976), p. 7. **165** The best book on French politics and

The female religious orders which came to Ireland included the Ursulines (1770s), Sacred Heart (1842), Faithful Companions of Jesus (1844), Good Shepherd (1848), Daughters of Charity (1855), Our Lady of Charity of the Refuge (1853), St Louis (1859), St Joseph of Cluny (1860), Little Sisters of the Poor (1860s), Sacré Coeur (1862), Bon Secours (1865), Sacred Heart of Mary (1870), Marists (1873) and Little Sisters of the Assumption (1891).[166] These schools presumably supplied the five hundred Irish girls who worked in Paris in 1920 as governesses, who were organised by the Irish clergy who staffed the anglophone church on the Avenue Hoche.[167]

THE 1916 RISING

Many flags flew in Dublin in 1916. At least three fluttered over the GPO. The Tricolour, with its revolutionary French connotations, was the choice of radical republicans. The Fenian Oath had been devised by James Stephens in Paris in 1859: 'I, A. B., in the presence of Almighty God, do solemnly swear allegiance to the Irish Republic, now virtually established; and that I will do my very utmost, at every risk, while life lasts, to defend its independence and integrity; and, finally, that I will yield implicit obedience in all things, not contrary to the laws of God [or 'the laws of morality'], to the commands of my superior officers. So help me God. Amen'.[168] French secular republicanism dictated key passages in the 1916 proclamation of 'the Irish republic now virtually established'. Its authors were intent on advancing Irish republicanism well beyond Whiteboyism and the hillside men, conferring on it historical and intellectual gravitas and emitting a whiff of French glamour.[169]

While the French Ambassador to London, Paul Cambon, recognised after 1916 that the future in Irish politics belonged to Sinn Féin, he felt bruised that the Irish had turned away so decisively away from their former friend France. J.F.X. O'Brien had noted: 'In 1855 the name of France would have worked enthusiasm in an Irish crowd in almost any part of Ireland ... I do not think that sympathy for France is now [1895] as vivid as it was in 1855 among Irishmen'.[170] In his dispatch of 3 May 1916, the ambassador noted:

> The Sinn Feiners have won over the sympathy of the majority of the Irish
> people. The question is no longer simply that of Home Rule for Ireland,

Catholicism of this period is Michael Sutton, *Nationalism, positivism and Catholicism: the politics of Charles Maurras and French Catholics, 1890–1914* (Cambridge, 1982).   **166** A.V. O'Connor, 'The revolution in girls' secondary education in Ireland 1860–1910' in M. Cullen (ed.), *Girls don't do honours: Irish women in education in the 19th and 20th centuries* (Dublin, 1987), pp 31–54.   **167** *Documents on Irish foreign policy*, i, p. 52.   **168** Ryan, *Fenian chief*, p. 92.   **169** Liam de Paor, *On the Easter Proclamation and other declarations* (Dublin, 1997). This short book is still one of the best on 1916.   **170** O'Brien, *For the liberty of Ireland*, p. 36.

but separation. The republican flag has been raised in Dublin; the clock has been put back fifty years in Ireland and one can safely say that the days of the Fenians have returned. The continuation of the policy of Home Rule is impossible.[171]

A later French delegation in June 1916 remarked on the efflorescence of Sinn Féin: it was like 'a rather narrow river, which had suddenly burst its banks and covers today a vast extent of territory'.[172]

DUBLIN, PARIS AND REVOLUTION

The most astonishing feature of the 1916 Rising was that it took place in Dublin, the city so long despised by Irish nationalism for its shoneenism and introversion.[173] Yeats excoriated the Dublin in which the Irish Revival started as 'a vile hole', 'torn with every kind of political passion and prejudice'.[174] And yet it was Dublin, rather than the vaunted nationalist heartlands of Cork or Tipperary, that initiated the Rising.

Dublin could also claim that the city instigated one of the seminal processes of twentieth-century history – the dissolution of the British Empire globally.[175] The Rising in Dublin marked a sea-change, initiating the process by which Ireland became the first successful secessionist from the British Empire since the American colonies. These facts heralded the advent of Dublin as an Irish capital rather than a British provincial town. The 1916 leaders had been determined to assert Dublin's role as an Irish city. Pearse's *War Bulletin* praised the Dublin insurgents: 'Already they have won a great thing. They have redeemed Dublin from many shames and made her name splendid among the names of cities'. A wrong-footed Yeats himself registered the shock: 'A bunch of martyrs (1916) were the bomb and we are living in the explosion'.[176]

Dublin now joined the ranks of other devastated European cities – Ypres, Louvain, Rheims – as an emblem of the First World War.[177] Dublin also joined Paris in 1870 and predated St Petersburgh in 1917 as global emblems of revolutionary cities. All three cities were incubators of cultural modernism and

171 Mark Tierney, 'A survey of reports of French consuls in Ireland 1814–1929' in L. Swords (ed.), *Irish-French connections, 1578–1978* (Paris, 1978), pp 130–41. **172** Tierney, 'French consuls', p. 138. **173** Mark Traugott, 'Capital cities and revolutions', *Social Science History*, 19:1 (Spring 1995), pp 147–68. His focus is especially on Paris in 1789, 1830 and 1848, and the ability of insurrectionists in the capital to impose their will on an unreceptive rural population. **174** W.B. Yeats, *The collected works of W.B. Yeats. Vol. X: Later articles and reviews*, ed. C. Johnson (New York, 2000), p. 255. **175** I trace this trajectory in Kevin Whelan, *Dublin in its global setting: from Wood Quay to Silicon City* (Dublin, 2015). **176** Yeats to Olivia Shakespeare, 1922, in *Letters of William Butler Yeats*, ed. A. Wade (London, 1954), p. 690. **177** Keith Jeffery, *1916: a global history* (London, 2015), pp 97–122.

hosted a surprising number of its major figures: St Petersburg (Pushkin, Gogol, Dostoevsky, Shostakovitch); Paris (Baudelaire, Proust, Picasso, Apollinaire); Dublin (Joyce, Yeats, Synge, Beckett).[178]

FROM EUROPE TO AMERICA

One result of the European descent into a world war was the inexorable ascent of America as the leading global power, marked by its participation in the war in 1917. The British entered the war as the dominant global power; the Americans exited it in that position – a seismic collapse in British imperial prestige.

America's ascendancy as a world power swelled an extraordinary surge of national pride, driven by disdain for a declining Europe. But America remained troubled by a nagging sense that while its democratic mass culture might be energetic it was also inherently vulgar, in contrast to the sophisticated high culture of old Europe. New York would be the business capital of the world but could it assume the role of capital of twentieth-century culture that Paris had performed with such verve across the span of the nineteenth century? The Armoury Show in New York in 1913 marked a turning point (with Irish-American input by John Quinn, and with paintings by John Butler Yeats on display) but it was only in the 1960s that New York indubitably became the capital of the global art market.

Irish nationalism pivoted away from Britain and Europe and towards the United States. 1916 was incubated in New York and Philadelphia rather than in Paris.[179] Of the signatories of the 1916 Proclamation, more had experience of New York than Paris. Only John MacBride had a lengthy Paris experience. In 1910, Thomas MacDonagh had gone there to live at 44 rue de Jacob, seeking the solitude of 'a hawk in the sky'.[180] Others associated with the literary and cultural revival that spent time in Paris included Constance Markievicz (who met her Polish husband, Count Casimir Markievicz at art school in Paris and married him in 1900), Padraic Colum and the novelist James Stephens. Markievicz, like her close friend Gonne, was financially independent, tall and cosmopolitan: she returned to Dublin from a Bohemian life in Paris and London in 1907 and plunged into full-blooded political activism around a political, social and feminist

---

178 One way in which Dublin did not follow Parisian precedent was in its refusal to Haussmanise the post-Independence capital. Patrick Abercrombie's modernist plan of 1922 advanced extravagant proposals for remodelling the city on those lines. 'Dublin today presents a similar spectacle to Paris prior to the operations of Napoleon III and Haussmann: it is a city of magnificent possibilities, containing features of the first order, but loosely co-related and often marred by the juxtaposition of incongruities and squalor. As at Paris central areas which should be of first-rate commercial importance are occupied by slums, and streets of noble architectural dignity are tenement ridden': Patrick Abercrombie, *Dublin of the future: the new town plan* (Liverpool, 1922), p. 3.   179 Miriam Nyhan Grey (ed.), *Ireland's allies: America and the 1916 Rising* (Dublin, 2016).   180 Shane Kenna, *Thomas MacDonagh* (Dublin, 2014), p. 90.

agenda. After 1916, Markievicz was described in the British press as 'a sinister figure who had a room in her house entirely filled with human skulls. She had, in fact, from the time of her [Paris] art-school days a human skull on the mantelpiece'.[181]

THINKING IN TENSES

Under colonialism, time-torn cultural nationalism always thinks in tenses – once we were like that, now we are like this, but in the future we could become something else. The French journalist Jules de Lasteyrie (1810–83) criticised the Irishman 'for not being able to accept defeat. In him, imagination has killed reason. He lives by dreams, fantasies, chimeras'.[182] Colonial conditions fermented the yearning for an alternative geography that sought access to a desire-drenched world imagined by what Yeats called 'the gazing heart'.[183] Yeats crepuscular mode in his Celtic Twilight phase presented Ireland as a place associated with the inner eye of reverie and prophecy, not the objective external eye of rationality. Mary Colum noted the poet's 'necromantic eyes sunk in dream', his 'dark sorcerer's eyes'.[184]

Irish cultural nationalism created ways of thinking in tenses, where the future (tiocfaidh ár lá) and the pluperfect (some day we will have arrived at that future and only then can we forget the nightmare of our history) tenses could compensate for the damaged past (a vanquished culture) and sordid present (a degraded post-Famine world). Kitty O'Doherty noted the 'steely eyes' in 'a courageous old face' of Thomas Clarke, the hard man of the Rising: 'He was looking into the future, he was not looking at you at all'.[185]

Dreaming accessed an interior richness as opposed to the analytical power that Yeats assigned to the commercial, the industrial and the scientific mentality. The inner eye connected with the ancient spiritual wisdom of the world, which modernity sought to extinguish. For Yeats spiritualism became the alternative religion to modernity.

Revival Ireland was bathed in this twilight atmosphere as opposed to the harsh light that glared across the modern cities of Europe – like Paris, the city of light. Joyce's friend Arthur Power observed that 'it is in Paris that modern life has come to its full realisation and splendour ... The centre and origin of modernism undoubtedly is Paris, ville de lumière ... radiant with intellectual

181 Mrs Sidney Czira, Witness Statement 909, Bureau of Military History.   182 Jules de Lasteyrie, 'Les Fenians' in *Revue des Deux Mondes*, T. 68, 1867.   183 In his poem 'In memory of Major Robert Gregory'.   184 Colum, *Life and the dream*, p. 99, p. 128.   185 Kitty O'Doherty, Witness Statement 355, Bureau of Military History. On the relationship between 1916 and literature, see the chapter 'Cyclical violence: the Irish insurrection and the limits of enchantment' in Sarah Cole, *At the violet hour: modernism and violence in England and Ireland* (Oxford, 2012), pp 131–95.

light'.[186] But only the binary released the dynamic of Yeats poetry, so that Paris and the west of Ireland were not opposites but necessarily and intimately yoked together.

PARIS/LONDON/DUBLIN

For Irish nationalists, Paris (as a shorthand for France) offered an alternative liberation geography, a world elsewhere where that coveted Irish future was already materialised, and open to Irishmen. The irresistible allure of Paris was simply that it was not London.[187] Thomas Moore in his early poem 'Corruption' had excoriated the malign influence of Britain 'that unpitying power, whose whips and chains/Made Ireland first in wild adulterous trance/Turn false to England's bed and whore with France'.[188]

Once that future had been actualised (the 1916 Rising, the advent of the Free State), Paris had served its function, and receded in time and space. Desmond Ryan recorded Pearse's vision of Dublin as he mused in the wrecked shell of the GPO:

> 'After a few years they will see the meaning of what we tried to do'. He rose, and we walked a few paces ahead. 'Dublin's name will be glorious for ever', he said with deep feeling and passion. 'Men will speak of her as one of the splendid cities, as they speak now of Paris. Dublin! Paris!'[189]

After independence, with the pronounced inward turn in Ireland, the influence of France faded. The artist J.B. Yeats concluded in 1922 that 'We must look to ourselves for the springs of our art. We must not look to Paris or London for a pacemaker'.[190]

A SURREAL POSTCRIPT

Dada was born in 1916 as an explicit protest against the slaughter of the war. Once Dada moved its operational base to Paris in 1920, surrealism emerged out of it, which was also vigorously anti-imperial. In the first line of their 1925

---

186 Power, *Old Waterford house*, p. 81.   **187** This point is well made in Michael Cronin, 'The shining tumultuous river? Irish perspectives on Europe' in E. Maher, E. O'Brien & G. Neville (eds), *Reinventing Ireland through a French prism* (Frankfurt-am-Main, 2007), pp 21–39. **188** Thomas Moore, *The works of Thomas Moore*, 6 vols (Paris, 1823), vi, pp 36–7. Moore later bowdlerised his poem when published in London, and the poem is now quoted in this softened version. The younger Moore exhibited gristly politics far from the sugary confections of his older life.   **189** Desmond Ryan, *The man called Pearse* (Dublin, 1919), p. 58.   **190** J.B. Yeats, *Modern aspects of Irish art* (Dublin, 1922).

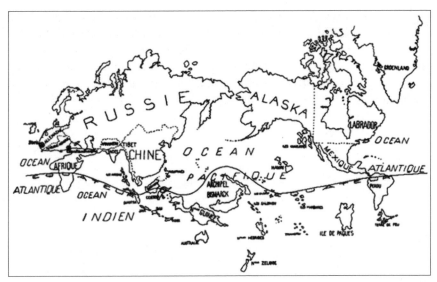

2.5 *Le monde au temps des surréalistes* ('The surrealist map of the world'). *Variétés* (Brussels, June 1929), pp 26–7. Ireland is shown at far left.

manifesto ('The Revolution first and always!') the French surrealists declared that 'the world is a crossroads of conflicts'. The surrealists castigated colonialism and declared that French entanglements in the Moroccan war had so disgusted them that 'for us France does not exist'.[191] *Le monde au temps des surréalistes* (The surrealist map of the world) first appeared in a special issue of the periodical *Variétés*.[192] The poet Paul Éluard (1895–1952) likely devised this first explicit counter-map that made an unequivocally anti-colonial riposte against a canonical map – *Les cinq parties du monde, planisphère, comprenant toutes les possessions coloniales*, a classic of the era that displayed colonial possessions in pastel colours – English yellow, French pink, Dutch orange, Italian mauve.[193]

On the surrealist map, an undulating Equator deviates from a straight line. The Pacific not the Atlantic occupied the cartographic centre, relegating a diminished Europe to the margins of the earth and the page. Asia looms large, as a potential destabiliser of empires ('it is now the turn of the Mongolians to pitch their tents in our place').[194] North America has been absorbed entirely by Alaska and Labrador from the north and Mexico from the south. Easter Island is prominent, as a primitive site of disruptive energy, as are the Arctic regions of the Inuit. France is simply erased from this map, while Paris has become the

191 *La Révolution surréaliste*, v, Paris (15 October 1925), pp 31–2. **192** *Variétés* (Brussels, June 1929), pp 26–7. Dedicated to 'Le Surréalisme en 1929', it featured René Crevel, Paul Éluard, Louis Aragon, Robert Desnos and André Breton. **193** Denis Wood, *Rethinking the power of maps* (New York, 2010), p. 199. **194** *La Révolution surréaliste*, p. 32.

capital of Germany. An oversize Soviet Union expresses its increased global weight in the wake of the Russian Revolution of 1917. Mexico expands because of its decade long revolution after 1910. But for our purposes, the most striking feature of this map is that Ireland towers over a puny England, an indication of its elevated status after Irish independence and the literary reputation of the island.[195]

195 This context may also inform Raymond Queneau's proto magic realist/pulp fiction novel on the 1916 Rebellion – *On est toujours trop bon avec les femmes* (Paris, 1947). Douglas Smith, 'Raymond Queneau's 1916 Easter Rising: *On est toujours trop bon avec les femmes* as (post-) historical novel', *Irish Journal of French Studies*, 13 (2013), pp 151–73.

Paris, 1796: birthplace of the first Irish Republic? Tone's mission to France and Irish sovereignty

SYLVIE KLEINMAN

Ce n'est point à Philadelphie, c'est à Paris qu'il faut préparer l'exécution de ce plan.[1]

On 23 June 1796, Theobald Wolfe Tone was engaged in one of many conversations about the logistics of a French expedition to Ireland with General Henri Clarke, a senior military advisor of Irish origin and head of the French Directory's Cabinet historique et topographique militaire. Tone, under the pseudonym 'James Smith', had been in Paris since February on a clandestine mission, relentlessly lobbying political and military decision-makers to establish the *encadrement* without which an Irish revolution and the creation of an independent Ireland could not succeed. He proposed that Irish prisoners of war in France (held as British) be released to form a vanguard of scouts and guides who would be landed in advance to inform locals of French intentions. Tone specified that they would be 'an Irish corps, in green jackets, with green feathers'.[2] Clarke 'seemed to relish' the idea, and took notes in French of Tone's description of the unit's 'green standard with the Harp, surmounted with the Cap of Liberty'. Tone concluded that his idea would be circulated and that his flag design would be commissioned. The same day, an internal army memo addressed to General Lazare Hoche, the recently appointed commander of the expedition, endorsed the potential of these symbols of Irish nationhood:

> The Irish, like every nation in the world, have a sort of religious respect for certain emblems and principally those that led their ancestors into battle. It is possible to turn this respect and attachment for their ancient emblems to the advantage of the revolution which is being prepared in their country.[3]

---

1 Charles Delacroix (minister for external relation) to the Directory, 27 Jan. 1796, reprinted in T.W. Moody, R.B. McDowell & C.J. Woods (eds), *The writings of Theobald Wolfe Tone, 1763–1798* (Oxford, 2001), ii, pp 38–40. For Tone's life, see Marianne Elliott, *Wolfe Tone* (Liverpool, 2012); for his military career, see Sylvie Kleinman '"Un brave de plus": Theobald Wolfe Tone, alias Adjutant-general James Smith: French officer and Irish patriot adventurer, 1796–1798' in N. Genet-Rouffiac & D. Murphy (eds), *Franco-Irish military connections, 1590–1945* (Dublin, 2009), pp 163–88; reprinted with illustrations in *Revue Historique des Armées*, 253 (2008), pp 55–65.   2 Tone, diary entry, 23 June 1796, in Tone, *Writings*, ii, p. 210. The French distinguished the Irish from other Britons at this time.   3 Service Historique de la Défense [SHD] (Vincennes), Armée: Directory to Hoche, Paris 23 June 1796: Registre de

This memo specified that the harp would be gold with silver strings, adding an iconic detail: the harp was to be placed above two branches of shamrock ('treffles'). One final defining feature of Irishness is not mentioned here. By the time that Tone resumed his real name after the outbreak of rebellion in Ireland in May 1798, his French officer's official notepaper included the motto *Erin Go Bragh!* above the words *Liberté Égalité*.[4]

Tone had found Clarke out of touch with the prevailing spirit of reform and unity in Ireland: in his diary, he offloaded his exasperation with Clarke's 'sad trash about monarchy, the noblesse and the clergy'.[5] The French-born son of an Irish officer of the old Irish Brigade in the service of the French king, Clarke was obsessed with the idea that the Irish still hankered after a Catholic aristocrat to reign over them. Tone's writings, both private and public, were unburdened by too much political theory, but when pressed by the French as to what type of regime should result from the *fait d'armes*, he was adamant that it could only be a republic. Ten days after arriving in Paris, Tone submitted his first memorial on Ireland to the Directory, asserting that there had been a 'revolution in the political morality' of the Irish nation since the French Revolution, as the unbounded liberty of conscience in France had mitigated Protestant fears of popery.[6]

This memorial, written in the relative security of exile but highly treasonable from an Anglo-Irish perspective, was reprinted in his collected works in 1826.[7] These assertions by Tone of Ireland's nationhood were thus in the public domain by the time that Young Irelanders like Thomas Davis were reaching adolescence, and they helped reignite an ardent spirit of nationalism that grew unrelentingly towards 1916. Its ideological bedrock was Tone's resolute commitment, finally expressed openly in February 1796, to 'establish the independence of Ireland and to frame a free republic on the broad basis of liberty and equality'.[8] The French Revolution had established 'unbounded liberty of conscience' and this had facilitated the 'cordial union' among the sects in Ireland. But only a disciplined and well-armed revolution could avert civil war. For this and other reasons, it was in France's interests to separate Ireland from England, and if 'the standard of the [French] Republic' were 'displayed' on Irish soil in the cause of Irish liberty, millions of Tone's compatriots would rally to it, he claimed.

Drawn in and gripped by the immediacy of his writings that continuously affirmed Ireland's right to be a sovereign nation, generations of nationalists assiduously read his diary and the brief autobiography started as he was waiting

---

Côtes de l'Océan B5*–97, f. 78v, letter 218, 23 June 1796; translated by François van Brock, 'A proposed Irish regiment and standard', *Irish Sword*, 11 (1973–4), p. 231.   4 Tone to Matilda Tone, 14 Aug. 1798: reproduced in Richard Hayes, *Irish swordsmen of France* (Dublin, 1941), p. 297.   5 Tone, *Writings*, ii, p. 157.   6 'First memorial to the French government on the present state of Ireland, 22 Feb. 1796' reprinted in Tone, *Writings*, ii, p. 64, et seq. 7 William Theobald Wolfe Tone (ed.), *Life of Theobald Wolfe Tone*, 2 vols (Washington, 1826). 8 'First memorial to the French government on the present state of Ireland, 22 Feb. 1796'

to embark on the Bantry expedition. Fused with letters and documents in various editions, it stood out as one of the most inspirational texts for nationalists. An enduring memory of Patrick Pearse is of him pacing the grounds at St Enda's wrapped in his schoolmaster's gown, totally absorbed in his reading of Tone's autobiography.[9] For James Connolly, Tone was one 'whose virtues we can only honour by imitation'.[10]

Yet 'Wolfe' Tone was absent during the 2016 centenary of the Rising, despite the irrefutable impact that his legacy had on its key ideologues and combatants generally.[11] Though his diaries cover other periods of his life, an unrivalled energy and conviction flow from the pages covering his historical mission in Paris during those initial interactions with French officials. In the corridors of power concentrated in the heart of the French capital, Tone arguably achieved official recognition of a first Irish republic by the most advanced state of the modern age. It is the key to understanding why Tone's legacy endured, and even unlikely figures acknowledged his 'absolute intrepidity and great persistence' at this time.[12] Conveying Tone's indomitable commitment and self-sacrifice helped propel Pearse into his role as 1916's most potent propagandist: for him, accomplishing what 'Tone's generation' had failed in achieving was 'the unspeakable privilege' of the patriots of 1913.[13] Throughout his adventurous life, Tone's mission to France stood out as a defining moment on the path to Irish sovereignty.

PARIS, 1796: BIRTHPLACE OF THE FIRST IRISH REPUBLIC?

My first step was in the rue du Bacq (sic), but my *second* was plump into the Luxembourg.[14]

In the specific context of 1793, Irish revolutionaries seeking military assistance and political support to achieve independence from Britain had only one choice

reprinted in Tone, *Writings*, ii, p. 64. **9** Denis Gwynn, 'Patrick Pearse', *Dublin Review* (Jan.–Mar. 1923), pp 92–105. Gwynn is referring to the edition of Tone's works by R. Barry O'Brien, *The autobiography of Theobald Wolfe Tone, 1763–1798*, 2 vols (London, 1893). It was the first to use the title 'autobiography', as Tone, borrowing Sterne's Shandian wording, had entitled his memoir 'Memorandums on my life & opinions': Tone, *Writings*, ii, p. 261. Brian Crowley confirmed that there are no extant editions of Tone's writings in the original library of St Enda's, now the Pearse Museum, Rathfarnham. **10** James Connolly, 'The men we honour', *The Worker's Republic*, 13 Aug. 1898. **11** He was only ever called by his patronymic surname, 'Tone', during his lifetime, even by his wife. Wolfe was a middle name, and the use of 'Wolfe Tone' after his death by those who had never known him also corresponds to his posthumous legend. **12** Augustine Birrell, 'Wolfe Tone', *The Contemporary Review*, 65 (Jan.–June 1894), p. 48; review of O'Brien, *Autobiography*. Tom Bartlett pointed me to the extraordinary paradox of this review. **13** Patrick Pearse, 'How does she stand?' (Address given at Tone's grave in Bodenstown, county Kildare, 22 June 1913), in *The coming revolution: the political writings and speeches of Patrick Pearse* (Cork, 2012), p. 57. **14** Tone to Matilda Tone, 27 Aug. 1797, in Tone, *Writings*, iii, p. 135.

of 'gallant allies': the first French republic, established in September 1792. Marianne Elliot asserted that Tone only assumed the role of a revolutionary when it was created for him in an atmosphere of 'unreality' in the spring of 1795, and that 'his French plans were as ill formulated as his political philosophy' when he left Ireland. Elliott suggested that Tone was a mere accidental revolutionary who at best only espoused republicanism at a late stage.[15] Today it is clearer that Tone's actions surpassed his words: his determination to seek French assistance inspired him to becoming the highly effective 'ambassador incognito' of the United Irishmen in Paris.[16] Before his exile, putting any plans of sedition on paper would have been highly dangerous.

Furthermore, the diary that he kept between February 1793 (the pivotal moment for Irish revolutionaries when France went to war against Britain) and February 1796 has not survived.[17] Therefore we need to reflect on cryptic phrases like the one recorded by Thomas Russell, his closest friend among the United Irishmen. Russell had just been examined by a secret committee of the House of Lords on 10 May 1793, and he used a nickname that Tone had adopted: 'Think of what is to be done. Mr H[utton] is willing, if the ↑ [United Irishmen?] be willing, to risque all he has [to] go to an *unanointed republic* via London'.[18] A codeword for being a United Irishman was to be 'up' (hence the arrow), and it seems clear that Russell is alluding to Tone going to France; this may only have been wine-induced bravado for which the latter left ample evidence in his journals.

Yet Tone's incrimination shortly afterwards in the Jackson affair (1794–5) is well-documented. He had assisted in drafting a memorandum for Jackson, a French agent in Dublin, but the document was intercepted and Jackson was arrested. The text speaks of Ireland as 'a conquered and oppressed and insulted country' where the 'name of England and her power is universally odious', of a 'convulsion' [uprising], levelling the government to the dust, and of Ireland being favourable 'to an invasion … if a force [i.e., an army] were present and sufficiently strong to resort to for defence'.[19] A vulnerable Tone negotiated perpetual exile and sailed to America, but as both French archives and Tone himself confirm, he called on the French representative in Philadelphia immediately after his arrival there in August 1795.

Tone, unlike many revolutionaries and insurgents, recorded the daily progress of his treasonable negotiations with the French government, a 'running commentary' enlivened with candour, jokes and self-mockery.[20] Tone had time on his hands in his solitary existence, in total contrast to later generations of Irish activists in Paris. While the Fenians freely mixed with French Republicans in

15 Elliott, *Tone*, p. 242, 249.   16 Pierre Joannon, 'Theobald Wolfe Tone à Paris: conspirateur exilé ou ambassadeur incognito?', *Cycnos*, 15:2 (1998), pp 5–18.   17 The last entry before exile is for 8 Feb. 1793: Tone, *Writings*, i, p. 404; the diary resumes in Le Havre on 2 Feb. 1796: Tone, *Writings*, ii, p. 40.   18 C.J. Woods (ed.), *Journals and Memoirs of Thomas Russell* (Dublin, 1991), p. 76.   19 Tone, *Writings*, i, pp 506–8.   20 Birrell, 'Wolfe Tone', p. 53.

their favourite cafés, singing the banned *Marseillaise* after hours, Tone spent his evenings alone or with a handful of trusted Irish exiles. The diary grew into a densely packed narrative, emitting a heartfelt patriotism and determination to achieve Irish independence, formulated in relative freedom in Paris. Yet in parallel to these private musings, laced with humour and doubt, a significant corpus of documents has survived and these can be consulted in parallel to Tone's version of his negotiations.[21] Many were republished by his son in 1826: read alongside his diary, they form the source of a compelling rhetoric on Irish sovereignty, and it is no wonder that later generations of nationalists were emboldened by his single-minded determination.[22]

Charting Tone's movements around the city mark out a section of the capital mostly concentrated on the Left Bank. On his arrival on 12 February 1796, Tone first stayed at the Hôtel des Étrangers on the rue Vivienne, near the Maison Égalité (the renamed Palais-Royal), and conveniently just a few minutes' walk from the residence of James Monroe, the American ambassador. Tone carried a coded letter of introduction to Monroe who received him warmly at the Hôtel Cusset, 95 rue de Richelieu (renamed rue de la Loi during the Revolution, and now a commercial hotel). His various addresses, and those of his few acquaintances 'indispensably necessary to the success of my business', were all located within a central and highly convenient sector spanning the Seine and mostly within what are today the 2nd and 6th arrondissements.[23]

After Monroe, Tone's first French contact was Charles Delacroix, at the ministry for External Relations at 'rue du Bacq (sic), 471'. It backed onto the sumptuous Hôtel Gallifet at 73, rue de Varenne in the 7e, and Tone noted that he had been brought into the minister's 'magnificent antechamber'.[24] Monroe had encouraged him to go directly to Carnot who, as a member of the Directory, held public audiences at the Luxembourg palace, the seat of government where Tone was to become a frequent visitor. His first visit gave rise to one of Tone's most enduring diary entries. Evidently written up that evening, its pacy audacity and theatricality reflect how nervous Tone must have felt earlier that day:

> Went ... in a fright to the Luxembourg, conning speeches in execrable French all the way. What shall I say to Carnot? ... Plucked up a spirit, as I drew near the Palace and mounted the stairs like a lion. Went into the first bureau that I found open, and demanded at once to see Carnot. The clerks

21 Most are in French archives and have been reproduced in the Oxford edition of Tone's *Writings*.   22 Sylvie Kleinman, 'Rhétorique de la souveraineté nationale irlandaise: Théobald Wolfe Tone et la République française, 1796–1798', *La Révolution française*, 11 (2016) La France et l'Irlande à l'époque de la république atlantique http://lrf.revues.org/1656. 23 Tone, *Writings*, ii, p. 212.   24 Tone, *Writings*, ii, p. 53. Currently the location of the Centre culturel italien, the hôtel is mostly associated with Delacroix's successor, Talleyrand. It is probably here that Robert Emmet and Malachy Delaney called on him in January 1801. Part of Emmet's legend was that he too had met Napoleon, but its visualisation by John D. Reigh

stared a little, but I repeated my demand with a courage truly heroic ...
The folding doors were now thrown open[25] ... and Citizen Carnot appeared,
in the *petit costume* of white sattin, with crimson robe, richly embroidered.

Tone returned to the Luxembourg for further meetings with various officials
(possibly entering at what is now the address of the French Senate, i.e., 15, rue
de Vaugirard), and in May to secure official permission as a foreigner to remain
in Paris, another source of anxiety alongside his worsening money problems.
From late May 1796 (as the Directory was on the point of officially agreeing to
the Bantry expedition), he called in nearly every day to Clarke at his Cabinet
Topographique, across the street from the Luxembourg at the Hôtel de la
Trémouille (now 50, rue de Vaugirard). Clarke was negotiating Tone's
commission in the French army, but the final decision rested with General
Lazare Hoche; this historic milestone defined his posthumous legacy, but it also
solved his immediate financial problems. A week before meeting Hoche, he had
written: 'So here I am, with exactly two louis in my exchequer, negotiating with
the French Government and planning revolutions. I must say it is truly original'.
That morning Clarke assured him that Hoche was due in Paris imminently
to confer privately with the Directory, at which stage Tone's army brevet would
be finalised.

Paradoxically, on 12 July 1796 (hence the diary entry defiantly starting with
'Battle of Aughrim!')[26], Tone was summoned to the Luxembourg and there met
Hoche, a scene vividly described in his diary and one of many demonstrating his
qualities as an eyewitness to history. When appointed to lead the Irish
expedition, Hoche was the only general who truly rivalled Bonaparte's meteoric
rise, and as France's foremost military commander possessed a brilliant 'political
acumen'.[27] While the two men discussed logistics and provisioning, Hoche was
also most eager for satisfaction on one 'important point', the political outcome:
'what form of government' would the Irish wish to adopt?[28] Tantalisingly, Clarke
then interrupted them, taking them both to join Carnot and fifteen others,
including Truguet, the minister for marine, for dinner. Afterwards, the senior
decision-makers retired for a three-hour 'council on Irish matters', while Tone
paced the gardens with the general secretary Lagarde and listened to a symphony
playing upstairs in the apartments of one of the directors.[29]

---

published in *The Shamrock* in 1895 belongs to the romanticised narrative genre of that age. It
seems highly improbable that as First Consul, Napoleon would have agreed to receive him,
and no sources even hint at such an encounter: Sylvie Kleinman, '"Unhappy is the man and
nation whose destiny depends on the will of another": Robert Emmet's mission to France' in
A. Dolan, P. Geoghegan & D. Jones (eds), *Reinterpreting Emmet: essays on the life and legacy of
Robert Emmet* (Dublin, 2007), p. 68.   **25** This *entrée* is aptly recreated as the setting for Hugh
Gough's contribution, filmed inside the Luxembourg palace, to *Rebellion: a television history
of 1798*, VHS video (Dublin, RTÉ, 1998); Tone, *Writings*, ii, pp 75–6.   **26** Tone, *Writings*, ii,
p. 232.   **27** Elliott, *Tone*, p. 287.   **28** Tone, *Writings*, ii, p. 226.   **29** Tone, *Writings*, ii, p. 235.

Before sitting down, Hoche had taken Tone aside and repeated his question, to which Tone answered firmly 'undoubtedly a republic'. Hoche also wanted reassurances that the Catholics would not want to 'set up one of their chiefs for king'. Tone was suitably annoyed at this outdated notion, but pleased that Hoche was 'so anxious on this topic', having pressed him more than the others had. Carnot then joined them, 'with a pocket map of Ireland in his hand' and after a lengthy discussion (in French) about troop numbers and landing places, concluded: 'it will be, to be sure, a most brilliant operation!' Tone, hopeful, introduced a hint of Hiberno-English in his translation of Carnot's optimism.

It is essential to consider the skipped heartbeats of nationalists, as Tom Bartlett put it, in the following century as they followed Tone on his quest through the corridors of power. Many vibrant passages of the diary show how successfully he wrote 'at the moment' to 'represent things exactly as they' struck him, this immediacy defining much of the writing of the age, and partially explaining his appeal.[30] Thus, he projected his experiences, anxieties, hopes and motivations onto his readers, and his writings helped place him in the pantheon of Irish patriotic heroes. Reading Tone created an impulse in Irish nationalists to honour his sacrifice, and for some to emulate it.

The nineteenth-century imagination was also shaped visually; historical narratives and emerging national foundation myths were especially effective in narrative books, and with major advances in printing technology, this prioritised *imagery*. Thomas Davis, a leading Young Irelander imbued with French historicism and a major champion of Tone's memory in the 1840s, deplored the lack of Irish national art, despite the abundance of national subjects. A list that he compiled of suitable topics based on written sources included 'Tone and Carnot', drawn from Tone's memoirs.[31] But an even greater encounter captured the imagination of the collective consciousness.

The legendary aura of Napoleon throughout the nineteenth century also gripped Ireland, and fascination with his military prowess even extended to those who normally found imperialism repugnant, notably Patrick Pearse.[32] In this case audacity totally overshadowed classical definitions of 'defeat'. In the immediate context of 1916, after the Entente Cordiale, France as a state could never be a gallant ally in a military alliance with Irish separatists. But in the 1790s, France's military strategy on Ireland was rooted in a desire to humiliate England and to reduce her to a secondary mercantile power on the seas, a reality that the ever-pragmatic Tone recognised. The military assistance from France that he negotiated in various places around Paris was indispensable to his supreme political goal, Irish independence. To the 1916 generation nurtured on 1798 and the 'Year of the French', the overwhelming legacy of Tone's mission was that

30 Tone, *Writings*, iii, p. 174.   **31** Thomas Davis, 'Hints for Irish historical paintings', *The Nation*, 29 July 1843.   **32** The fine engraved portrait of Napoleon in the headmaster's study at St Enda's is said to have been Pearse's own: information from Brian Crowley.

Ireland's right to sovereignty had been recognised by the first French republic. Contemporary documents abound with French interrogations about the socio-political composition of Irish society, and though these texts emit a steady stream of laboured ideological rhetoric on rights and liberties, they also promoted the case for Irish nationhood.

After the return of General Bonaparte to Paris from Italy in December 1797, England remained France's sole enemy and Ireland once again became significant in French military strategy. On 12 November, Tone wrote to Bonaparte, now commander of the Armée d'Angleterre, offering his services.[33] Tone was summoned to meet Bonaparte at his domicile in the famous little *hôtel* in the garden at 60, rue Chantereine, where Josephine had set a trend by redecorating in the fashionable neo-Roman style. It was a brief walk from the rue Vivienne where Tone had first stayed in Paris in 1796. While Tone states that 'all the furniture and ornaments [were] in the most classical taste', one would have welcomed his impressions on entering the house via the famous semi-circular striped 'Roman' military tent on the porch.[34] Tone's three meetings with Napoleon are discussed elsewhere, but the tilt towards Egypt in the great man's strategy did not diminish Tone's legend in the making. His encounter with the man immortalised as one of the greatest military commanders of all times easily lent itself to the Irish national narrative. Their second meeting was rendered in a bold chromolithograph print depicting Tone and Bonaparte in full uniform, poring over a map of Ireland, Britain and France. Published exactly one century later, it visually inaugurated the centenary of 1798, and ensured that their encounter would become, in the true sense of the word, iconic.[35]

But Tone had at least *seen* Napoleon before their first meeting, a fact overlooked until now. In an uncharacteristically brief diary entry, he recalled a 'superb ... grand fête' held to receive the peace treaty from the Emperor [of Austria] which 'had been b[rought up by Buonaparte in person to the Directory'.[36] Tone's throwaway entry belies the solemnity of the occasion, immortalised by every scholar of Napoleon. These include Madame de Staël, who was present and for whom it was 'an epoch in the history of the Revolution'.[37] The ceremony was held in the courtyard of the Luxembourg palace because no chamber would have been spacious enough to hold the vast throng of spectators: outside people hung out of every window and roof, and excited crowds surged through the gardens and streets. A celebrated print captured the scene as Tone had witnessed it, possibly seated at the back of the

33 Tone, *Writings*, iii, p. 173. An original in Tone's hand is in Trinity College, Dublin.
34 Marie-Lys de Castelbajac, Elisabeth Caude et al. (eds), *Josephine et Napoléon, L'Hôtel de la rue Chantereine* (Paris, 2013). The street was shortly after renamed rue de la Victoire, and the house was demolished in 1857.   35 John Fergus O'Hea, 'Tone's interview with Napoleon', *Weekly Freeman and National Press*, 11 Dec. 1897; reproduced in Sylvie Kleinman, 'Rough guide to Paris: Wolfe Tone as an accidental tourist', *History Ireland*, 16:2 (2008), p. 39. 36 Tone, *Writings*, iii, p. 181.   37 Germaine de Staël-Holstein, *Considérations sur la Révolution*

diplomatic corps.[38] He was delighted with the 'spirit of the most determined hostility to England' that permeated the speeches.[39] Bonaparte had been brief but affirmed that while religion, feudalism and royalty had governed Europe for over twenty centuries, now a turning point had arrived, as the peace just concluded inaugurated the new age of representative governments. Europe would only be free once the happiness of the French people rested on organic laws. The five directors appeared in Roman republican costume, bowing before a patriotic altar with statues of Liberty, Equality and Peace, and Talleyrand's speech was also imbued with republicanism. It was a critical juncture in the career of Napoleon and the role of the army in France's increasingly aggressive expansionism, which also had significant implications for Ireland; Tone's silent presence is surely noteworthy.

SINGING THE 'MARSEILLE HYMN': PARIS AS THE CAPITAL OF A
NEW REPUBLICAN CULTURE

Tone has overwhelming appeal as a chronicler of French history and a well-informed and significant anglophone *flâneur parisien*, but he also vividly captured Paris' role as the capital of a new republican state.[40] Due to the gap in his diaries, caution must be exercised when evaluating the influence that America exerted on him, and we would welcome knowing on what occasion he had 'seen' Talleyrand 'in Philadelphia', given the brevity of his time there.[41] Tone was not a consistent political thinker and, for obvious reasons, concerns in his Paris diary about the first, and necessary military, phase of the French expedition far outweigh consideration of the institutions that a democratic Irish republic might rest on. Tone was a radical lawyer seeking to replace an antiquated system of governance with a republican one, so it is unsurprising that the first book he mentions purchasing was France's *Constitution* (1795). He recorded the charms of Lodoïska, wife of the politician and bookseller Louvet, who handed the volume to him in their shop at 24, Galerie Neuve, Maison Égalité, but he never commented on this fundamental written pillar of modern democracy. Let us assume that he had read it before attending a session of 'the *Conseil des Cinq-Cents*, or the French House of Commons.'[42] Tone found 'the first assembly in Europe' to be horribly accommodated in a 'mean, dirty' and ill-contrived room, and its members to be surprisingly disorderly, given that they had six years

française, 2 vols (Paris, 1862), i, pp 497–8.   **38** *Fête donnée à Bonaparte au Palais National du Directoire, après le traité de Campo Formio, le 20 Frimaire An 6e de la République*: N°131, Inventory Nr G. 31929 Musée Carnavalet, Paris: Abraham Girardet (artist), Pierre-Gabriel Berthault (engraver).   **39** Tone, *Writings*, iii, p. 173.   **40** Sylvie Kleinman, 'Ambassador incognito and accidental tourist: cultural perspectives on Theobald Wolfe Tone's mission to France 1796–8', *Journal of Irish and Scottish Studies*, 2:1 (2008), pp 101–22.   **41** Tone, *Writings*, iii, p. 110, p. 175.   **42** Tone, *Writings*, ii, p. 139 [1 April 1796].

experience of 'public assemblies'. But characteristically, he waxes lyrical about French *esprit*: 'it is the same impetuosity which makes them redoubtable in the field and disorderly in the Senate' (figuratively an allusion to ancient Rome, given that the *Conseil* was the lower chamber of a bicameral system). The members reminded him strongly of the General Committee of the Catholic Convention of 1792, who appeared in retrospect as 'gentlemen' and 'ten times more orderly'.

Where precisely on the pavé of Paris did the paths of various Irish soldiers of destiny (constitutional and otherwise) cross? In 1796, the *Conseil* sat in the (former) *Salle du Manège* in the Tuileries palace which had housed the celebrated Constituent Assembly in 1789 and where France's first republican assembly, the Convention, opened in September 1792 after the fall of the monarchy. Today a plaque on the railings of the Tuileries gardens marks the entrance to this long-gone building, facing 230 rue de Rivoli. When John Mitchel arrived back in Paris in November 1865 as financial agent for the Fenians, he was among many Irishmen who frequented the popular English-language reading rooms at Galignani's, a few strides away at 224. Parnell stayed at both the Hôtel Meurice (228) and also the Brighton, further down at 218, and presumably strolled in the gardens, unaware that it was here that Tone had enjoyed his first taste of representative government.

In sharp contrast to later generations of Irish nationalists, Tone's early experience of Paris was of anonymity and isolation, especially during the first five months before his enlistment in the French army. While his days were filled with meetings and parleys within the corridors of power of the most prestigious venues in the capital, his evening meals and entertainment were solitary. He attended the theatre regularly, and his descriptions of republican *divertissements* inspired by classical antiquity resemble the Irish-themed *tableaux vivants* made popular in the 1890s, although by then they were steeped in the Gaelic Revival. On his first night in Paris, Tone attended a performance of an elaborate ballet, *L'Offrande à la Liberté*, at the Théâtre des Arts a few minutes walk from his hotel, and left a vivid account in his diary. We tend to associate state-orchestrated rituals and ceremonies in the public sphere with the abolition of the monarchy and the fearsome Robespierrist phase of the Revolution. But republicanism reasserted itself during the Directory and promoted a concerted programme of public festivals, rituals and ceremonies to unite and instruct citizens on the common political values which embodied France.

Tone vividly describes the Statue of Liberty centre stage 'with an altar blazing before her' and the characters decked out in Grecian attire.[43] Whenever the word

---

43 Tone, *Writings*, ii, pp 49–50. The *Offrande* had been performed continuously from 1792 to 1799 and it was famous for its orchestration by Gossec of the 'Marche des Marseillais'. Tone's precise wording so echoes another critical review, which also refers to the electrifying effect, that it can hardly be a coincidence: André Tissier, *Les spectacles à Paris pendant la Révolution: répertoire analytique chronologique et bibliographique* (Geneva, 2002), p. 48, quoting a review in

3.1 The five dollar Fenian Bond was issued by John O'Mahony as treasurer of 'The Irish Republic' on 17 March 1866, and was redeemable 'six months after the acknowledgment' of the independence of the Irish nation. O'Mahony was familiar with the Paris frequented by Tone and no doubt felt honour bound as he walked the streets to fulfil his unfinished mission. Anyone intimate with Tone's diary – as O'Mahony was – knew how utterly penniless Tone was before his enlistment, and the cherished hero's portrait was chosen for the lowest denomination of the bond. Recess printed by Continental Bank Note Co., New York. The names of the Irish counties are threaded into the border (National Museum of Ireland).

'esclavage' (slavery) was sung from the then dominant civic air *Veillons au salut de l'empire*, 'it operated like an electric shock'. The Marseilles Hymn was next sung and produced still greater enthusiasm. At the words 'Aux Armes, Citoyens!', the performers drew their swords and the females turned to them in encouragement. After a procession and several changes of tempo in the music, and two females lighting tripods on the altar, the verses 'Amour sacré de la patrie' and 'Liberté, Liberté chérie' were sung. Tone was 'powerfully affected' and continued to be so when the music changed to a martial style and the National Guards rushed onto the stage with their bayonets drawn and 'the Tricolour flag flying'. Tone was mesmerised by this spectacle 'worthy of a free republic'. The *Marseillaise* was sung communally at the end of theatre performances, but the French were growing weary of public festivals and the police were monitoring the crowd's enthusiasm. Yet Tone's account remains unique in terms of the powerful emotional charge of patriotism that he conveys, which was revived and scaled new heights under the Third Republic.

Equally detailed, but more significant in terms of conveying Tone's sense of the French as a regenerated society of citizens with rights and obligations, was an official coming of age festival that he attended at the Church of St Roch (24, rue St Roch). Repurposed as a Temple of Liberty, it too had an altar 'decorated with the national colours and a statue of liberty'.[44] Local youths who had reached sixteen were presented to the municipal authorities to receive their arms, and

Petites Affiches, 2 Oct. 1792.   **44** Tone, *Writings*, ii, p. 136.

those now twenty-one were enrolled as citizens. The processions and rituals were dominated by martial honour and glory, and a musing Tone noted that the Irish were equally brave as a people. It 'would not be impossible' to fire the enthusiasm of the Irish to equal the French and he wished that his beloved wife Matilda had 'heard the burst of *Aux armes, Citoyens!*'. Tone attended other patriotic entertainments and official events, and in Bonn the following year took part in the ceremonial planting of a Tree of Liberty. His diary monitored history in the making, as men took action to shape their own destiny and reverse centuries of political injustice.

TONE'S AFTERLIFE

'This French mission and what came of it is the great event of Tone's life'.[45] These words came from a review of R. Barry O'Brien's widely read 1893 edition of Tone's writings. It was written by an English Liberal politician who was provoked by the rebel but sensitive to this 'lover of adventure and intrigue', with his 'quick wit' and 'ready pen'; the reviewer concluded that 'a more agreeable person to read about hardly exists'.[46] He was Augustine Birrell, more famous as chief secretary for Ireland in 1916, but also a reputable critic who recognised Tone's literary qualities and noted how 'persuasively written' his memorials to the French government were. Openly favourable to Home Rule, Birrell was eventually blamed in British circles for the Rising for having been caught unawares and unprepared. He had underestimated the conspirators, and so it is paradoxical that he knew about, and in his own way admired Tone, who was one of the models of martial bravery for the rebels.

On his thirty-third birthday, Tone recorded his thoughts: at that age Alexander had conquered the world, but the cause to which he was devoted was 'so just' and the end so 'sacred', that he 'would push everything' in Paris, as far as he could. Tone's jottings are flecked with a gloomier, perhaps more realistic, sense of his situation: his birthday musings continue: 'The liberty and independence of my country first … my wife and our darling babies next; and last, I hope, a well earned reputation'.[47] He had presumably discussed with Matilda his possible fate, death, and his actions thereafter demonstrate – as Birrell acknowledged – his absolute persistence, especially in the teeth of adversity. After his enlistment in the French army, Tone was comforted by the thought that his French contacts would look after his family's welfare: he issued detailed instructions in his last frantic letters to his wife about which Irish exile or ministry she should go to in Paris for assistance.[48]

---

45 Birrell, 'Wolfe Tone', p. 53.   **46** Birrell, 'Wolfe Tone', p. 47.   **47** Tone, *Writings*, ii, p. 207 (20 June 1763). He was then living at 7, Petite rue Saint-Roch Poissonnière, now the rue des Jeûneurs in the 2e.   **48** Sylvie Kleinman, 'Matty and the daffs: the family life of Theobald

On Easter Monday, 24 April 1916, the most significant political act of the insurgents was the reading of the Proclamation of the Irish Republic in front of the General Post Office. Asserting their strong desire to be recognised as legitimate combatants, they hoisted their flags onto its roof, one of the city's tallest buildings. One succinctly announced their goal in two English words: 'Irish Republic'. That flag was later seized by the British army, who triumphantly posed with it at the base of the Parnell monument, holding the flag upside down as a gesture of disrespect. In 1966, it was presented to the Irish state and the centenary in 2016 revealed a compelling detail. It was crafted by a house painter out of domestic green and gold paint, whose name was Theobald Wolfe Tone Fitzgerald: clearly, his parents had been ardent nationalists. History has come full circle, as the flag is now kept in the former Royal Barracks where Tone expired in his prison cell.[49]

In Paris in the spring of 1796, Tone and Clarke discussed what future generations would recognise as the first 'Erin go Bragh' [Éireann go Brách – Ireland Forever] flag, aware that displaying the harp without the crown would have been regarded as treasonable by Dublin Castle. The French implemented Tone's proposal, and one flag was seized aboard the *Hoche*, on which Tone had sailed to Ireland in September 1798 on his fatal journey. After the French defeat at Lough Swilly in October, and Tone's imprisonment in Derry, a jubilant earl of Cavan announced to Edward Cooke, under-secretary in Dublin Castle, that he was sending down 'a green flag without the crown' for his 'museum of French curiosities'. There had been one such flag, imported for 'the revolution in this country' on each French ship, he wrote.[50] During the brief occupation of Mayo in August that year, two eyewitnesses were provoked by the French audaciously hoisting such 'a green flag ... inscribed ERIN GO BRAGH', which clearly 'displayed a Harp without a Crown'.[51]

The roots of martial heroism underpinning nationalist struggles – but also British patriotic culture – were moulded in the Western world during the American and French Revolutions and throughout the Napoleonic wars. Tone's sense of himself as a patriotic soldier, an identity that flourished during his French mission, was emblematic of this legacy and survived to inspire Pearse and his comrades.[52] France's recognition of Irish nationhood was personified by Tone, as even Birrell had recognised, and Paris provided the matrix for Tone's writings, which transmitted key elements of Irish nationalism to later generations. In one entry, Tone relates a day spent visiting Paris with a former

Wolfe Tone in exile' (1795–1798)' in M. Hatfield, J. Kruse & R. Nic Congáil (eds), *Historical perspectives on parenthood and childhood in Ireland* (forthcoming, 2017), Chapter 1.   **49** *Irish Times*, 15 Mar. 2016.   **50** Earl of Cavan to Edward Cooke, 7 Nov. 1798: NAI, R.P., 620/41/23, cited in Tone, *Writings*, iii, p. 367.   **51** [Joseph Stock], *Narrative of what passed at Killalla in the county of Mayo during the French invasion* (Dublin, 1800), p. 23; [James Little], 'Little's diary of the French landing', ed. Nuala Costello, *Analecta Hibernica*, 11 (July 1941), p. 84.   **52** Sylvie Kleinman, 'Revolutionary commemoration and the mythologisation of

French aristocrat that he had befriended during his crossing from America. They visited the Pantheon, described by Tone as a repository sacred to everything that is 'patriotic'. However, while Tone believed that the Irish should build one when they became a republic, they should not rush to fill it with the remains of their illustrious dead, he thought. Which of his readers could not have been deeply moved by how prophetic that day of sightseeing had been.

During the 1898 centenary, the northern patriot Alice Milligan was indefatigable in projecting Tone's memory, and she welcomed the use of decorated banners during street parades, as these 'were infinitely more effective for young people in conveying national history and forging anti-colonial resistance than any text book'.[53] At one Wolfe Tone procession in Dublin, colourful banners displayed inspirational scenes portraying the United Irishmen. Milligan's way of embodying the past through living pictures was also 'a means of envisioning the future of an independent Ireland'. Among them was the iconic 'Tone meeting Napoleon', based on the colour illustration from the *Weekly Freeman*: his Paris mission had been relived by countless readers, and this visualisation now supported pageantry and proclaimed his determination. In Paris, Tone could finally 'speak the truth' as 'a friend to the liberty and independence of Ireland', without fear of arrest from 'his Majesty's attorney general'.[54] Tone's French mission was a seminal moment, easily converted into the stuff of legend and hero quest, but also functioning as a grounded guide to direct action. Its legacy fuelled the resolve of future revolutionaries and helped them to escape the culture of defeat that permeated Irish life across the long nineteenth century. They rose to complete Tone's task, which shifted from a conspiracy to feasible revolution in Paris in 1796.[55]

history', *Studies* (Spring 2016), pp 31–40.   **53** Catherine Morris, 'Alice Milligan, republican tableaux and the Revival', *Field Day Review*, 6 (2010), p. 147, citing *Shan Van Vocht*, 2 Sept. 1898.   **54** Address to the people of Ireland, Tone, *Writings*, ii, p. 376.   **55** I wish to thank Claire Batt, Tom Bartlett, Mathieu Ferradou and Pierre Joannon for their unfailing support while writing this essay.

Was Bonaparte in the GPO? The legend of Napoleon in Irish history, 1796–1916

THOMAS BARTLETT

NAPOLEON AND IRELAND, 1796–1815

The involvement of Napoleon Bonaparte with the plans of Theobald Wolfe Tone and Robert Emmet to bring a French army of invasion into Ireland during the revolutionary and Napoleonic wars is well known. These projects are documented in the historical record. More elusive, however, is the historical significance of Napoleon, his meaning, first, in Irish popular consciousness in the 'long' nineteenth century; then, second, his place in Irish revolutionary thinking in terms of obtaining military assistance from abroad. In an Irish context, these twin aspects of Napoleon's legacy – the popular and the revolutionary – can be separated and seen as *Napoleonism* and *Bonapartism*. Napoleonism was a sentimental, nostalgic and romantic view of the Emperor, preoccupied with his victories, his achievements, his sayings and the affecting circumstances surrounding his exile on St Helena and his death. Who could not fail to be moved by his tumultuous fall from being emperor of half the world to being confined to a barren lump of rock in the south Atlantic? This Napoleonism largely lacked political content. Against that, there is *Bonapartism* which was overtly political and potentially revolutionary.[1] It equated Bonaparte with the French Revolution, with republicanism and with liberalism and it admired his brilliant blend of martial vigour with civic virtue. This blithely ignored the inconvenient truths about Napoleon: apart from waging war all over Europe, he was, as one critic noted, 'the man who terminated the first French Republic, suppressed all legislative opposition, practised the most draconian censorship in French history, organised a police force of redoubtable efficiency, re-established a nobility, and reimposed slavery in France's Caribbean colonies'.[2] These two paths – Napoleonism and Bonapartism – converged in Ireland in 1916.

As in all assessments of Napoleon and his impact, the primary difficulty lies in separating fact from fantasy, myth from reality, and prising apart the legacy, the legend and the whimsy. It was recorded in 1819 that the world would never have heard of Napoleon but for the quick-thinking actions of an Irish priest, Edward Redmond, parish priest of Ferns (County Wexford) from 1786 until

1 On the Napoleon legend in nineteenth-century France, see especially Sudhir Hazareesingh, *The legend of Napoleon* (London, 2002). 2 David Bell, 'Napoleon in the flesh', *Modern*

1818. Redmond, as a student in France, had dramatically rescued the boy Bonaparte who had fallen into a river near to the college where Redmond was studying. Redmond had pulled him to safety and the rest is what – history? or fantasy?[3] Then there are the complicated Irish connections of Napoleon's family. We can disregard the claim that Napoleon's grandfather on his mother's side was an O'Donovan from Kilkenny – there is no evidence[4] – but we are on firmer ground in pointing out that Napoleon's older brother, Joseph, married the daughter of Francis Clary, an Irish merchant in Marseilles; she eventually became queen of Spain. Jérôme, the youngest of Napoleon's brothers, married Elizabeth Patterson, daughter of an Irish merchant in Baltimore, Maryland – much to Napoleon's displeasure. As for Napoleon himself, in his youth he was rejected by Désirée Clary, another daughter of Francis Clary and the sister of Joseph's wife. According to Montholon, the exiled Napoleon's Boswell, Désirée remained thereafter Bonaparte's one true love. She subsequently married Marshal Bernadotte, his bitter rival, and eventually became queen of Sweden. One writer has speculated 'whether the career of Napoleon might have been different if he had married [Désirée] with her splendid character and qualities, rather than Joséphine – an adventuress of dubious morals'.[5]

The well-known silversmiths, Bradford's of Clonmel, County Tipperary, claimed that Napoleon shaved with razors made by them.[6] Who would want to refute this charming boast? And then there is Marengo, Napoleon's favourite stallion, named after his famous victory in Italy in 1801, a horse that carried him through Austerlitz, Wagram, the Russian campaign of 1812 and Waterloo, despite being wounded many times. Marengo, who died aged 38 years, remained a prime attraction in circuses and shows, and its skeleton was for many years on display in the National Army Museum in Chelsea. Some years ago it was the subject of an admiring biography.[7] Given the well-attested Irish love for horses, it was inevitable that a claim would be made for Irish ownership. Marengo is frequently asserted to have been bred at Ballinkeele in Wexford and purchased at the horsefair at Ballinasloe, County Galway, for 100 guineas.[8] The local tourist office promotes the connection, and today a rather grand restaurant in the town – the Marengo – celebrates the Napoleonic link. Can any of this be true? The

Language Notes, 120:4 (2005), pp 711–15.   **3** The source of the story is J.B. Trotter, *Walks through Ireland* (London, 1819), pp 31–2. (My thanks to C.J. Woods for this reference.) The story is repeated in P.F. Kavanagh, *A popular history of the Insurrection of 1798* (Dublin, 1870), p. 303. Richard Hayes ('Irish links with Napoleon', *Studies* (March 1946), p. 43) dismisses the claim as lacking 'authenticity'.   **4** John O'Donovan, the foremost Irish scholar of the nineteenth century, investigated this claim 'in vain': Hayes, 'Irish links', p. 63.   **5** Hayes, 'Irish links', pp 63–74.   **6** Cited in article on Clonmel in *Béaloideas*, 10, pp 292–3.   **7** Marengo's skeleton is currently being reconstructed (*Guardian*, 26 Dec. 2016) and will be displayed in the refurbished National Army Museum. Stephen Fry wrote a radio play about a love affair between Marengo and Wellington's horse, Copenhagen. Jill Hamilton, *Marengo, the myth of Napoleon's horse* (London, 2000).   **8** Hayes, 'Irish links with Napoleon', p. 72. Wellington's horse, Copenhagen, was also allegedly purchased at the Ballinasloe horsefair.

family details are supported by the evidence, but the rest is problematic. Intriguingly, Bonaparte claimed to have suffered a near-death experience as a seventeen-year-old youth in France, and the story of a near-drowning surfaced in Barry O'Meara's *Napoleon in exile or a voice from St Helena* in 1822.[9] However, in this version Bonaparte maintained that he struggled ashore unaided and there is no mention of a priest. On the other hand, the story was certainly current in Wexford in 1812 and Father Redmond died in 1818, four years before O'Meara's book came out. The story is best regarded as unproven. As for Marengo, the available evidence points to a horse of Barbary stock captured or purchased in the aftermath of the battle of Aboukir Bay (1798) in Egypt. The Ballinasloe connection may date from the publication of Thackeray's Napoleonic novel, *Vanity Fair* (1847), where the words Marengo, Ballinasloe and horse appear close together.

We are on firmer ground in addressing Bonaparte's connection with the United Irishmen.[10] From the 1690s on, successive Irish governments had kept a close eye on French military planning that might conceivably include an invasion of Ireland, and French officer cadets in the French military academies were routinely set as an exercise an incursion into Ireland. Little had come of these fears.[11] However, by the mid-1790s, the French revolutionary authorities had finally begun to contemplate a descent on Ireland: at the very least, a small French force might tie up many British soldiers. An invasion might even succeed, considering what Bonaparte had done in Italy in 1796–7. Ireland could prove another Italy for a lucky French general, the island would then be detached from Britain and thus Britain would be deprived of a vital supply of recruits and provisions for her army and navy. The future Hibernian Republic would join the Cisalpine Republic, the Batavian Republic and the Parthenopean Republic and others as satellite republics of France. An encircled Britain would have no alternative but to concede. In addition, an invasion of Ireland could ignite a civil war – a well-deserved payback for Pitt who had infamously stirred up counter-revolution in the Vendée and had acted as paymaster to the agrarian insurgency there, *la chouannerie*. Ireland could be Pitt's Vendée.[12]

Theobald Wolfe Tone had several meetings with Napoleon Bonaparte between December 1797 and January 1798. As the recent conqueror of Italy, Napoleon's reputation was soaring and news of his victories over the Austrians penetrated to remote parts of Europe. Miles Byrne, United Irishman and later soldier in the Grande Armée, more than sixty years later recalled the 'happy

9 Hubert O'Connor, *The Emperor and the Irishman: Napoleon and Dr Barry O'Meara on St Helena* (Dublin, 2008), p. 151. 10 Marianne Elliott, *Partners in revolution: the United Irishmen and France* (New Haven, 1982). 11 James Kelly, '"Disappointing the boundless ambitions of France": Irish Protestants and the fear of invasion, 1661–1815', *Studia Hibernica*, 37 (2011), pp 27–105. 12 Hugh Gough, 'Total war? Revolutionary France and United Irish strategy in the 1790s' in D. Murphy & N. Genet-Rouffiac (eds), *Franco-Irish military connections, 1590–1945* (Dublin, 2009), pp 150–63.

days' in Monaseed, County Wexford, when, with pulse racing, 'we used to read at the chapel the newspapers giving an account of [Napoleon's] brilliant campaigns from 1795 down to the peace of Campo Formio in 1797'.[13] Around the same time, a man was arrested in Oranmore, County Galway, for drinking this toast: 'Go bhfeicimid Seoirse a chrocadh le corda/ agus a chraicean mar bhróga ar Bhonaparte' ('May we see George hanged by a rope/ and his skin as boots for Bonaparte').[14] Henry O'Kane disembarked with General Humbert at Killala, County Mayo, in August 1798: when he wanted to impose his will, he waved his sword and claimed that what 'he had in his hand was given to him by General Bonaparte'. Indeed in the folklore associated with the French raid in 1798, it was Bonaparte who was at its head, not the obscure Humbert:

> Tá na Francaigh anois istigh i gCill Ala
> Agus béimid go leathan láidir
> Tá Bonaparte i gCaisleán an Bharraigh
> Ag iarraidh an dlí a cheap Sáirséal.[15]

> [The French are now in Killala
> And we will be broad and strong
> Bonaparte is now in Castlebar
> Seeking to enact Sarsfield's law]

More elevated witnesses could also be swept away by Napoleon's awesome reputation: in May 1798, Lieutenant General James Stewart rashly announced that he had in fact captured Napoleon Bonaparte off the Cork coast.[16] Given Napoleon's extraordinary military standing throughout Europe, Tone commented in his diary in November 1797 that 'it is droll enough' that he, an Irish exile, a relative unknown, with no military standing, travelling under the *nom de plume* of James Smith, 'should be writing to Buonaparte' seeking an interview. The pair duly met during the third week of December 1797 at Bonaparte's house in the rue Chantereine. Here is Tone's account:

> December 18–21, 1797. He lives in the greatest simplicity; his house is small but neat and all the furniture and ornaments in the most classical taste. He is about five feet six inches high and well made, but stoops considerably; he looks at least ten years older than he is owing to the great fatigues he underwent in his immortal campaign of Italy. His face is that of a profound thinker but bears no mark of that great enthusiasm and

---

13 Thomas Bartlett, 'Miles Byrne; United Irishman, Irish exile and *Beau Sabreur*' in D. Keogh & N. Furlong (eds), *The mighty wave: the 1798 rebellion in Wexford* (Dublin, 1996), p. 129. 14 Guy Beiner, *Remembering the Year of the French: Irish folk history and social memory* (Madison, WI, 2007), p. 112.   15 Guy Beiner, 'Who were the men of the west? Folk historiographies and the reconstruction of democratic histories', *Folklore*, 112:2 (2004), p. 206.   16 Beiner,

unceasing activity by which he has been so much distinguished. It is rather to my mind the countenance of a mathematician than of a general. He has a fine eye and a great firmness about his mouth; he speaks low and hollow. So much for his manner and figure.

As for Ireland and Irish affairs, Tone recorded his disappointment that Bonaparte 'appears a good deal uninformed; for example he seems convinced that our population is not more than two millions which is nonsense. Buonaparte listened but said little'. (Another of Bonaparte's Irish visitors recorded that the great man believed that Ireland was infested with wolves. And yet another recalled that Bonaparte 'seemed to understand nothing of this noble island of Ireland more than to have a general idea of its religious differences with England. He erroneously thought the entire country Catholic. I afterwards knew that he entertained a very poor idea of the Irish nation').[17]

A further meeting on 23 December lasted just five minutes during which Bonaparte asked for further materials on Ireland. Tone wrote in his diary:

> His manner is cold and he speaks very little; it is not however so dry as that of [General Lazare] Hoche but seems rather to proceed from languor than anything else. He is perfectly civil however to us; but from anything we have yet seen or heard from him, it is impossible to augur anything good or bad. We have now seen the greatest man in Europe three times and I am astonished how little I have to record about him … Yet after all it is a droll thing that I should become acquainted with Buonaparte.

A final meeting took place on 13 January 1798. Tone and Edward Lewines, another United Irishman, met Bonaparte and handed over further Irish memoranda and maps of Ireland. Tone told him that the United Irishmen in Paris were eager to be involved in any invasion by the Armée d'Angleterre: 'Finally [writes Tone] I spoke of myself'. Tone expressed his great desire to be on the staff for the forthcoming invasion. Bonaparte assured him he would be, but Tone then had to make the humiliating disclosure that he had next to no military experience or knowledge. Bonaparte replied in a phrase which set Irish nationalist heart's pounding during the nineteenth century: 'Mais vous êtes brave'. Tone modestly replied that when the opportunity offered he hoped that would be the case. Bonaparte rejoined – 'Eh bien, cela suffit'.[18] They parted, never to meet again: Napoleon within a matter of months would go off to Egypt – not Ireland; Tone sailed for Ireland in September 1798, only to be captured and to die in prison by his own hand.[19]

Remembering the Year of the French, p. 146.   **17** Hayes, 'Irish links with Napoleon', p. 64; J.B. Trotter, quoted in T.W. Moody, R.B. McDowell & C.J. Woods (eds), *The writings of Theobald Wolfe Tone*, 3 vols (Oxford, 1998–2007), iii, p. 185.   **18** Thomas Bartlett (ed.), *Life of Theobald Wolfe Tone* (Dublin, 1998), pp 815–20.   **19** Sylvie Kleinman, 'Un brave de plus'; Theobald

Twelve years later, Tone's widow, Matilda, encountered Napoleon. Since her husband's death she had lived quietly in France, subsisting on the pension paid to her by the French government, awarded after some prompting by Lucien Bonaparte, Napoleon's brother. She spent her time caring for her family, but suffered the heartache of seeing all of her children, save William, die of consumption. William was to be her sole surviving child and she was determined that he be enrolled in the Imperial army's prestigious School of Cavalry. Accordingly in 1810 she applied to the Duc de Feltre, minister of war, to place her son there. Feltre (previously Henri Clarke) was of Irish Jacobite stock, and he had worked closely with Tone in preparations for a French invasion of Ireland. Despite these connections, Feltre felt that he owed the Tones no special favours and he ruled that young William would become an officer cadet in Napoleon's Irish Legion, at that time serving in Spain. With formidable resolve, the affronted Matilda decided to bring her case to the Emperor's personal attention.

It was well known that Napoleon hunted regularly in the forest of St Germain when in Paris. Matilda conceived a plan to ambush the Emperor when his carriage halted to change horses and to thrust a bound essay by William, along with her memorial detailing her claim on France, into his hands. Matilda Tone continues …

> Very soon the carriage with the Emperor and Empress drove into the circle [in the forest]; the horses were changed as quick as [I had] thought, but I stepped up and presented the book and the memorial. [The Emperor] took them and handing the book to his écuyer [equerry], opened the paper. I have said it commenced by recalling Tone to his memory. When [Napoleon] began [to read], he said 'Tone!' with an expressive accent, 'I remember him well' (Je m'en souviens bien).

Napoleon asked Matilda about her circumstances and she described her modest life at St Germain and explained further about her son. The Emperor promised to investigate and his carriage departed. The incident was the talk of St Germain; who was that strange woman who had taken the Emperor of France by his collar? Matilda's effort proved successful, for William obtained his government scholarship and he never did serve in the Irish Legion.[20]

Napoleon's later dealings with the United Irishmen proved less happy. After the failure of the 1798 rebellion and the non-arrival of a large French force, the surviving United Irish leaders were reluctant to put too much further trust in French promises. Robert Emmet travelled to France in the aftermath of the 1798

Wolfe Tone, alias Adjutant General James Smyth: French officer and patriot adventurer, 1796–8' in Murphy & Genet Rouffiac (eds), *Franco-Irish militay connections*, pp 163–88. **20** Bartlett (ed.), *Life of Tone*, pp 916–17.

UNE CÉRÉMONIE FRANÇAISE EN IRLANDE

Le Centenaire de la descente en Irlande des Soldats français en 1798

LES IRLANDAIS PORTANT DES COURONNES AU MONUMENT COMMÉMORATIF DU CHAMP DE BATAILLE DE CASTLEBAR

1 The 1898 image from *Le Petit Parisien* is a collaboration between Tony Beltrand and Eugène Dété. It depicts 'une cérémonie française en Irlande', at the 1798 monument (erected 1876), at French Hill, Castlebar, Co. Mayo, commemorating 'le centenaire de la descente en Irlande des soldats françaises 1798'. The caption reads 'Les Irlandais portant des couronnes au monument commémoratif du champ de bataille de Castlebar'. The monument reads 'Aux braves soldats Français qui périrent ici pour la liberté de l'Irlande' (Collection Pierre Joannon).

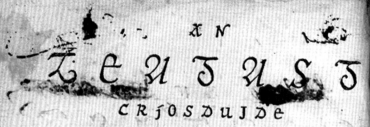

AN TEAGUSG

CRÍOSDUJÐE

DO RÉJR

ceasda agus freagarta,

air na tarruing go brmobarac ar

bréjtir hsojlléjr ðé,

agus

As tojbreacajb fjorg-lana ojle.

Ejro ne Comajple, agus glac Teagarg, cvm
go mbja tr gljc ann do Chpjc óéjzjonvjg.
Prov. 19. 20.

A BPAJRJS,

Ajn na crp a gClóð ne Sevmry JUERJN, ag
San-Tomas ó Acvn, a Spájo Sajn-Sevm.

M. D. CC. XLII.

Ré Ceað an Rjg, agus ne Déjgtejro na
nOllamyn ne Djagact.

2 Andrew Donlevy, *An Teagasg Críosduidhe do réir ceasda agus freagartha, air natharruing go bunubhasach as bréithir hsoilléir Dé agus as toibreachaib fiorghlan aoile. AbPairís air nachur a gclódh re Seumus Guerin, ag San Tomás ó Acuin, a sráid Sain-Seum [as]. M.D. CC. XLII Ré Cead an Rígh, agus re Déightheisd na nOllamhun re Diaghacht* (Paris, 1742). The Sráid Sain Seam. – Saint James's Street – is a subtle nod in a Jacobite direction, discreetly veiled by the abbreviation. Dunleavy was prompted by 'a great desire of contributing to the instruction of the poor Irish youth … The plainest and most obvious Irish is used therein, preferring, after the example of S. Augustin, rather to be censured by grammarians than misunderstood of the people' (Gilbert Library, Dublin).

3 Flamboyant artists in Paris, 1914 (Musée Albert-Kahn, Département des Hauts-de-Seine).

Tone's Interview with Napoleon,
December 23, 1797.

4 'Tone's interview with Napoleon, December 23 1797'. A cartoon by John Francis O'Hea in the *Weekly Freeman*, 11 December 1911. This chromolithograph was printed by James Walker & Co., colour printers, Dublin (National Library of Ireland).

NO. 3. SIXTH YEAR

A BROADSIDE

FOR AUGUST, 1913.
PUBLISHED MONTHLY BY E. C. YEATS AT THE CUALA PRESS,
CHURCHTOWN, DUNDRUM, COUNTY DUBLIN.
SUBSCRIPTION TWELVE SHILLINGS A YEAR POST FREE.

NAPOLEON BUONAPARTE'S FAREWELL TO PARIS
I visited the splendid city the metropolis called Paris,
Situated every morning by Sol's refulgent beams,
Conjoined by bright Aurora advancing from the Orient,
With radiant lights adorning in fire shining ray.
Commanding Scethua to retire, then the windows glance like fire
And the universe admire their merchandise in store,
While floral spreading fragrance the fertile plains to decorate,
To illuminate the royal Corsican again on the French shore.

I am Napoleon Buonaparte, the conqueror of nations,
I banished German legions — drove kings from their thrones,
I've trampled Dukes and Earls and splendid congregations,
For which I am transported to St. Helena's shore.
Like a Hannibal I crossed the Alps o'er burning sands and rocky cliffs,
Over Russian hills through snow and frost I still the laurel wore,
Now I am in a desert Isle, the very devil it would fright,
I thought to shine in armour bright thro' Europe once more.

300 copies only.

5 'Napoleon's Buonaparte's farewell to Paris'. 'I visited the splendid city, the metropolis called Paris'. A broadside published by the Cuala Press in Dublin, August 1913 (Collection Anthony J. Mourek).

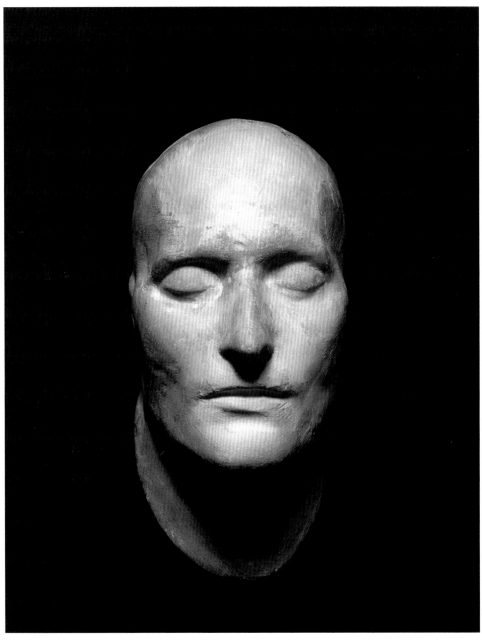

6 The death mask of Napoleon, known as the Antommarchi-Burghersh mask. It was created on 7 May 1821, a day and a half after his death. This is regarded as the closest example to the first cast taken from Napoleon's face (Musée de l'Armée, Paris).

7 Napoleon at the Camp de Boulogne, by Jacques Onfroy de Bréville (1858–1931) (known by the pen
name Job after his initials). This is one of thirty-six chromolithographs in the folio edition of *Bonaparte*
(Boivin & Cie, Paris, 1910)– an illustrated biography in French. These are rendered in the flowing lines
of Art Nouveau. Job was a well-known children's illustrator for heroes of the nation like Napoleon.
Among other books on Napoleon illustrated by Job are *Le Grand Napoléon des petits enfans* (1908),
Napoléon (1921) and *Quand le grand Napoléon était petit* (1931) (Collection Pierre Joannon).

8 Charles Baudelaire (1821–67) photographed in 1862 by Étienne Carjat.

9 Émile Zola (1840–1902) photographed in 1862 by Étienne Carjat.

10 Victor Hugo (1802–65) photographed in 1876 by Étienne Carjat.

11 Gustave Courbet, 'L'atelier du peintre' (The artist's studio). 1855, oil on canvas. The left side shows ordinary life in Paris, while elite Parisian figures, including Charles Baudelaire, Champfleury and Pierre-Joseph Proudhon, are shown on the right. Courbet claimed that the painting 'represents society at its best, its worst, and its average' (Musée d'Orsay, Paris).

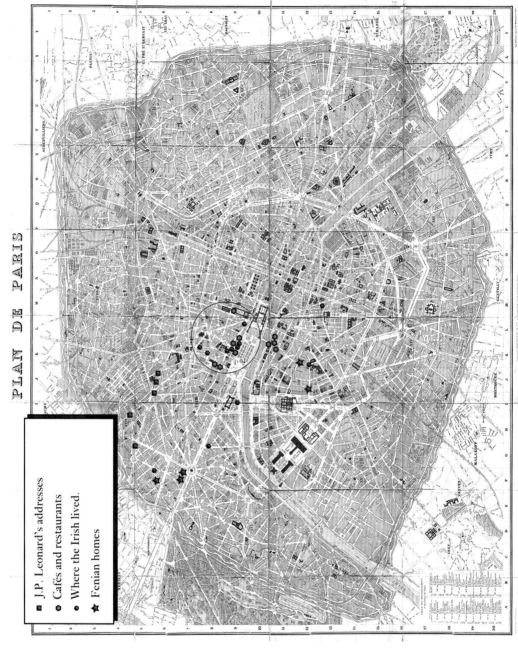

PLAN DE PARIS

- ■ J.P. Leonard's addresses
- ◉ Cafés and restaurants
- ● Where the Irish lived.
- ★ Fenian homes

12 Irish Paris 1850s–1860s (Matthew Stout).

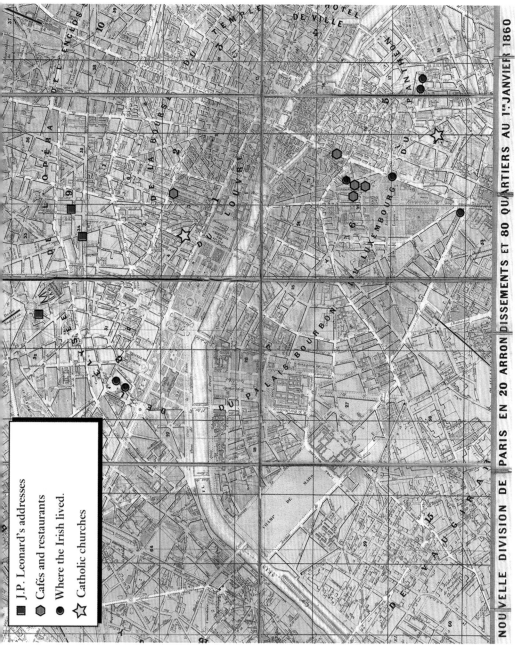

13 Irish Paris 1870s–1880s (Matthew Stout).

NOUVELLE DIVISION DE PARIS EN 20 ARRONDISSEMENTS ET 80 QUARTIERS AU 1ᵉʳ JANVIER 1860

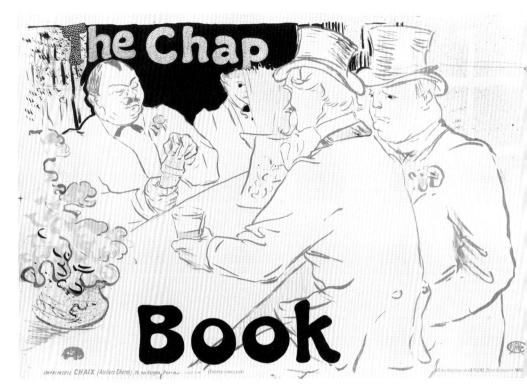

IMPRIMERIE *CHAIX* (Ateliers Cheret), 20, rue Bergère, PARIS.   (Encres Lorilleux)

14 The Irish-American bar, 1895. Eugene Davis noted in 1886 that 'To the pleasure seeker or epicurean, Paris is a bewitching fairyland'. The Corkman especially liked the Irish-American bar at 33 Rue Royale, because it served Guinness and Jameson. This 1895 poster by Toulouse Lautrec was published by the magazine *La Plume* to advertise the American literary periodical *The Chap Book*. Ralph (Randolph), the imperturbable barman, of mixed Indian and Chinese background, was highly regarded for his inventive cocktails. Lautrec shows Ralph, behind the gleaming mahogany bar, serving Tom, the portly coachman of Alphonse de Rothschild (Collection Kevin Whelan).

15 (*opposite*) 'En Irlande. Manifestation contre M. Chamberlain' in *Le Petit Journal*, 31 December 1899. The flag is that of the Transvaal. The text in translation reads: 'Trinity College Dublin, with a questionable attitude, deemed it acceptable to confer an honorary doctorate on Mr. Joe Chamberlain. While the English ministers met as a matter of urgency to impose the most serious measures, he was travelling light heartedly to the oppressed island to pompously receive his degree'. When the Boer War broke out in October 1899, it was received enthusiastically within nationalist Ireland as an anti-imperial struggle. James Connolly noted that a police raid on his offices before the Chamberlain demonstration seized 'one red flag, one green flag, two Boer flags, and the historic black flag which led the anti-Jubilee procession of 1897'. Leopold Bloom recalled the lively scenes outside Trinity on that day in *Ulysses*: 'That horsepoliceman the day Joe Chamberlain was given his degree in Trinity, he got a run for his money. My word he did!' (Collection Pierre Joannon).

Le Petit Journal

Le Petit Journal
CHAQUE JOUR 5 CENTIMES

Le Supplément illustré
CHAQUE SEMAINE 5 CENTIMES

SUPPLÉMENT ILLUSTRÉ

Huit pages : CINQ centimes

ABONNEMENTS

	SIX MOIS	UN AN
SEINE ET SEINE-ET-OISE	2 fr.	3 fr. 50
DÉPARTEMENTS	2 fr.	4 fr.
ÉTRANGER	2.50	5 fr.

Dixième année   DIMANCHE 31 DÉCEMBRE 1899   Numéro 476

EN IRLANDE

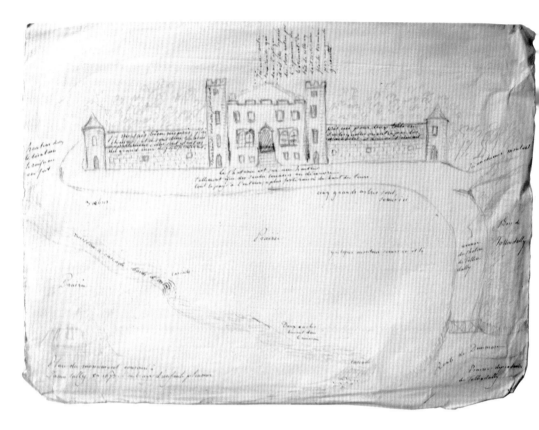

16 The Lally-Tolendall home farm at Tullinadaly, Co. Galway. The ancestral Lally castle of Tullinadaly stood in the modern townland of Castletown, north of Tuam. The estate was forfeited due to Jacobitism in the 1690s, and the family, then headed by James Lally, followed King James into French exile. James's son Thomas was viceroy in India under King Louis XV, and he was executed in 1766 in a scandalous manner. His son Trophime-Gérard, Marquis de Lally-Tollendal (1751–1830), was a French politician. Remarkably, Lally-Tollendal actively contemplated repurchasing Tullinadaly in the 1820s, and sent a French surveyor to map the estate. This drawing is from that survey. The house is currently a substantial ruin (Collection Rolf Loeber).

rebellion and made contact with leading members of the Consulate. It is unclear whether he ever met Napoleon. His biographers are divided on this point, but it seems unlikely; there is no evidence to support a meeting.[21] Emmet and others did meet French officials, but their abiding impression from these contacts was deep suspicion concerning French intentions towards Ireland. Certainly, Thomas Addis Emmet, Robert's eldest brother, hated Napoleon for, as he saw it, his betrayal of republicanism, and he doubted whether Napoleon had ever had any intention of liberating Ireland. Arthur O'Connor, although a bitter enemy of Thomas Addis Emmet, equally denounced 'that enemy of anything like liberty, Bounaparte'.[22] Robert Emmet came to share this verdict. However, despite doubts over Napoleon's intentions or whether he and Robert Emmet had ever met, Irish nationalists in the late nineteenth century had no hesitation about shoehorning Robert Emmet and Napoleon Bonaparte into their patriotic iconography. Where the legend and the facts conflict, print the legend.

Finally, in terms of the historical record, there is the Irish Legion, renamed in 1809 *le 3eme Régiment Étranger – Irlandais*, which was raised by Napoleon Bonaparte on the resumption of war with England in 1803 and disbanded on his defeat in 1815.[23] The Irish Legion's story is unhappy; it had an undistinguished, even unfortunate history. No Fontenoy or Cremona adorns its battle honours. While its officers were (initially) Irish-born or of Irish extraction, its rank-and-file consisted mostly of Polish or Prussian conscripts, with a leavening of British, Irish and Scottish deserters, or former prisoners-of-war. The Legion in its short history had a notorious reputation for indiscipline, insubordination and rancorous feuding that left at least one man dead, a number wounded, and caused others to give up in despair. At least one colonel – Jeremiah Fitzhenry – deserted to the British. Raised specifically for service in Ireland, it never saw action in that country and instead spent its early years kicking its heels in enforced idleness in Brittany. All in all, its disbandment under the restored Bourbons (possibly at the insistence of Castlereagh) offered relief from its dispiriting squabbles and factionalism.[24]

21 Patrick Geoghegan, *Robert Emmet: a life* (Dublin, 2002), p. 101 maintains that he met Napoleon; Marianne Elliott, *Robert Emmet, the making of a legend* (London, 2003), claims that there is no evidence that he did (p. 34), and Ruán O'Donnell, *Robert Emmet and the Rebellion of 1798* (Dublin, 2003), is non-committal (p. 169). **22** Alex. Marsden to – Wynn, 7 March 1806 (TNA HO/100/135/61). Some Presbyterian reformers and radicals clustered in and around Belfast – the Drennans, Tennents and Simms' connection – maintained a qualified fondness for Napoleon, on occasion 'utilising him rhetorically in their battles with the forces of reaction'– they were regularly denounced by their opponents as 'friends of Bonaparte' or 'Bonaparte-Protestants'. J.J. Wright, *'The natural leaders' and their world: politics, culture and society in Belfast, c.1801–1832* (Liverpool, 2012), pp 106–11. **23** J.G. Gallaher, *Napoleon's Irish Legion* (Illinois, 1993); Thomas Bartlett, 'Last flight of the Wild Geese? Bonaparte's Irish Legion, 1803–1815' in T. O'Connor & M.A. Lyons (eds), *Irish communities in early modern Europe* (Dublin, 2006), pp 160–71. **24** For details of the composition of the Irish Legion, see N. Dunne-Lynch, 'The Irish Legion of Napoleon, 1803–1815' in Murphy & Genet-Rouffiac (eds), *Franco-Irish military connections*, pp 189–218.

Little of these disputes was known about in Ireland, nor indeed of Napoleon's vagueness where Ireland was concerned. Despite a concerted British effort to demonise him in pamphlet, broadside and print, and to detail the misery visited on the countries he had invaded,[25] the Irish Catholic reaction to Napoleon's exploits, adventures and victories was overwhelmingly favourable. 'The success of Bonaparte on the Continent has occasioned great joy and exultation among many of the Catholics', wrote one official in 1806.[26] And another reported in the same year that 'the country people are becoming greater politicians of late and meet in clubs to read the accounts of Buonaparte'.[27] Agrarian insurgents in County Waterford reportedly drank to the 'health and success to Bonaparte' and elsewhere in that county the toast was 'Bonaparte and our religion'.[28] Despite the efforts of some Catholic priests to label Napoleon as an infidel,[29] his rough treatment of the Pope and the Catholic church was simply ignored: in fact, wrote one Dublin Castle official rather wearily: 'If Bonaparte could bring the Pope to the top of Tara Hill and guillotine him there in the face of day, he would not have ten followers and friends the less for it'.[30]

The progress of the war in Spain was followed with rapt attention by both Dublin Castle and 'the whole population of Ireland ... understood to mean the Catholics'. People, 'even poor people', claimed Joseph Trail's source (an ex-1798 rebel) talk and think of nothing but Napoleon's successes and the expected invasion.[31] 'The minds of all the parties in the Catholic body are directed towards the events in Spain', noted chief secretary, Edward Littlehales.[32] Whenever bad news arrived from the Iberian peninsula, wrote the veteran Orange champion, John Giffard, in 1809, the 'walls [in Dublin] are immediately covered with *placards* and you can see joy in every popish countenance, insolence in their eyes and malice in their manner. When things are better as now they are supposed to be, all is stillness and tranquillity'.[33] Five years on, the news from the front was better still: 'The prospect on the Continent has again brightened', wrote Lord Sidmouth to Peel, 'and the barometer of turbulence and disaffection on your side of the water has, I suppose, again fallen'.[34] Whitworth, the lord lieutenant, looked forward to Bonaparte's demise as 'the best remedy for Irish disaffection'.[35]

---

25 Stuart Semmel, *Napoleon and the British* (New Haven, 2004), chapter 2, 'National character and national anxiety'. **26** William Elliott to Lord Spencer, 5 Dec. 1806, BL MS 75,904. **27** A. Trail to —, late 1806, TNA HO/100/138/396. **28** John Palliser to Bagwell, 31 Jan. 1809; Saxton to Beckett, 21, 31 Jan. 1809, TNA HO 100/153/37, 151–2. **29** In Eyrecourt, County Galway, in September 1813, the local parish priest, Fr Costello, allegedly ordered his parishioners to extinguish candles lit to celebrate Wellington's victory at Vitoria, Spain. Bishop of Clonfert to [Sidmouth], 19 Sept. 1813, TNA HO/100/172/60–2. **30** Joseph Pollock to Wellesley, 12 Jan. 1809 in *Wellington Supplementary Dispatches*, v, pp 534–5. **31** Trail to Wellesley, 16 July 1807 in *Wellington Supplementary Dispatches*, v, pp 119–21. **32** E.B. Littlehales to —, 27 Nov. 1808, TNA HO100/149/227. **33** Giffard to Archbishop of Cashel, 20 May 1809, PRONI, T3719/c 43/97. **34** Sidmouth to Peel, 10 Mar. 1814, TNA HO/100/177/172. **35** Whitworth to Sidmouth, 16 Feb. 1814, TNA HO/100/177/97.

Accordingly, news of Bonaparte's escape from Elba and the ensuing 'hundred days' of frenzied political, diplomatic and military activity, culminating in the decisive battle of Waterloo, was followed avidly in Ireland. Loyalists cheered his defeat. The Gothic novelist (and clergyman) Charles Maturin noted that 'the appalling supernatural greatness of Buonaparte had terrified even those who wished him well, and men seemed relieved, as from the spell of an enchanter'.[36] By contrast, 'the lower orders' were 'highly gratified' at his progress and adventures which had caused 'a ferment' in Ireland.[37] Nor were the disaffected in Ireland all that despondent about Bonaparte's exile to St Helena: in September 1815 – three months after Waterloo – it was said that insurgents in Tipperary 'still expect Bonaparte', and in November of that year, a correspondent of under-secretary William Gregory wrote that the disaffected still clung to the 'absurd idea of French help' as a result 'of false prophecies circulated among them for the purposes of delusion'.[38]

However, even before Waterloo, Napoleon Bonaparte had passed into legend in Ireland. In France and in Britain, the Napoleonic legend rested almost entirely on his actions during the 'hundred days' when the great man attempted to follow what might be called a liberal agenda in French politics, but in Ireland, long before this, he was regarded as a messianic figure destined to bring deliverance to the Catholics. This French messiah travelled a well-trodden Irish road. In 1810, near Dunlavin in County Wicklow, a large crowd had gathered to hear Doyle, a local poet: at his performance, two figures duly appeared, none other than Napoleon and his Empress (in effigy). In August 1815, as news of Bonaparte's fall was confirmed, a Catholic leader, Rafferty, promised the crowd at a gathering near Omagh, County Tyrone, that those who stuck with him 'shall get a townland in some part of Ireland. They then cheered [Rafferty], at first called him King James and afterwards Bonaparte'.[39]

THE EMPEROR AND HIS IRISH DOCTOR

Napoleon was accompanied to St Helena by Dr Barry O'Meara, an Irish medical doctor who had been trained in the Royal College of Surgeons, Dublin, and then served in the Royal Navy. Napoleon was taken with O'Meara's command of Italian – one of Bonaparte's languages – and asked for him to stay on, and the two men subsequently became respectful friends. St Helena was a desolate chunk of volanic rock in the South Atlantic, populated largely by vast numbers of pink-eyed rats, and with an inhospitable climate. The Irish-born governor,

36 Quoted in David Dickson, *Dublin: the making of a capital city* (London, 2014), p. 274.
37 Abstract of Reports, March 1815, TNA HO/100/183/411; Whitworth to Sidmouth, 1 April 1815, TNA HO/100/183/364.   **38** Samuel Jacob to Attorney General, 10 Sept. 1815, TNA HO/100/185/442–4; D'Arcy Mahon to Gregory, 16 Nov. 1815, TNA HO100/187/149–50.   **39** Brig. Maj. Eccles to W.W. Pole, 31 July 1810, TNA HO/100/159/104–5; Sir

Hudson Lowe, quickly turned against his fellow Irishman, O'Meara. Lowe, a martinet and a deeply insecure man, feared that an attempt would be made to rescue Bonaparte: to prevent such an escape, he would make Napoleon's life miserable and visit as much humiliation on him as possible.[40] He insisted that O'Meara, as a British officer, must forget his medical duty of care to his patient and spy on the Emperor. O'Meara indignantly refused, and until 1818 when he was sacked, a battle of wits ensued between the doctor and the governor. O'Meara, however, had the last laugh. Removed from his position, and then cashiered from the Royal Navy (with loss of pension), O'Meara published his detailed diaries of his stay on St Helena in 1822 as *Napoleon in exile or a voice from St Helena*.[41]

The work, like that of Las Cases on Napoleon's exile, *Mémorial de Sainte Hélène*, was received enthusiastically by an English-reading public that had remained fascinated by Napoleon.[42] O'Meara became an unquestionably authentic source of quotations and opinions that the general public, starved of news of the great man, wished to hear. According to Napoleon, as reported by O'Meara, the French revolution offered 'the career open to talents', the English were nothing but 'a nation of shopkeepers' and as for the military – with perhaps a nod to Theobald Wolfe Tone – 'I love a brave soldier who has undergone the baptism of fire whatever nation he may belong to'. Bonaparte treated O'Meara as an *English* officer and scarcely realised that he was Irish. The Emperor's much-quoted regret that he had not invaded Ireland instead of Egypt (a quotation that found its way into Lady Gregory's *Kiltartan history book* in 1909) originated with Las Cases, not O'Meara. More pertinent was Napoleon's verdict on the United Irishmen that he had encountered. O'Meara revealed that he was dismissive of them:

> If the Irish had sent over honest men to me I would certainly have made an attempt upon Ireland. But I had no confidence in either the integrity or the talents of the Irish leaders that were in France. They could offer no plan, were divided in opinion and continually quarrelling with one another. I had but a poor opinion of that [Arthur] O'Connor who was so much spoken of amongst you.[43]

John Stewart to Abercorn, 27 Aug. 1815, PRONI T2541/1B3/21/9.   **40** Desmond Gregory, *Napoleon's jailer: Lt. Gen. Sir Hudson Lowe, a life* (Madison, NJ, 1966) offers a vigorous defense of Lowe against 'the venomous surgeon, Dr O'Meara'.   **41** Barry O'Meara, *Napoleon in exile or a voice from St Helena*, 2 vols (London, 1822). The affecting details in the book concerning Napoleon's captivity, and his stoic dignity in the face of provocation, made an impression on two youthful historians, T.B. Macaulay and Thomas Carlyle. Semmel, *Napoleon and the British*, pp 217–18.   **42** For the impact of Las Cases' work on the Napoleon legend see Hazareesingh, *Legend of Napoleon* and Semmel, *Napoleon and the British*.   **43** O'Connor, *The Emperor and the Irishman*, p. 120: Napoleon's 'amongst you' is a rare acknowledgement that O'Meara was actually Irish.

As for Theobald Wolfe Tone – despite the 'je m'en souviens bien' of earlier times – he figures nowhere in Napoleon's table talk, nor is there any reference to him in Napoleon's voluminous correspondence, published during the Second Empire.

O'Meara's book had a huge success, and his earnings from it – and from the rapid French translation – more than compensated for his loss of employment and pension. Hudson Lowe sued for libel, but the case collapsed because of delays. O'Meara married the much older Lady Theodosia Leigh (née Broughton), a wealthy and twice-married widow (her first husband had been hanged for murdering her brother, and her second marriage had ended in divorce in 1818). O'Meara was taken up by the Whig opposition centred on Holland House and he was befriended by Daniel O'Connell who regarded Napoleon as an 'unfortunate great man'. O'Meara went on to help found the New Reform Club. He died in 1836, apparently of a chill caught at one of O'Connell's meetings. Long before then Napoleon Bonaparte (d. 1821) had passed from history into mythology. In death, he was to achieve a reputation, an apotheosis even, that had been denied or disputed in his lifetime. He achieved this inside and outside France but especially in Ireland.

IRISH REPRESENTATIONS OF NAPOLEON

Napoleon Bonaparte was remembered in Ireland in the nineteenth century – in Irish-language poetry, in ballads, in folklore, in folk plays, in the theatre and, in the early twentieth century, in film.[44] Curiously, Irish novels about Napoleon are few and far between.[45] But this does not mean that the revolutionary and Napoleonic period was neglected by authors, but the scores of novels set in those times were consumed by the 1798 rebellion and Robert Emmet. However, if novels featuring Napoleon were scarce, such was not the case with poetry in Irish. The Royal Irish Academy's *Corpus na Gaeilge, 1600–1882* has many references to poems in which, variously, 'Bóin', 'Bóna' and especially 'Bónaí' or 'Bónapartaidh' appear. Almost all of these poems praised him as among other things as 'an gaiscíoch ríúil sin Bónaí' (that regal hero Boney) who had laid low Oliver Cromwell, William III and Henry VIII, and who, it was predicted, would return to Ireland one sunny day (lá gréine).[46]

In the English language, numerous ballads were published in Ireland relating to Napoleon Bonaparte, vivid testimony to his hold on the public imagination

44 See Napoléon I in Daithí Ó hÓgáin (ed.), *The lore of Ireland* (Dublin, 2006), pp 371–2; Hayes, 'Irish links with Napoleon'; Alan Gailey, 'The folk play in Ireland', *Studia Hibernica*, 6 (1966), pp 113–54; G-D. Zimmermann, *Songs of Irish rebellion: political street ballads and rebel songs, 1780–1900* (Dublin, 1967). 45 The invaluable bibliography of Irish fiction compiled by Rolf and Magda Loeber, *Guide to Irish fiction, 1650–1900* (Dublin, 2006) locates only two or three concerning Napoleon compared to over 100 on the 1798 rebellion. 46 Vincent Morley,

long after his death. Some of these ballads were probably written in England, where a cult of Bonaparte existed until the 1850s,[47] and were subsequently adapted to Irish circumstances; some were older Irish ballads or poems (frequently sung rather than recited) duly updated to include Bonaparte. A central theme in Irish poetry was the notion of the deliverance of oppressed Ireland by foreign intervention. At one time, James II or Bonny Prince Charlie had been the deliverer or messiah who would free Ireland; now Napoleon passed seamlessly into this tradition. Here is one example from the 1850s:

> One night sad and languid I lay on my bed
> and I scarce had reclined on my pillow
> when a vision surprising came into my head
> I thought I was crossing the billow
> [Napoleon appears, and speaks]
> On the plains of Marengo, I tyranny hurled
> wherever my banner the eagle unfurled
> 'Twas the standard of freedom all over the world
> To liberty's temple I guided mankind
> And slavery sought to keep under
> the fetters of bondsmen I oft did unbind
> Tyrants' treaties I tore them asunder.[48]

The image of Bonaparte as a universal liberator, friend of the people and democrat was being created, cemented and passed on to posterity.

The accomplished traditional singer, Frank Harte, working with Donal Lunny, produced a double CD entitled *My name is Napoleon Bonaparte* consisting of twenty-six Irish ballads on Napoleon.[49] These included: *The Bonny bunch of roses, The Green Linnet, Napoleon's farewell to Paris, I am Napoleon Bonaparte, Napoleon is the boy for kicking up a row, Bonaparte's farewell.* Not all were tributes to Napoleon; some were traditional anti-war songs, while several blamed him for the death of a loved one who had taken the King's shilling and enlisted in the British army, only to perish or suffer mutilation – pegs replacing legs – as a result of Waterloo. But most lamented the lost hero, the 'Green Linnet', a gallant ally who would surely one day return to 'sting the bonny bunch of roses', i.e., the British army.

James Joyce was sufficiently impressed with the Napoleonic cult to include a mention of Bonaparte in *Portrait of the artist as a young man* (1916), where

Ó Chéitinn go Raiftearí (Baile Átha Cliath, 2011), p. 258.   **47** For discussion of Napoleon's place in British balladry, see Vic Gammon, 'The grand conversation: Napoleon and British popular balladry', *Royal Society of Arts Journal*, 137 (1989), pp 665–74.   **48** National Library. Zimmerman, *Songs of Irish rebellion*, especially 'I am Napoleon Bonaparte, conqueror of nations', p. 103. Samuel Lover, *Legends and stories of Ireland* (Dublin, 1834), pp 253–9 for other ballads on Napoléon.   **49** HDCD0027 Hummingbird Records, Dublin 2001.

Napoleon's alleged statement that 'the happiest day of my life was when I made my first holy communion' is quoted without comment. In *Ulysses* (1922), there are eleven references to Bonaparte including one where the great man is listed as one of the 'many Irish heroes and heroines of antiquity' alongside Shane O'Neill, Father Murphy of Boolavogue and Tone. However Joyce, mischievous as ever, somewhat spoiled the effect by also including in his roll of Irish heroes 'The last of the Mohicans', 'The man who broke the bank at Monte Carlo' and the Queen of Sheba. More to the point, and tellingly, he described Leopold Bloom as sporting a 'Napoleonic forelock'.[50]

Irish balladry kept Bonaparte's name alive, and helped in the creation of the image of Napoleon as a benevolent ruler and liberal democrat, as did the popular memory of Bonaparte as revealed in the folklore archive in the Department of Irish Folklore in University College Dublin. Daniel O'Connell, another 'Deliverer', features in a large mass of references in folklore, Oliver Cromwell is next with much fewer, but Napoleon is a respectable third, probably ahead of Tone and certainly of Emmet. In Irish folklore, stories about Napoleon appear that were found elsewhere in Europe: that he was unaffected and had simple tastes, that he was gentle to his soldiers (no flogging, as in Wellington's army), and that he allowed his men to address him using the familiar 'tu'.[51] A story, common in France, but found in Ireland and elsewhere, was that Napoleon had never in fact died; or in Irish folklore 'níor cailliú aríú é'.[52] A French traveller in Ireland in the 1840s was told by a turf-cutter that Napoleon was not dead: 'that fellow on St Helena was not really him at all; Bonaparte was hidden away in some impenetrable place and would emerge when the time was come'.[53] Other stories represent Napoleon as the all-forgiving, wise ruler, literally a gentle man. Here is one from West Kerry, an Irish-speaking area, and collected in the 1930s, *An Fear Faire 'na Chodhladh* (the sleeping sentry), a story that is found in France as 'La sentinelle endormie', and elsewhere in Europe. It begins: Bhí cath mór idir Bonaparte leis na sluagh Francach 's na h-Astrians uair san Iodáil …

> There was a big battle one time between the French and Austrian armies in Italy. The Austrians were defeated and the day went to the French. That night the French slept soundly in the open air and Bonaparte posted sentries around them in case the Austrians returned. Just before midnight

50 H.W. Gabler, *Ulysses: a critical and synoptic edition*, 3 vols (New York, 1984), iii, pp 185, 363. In 1897, George Bernard Shaw wrote a play *The man of destiny* about Napoleon, and in 1904 W.B. Yeats lectured on Robert Emmet, claiming that Emmet and Napoleon had plotted a simultaneous landing and uprising in Ireland: W.B. Yeats to John Quinn, 1 Feb. 1904 in J. Kelly & R. Schuchard (eds), *The collected letters of W.B. Yeats*, vol. 3, *1901–1904* (Oxford, 1994), p. 54.   51 David Bell, *The first total war* (London, 2008), p. 247.   52 Folklore Dept, UCD, collected in Galway: vol. 182, p. 492. Hazareesingh, *Legend of Napoleon*, pp 69–70, for rejection of the claim that Napoleon had died; and p. 51 for discussion of the large number of Napoleon impersonators and of insane people who claimed to be Napoleon.   53 Cited in J.J. Prévost, *Un tour en Irlande* (Paris, 1846), p. 126.

Bonaparte rose from his bed to check that everything was in order around his camp. On his walk around the camp perimeter he came across a sentry fast asleep, his musket on the ground. Napoleon took up the sentry's weapon and stood guard in his stead. After about an hour the sentry awoke and was startled to find that his musket was missing. He was also taken aback to see Napoleon in front of him with the gun in his hands. Understandably, he reckoned that he would pay dearly for his transgression. But no, gentle Napoleon merely said that he understood that the sentry was tired after the hard day's battle – no harder battle was ever fought – but that from now on he would have to do his duty, for the enemy could yet destroy the French with a surprise attack. The sentry thanked Napoleon, resumed his post, and never again failed in his duty.[54]

Here is another example, a delightful one, of the meek and mild emperor. It was collected as part of the nationwide Irish Folklore Schools' Scheme, undertaken in 1938. It is entitled *Napoleon and his Bird*:

Long, long ago when Napoleon was advancing on Moscow he had a small bird that sang on his table every morning at breakfast. One morning he asked for it but the serjeant said it was dead and Napoleon was very sad for he had grown to like it in the passed [sic]. When an old clockmaker saw how sad he was about his bird he said he would make him a clockwork one that would sing for him every morning. So after three weeks the old clockmaker brought an artificial bird that sung when he wound it. Then Napoleon said that he would like five more, that way he could set all six singing together. One day when my father was in the city he was lucky to buy one and it still sings its song since the clockmaker made it. Told to me by my father.[55]

Alongside ballads, poems and folklore, there is the public memory of Napoleon, Joséphine, Marengo, his horse, and the Battle of Waterloo. In numerous re-enactments, re-stagings, circus acts, and popular melodrama, Napoleon or a version of him and his entourage lived on long after his death. In 1816, to great acclaim, Bonaparte's carriage was exhibited in London, along with his personal wardrobe, his horses and his Dutch coachman, Jean Hornn. The exhibition later moved to Dublin where it was equally enthusiastically received.[56] Among other examples of the Irish public's fascination with Napoleon we may note the bizarre exhibition staged in the 1840s at 153 Capel Street, Dublin. This was nothing less

---

54 Folklore Department, UCD, collected in Corca Dhuibhne: Vol. 11.   55 Schools Manuscripts, No. 797. 'Bird' is possibly code for Napoleon, who was known as 'the Green Linnet'.   56 The exhibition also toured to Bristol and Edinburgh: Semmel, *Napoleon and the British*, p. 226.

After which (LAST time in this Kingdom) a Grand Military Equestrian Spectacle, in 3 Acts, called

The BATTLE of Waterloo.

With NEW and APPROPRIATE SCENERY, MACHINERY, DRESSES and DECORATIONS—The Scenery designed and painted by Mr. WHITMORE and Assistants—The Machinery by Mr. STEDMAN—The Properties, &c. by Mr. BEADWELL—The Dresses and Military Costumes by Mr. MURPHY, Mrs. POWERS, and Mrs. PARSONS—The whole of the Cavalry Movements, Evolutions, & entire of the Equestrian department under the immediate superintendance and management of

Monsieur DUCROW.

The OVERTURE, by Mr. BARTON,

The whole arranged and produced under the immediate direction of **Mr. NORMAN.**

His Grace, the Duke of Wellington Mr. SOUTHWELL, Duke of Brunswick Mr. MACKINTOSH, Shaw (THE LIFE-GUARDSMAN) Mr. BARTLETT, Corporal Standfast (OF THE HIGHLANDERS) Mr. BRINDAL, Molly Malony (A CHARACTER WELL KNOWN TO THE OFFICERS AND PRIVATES OF THE 92D) Mr. R. HAMERTON, Jean de Costa (NAPOLEON'S GUIDE) Mr. SMOLLET, Henri Master ST. PIERRE, Kouac Mr. A. LEE, in which he will sing " DEEDS OF THE BRAVE," Bredowski (A PRUSSIAN OFFICER OF THE LANDWHER) Mr. NORMAN, The Emperor Napoleon .... Mr. GOMERSAL, Bonaparte's Favorite Mameluch .... Mons. DUCROW, In which Character he will Ride,,

THE HORSE, MARENGO,

Marshal Ney Mr. JACKSON. Gen. Vandamme Mr. BUCKLEY, Mons. Maign Maladroit Mr. TALBOT, Phedora (WIFE TO BREDOWSKI) Mrs VAUGHAN, Mary Cameron (DISGUISED AS A SOLDIER) Miss CURTIS, Marinette (A BRUSSELS GIRL) Mrs. H. CORRY, Annette Miss ST. PIERRE, Rose (A BRABANT GIRL) Miss CUNNINGHAM, De Costa's Wife Mrs. BROAD, Imperial Guards—Cuirassiers—Red Lancers—Black Brunswickers—Artillery—Sappers—British Infantry—Life-Guards—Highlanders—Prussians—Hanoverians, &c. by a numerous Train of Auxiliaries.
At the opening of Act 2nd—A COMIC FRENCH JIGG by Master & Miss St. PIERRE.

THE FOLLOWING SCENES AMONG MANY OTHERS WILL BE POURTRAYED:

BATTLE OF LIGNY.
QUATRE-BRAS
Splendid Engagement of the ENGLISH and FRENCH——Perilous Situation of the HIGHLANDERS
IN THE FIELD OF RYE,
DESTRUCTION OF THE FARM HOUSE, WITH THE INTERESTING
DEATH of the DUKE of BRUNSWICK.
THE BATTLE—
Explosion of Ammunition Waggon.

| Death of Shaw, the Life Guardsman. | Capture and Re-capture of Capt Sandy's Brigade of Guns. | The Imperial Guard, Napoleon's last hope completely routed. |

Tickets and Places to be had of Mr. GOMERSAL, 84, S. Great Georges-st ; of Mr. TYRRELL, 17, College-Green ; and of Mr. LOWTHER at the Theatre.

WM. HENRY TYRRELL, Printer, Colleg.-Green

4.1 A poster for a benefit performance on 26 January 1825 for 'Mr Gomersal Bonaparte' in the Theatre Royal, featuring 'a great equestrian spectacle', The Battle of Waterloo, and Marengo, allegedly 'the property of Napoleon's chief mameluke'. Napoleon was played by Edward Gomersal, who bore a remarkable likeness to Bonaparte (National Library of Ireland).

than 'A beautiful mechanical group The Death of Napoleon'. Underlining the macabre Victorian obsession with the last moments of great men, this machine, replete with compression tubes, offered a breath-taking experience in which Napoleon's deathbed scenes were re-enacted:

> Napoleon is shown lying on a correct model of his famous bedstead surrounded by his attendants and confessor; he opens and shuts his eyes, turns his head on the pillow, the heaving of the chest or breathing very languidly [sic]. This melancoly scene defies description! It must be seen to be duly appreciated.[57]

Other playbills advertised the re-enactment of Waterloo using regular soldiers of the Dublin garrison as extras, and with loud explosions promised. As always Marengo, Napoleon, Joséphine and Tone were much in evidence. Edward Alexander Gomersal (d. 1862), an actor who bore an uncanny likeness to Bonaparte, made an entire career out of playing him, and he often took the lead role.

In the last years of the nineteenth century and the first decade of the twentieth, film made its appearance in Ireland, with patriotic themes very much to the fore and with frequent representations of Tone, Bonaparte and Emmet (be it said, with extravagant liberties taken with the historical record).[58] Around the same time, the indefatigable theatre impresario, Kennedy Miller, was staging a remarkable number of melodramas of a strongly nationalist bent in the Queen's Theatre, Brunswick Street: among them 'Peep of Day', 'Theobald Wolfe Tone' (Tone survives the rebellion and sails off to Australia with Napoleon and Joséphine), 'A true son of Erin', 'The Ulster hero' and 'Sarsfield'.[59] By coincidence the play *Napoleon and Josephine* opened in the Queen's Theatre on Easter Saturday, 22 April 1916, only to be upstaged (and shut down) by another performance nearby two days later on Easter Monday: the Irish Rebellion. *Napoleon and Josephine* re-opened three weeks later, but to an Ireland that had changed dramatically.

THE CORSICAN AND THE 1916 RISING

Was there a connection between the cult of Bonaparte and the Easter Rising? Was Bonaparte in the GPO? At least some Irish Volunteers were admirers of Napoleon Bonaparte. Sean McKeon, later officer commanding the IRA in Longford, in his witness statement to the Bureau of Military History, recalled thinking that 'we thought ourselves as valiant as Napoleon', only to be sharply

---

57 NLI playbill, no. 2/108.   58 Kevin Rockett, 'Emmet on film', *History Ireland*, 11:3 (2003), pp 46–9; Pat Johnston, 'Ireland a nation', *Dublin Historical Record*, 40:4 (1987), pp 145–7. 59 Christopher Fitzsimons, *Mr J. Kennedy Miller's very capable company of Irish players*

reminded by a superior that he was no 'pocket Bonaparte going over to conquer England'. For his part, Volunteer C.J. McAuley, after observing Joseph Mary Plunkett from his sickbed addressing the Volunteer officers gathered around him with their notebooks and pencils poised, caustically remarked that the scene was like 'Napoleon dictating to his marshals'. When Joseph Good was bitten on the ear by Michael Collins, he shrugged it off by recalling that 'Napoleon had a trick of pinching ears'. Even Helena Molony, recollecting the valour of the Cumann na mBan women during the Rising, wrote that at least one of them had done 'something for which Napoleon would have decorated her'. And when Felix O'Doherty from Cork set down his thoughts on the confusion that prevailed in Volunteer ranks on Easter Saturday, he remarked that he could vividly recall that day because he was engrossed in a novel, *The sword hand of Napoleon*, set amidst Bonaparte's retreat from Moscow.[60]

So much for the rank-and-file Volunteers; but what of their superiors? Here the evidence, while sparser, is suggestive. James Connolly was a perhaps unlikely admirer of Napoleon, praising the ousting of Redmondites from the Volunteers in 1914 as quite a 'Napoleon-like stroke'.[61] It was, however, Patrick H. Pearse whose enthusiasm for Napoleon Bonaparte knew no bounds. At St Enda's, his school in Rathfarnham, he decorated the classrooms with pictures and miniature statues of Bonaparte, and in his study he had what amounted to a shrine to the great man. Padraic Colum recalled that Pearse's prized possession was a lock of Bonaparte's hair. Pearse, according to Colum, used to say 'hold your breath now while I'm showing you this'.[62] In the GPO, one witness recalled that Pearse affected a very solemn 'Napoleonic attitude with his right hand on his breast'. Not surprisingly, Desmond Ryan, Pearse's first biographer, accepted that Pearse had a Napoleonic complex that 'expressed itself in a fanatical glorification of war for its own sake'.[63]

In other ways too, Pearse expressed his admiration for Bonaparte. He added lines to the 'Old Gray Mare', a ballad that had been around for some time, that brought Bonaparte into it:

> At break of day I chanced to stray
> All by the Seine's fair side
> When to ease my heart young Bonaparte

(Dublin, 2011). **60** Bureau of Military History, Witness Statements, No. 1716 [McKeon]; No. 735 [McAuley]; No. 391 [Molony]; No. 739 [O'Doherty]. C. Townshend Brady, *The sword hand of Napoleon: a romance of Russia and the great retreat* (New York, 1914). **61** Quoted in Austen Morgan, *James Connolly: a political biography* (Manchester, 1988), p. 149. **62** Padraic Colum, *The road round Ireland* (New York, 1926), p. 158. **63** Quoted in Ruth Dudley Edwards, *Patrick Pearse, the triumph of failure* (London, 1977), p. 342. An interest in Bonaparte, even an obsession with him, was commonplace among military folk at this time. Sir John French, commander of the British Expeditionary Force to France in 1914, was a noted collector of Napoleonic memorabilia while his successor Sir Douglas Haig claimed to

> Came forward for to ride
> On a field of green with gallant mien
> He formed his men in square
> And down the line with look so fine
> He rode his Old Gray Mare.[64]

And to the Irish poem, *O Bhean an Tighe* (Woman of the house), he added the line 'Beidh Boney in Eirinn le fáinne an lae' ('Boney will be in Ireland at the breaking of the day').[65] Pearse was in absolute thrall to R.M. Johnston's book *The Corsican*,[66] a compilation of a diary by Bonaparte 'derived entirely from Napoleon's own words, written and spoken'. While its editor candidly admitted that 'it avowedly contravenes ... those rules for the treatment of historical documents', he claimed that the book still offered 'psychological illumination of a great career'. It also contained reassuring words of advice for aspiring soldiers: 'The art of war does not require complicated manoeuvres: the simplest are the best and common sense is fundamental'.[67] Pearse carried this book everywhere with him. Colum recalled 'being with [Pearse] in the Abbey Theatre and seeing him read during the intervals a book called *The Corsican* that was made up from diaries, proclamations and despatches of Napoleon'.[68] Napoleon's pronouncements would have been useful to Pearse who despite being appointed Director of Military Operations in the Volunteers had no military experience whatsoever.[69] Did Pearse carry *The Corsican* with him into the GPO? We cannot know, but it is possible.

Lastly, are we certain that the phrase in the Easter Proclamation referring to 'our gallant allies in Europe' applied simply to Germany and the other axis powers? Germany was not named (nor Germany's allies, Austria-Hungary, Turkey or Bulgaria) and, at his court martial, Pearse flatly rejected the charge that the Rising was intended to assist the German war effort: 'Germany is no more to me than England is', he declared.[70] Could the phrase be a reference to the historic Irish expectation of military assistance from abroad, notably from France, an expectation nurtured over the centuries, brought forward by the

---

have spoken to Napoleon during a spiritualist séance. Robert and Isabelle Tombs, *That sweet enemy: the French and the British from the Sun King to the present* (London, 2006), p. 484. **64** Raymond Porter, *P.H. Pearse* (New York, 1973), p. 153. **65** Desmond Ryan (ed.), *P.H. Pearse collected works: scríbhinní* (Dublin, [1917]), p. 215. **66** First published in New York in 1910. The French writer Louis Le Roux claimed that Desmond Ryan gave Pearse the book. Le Roux, *Patrick H. Pearse* (translated by Desmond Ryan) (Dublin, 1932), p. 47. **67** Johnston, *The Corsican*, p. 499. **68** Maurice Joy & Padraic Colum (eds), *The Irish Rebellion of 1916 and its martyrs* (New York, 1916), p. 285. **69** Kathleen Clarke (widow of Thomas Clarke) remarked in 1966 that Pearse 'knew as much about command as my dog': quoted in Joost Augusteijn, *Patrick Pearse: the making of a revolutionary* (Basingstoke, 2010), p. 333. **70** Quoted in Augusteijn, *Pearse*, p. 320. Roger Casement and John Devoy were the most notable advocates of a German alliance, although Casement quickly turned against the Germans. Jerome aan de Wiel, *The Irish factor, 1899–1919* (Dublin, 2008), p. 53.

recent close study of the revolutionary period, and kept alive by the admiration for Bonaparte?[71] France had been Britain's staunch ally since the *Entente Cordiale* of 1904, and was now embarked in a horrific war alongside her, and yet there was still a view in Irish circles that France remained Ireland's historic friend. Here is Connolly in his 'Notes on the Front' dated 23 October 1915: 'France is the mother of European democracy, the apostle of the right of rebellion, the century-long sword of the revolution of peoples'.[72] There is nothing here to suggest that he reviled France as England's steadfast ally and thus the enemy of a free Ireland. On the contrary, a preoccupation, amounting in some cases to an obsession with Bonaparte and his times, and with his contemporaries, and by extension, a corresponding familiarity with the notion of deliverance from abroad, surely meant that a role by 'our gallant allies in Europe' was all that easier to contemplate and accept? Perhaps Bonaparte stalked the GPO after all.[73]

71 In Pearse's final examination in French at the Royal University, six of seven passages for translation related to French invasion attempts on Ireland in the 1790s. W.J. McCormick, *Dublin 1916: the French connection* (Dublin, 2012), p. 202.   72 *James Connolly: the lost writings*, ed. A. Ó Cathasaigh, (London, 1997), p. 178.   73 I would like to thank Mary Broderick of the Department of Prints and Drawings, National Library, the late Daithí Ó hÓgáin and the staff of the Department of Irish Folklore, University College Dublin, C.J. Woods, Sylvie Kleinman, Anne Dolan, Hugh Gough, David Dickson and Vincent Morley for their assistance.

Catholicism, Republicanism and race: Ireland in nineteenth-century French thought

SEAMUS DEANE

The French and the Irish Catholic communities of the first half of the nineteenth century gathered around Daniel O'Connell as the great historical figure in whom they vested their hope and their admiration. This admiration became the nucleus of a reviving Catholicism in both countries. Republicanism as a political ideal was also often claimed as a shared heritage, but it remained ever-elusive because so differently imagined, especially within France in the years between 1830 and 1870. By the time the Third Republic was established, after the Germans arrived on the first of their three visits (1870, 1914, 1940), no French person, however learned or politically alert, could possibly claim that they knew any longer what Republicanism actually meant, although at a minimum it still retained a settled animus towards Catholicism.

Yet 1830, 1848 and 1870 were three decisive moments in French history, and all in their different ways concerned Republicanism. The problem was that people on opposite sides regarded themselves as equally republican. As early as 1834, Republicanism was claimed by Lamennais as a political belief through which the mass of the people should share in the prosperity of the country. While that remained a belief, it increasingly became a fiction; the hope of realising it receded, while the desire to realise it was increasingly regarded as a foolish or even dangerous aspiration. That sense intensified after the 1848 revolution, largely on account of its utopian-socialist elements, not to speak of the bloodshed that characterised its exclusively Parisian action.

A major transition in French history started with the destruction of the Church of St Germain in central Paris by a Republican mob on 13 February 1831, and rioting over the next two days. No weaponry was used, just the unbridled fury of hands, feet and crowbars. The destruction of that particular church prompted a certain revival in the church in France, in French Catholicism and in Irish Catholicism. The three main interpreters of this event were all friends – Félicité de Lamennais, Henri Lacordaire and Charles de Montalembert. Montalembert visited Ireland in 1830, and wrote extensively on Irish Catholicism and the oppression of Irish Catholics by the British establishment, which he claimed was unprecedented in its bigotry. He was followed in a different vein by Gustave de Beaumont, the companion of Tocqueville, who also described the Protestant Ascendancy in Ireland as the cruellest and most unjust regime that Europe had ever seen, even in its darkest ages.[1]

Montalembert wrote on Ireland in a new journal, *L'Avenir*, a short-lived (1 September 1830 to 15 November 1831), experimental, Catholic literary journal. A fire had been lit that flared briefly before the Pope stamped it – and them – out. Montalembert and Lamennais never fully recovered from the Pope's reactionary squelching of their enterprise in 1832. French Catholicism, in the midst of the political maelstrom of the revolution in 1830, was shocked by the destruction of the St Germain Church; at Montalembert's prompting, it began to take the Irish church as an emblematic counter-example of survival and revival. Montalembert argued repeatedly that the Irish church experienced extreme material deprivation and that Irish Catholics owned no stake of any importance in the economic system under which they lived; nevertheless, they clung to their religious belief, and to the structures and the rituals of the church in a way which shamed France, which in the eighteenth century and the revolutionary period was at first sceptical of and then hostile to the Catholic church. The destruction of St Germain in 1831, this church in the centre of Paris, not far from Notre Dame, had itself been inspired by fury at the latest stupidities of the outgoing French king, Charles X. Among these, he tried to return to the church powers that it would not have dared to exercise in the eighteenth century. He introduced other unpopular ordinances on 25 July 1830 and the inflammable populace exploded in fury at these 'villainous' laws.

In St Germain Church, an annual commemorative requiem Mass was being celebrated for the duc De Berry, one of the last descendants of the Bourbons, stabbed to death in a lurid street incident in 1820. He had been a member of the Royal family, and next successor to the King. This requiem Mass occupied an elevated place in the monarchist calendar. During it, royalists unfurled flags and emblems associated with the monarchy, making a political statement in favour of Bourbon royalism. This prompted uproar inside and outside the church, sparking off a destructive riot that raged for three days. The destruction then moved to the Archbishop's palace, a notable building with a famous library in the lee of the cathedral of Notre-Dame. That library was specifically targeted, and its books were flung out the window, choking the Seine below the wrecked palace with precious books and sacred vestments, floating between banks with a seething mob rampaging on one side and the National Guard parading nervously down the other, ostentatiously not crossing the river. The government was at an impasse, the destruction raged. The fury was understood by French conservatives as the violation of a sacred heritage, yoking the melancholy fate of a deposed royalty and a pillaged religion. Churches and libraries were the most

1 Gustave de Beaumont, *Ireland: social, political, and religious*, edited and translated by W.C. Taylor (Harvard, 2007).

highly evolved examples of civilisation, which an ignorant, irruptive and unleashed barbarism could suddenly destroy with impunity, abetted by a French liberalism that prided itself on France being the most secular of modern nations.

Montalembert described this behaviour as resembling that of the Cossacks in Warsaw; they destroyed and ransacked libraries because they were specifically anti-civilisation. The rioters were as ignorant as the Cossacks before them; in transporting the Warsaw library to St Petersburg, they sliced in half books that were too big to fit in their saddle bags and squeezed the mutilated works in with brutal indifference. Paris, he claimed, now confronted a similar violent ignorance – the spreading stain of barbarism. In fact Montalembert and the press spoke more truth than either knew. During those particular weeks of violence, Russia was arriving in Paris in the form of cholera, carried by the Russian army which was then besieging Warsaw. Russia was coming to Paris. The Polish emigrés from Warsaw came to plead with the French for help, bringing this unknown disease with them. It spread like wildfire and sowed panic. Supporters of Napoleon said that if you gazed up at his statue on the column at the Place Vendôme, you would be immune. Others claimed that if you were a Saint-Simonian liberal, you would avoid contracting this ancient disease, because that political party supported progress. The cholera arrived anyway, and killed Hegel, Casimir-Perier, the prime minister of France, and Général Jean Maximilien Lamarque, a hero of Napoleonic days; his funeral provoked further disorder.[2] For several weeks, 700 people a day in Paris died of the disease and it eventually killed 18,000 people. Rumours swirled about it, since it was the poor of Paris who suffered most. They inhabited the infected centre of the city, they could not flee, and many decided that the cholera was a conspiracy of the establishment against the poor. This intensified the hatreds within the various classes and parties.[3]

When Louis Philippe ascended the throne, he made a fuss about his 'choosing' to call himself not the King of France but the King of the French, a step towards 'democracy'. Louis XVI had been obliged to call himself 'the King of the French' since 1791. Louis Phillipe embraced the title as if the Revolution were being reborn in him. Further, he said that he would never, as king, attend Mass, he would remove the fleur-de-lys from the royal decorations, he would change the songs that the troops sang, including the Marseillaise. It was a series of cosmetic emblematic gestures, signalling that the Royalist system was being replaced by the new capitalist business world, a transition so memorably represented in the novels of Honoré de Balzac (1799–1850). The Orleanist 'July monarchy' lasted from 1830–48; it was the last monarchy in French history and

2 Eric Hazan, *The invention of Paris: a history in footsteps*, trans. David Fernbach (London, 2010), pp 249–50. 3 The correlation between political unrest and epidemics in Paris in 1832 and 1849 is explored in Francis Delaporte, *Disease and civilization: cholera in Paris 1832* (Cambridge, MA, 1986), Catherine Kudlick, *Cholera in post-revolutionary Paris: a cultural history* (London, 1996) and Jan Goldstein, 'The hysteria diagnosis and the politics of anticlericalism in nineteenth-century France', *Journal of Modern History*, 54 (1982), pp 209–39.

the first modern example of big business and politics in that incestuous embrace which has become a normal, indeed a required, spectacle in the western world. Balzac, himself a monarchist, became the most celebrated analyst of this successor world.

In a letter to his Polish lover Madame Hanska, Balzac announced:

> In short, this is the game that I play: four men will have had, in this century, an immense influence – Napoleon, Cuvier [scientist], O'Connell. I should like to be the fourth. The first lived on the blood of Europe; he inoculated armies; the second had married the natural world; the third had incarnated a people; I – I shall carry a whole society in my head.

According to Henry James, the 'great money question' was 'the supreme inspiration and the aesthetic alloy' of Balzac's life, which generated the 'fantastic cohesiveness' of his work: 'A French brain alone could have persisted in making a system of all this ... *La Comédie Humaine* is in the imaginative line very much what Comte's *Positive Philosophy* is in the scientific'.[4] Further, Balzac's concentration on Paris showed his 'sympathy with the French theory of centralization'.[5]

Lamennais, above all, regarded centralisation as a blight upon French civilisation, as a scientific, bureaucratic uniformity which threatened to obliterate its diversity and richness. The railways were the most visible representation of that co-ordination. But in Balzac we experience a magnificent effort to encompass all the variety of human experience in a single vision that it took into its purview every detail of the social and financial structure, of streets, building, individual dress, faces, the workings of passion, the passage of time. The English World's Classics 1992 translation of one of his latest and greatest novels, *La cousine Bette* (1846), devotes a specific appendix to 'The money plot' of the novel; no other novelist would need such an intricate aid. Wealth for Balzac remained the tried, trusted and reassuring solidity of inheritance, land and fortune, not the volatile modern version of profit, investment, wages and interest.

The Balzacian worlds of Vautrin, Goriot, Lucien De Rubempré, Crevel, Valérie Marnesse, worlds so much more indelibly etched than Hugo's flashy version in *Les Misérables*, have in common the recognition that the poor of Paris lived in such poverty that the abyss that separated them from even the most impecunious of the middle classes was unbridgeable and no less so in 1870 than in 1848 or 1830. Only the Catholic charities helped. Balzac gives us the example of one towards the end of *Cousin Bette*, in Chapter 124, when he writes of one of 'the many admirable organisations founded by Catholic charity in Paris'; yet he also emphasies the general lack of belief among Parisians of all classes, among

---

4 Henry James, *French poets and novelists* (London, 1878), p. 102.   5 James, *French poets and novelists*, p. 93.

prostitutes and their customers, politicians and ecclesiastics. It was a problem that could only be solved, Lamennais and his followers urged, by Christianity allying itself with socialism, thereby allaying poverty and bringing the church into line with at least some approximation of Christian teaching.

When the government exercised control over newspapers, alternatives to them were found in political clubs, in short-lived but sometimes influential journals, and in various social projects dedicated to a particular cause. The Catholic church and socialism were the most effective organisations in finding these alternatives, although the socialist or proto-socialist ventures, like Saint-Simonianism, were offered as alternatives to or replacements for Catholicism.

Montalembert, Lamennais and Lacordaire (who became famous as a preacher in Notre Dame) sought to reinvigorate Catholicism, with journals, with restoration projects on ruined churches, with the renovation of the great teaching orders, including even the disgraced Jesuits. It took quite a while for the Jesuits to be rehabilitated, but nevertheless they were. By the 1840s, at least four major religious orders were re-established in France. Some of the greatest buildings of French Catholicism had finally recovered from the ruin visited on them during the revolution in early 1789.

The Church of St Germain, an exemplary Gothic restoration, was the emblematic centre-piece of this new crusade. The Gothic revival style offered a unified vision that 'restored' a door, a window, an arch, stained glass, in pursuit of a purity that balanced every harmonised detail.[6] The therapeutic restorations[7] – of buildings, of stained glass windows, of a pillar, of an altar, in a faux medieval Gothic style – mocked by purists as 'le style goddique' – materialised the belief that this was the restoration not just of an object but of a church, the Church, the ancient Church of France. France – 'the most Christian, the oldest daughter of the Church'[8] – with all these glorious titles attached to it, had had the Revolution to contend with and yet, it was claimed, it had survived. A restored and impeccably French Paris was portrayed as central to the heritage of Europe. The chief propagandist for this perspective was Montalembert, increasingly the political leader of French Catholicism.

Lamennais, whose work is scarcely read anymore, was the only one of the three who really deserves the title of thinker.[9] Montalembert was a populariser while Lacordaire was a preacher pure and simple. At Notre Dame in his public

6 See Montalembert's famous description of the evolution of the round arch of the Roman basilica into the pointed arch of the Gothic, in which the renewed faith (like that of the 1830s) first found expression in the columns that soared up into the Christian basilica and, like prayers finding themselves in the presence of God, ('lean towards one another and embrace, like sisters; in that embrace, they discover the ogival arch'); *Histoire de Sainte Elisabeth de Hongrie (1207–1231)* (Paris, 1836), p. lxvi.   7 Jukka Jokilehto, *A history of architectural restoration* (Oxford, 2002).   8 Montalembert invoked 1,500 years 'of glory', saying it is by these titles only that France marches at the head of the nations: 'the very (most) Christian people (or king), the eldest daughter of the Church'; *Oeuvres* 1, *Polémiques* 1, 551.   9 Georges Hourdin, *Lamennais: prophète et combattant de la Liberté* (Paris, 1982).

lectures of 1835–6, he was incomparable, and hailed as 'a new prophet'.[10] His already terrific presence – the ravaged face, the emaciated look, the beautiful speaking voice – intensified when he reappeared, tonsured and in white robes, on 14 February 1841 as a Dominican monk, in the pulpit of Notre-Dame, witnessed by a congregation of 6,000. All three spoke on behalf of the poor, the deprived, the underprivileged, using Christianity in its most radical sense as the religion of the poor. In this way, they sought to suture Catholicism to democracy in a novel configuration.

They all agreed that to revive the religion of the deprived, which embodied the religion of the early gospels, one should look across the sea to Ireland, a heartening example to French Catholics. There you had the outstanding example in Europe of original and true Christianity surviving – as it was built to survive – oppression. Authentic Christianity should be a purely spiritual possession. There could be no corruption in a church that owned no land, that sought only to own the hearts of the people. The Irish Catholics were accordingly 'forts dans leur faiblesse' (strong in their weakness) – spiritually strong, despite their material deprivation. Lamennais claimed that, as the early church of the Apostles grew under the sword of persecution for three centuries, so too did the Irish Catholic church.[11] This highly idealised version of Irish Catholicism was politicised by the French because it gave impetus to the idea of a radical religious and anti-heretical revival, carried by 'these small communities so faithful to the old law and faith'.[12]

Catholic Europe had lost the energy of the true faith, except for this one little isolated island marooned in the midst of the northern heresy, as they called Protestantism, and immured too within the English language and its violent empire. And yet, despite the fact that Ireland was decimated and impoverished, it still retained a more vibrant Catholic spirituality than any of its richer southern neighbours. Compare France: 25 million Catholics, 1,500 years of service, 50,000 priests, 80 bishops, and yet, Montalembert fumed in 1844, the French clergy remained mute because they have 'a duty to be silent and servile' as paid functionaries of the political establishment.[13]

The celebrated figure of Irish Catholicism, the man who represented it most to the world, was Daniel O'Connell, whom Montalembert admired and defended all his life, and who was called the 'Irish Pope' by Lacordaire in 1831.[14] O'Connell was visited by Montalembert when he came to Paris in 1847, and his

10 Montalembert, 'La Père Lacordaire', 1862, *Oeuvres* 9, *Polémiques* 3, pp 450–9. 11 Lamennais, *Réflexions*, *Oeuvres*, vi, pp 1–3. Lamennais insisted that persecution actually favoured the growth of the faith: Christians can calibrate the ratio between persecution and victimisation of the faith as an index of an authentically Christian historical narrative. 12 'Deuxième Lettre à *L'Ami de la Religion*', 21 Oct. 1848, in Montalembert, *Oeuvres 4, Polémiques* 1 (Paris, 1860), p. 523. 13 'Liberté d'Église: Discussion sur le Projet de Loi sur les Fonds Secrets', 16 April 1844, in Montalemebert, *Oeuvres* 1, *Discours* 1, 1831–1844 (Paris, 1860), pp 366, 369, 388. 14 Lacordaire, 'Mouvement d'Ascension du Catholicisme: Réponse

fight in the British parliament for Catholic rights was deeply admired.[15] Lacordaire's soaring oration in Notre Dame in 1847 after his death called O'Connell 'the first mediator between the church and modern society' and praised the power of his oratory: while an O'Connell could speak so intrepidly, uneasy lay the head that wore the despot's crown. Montalembert affirmed the scale of O'Connell's achievement: 'The nineteenth century will be remembered for the regeneration of oppressed peoples; Greece after 400 years, Ireland, long-forgotten, never mentioned by the eighteenth-century *philosophes*, reborn in the voice of an orator of genius, has bit by bit recovered all her rights'.

Regarded from a French perspective, a politically valuable feature of his politics was that O'Connell opposed violence. He recognised the inevitable feature of a colonial situation: if you are colonised and oppressed, and you rebel, your people will be visited by a violence far greater than you could ever imagine. We must recall here the beginning of France's own imperial career in Algeria. France had already committed the crime of invading and claiming Algeria in 1830 and thereafter colonising it with a spectacular violence. Similar examples in the British empire in Asia and Africa were numerous and Ireland provided its own melancholy parallel.

So here we have an attempted revival led by three Catholics who were reviving France on the ground that material welfare was not the primary goal. Their aim was to achieve a new non-violent aesthetic for French religion, the signs of which were to be restored churches, restored Roman ritual, a single ritual for all Catholic churches, the adoption of Latin, and the revival of everything that attached to ancient France, except its political manifestations. The crowning of bishops and the celebration of Mass were stripped – and remained stripped – of the ritual and political features that once attended them. At any celebration, when a prince of the church, a cardinal, the Pope, or any great church figure was being crowned or ordained, the French king was always separated from the church hierarchy by an assemblage of ordinary French people. The French king walked behind them to demonstrate that he too was regarded by the church as just one member of the church among many.

All that ritual, so despised by the atheists, was abandoned. But it was remembered in sermons, especially in Lacordaire's sermons, that boomed so beautifully from the elevated pulpit of Notre Dame. Lacordaire considered that the present materialist system of business, all that sordid moneymaking, was a pagan system that was bound to explode finally in revolution because it was immiserating the mass of people in the name of riches, in violation of the true essence of Christianity. The most violent years were 1831, 1832 and 1835. The worst was 1832. The bloodshed was incredible. The method of war, innovated in

au Globe', 7 Jan. 1831.   **15** Laurent Colantonio, 'Daniel O'Connell: un Irlandais au coeur du discours républicain pendant la Monarchie de Juillet', *Revue d'Histoire du XIXe Siècle*, 21 (2000), pp 39–53.

this fashion in the 1820s, saw the populace rise against the military and the police, and defend themselves by building barricades. Barricades of cobbles and slab stones were thrown up at strategic points where streets bent or where a spider web of streets converged. The geography of modern Paris emanated from the streets that were razed to make space for the broad boulevards by Haussmann, who built them sufficiently wide to ensure that they could never again be blocked by any revolutionary barricades. Paris became one giant building site from 1853 to 1870.

> Paris change! mais rien dans ma mélancolie
> N'a bougé! palais neufs, échafaudages, blocs,
> Vieux faubourgs, tout pour moi devient allégorie
> Et mes chers souvenirs sont plus lourds que des rocs.[16]

> Paris may change but my melancholy never stirs.
> New palaces, scaffolding, blocks,
> Old quarters, all become symbolic for me,
> And my cherished memories are heavier than rocks.

One of Baudelaire's recurrent images of hell was of a person lying under a pile of freshly shot corpses, someone who had survived the slaughter and who was trying to swim through the lake of blood into which s/he has been asphyxiatingly pressed, a body becoming a corpse. This Baudelairian image for hell is redolent of the studied melodrama of Edgar Allan Poe (whom Baudelaire translated into French). Poe was obsessed by the trope of being buried alive. This becomes, in Baudelaire, an existential condition, of which 'Le Cygne' is one of the most memorable explorations. Its initial references to Andromaque (the Racinian play as well as the Greek original) and to Ovid in his exile (see the 1859 Delacroix painting 'Ovid among the Scythians') set the pace for the accelerating sense of exile, from Troy, from Rome, from civilization, from the possibility of being any longer alive, yet still living, forever entombed. Racine's *Andromaque* (1667), like all of his tragedies, extinguishes space; in the emptiness, the increasingly eloquent and desperate speeches become more echoic, sounding in myth, not history, for history would be too velveteeen a fabric in which to familiarise these recognitions. Only the staringly mythic and the monstrous are on the stage and the myth prevails only when the individual is destroyed by the monster. This is absolutism, the only alternative to (yet also the producer of) annihilation. This

16 Baudelaire, 'Le Cygne' in *Fleurs du mal*. Baudelaire is notoriously difficult to translate. The nuance here is that the changing Paris (of Haussmann) is an allegory, in its alterations, of unchanging sorrow. That which changes is the image of what does not; the swan was once, in its death song, the traditional image of that 'harmony with sadness' (Ovid). This translation in pursuing a clarity loses the anguish, the cello darkness, the plangency that Baudelaire keeps in balance in his lines.

seventeenth-century classicism is transposed and inflected, grandeur and sordidness combined, in the ruined figure of the demolition of Paris, the building site for modernism and the pathetic swan staggering in the broken streets in which it can no longer represent anything but its own extinction. Modernism is not only the ruin of the past; it is the moment of recognising that the ruin has arrived while still remembering what the past once was, what the earth was like before it was swallowed in the opening sink hole of hell.

This infernal moment has its specific experience – that of being on the barricades in Paris in 1830, 1832, 1848, after the troops open fire. It has one, ultimately unavailing, effort at redemption. Baudelaire reminds us of one of the strange things that happened on 5 June 1832 at the funeral of the popular Napoleonic general, Lamarque. A large crowd had followed the cortège, and some students seized the carriage bearing the coffin and diverted it to the Place de la Bastille, where cries rang out: 'down with Louis-Philippe, long live the Republic'. A horseman suddenly forced his way into the centre of the crowd, and raised a red flag, bordered in black, bearing the words 'liberty or death'. This was acclaimed by the crowd and the man, who has never been identified, raised his flag and then dipped it in honour of the dead general.

From then on, the red flag became the flag of the people, whereas before it had been, since 1789, the symbol of martial law, hung on the orders of the 'Constituent Assembly' from the gates of the Hotel de Ville and carried from there by the soldiers through every street they patrolled. Traditionally, when the army or police were going to fire on a crowd, as in the martial law passed by the Convention, they raised the red flag to signify that everyone on the street was now, by that act, rendered criminal and subject to lethal violence. Therefore, they could now legally open fire, as in the Champs de-Mars in 1790, under Bailly and Lafayette, killing an indeterminate number of people. This red flag of security had morphed into the red flag of rebellion and the tricolour became the flag of the establishment.[17]

It remained a problem for empires – even as you put them down, how do you delegitimise the poor who make up the armies of the dispossessed, who took part in fighting and died in their thousands? How do you handle this revolutionary process so that government may continue? Some sought reforms, but they could not equal the Catholic liberals, who won over radical groups by sponsoring them through sermons and speeches and by disassociating them from the more secular left wing Europeans that were promoting utopian communism.

17 My parents told me all those years ago in the Bogside that our tricolour was modelled on the French tricolour, which had been brought back to Ireland by Thomas Francis Meagher, and that it was the Irish flag of rebellion. They also explained the significance of the green and orange being conjoined by the white. The position of red in the spectrum was not understood. In fact, when Meagher brought that flag back to Ireland in 1848, he carried a flag understood to be the flag of governmental powers, the flag of the reaction, which was then busy crushing yet another rebellion and doing it in an even bloodier manner than in 1832.

France in this period was famed for the new positivist sociology producing the utopian thinking associated with Charles Fourier. He claimed that the possibility now existed for the whole fabric of human society to be renovated so that injustice was vanquished. This could be achieved through the exercise of reason, but for reason to work its secular magic, the country would first have to be disabused of the illusions of religion, of armed might, monarchical splendour, of fighting for one's country, or dying for the sake of oppression.

Fourier in *Théorie des quatre mouvements* diagnoses the revolutionary condition of society which can only be eliminated through social reform:

> Yes, the civilised order is becoming more and more shaky; the volcano created by philosophy in 1789 is only in its first eruption; others will follow as soon as a weak rule favours the agitators; the war of the poor against the rich was so successful that the intriguers of all countries dream only of resuming it. It is useless to try to avert it; nature ridicules our enlightenment and our foresight; it will be able to bring forth revolution out of the same measures which we adopt to ensure social tranquillity.[18]

Saint-Simon and Fourier were among the most radical thinkers before Marx, and along with them we should also rank Lamennais, who is never mentioned among these socialist thinkers because he was a Catholic priest. Lamennais in his 20s was writing in defense of the counter-revolution. But by 1834, in his *Paroles d'un croyant*, he denounced what he called the conspiracy of kings and priests against the people – and broke with the church. Later, he served in the city on his own in the French parliament – a member of no party, disowned by his former friends. When he died in 1854, he was buried at Père Lachaise in a common grave, without any ecclesiastical rites. Lamennais was the chief figure who sought to harmonise Catholicism and socialism. An alarmed conservative in Dostoevsky's *The brothers Karamazov* (1880) thought that this attempt was especially dangerous to the established order: 'The socialist who is a Christian is more to be dreaded than a socialist who is an atheist'.[19]

According to one hostile commentator, Lamennais finally chose democracy over Christianity because he found them ultimately incompatible, partly because in the division between Paris and the peasantry, the latter always sided with the church and reaction. And in the new age of the railways, the peasantry could be more effectively mobilised. The railway saw off some of the worst revolutionary

18 Charles Fourier, *Théorie des quatre mouvements et des destinées générales* (Paris, 1841), p. 8.
19 Book II, Chapter v. The quotation from a police inspector (on the brink of Louis Napoleon's imperial usurpation of 1851) is reported by the Frenchified Miusov. Dostoevsky's novels are themselves a good index of the power of French influence as the model for modernity, secularism and revolution, at the moment (just before the Franco-Prussian War of 1870–1 weakened it) when Russian orthodoxy struggled to define itself against this great military and cultural power.

Gargantua.

5.1 Honoré Daumier (1808–79). The name Gargantua is derived from Rabelais's *Gargantua and Pantagruel* (1532), and it embodies obscenity, crudity and vulgarity. A bloated Louis-Philippe is seated on his toilet/throne, gorging himself on bags of coins extracted by his minions from the tattered emaciated poor. About the throne throng fat little favourites scooping up honours and commissions, defecated through the Royal arse, into which the coerced taxes are converted. The favourites then rush off to the National Assembly, shrouded in darkness. In the sunlit distance are the old reliables of maritime and agricultural trade – a port and windmills. Louis-Philippe awarded himself eighteen millions francs annually, almost forty times more than what Napoleon did. Although 'Gargantua' was never actually published (the censor and the police stopped publication of *La Caricature* of 15 December 1831), Daumier was sentenced to six months in prison. The pear-shaped head and spindly legs established a visual identity for the king. This abrasive lithograph established the reputation of the twenty-four-years-old Daumier.

moments in Paris, from the government's point of view, by facilitating peasant armies being ferried in from the provinces to counteract the street radicals. Paris and France were two different countries, as revolutionary episodes always clarified.

No comparable division existed in Ireland, although shadowy versions of it persisted and became more tangible in the twentieth century. But for the nineteenth century, Daniel O'Connell incarnated for Europe the idea of the constitutional Christian rebel. The colonial conditions in Ireland, and the suffering of Ireland were exemplary for the growth of a reinvigorated religion, although Ireland had to be rearranged, as it were, to accommodate radical Catholic theory about Christianity. Some of the most radical left-wing clerical movements began in Paris. Lamennais, the most distinguished thinker among them, looked to O'Connell and to Ireland for inspiration, at those moments when the French army went berserk, when they used what they themselves openly called 'African methods', that is brutal oppression, perfectly familiar also in the British system which had put down so many rebellions, with the suppression of the Indian Mutiny the most barbaric of all.

A notorious regiment in the French army, the 25th, was commanded by General Bugeaud, a veteran of Algeria, whose name is still spat out with venom in both Algeria and in Paris. As it was withdrawing after a foray into the small streets, a shot rang out from a house on the Rue Transnonain in April 1834. Bugeaud ordered the extermination of everybody in it. His obedient soldiers killed every man, woman and child; this massacre was commemorated in a piercing lithograph by Honoré Daumier, that was described by Baudelaire: 'It is not precisely caricature, it is history, the terrible and trivial reality'.[20] It is because of Daumier and Baudelaire that we now particularly remember this slaughter.

It reminds us that in these barricade battles, colonial violence was deplored not because it was in itself outrageous but because it was happening on the streets of Europe. Lamennais was not the first to point out that behind the corpses of Paris and Ireland, behind all these European dead, lay the piled corpses of the colonial dead and this cried out to heaven as an injustice. Invisible peoples – the Indians, the Irish, the Algerians – were major victims of the two big European empires at that time: to do at home what empires regularly did abroad was risky because it laid bare the hypocrisy of empire – a hypocrisy that exposed the gap between the 'people' and their governments.

Lamennais concluded, therefore, that if there was to be a new Christianity, there had to be a new political cognition. The French cannot exist as a nation if they exist as an empire, he claimed. No nation that calls itself decent, moral or honourable can be an imperial centre. A never-ending wave of hostility lashed Lamennais for this argument; it was one of the main reasons why he ended up so isolated. Lamennais sought to found a new missionary church, which proposed not the conversion of the heathen but the conversion of the French government to Christianity. Only this conversion would redeem the soul of France. Colonialism had conferred a cruel favour on the Europeans by opening their eyes as to how savage they actually were, their cherished idea of civilisation an occult configuration of violence. We live, Lamennais concluded, in a society

20 Charles Baudelaire, *Curiosités esthétiques; Quelques-uns de mes contemporains*, ed. Louis Conard (Paris, 1923).

5.2 *Rue Transnonain le 15 avril 1834.* In April 1834, public disorder in Paris centred on rue Transnonain in the working-class district of St Martin. Number 12 on the street was close to a barricade and the French army claimed that a shot was fired from there, killing a soldier. The army swarmed into the building and slaughtered nineteen men, women and children. The lithograph shows the bloody aftermath in a spare realist style. The viewer sees the scene as if just opening the door of the bedroom. The eerie stillness is foregrounded by a man slumped against his empty bed, crumpled up in the bed sheets. Only slowly does one make out the dead child under him, with blood seeping from his head. In the shadows lies the slaughtered mother on the ground and in the right foreground, an elderly man, yet another victim. Haussmann later merged rue Transnonain with the larger rue Beaubourg. Although the street name was erased, Daumier's lithograph preserved the memory of the 1834 atrocity.

which has rules, regulations and structures that were established before mass industrial society. Look at where the worst violence had occured in France, in Lille among the silk workers, in Paris among the printers, who were forever being shut down and subjected to heavy censorship. Anywhere there was mass employment depending on one industry, or another shut down because the wages were intolerably low, there violence erupts. We must generate, Lamennais argued, a renewed society which is not colonial, a form of society which preaches Christianity to the new society that has emerged in Europe, a rough beast increasingly lurching towards a barbarism as brutal as any colonial society.

For Montalembert, Ireland also represented the shadow of an atoning vengeance delivered on England: 'Ireland, the avenger of Catholicism, confronted England and demanded an accounting for 300 years of anti-Catholic oppression'.[21] O'Connell used similar rhetoric about the British in Ireland, although he always had a modifying clause or two to fall back back on. He was forever threatening violence which he never actually practiced, but he was a leader of a mass movement and Lamennais stressed this point. O'Connell was at one time the leader of a mass society, but never the leader of one that was being brutally modernised, as was France. (Both were mistaken on that score, as the Irish Famine proved to be a more calamitous and successful form of modernisation than France had ever experienced.)

Yet it is also true that the new barbarism, a phrase that resonates in France to the present day, is European. The new society is mass society. The new mode of war, in Paris as in Lille, is extermination, deploying the new technology of artillery. The French used artillery to clear the streets of Paris; it had, after all, Napoleon's infamous 'whiff of grapeshot' as an example to follow. Lamennais preaches, Lacordaire echoes him, Montalembert (a member of parliament for the (roughly-speaking) conservative right wing group), all regard France as experiencing a series of convulsions which are attempting to birth a new society, but retaining many structures of the old society while doing so. For them, religious belief is the only possible centre of energy left for the necessary conciliation and renovation, a real belief in actual Christianity. That demand might prove too much for most of the French, as it might prove too much for most human beings, but if Europe cannot rediscover that core belief, Lamennais in particular declared, Europe is doomed to recurring violence.

The Famine in Ireland, and the resulting reaction against the extermination of a people – the whole levelling of a country – became an apocalyptic omen, not just for the Irish, whose Fenian movement was one of its consequences, but in France too, where the Famine was treated as an apocalyptic demonstration of what colonial civilised society was capable of and culpable for. In general, French commentators agreed with John Mitchel that God sent the blight, but the British made the Famine. There was enough food in Ireland to feed the people, but the colonial system denied them access to it, exporting food while their subjects died. For Lamennais, this was not just the first modern famine, it was also the first apocalypse of industrial modern society, and as usual the blows rained down hardest on those who were weakest, least able to defend themselves. At least the Irish had not died in a pointless bloody war, he claimed, but for the sake of a truth, for a religion. This view found little purchase in the Anglosphere.

John Mitchel, on the other hand, was enraged that the Irish had not rebelled, as the French would have done. Why did the Irish not rebel? Because their priests taught them to be obedient, taught them that this was fate, that this was

21 Montalembert, *Oeuvres* 1, *Discours* 1, *1831–1844* (Paris, 1860), p. 400.

5.3 These three images are from *Impressions lithographiques de voyage par M.M. Trottman &
Cham* (Paris, 185[0?]). This rare book covers travels in Belgium, Holland, Russia, England,
Scotland and Ireland. The two images at the top show the O'Connell Collection being taken
up: Trottman gives one sou to O'Connell, two to the ragged collector himself. The bottom
image shows a Repeal meeting degenerating into a brawl. The drawings are by Cham (Charles
Amédée de Noé (1818–79), known as Cham, an amalgam of his Christian names). It is
unlikely that Cham ever set foot in Ireland, and the images use a visual vocabulary derived
from Famine illustrations in the *Illustrated London News* (Collection Anthony J. Mourek).

destiny, that this was God's will, that this was God's punishment on them for
being insufficiently faithful. That argument persisted until at least the twentieth
century. If we read, for instance, the memories of the famine in the University

College Dublin Folklore Department, collected in the 1930s, you find the concept that the decimating famine was their own fault. There must have been some toxic strain within their civilisation that had to be exterminated. Therefore nothing could be done about Famine except acquiesce in it, displaying that passivity that brought Mitchel to the level of aploplexy.

Mitchel was writing on a prison ship making its laborious passage to Australia, transported for having incited rebellion in 1848 in Ireland in a desperate attempt to rouse violence against what was being inflicted on his fellow countrymen. Mitchel at least had the distinction of being sent to Australia as a criminal. The British had been forced to introduce a new crime, treason felony, section three of which made it a crime to be a republican. In the year 2000, the *Guardian* newspaper sought to have that bill repealed but failed, on the grounds that it does not really matter anymore, even if you are a republican. But the British tabloid red tops, which are among the worst in the world, screamed that any attempt to remove the treason felony bill posed a threat to the Queen's life. The Queen would no longer be safe if republicans could roam free in Great Britain. Three senior British judges ruled that it was still too dangerous to remove that piece of legislation, moulded specifically for John Mitchel, from the statute book.

Mitchel was banished to Australia and endured that terrible journey during which he wrote *Jail journal*, which gives us the first global glimpse, from the Irish perspective, of the British Empire. Mitchel had never conceived quite how big it was before then. Now he learned about its scale as he sailed from Cork to the middle of the Atlantic, then down toward South Africa (where the British were refused permission to set up a prison camp), then to the West Indies, and thence to Australia. Mitchel recognised, 'here is a truly global empire'. The question Mitchel then posed becomes: how can we Irish ever overcome an empire which enslaves so many with such ease because it enjoys such enormous wealth, is so all-encompassing and acts with such brutal clarity? How can the Irish, the primary victims of this empire, ever overthrow it? How are they even going to survive, never mind resist, after the Famine?

This is the point at which France and Ireland criss-cross again. Mitchel evokes various scenarios for overthrowing an empire before concluding that the solution actually lay in the hands of the imperialists themselves. They prided themselves on the notion that they were chosen by God to dominate the world, because they have certain features and qualities that single them out. They are good at business, at the material things of this world, they are Anglo-Saxons, a privileged group, they have certain gifts which they were generously offering to the world. In order to deliver these gifts, they had to conquer the world first. Anybody who rejected their gifts obviously lay outside the Pale of civilisation, like the Irish.

After the Famine, John Henry Newman drew attention to the Irish in America, who in the US became as relentlessly 'Anglo-Saxon' as any WASP

ACTUALITÉS.   239.

5.4 'Le Fenian Stephen se faisant suivre par toute l'Irlande, s'il sait bien choisir son costume' ('The Fenian [James] Stephens being followed by all Ireland, if he knows how to choose his costume'). Drawn by Cham in *Le Charivari*, 24 December 1866 (Collection Pierre Joannon).

native. If they could flourish in America, then their Irish condition could not have stemmed from their terrible fate of being Irish. The Irish, the Italians, the German immigrants were showing that America was developing into a huge, powerful conglomerate civilisation, which no longer depended on the virtues of any single race.

So what race were the Irish? Mitchel was an early proponent of the idea that they were Celts and therefore different. At the same time, Lamennais, during the terrible 1848 revolution in Paris, concluded that the problem with France, and with Europe generally, was that it had a mongrel mix of incompatible races, and that these naturally antagonistic races could not but generate friction and rebellion. Among these newly discovered races were the Celts, especially the Bretons of France, all too willing to 'sulk on his own rocks, revolving in his own little mental orbit' (Arnold) rather than enjoy the benefits of an enlarged French civilisation. The Celts were melancholic dreamers, living at the edge of wakefulness, of the eternal ocean, of the capitalist system and on the edge of their Teutonic and Saxon antipodes. In this sense, Brittany like Ireland occupied a rim position. Arnold produced the fascinating, highly informed, sympathetic and intellectually woeful pages of 'On the study of Celtic literature', a landmark essay that in retrospect made Yeats unavoidable.[22]

The French and the Irish had converged via a shared idea of a revival in Catholicism. They now came together again on the idea that they were also partly Celts, and being Celts, that they were everything opposite to what the British were. The Celts enjoyed, as a particular possession of their own, the empire of the imagination. The martyrs were mutating into dreamers. Those elusive, long-ignored and marginalised figures – Gauls, Bretons, Irish – became the beneficiaries of a restoration, merging a new politics with an ancient culture. Vercingétorix was 'recovered' for the Gauls and for France as a national hero, as Cuchulainn was soon to be for the Irish. We are travelling on the fringes of Yeats country here but if being Celts confers a territory of your own, and that territory exists not in terra firma under your feet, but in your imagination, then it belongs to past history, and if it only exists in past history, then reviving past history, reviving the past religion, reviving everything that is ancient and traditional, can rescue us from our present plight. The Irish Celts can achieve revitalisation, through Catholicism.

By this time, the period of the Irish Revival, the French revolutionary phase had more or less died. After 1848, it was perfectly obvious that middle classes and the working classes no longer shared anything in common but were deadly enemies. No class accommodation was possible. The working-class political experiment with revolutionary politics of the modern kind, which began in the 1830s in the reign of Louis Philippe, died definitively with the arrival of Louis Napoleon's adventurist empire and ended with the Second Empire's defeat by the Prussians. Then the conquering Prussians helped the bourgeoisie of France to terminate the socialist and proto-socialist experiments of the previous decades, confirming the verdict of 1848 in the ghastly final days of the Commune when

---

22 Matthew Arnold, *The complete prose works of Matthew Arnold, vol. 3* ed. R.H. Super, *Lectures and essays in criticism* (Ann Arbor, MI, 1962).

tens of thousands were slaughtered on the streets of Paris. The battle was between Versailles and Paris, and rivers of blood flowed.

In the aftermath of both the Famine and the Commune, the Irish were busy becoming Celts and/or Gaels. Read Pearse on O'Donovan Rossa, that's the Gael. Read Michael Davitt on Parnell not really being Irish, and you learn by negative stress what to be Irish really means, and it is not being Protestant, it is not being a landlord, it is not being proudly ignorant of your own history, although of Parnell he also said 'and yet this man was our leader'. Why was he our leader? 'Because he was unlike the Irish'. Davitt says that Parnell shows how far the Irish have travelled. By the time of the great revolution of 1916, the Irish learned to be leaders of themselves.

Finally, let us revert to John Mitchel. When did Mitchel become himself? He says that it was when he was first arrested and the prison guard at Newgate brought him prison clothes.

> I had returned to my cell and taken leave of my wife and two poor boys. A few minutes after they had left me, a gaoler came in with a suit of coarse grey clothes in his hand. 'You are to put on these', said he, 'directly'. I put them on directly. A voice then shouted from the foot of the stairs, 'Let him be removed in his own clothes'; so I was ordered to change again, which I did.

He was taken to Spike Island in Cork, where he was once again instructed to take off his clothes and put on the prison clothes.

> Mr Grace excused me for putting me into convict dress ... he was afraid to refuse when the Smithfield jailer required to see me in felon array, that he might report it in Dublin. Curious that this should have happened twice. In Dublin also I had to put on convict dress and strip it off again instantly.

The governor said to him, 'We don't know what you are. You are not a normal convict'. Mitchel replies: 'I am a villain, am I not? After all, they passed a special act in parliament to make me one'.

Mitchel's dispute over his clothes reminds us how important wearing convict clothes has been in Irish prison history, provoking hunger strikes. Nakedness, Mitchel concluded, was the proper condition for someone who enjoys no political existence. When he got to Australia, he found lots of Irish there, but they were like shadows in Hades, in an underground antipodean hell, people scurrying around physically but politically non-existent in 'a land where men are transformed into brutes'.[23] Mitchel concluded that they were in a state of nudity,

---

23 John Mitchel, *Jail journal* (Dublin, 1918), p. 218.

the state that the Irish under British rule have always been in. Mitchel is finally able to connect the idea of the Celt and the idea of the criminal, the person who is criminal, that nobody can understand because they have no suit of clothes that fits that kind of criminal – a monarch can have clothes, an army can have clothes, but not an Irish non-citizen.

One of the great descriptions of that condition is Ernie O'Malley's magnificent book *On another man's wound*. O'Malley is constantly, apparently casually, noting 'how that flock of birds flashes from the bush'. Next time you hear about those birds, he's actually talking about the flash of bullets into that bush during an ambush. He offers a vivid description of the RIC, the police uniform, given in enormous detail, different colours – the fat neck of a policeman, the thick serge of his uniform. Beside him are the volunteers whom he does not know are volunteers, because they wear no uniform, they have no formal clothes, and they are therefore invisible to the man in uniform, while the man in uniform is all too visible to them. The only people who deserve to wear recognisable clothes are those who rule on behalf of the established system. The oppressed remain naked or invisible, both an advantage and a disadvantage.

Lamennais celebrated that invisibility in his last days when he no longer wore a uniform that proclaimed his vocation. He had left his religious order, he had left all political parties, he was leaving France, not physically, but internally. He was leaving all behind and he was dying, and he was proud to die naked, because there was no role or place left for him in this world that would allow him to wear the clothes of a Christian.

It is in these criss-crosses that you can see the connections between a very disturbed France and an equally disturbed Ireland. Yet central to the experience of both is the idea of a renovation that is sufficiently transformative to make a new community of a people almost entirely erased because of their particular religion, class and nationality.

Daniel O'Connell, a model for France; Paris of the barricades, an example for Young Ireland

LAURENT COLANTONIO

INTRODUCTION

This chapter interrogates the complicated interactions between the two nations in the second quarter of the nineteenth century. Throughout the 1830s and 1840s, Daniel O'Connell (1775–1847) was undoubtedly the most celebrated foreign politician in France. The Irishman imposed himself into the heart of French political debate, in proportions now difficult to imagine. How was it possible that this 'moment O'Connell' so penetrated political discourse that it became inescapable for anyone with an interest in French politics? The Irish experience – which O'Connell incarnated for his contemporaries – offered a socio-political laboratory. Playing out on Irish soil were the great stakes of revolutionary society: national identity, popular sovereignty, mass mobilisation, peaceful agitation, social progress without revolution, the dangerous intersection between religion and politics. Gustave de Beaumont in 1839 described Ireland as a 'small country in which the greatest questions of politics, morals, and humanity were debated'.[1] Through its reaction to O'Connell, France revealed its own conflicts, its own neuroses, and its own hopes. The O'Connell moment was also a pivotal moment in France after the revolutionary rupture, the Napoleonic moment, and monarchical restorations, where it became an urgent necessity to rebuild fraying social bonds.

The first section of this chapter considers the O'Connellite model for France.[2] The second section explores the other reflection of this game of mirrors; an episode at once brief and exciting, following the Parisian revolution of February 1848, whose shock waves suddenly galvanised the nationalists of Young Ireland, against a background of grim famine.

AN EMBLEMATIC FIGURE (1823–40)

French interest in Ireland was not born with O'Connell. It is sufficient to mention the last decade of the eighteenth century, or the romantic generation

---

1 Gustave de Beaumont, *L'Irlande sociale, politique et religieuse* (Paris, 1839), i, preface. The preface was not reproduced in the 1839 English translation.　2 Laurent Colantonio, 'Daniel

6.1 Daniel O'Connell, 1842. An image from the Paris newspaper *Le Charivari* (Collection Kevin Whelan)

who discovered the 'Celtic soul' of oppressed but unabashed Ireland in the 1820s.[3] The initial references to O'Connell surfaced in diplomatic correspondence between 1823–1824, shortly after the birth of the Catholic Association, which prompted reporting from the French consuls stationed at Dublin and Cork.[4] O'Connell, 'the advocate of the people', involved in political debate for more than two decades, had already attained the status of the essential figure within Irish nationalism.

O'Connell: un Irlandais au cœur du débat politique français, des dernières années de la Restauration à la Deuxième République' (PhD, Université Paris 8–Saint-Denis, 2001). **3** Richard Bolster, 'French romanticism and the Ireland myth', *Hermathena*, 99 (1964), pp 42–8; Jean Noël, 'Images de l'Irlande et des Irlandais dans la France de la Restauration', *Études Irlandaises*, 14:1 (1989), pp 147–71. **4** Dispatch from Romain (French consul in Dublin) to Chateaubriand (minister for foreign affairs), 16 July 1823, Archives du Ministère des Affaires Etrangères (MAE), Correspondance consulaire et commerciale (CCC), Dublin, vol. 2;

The campaign for Catholic Emancipation unveiled O'Connell to a wider French audience. The Catholic question in Ireland – posed in dramatically different terms in France – fed the politico-religious jousts of the Restoration. In 1824, *L'Étoile*, an influential ultra-royalist newspaper led by the Abbot of Genoude, described the Irish as the spearhead of the Catholic reconquest of Europe, struggling against the British Protestant power that wanted 'blacks to be free and the Irish to be slaves'.[5] Initially, O'Connell's extravagantly Catholic profile alienated French liberals, even when they supported Catholic emancipation.[6] Prosper Duvergier de Hauranne (1798–1881), a young liberal aristocrat, friend of Stendhal and Hugo, visited Ireland and met O'Connell in 1826. He was impressed despite himself by the charisma of this 'extraordinary man'.[7] In a second phase, after the equalisation of political rights between Catholics and Protestants in 1829, the French liberals revised upwards their estimate of O'Connell, the 'Liberator' (as he was now increasingly called). He was regarded as the man who had fought tenaciously for civil liberties, and without whom reform would have been impossible. Three major versions of his achievement were promulgated by the French press: as a victory of Catholicism for some, as a victory for freedom for the others, and as a prelude to revolution for the Republicans.[8]

In the 1830s, O'Connell's French popularity soared, although his profile was largely disconnected from actual developments in Ireland. O'Connell did not comment directly on French politics, and on the few occasions when he did speak about France, he was unflattering. On the eve of the revolution of July 1830, he condemned the oppressive regime of the Bourbons. He expressed similar hostility to the July Monarchy in 1832, which he dismissed as anti-clerical and dominated by 'pretended liberals who are the enemies of religion rather than friends of liberty'.[9] The Republicans, associated with the revolutionary violence, which he always abhorred, did not obtain his benediction either. Nevertheless until the early 1840s, O'Connell served as a beacon, an inspiration, a model in action, whose name was brandished by every major political project in France, in the name of 'universal principles', to mobilise its supporters or to demonise its opponents. Thus, the Irishman was draped in diverse French political costumes: from the liberal respectful of the law, to the rebellious revolutionary, from the champion of Catholicism to the democratic patriot, from the advocate of the oppressed to the standard bearer of the middle class.

Romain to Damas (minister for foreign affairs), 23 Oct. and 28 Dec. 1824, MAE, CCC, Dublin, vol. 2; chevalier de MacMahon (French consul in Cork) to Villèle (minister for foreign affairs), 1 July 1824, MAE, CCC, Cork.   **5** *L'Étoile*, 9, 10 and 12 Dec. 1824.   **6** *Le Courrier français*, 23–4 May 1825.   **7** Prosper Duvergier de Hauranne, *Lettres sur les élections anglaises et sur la situation de l'Irlande* (Paris, 1827), pp 167–84.   **8** *Le Globe*, 22 Apr. 1829; *La Gazette de France*, 18 Apr. 1829; *La Tribune des départements*, 20 June 1829.   **9** Daniel O'Connell to a friend in Rome, 1837 in M. O'Connell (ed.), *The correspondence of Daniel O'Connell*, 8 vols (Shannon, 1972–80), vi, letter 2369 b.

The story of the French liberal Catholics, grouped around Lamennais, Lacordaire and Montalembert in the aftermath of the July Revolution, is well documented and reveals a real proximity of thought with O'Connell.[10] In Europe, where the church was inflexibly chained to reaction, Ireland provided liberal Catholics with welcome proof that their project – reconciling Christianity with liberal modernity – could triumph. *L'Avenir*, their daily newspaper between 1830 and 1832, devoted many pages to O'Connell's Ireland.[11]

The Irish precedent also inspired the creation of the General Agency for the Defence of Religious Freedom on 18 December 1830 in Paris. A few days after the birth of the Association, Montalembert wrote:

> We laymen are born in a century in which it is so hard to live, but so glorious to fight. If ever despair descended on us, if our weary hearts doubted God and his eternal solicitude, think of the wonders of the Catholic Association, which began with only seven members, and which, after fifteen years of struggle, has achieved the religious independence of Ireland, and laid the foundations of its national independence.[12]

In many respects, the General Agency was strongly influenced by the Catholic Association. It was financed by the subscribers' contributions, a modest individual contribution of ten francs a year, a popular subscription comparable to the Catholic Rent.[13] This financing allowed it to become a pressure group, and to campaign for the freedom of education. Like much else within the liberal Catholic project, the General Agency did not survive the crushing papal condemnation of 1832.

Gustave de Beaumont (1802–66) was also enchanted by O'Connell. *L'Irlande, sociale, politique, et religieuse* (2 vols, 1839) contains long disquisitions on the 'Liberator'.[14] Through his visits to the island, one with Tocqueville in 1835, and another with his wife Clémentine de Lafayette (grand-daughter of the celebrated general) in 1837, Beaumont refined his prototype of the quintessential modern politician. O'Connell was attentive to his people's wishes while knowing how to channel them; he respected the existing social order while not being averse to social reform; he was capable of leading his country to a 'reasonable' democracy

---

10 Henri Rollet, 'The influence of O'Connell's example on French Liberal Catholicism' in D. MacCartney (ed.), *The world of Daniel O'Connell* (Dublin, 1980), pp 151–62; Pierre Joannon, 'O'Connell, Montalembert and the birth of Christian Democracy in France' in M.R. O'Connell (ed.), *Daniel O'Connell. Political pioneer* (Dublin, 1991), pp 98–109. 11 Most articles on Ireland were signed by Lamennais, Lacordaire or Montalembert. Montalembert published a distinguished 'Lettre sur le catholicisme en Irlande', *L'Avenir*, 1, 5 and 18 Jan. 1831. 12 *L'Avenir*, 18 Jan. 1831. 13 *Rapport sur les opérations du second semestre de 1831*, Paris, aux bureaux de l'Agence, 1832. This report gives a detailed presentation of the Agency's organisation and procedures. 14 Beaumont, *L'Irlande*. Twenty pages were dedicated to O'Connell (vol. ii, pp 28–45 in the original French edition).

achieved without violence. Beaumont, like his bosom friend Alexis de Tocqueville, believed that the advent of democracy was both inescapable and potentially destructive.[15] He discovered in Ireland an unprecedented situation that captivated him.

> Is not the power of O'Connell one of the most extraordinary that can be conceived? [Ireland] did not need a general to lead an army, but a citizen to direct a people; it sought a man whose power would be established by peaceable means, able to win the confidence of Ireland, without giving alarm to England. His power [is] entirely founded on the frail base of popular favour, a popular assent, every day required, and every day given.[16]

For the young liberal aristocrat, O'Connell solved the volatile equation – how to balance the eruption of 'numbers' onto the political scene without generating the predicted revolutionary explosion. This Irish experiment created a solution for how France could avoid anarchy.

To the left of the political spectrum, the Republicans admired O'Connell as the voice of the oppressed in their struggle against tyrants and kings, and they sought to emulate his popular status in France. They regarded O'Connell as the man who led the masses not in a desire to bridle their energy (as Beaumont had argued) but instead to encourage popular mobilisation. Lamennais, newly republican, described O'Connell as a 'revolutionary colossus'.[17] This subversive and radical reading of his political project mesmerised the Republicans of the 1830s, and in 1835 they solicited him to act as a lawyer for the Paris insurgents of April 1834.[18] O'Connell replied that he was proud to have been considered for so important a role in a trial that once again highlighted the tyranny of the July regime: 'France has no sufficient guarantees for her liberties – nay, scarcely any at all. The French are the slaves of [Louis-Philippe], who ought to be their servant'.[19] However, while conceding that contemporary republicans differed from their bloody predecessors of the Terror, O'Connell sought to distance himself – and by extension Irish Catholics – from any taint of being heirs to the horrors of the First Republic: 'Whilst I express my sympathy for your sufferings, let me not be misunderstood, as I should be, if I were conceived to concur in your political views as republicans'. This polite but firm refusal illustrated the

---

15 De Tocqueville's views on Ireland and O'Connell can be found in Emmet Larkin (ed.), *Alexis de Tocqueville's journey in Ireland, July–August 1835* (Washington, 1990).   **16** Beaumont, *L'Irlande*, ii, pp 29–31 and pp 37–8.   **17** Lamennais to Montalembert, 6 Oct. 1835 in Louis Le Guillou (ed.), *Correspondance générale de Lamennais* (Paris, 1976), vi, p. 495.   **18** This 'monster trial' followed the insurrections in April 1834 in Lyons and Paris. Repression was fierce. Police arrested 2,000 republicans, of whom 164 were arraigned in a lengthy Paris trial that caught the attention of the press and the public, between November 1835 and January 1836.   **19** The full letter is in W. Fagan, *The life and times of Daniel O'Connell*, 2 vols (Cork, 1847), ii, pp 480–5. Partial French translations in *Journal des débats*, 17 Dec. 1835 and

gulf which separated O'Connell from the figure imagined by the Republicans, fascinated by the extent of Irish popular mobilisation. It also exposed the chasm between two divergent visions of political change and social transformation, both claiming popular sovereignty.[20]

The testimony of Jean-Gabriel Capo de Feuillide (1800–63), journalist, poet and friend of Balzac, offered a dissonant voice. The author of *L'Irlande*, a massive travélogue published in 1839,[21] Capo de Feuillide expressed sympathy with Ireland and cast a stern eye on British rule. Unsurprisingly, he devoted many pages to O'Connell, 'more than a man, more than a prophet', always carrying the hopes of his ragged people on his broad shoulders.[22] Capo de Feuillide distinguished himself by adding critical reflections on the great man, identifying his social conservatism, although the Republicans failed or refused to notice it. By obeying 'the political wind that blows over his century', O'Connell was mistaken, because he believes that 'political reforms are enough to make nations flourish and be happy'. In Capo de Feuillide's estimation, O'Connell sought 'to repair the edifice at the head when it is at the base that it cracks'.[23] He criticised O'Connell's reduction of the social question to two crude identities: the aristocracy was English and the democracy was Irish. And he disagreed that it would be sufficient to overthrow the aristocracy to see the democracy triumph. Capo de Feuillide inquired about the difference 'between the ancient Toryism of the Protestants and the new Toryism of the Catholics?'[24] Instead, the real urgency was for indispensable social reform, which alone could restore the people to their rights. If it was impossible to restore the lands plundered from the Irish during the conquest, they should at a minimum be compensated for this past injustice:

> Justice for Ireland must henceforth contain the double cry of *Reform and indemnity!* O'Connell only heard the first; Let him utter the second! Otherwise, O'Connell will not be the liberator of his country.[25]

The contemporary journalist Charles Monselet claimed that Capo de Feuillide's *Lettres sur l'Irlande* 'had awoken the sympathy of Europe' to the plight of the Irish poor.[26]

Quantitative analysis of French books that mention O'Connell reveals a significant surge in publications from 1841, including two peaks in 1843 and 1847. There is also, however, a notable step-change in the reception of O'Connell

Le National, 18 Dec. 1835. **20** Laurent Colantonio, 'Daniel O'Connell: un Irlandais au cœur du discours républicain pendant la monarchie de Juillet', *Revue d'histoire du XIXe siècle*, 20–1 (2000), pp 39–53. **21** Jean-Gabriel Capo de Feuillide, *L'Irlande*, 2 vols (Paris, 1839). **22** Capo de Feuillide, *L'Irlande, i*, pp 32–5, *ii*, p. 312. **23** Capo de Feuillide, *L'Irlande, ii*, pp 294–5. **24** Capo de Feuillide, *L'Irlande, ii*, p. 319. **25** Capo de Feuillide, *L'Irlande, ii*, p. 336. **26** Charles Monselet, *La lorgnette littéraire. Dictionnaire des grands et des petits auteurs de mon temps* (Paris, 1857), p. 40.

in France between 1840 and his death in 1847. The Irishman was no longer regarded as the friend of all political traditions. From now on, he was regarded as a foil as much as an example. This inflection became particularly pronounced from 1843 to 1844, when sensational Irish political news – popular agitation for Repeal, monster meetings, O'Connell's trial, his incarceration and his early release – coincided with fresh commentary by the Irish leader on France, which in turn reinvigorated a reciprocal French interest in his political ideas.

In 1843, on the resonant date of 14 July, French Republicans organised a 'democratic demonstration' for Ireland in a Parisian restaurant, in support of Repeal of the Union. At the end of the evening, Ledru-Rollin was invited to carry a message of solidarity to O'Connell, and to assure him that if 'the English aristocracy draws the sword', a battalion of French democrats stood ready to come over and defend him.[27] This proposal for military assistance was indignantly rejected by O'Connell, in a letter first read in public at a meeting of the Repeal Association, before being sent (translated) to France:

> The visit you have intimated that you might make to this country, whilst it would be of no practical utility, would afford opportunity for further calumny, and for mischievous (though utterly false) insinuations. Upon these grounds we deem your contemplated visit to Ireland in anything resembling a public capacity as being, to say the least of it, premature.[28]

In October 1843, in opposition to the hated July Monarchy, O'Connell proposed instead to augment the army of the legitimist pretender Henri V with an Irish Brigade.[29] While this gratuitous provocation never happened, it inflamed French debates.[30]

For the Republicans, these two statements, only a few months apart, translated and relayed by the press, were revelatory. Their happy illusion, maintained since the early 1830s, that O'Connell was a covert republican, was shattered. Once the scales had dropped from their eyes, they launched sharp tirades at the Irishman. When he died in 1847, *Le National* drew his portrait as an impostor: 'O'Connell become the indefatigable echo of pains he did not feel, passed for a tribune of the people, while he was merely the powerful advocate of the bourgeoisie'.[31]

O'Connell's repeated diatribes against Louis-Philippe and support for the Bourbons equally discredited him in the Orleanist and Conservative ranks. This cooling was reinforced by their conclusion that repeal of the Union, the priority

---

27 *Le National*, 16 July 1843. The entire front page was filled by this report.   **28** *Dublin Evening Post*, 5 Aug. 1843.   **29** *Dublin Evening Post*, 30 Sept., 5 and 12 Oct. 1843. **30** According to the French consul in Dublin, one reason for his bravado was that the recent Franco-British diplomatic rapprochement had provoked O'Connell. Herbet to Guizot (minister for foreign affairs), 28 Sept. and 11 Oct. 1843, MAE, Correspondance politique des consuls (CPC), Angleterre, vol. 13.   **31** *Le National*, 24 May 1847.

for the Irish nationalists, would weaken Great Britain, while the anglophile Guizot worked to consolidate the 'cordiale' but fragile 'entente' between the two monarchies. O'Connell, the avatar of so many possible achievements, was dismissed as a mountebank selling impossible dreams.[32] A democratic mass movement in Ireland gathering together thousands of people – mostly non-voters – carried the unmistakeable whiff of an insurrectionary movement, and this worried supporters of the census suffrage. In May 1843, the consul Herbet was apprehensive about the surreptitious 'substitution of the dictatorship of the meetings for the regular government of the Chambers, the most serious fact that could arouse the solicitude of the ministry'.[33]

The Orleanist and Republican disapproval of O'Connell followed the same logic. In both cases, the exemplary figure turned into a foil, in the name of values that had once made O'Connell a model but for which he was now reproached. The Irishman's image had degenerated into that of a noisy demagogue. For the Orleanists, he flattered popular passions instead of containing them, plunging Ireland into chaos. For Republicans, he deceived the people into pursuing vain chimeras, deepening his own despotic power at their expense.

However, some identifications persisted and even strengthened. Since the early 1830s, O'Connell personified the political commitment and vigour of regenerated Catholicism. Over the next decade, the project of building a 'Catholic party' on the model of the Irish Catholic Association was more than ever in their minds, despite the obvious constraints: how could one gather under the same banner supporters of liberal modernity (Montalembert), democracy (Lacordaire),[34] a theocratic society (Veuillot), and Gallican legitimists favourable to the Bourbons? One possibility was to unite around the prestigious 'Irish Moses'.[35] This permitted a (fragile) show of cohesion by the Catholic party, which became the Electoral Committee for the Defence of Religious Freedom in 1844.[36] On 10 February 1848, a Parisian tribute to the deceased 'great man' was one of the last public occasions that presented a united front in public for a political movement on the brink of implosion. On that day, the Electoral

---

32 This observation was expressed in several consular dispatches from Ireland to Guizot in 1843 and 1844. Jean Lemoinne sneered at 'the utopia of the Repeal ... this great bluster [that] no one takes seriously' in *Journal des débats*, 27 August 1843. The expression 'cordiale entente' appeared in Louis-Philippe's speech during his royal visit to London in 1844: Philippe Chassaigne, *La Grande-Bretagne et le monde de 1815 à nos jours* (Paris, 2009), pp 32–3. 33 Herbet to Guizot, 13 May 1843, MAE, CPC, Angleterre, vol. 13. *Journal des débats*, 27 Aug., 23 Sept. and 6 Oct. 1843. 34 Lacordaire delivered a vibrant funeral eulogy for O'Connell at Notre-Dame Cathedral in Paris: Henri-Dominique Lacordaire, *Éloge funèbre de Daniel O'Connell, prononcé à Notre-Dame de Paris, le 10 février 1848* (Paris, 1848). 35 Article by Louis Veuillot in *L'Univers*, 23 July 1843. 36 Charles de Montalembert, *Du devoir des catholiques dans la question de la liberté d'enseignement* (Paris, 1843); *L'Univers*, 13 July 1844; Comité électoral pour la défense de la liberté religieuse, *Compte rendu des pétitions présentées à la Chambre des députés (session 1844–1845)* (Paris, 1845); Charles de Montalembert, *Du devoir des catholiques dans les élections* (Paris, 1846).

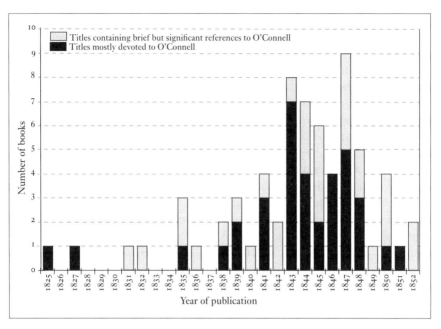

6.2 O'Connell in French books, 1825–52. Analysis of French books that mention O'Connell reveals a significant surge in publications after 1841, with notable peaks in 1843 and 1847.

Committee, in all its diversity – as witnessed by the guest list – solemnly honoured the memory of O'Connell in the presence of his eldest son and successor, John, who thanked the 'friends of Christian peace and social order'.[37]

In the years after his death, the memory of O'Connell endured in conservative French Catholic circles, as highlighted in *Le Libérateur de l'Irlande*, a biography published in 1848 by Joséphine de Gaulle, which was reprinted several times.[38] This book exalted the Catholic hero. Between the tyranny of number and the tyranny of the despot, a third way existed – the providential man, 'moved by inspiration', a 'divine mission', in whom a whole people recognised each other.[39] Charles de Gaulle, grandson of this biographer, repeatedly drew attention to this work, one of the bedside books of his youth.[40]

During the 1840s, O'Connell also influenced some social reformers such as the Christian socialist Philippe Buchez (1796–1865), the proto-feminist Flora Tristan (1803–1844) and the utopian socialist Étienne Cabet (1788–1856). Why were these thinkers on social transformation, in quest of a new harmony, drawn to O'Connell, who always reiterated that he 'desire[d] no social revolution, no social change'?[41] They recognised him as a leader who transformed an oppressed

37 Henri de Riancey, 'Honneurs rendus à la mémoire et à la famille de Daniel O'Connell' in *Le Correspondant*, 25 Feb. 1848, vol. xxi, pp 587–611.   38 Joséphine De Gaulle, *Le Libérateur de l'Irlande, ou vie de Daniel O'Connell* (Lille, 1848).   39 De Gaulle, *Le Libérateur*, p. 7. 40 Pierre Joannon, 'De Gaulle et l'Irlande: un retour aux sources', *Études Irlandaises*, 15:2 (1990), pp 113–25.   41 Daniel O'Connell to P.V. Fitzpatrick, 21 Feb. 1833, in O'Connell (ed.),

and destitute group into a powerful popular and organised movement, with the ability to articulate, in his resounding and inexhaustible voice, the grievances of the silenced and the marginalised, even in the halls of Westminster, where he was the pre-eminent voice of the voiceless.[42] They also admired his non-violent methods, which did not stifle his unwavering pursuit of constant agitation, while always being able to control and canalise popular energy. They shared with him a desire for reform without a nihilistic violence, destructive of the social fabric and which might unleash a nasty form of barbarism. Finally, in search of social regeneration, they applauded his constancy to the morals of primitive Christianity, regarded in France as a religion that favoured the 'multitude' and sought its emancipation.[43]

After 1848, French interest in the Irish political laboratory faded. When O'Connell died, his movement, already losing impetus, ground to a shuddering halt. The Great Famine ravaged the island and stalled political momentum, even as the masses entered onto the public political stage elsewhere in Europe. In France, Ireland once more became identified with older long-term images of poverty and subordination – political, social and economic.[44] In 1854, the artist Gustave Courbet illustrated this reversal. In *L'Atelier du Peintre* (now hanging in the Musée d'Orsay in Paris), he represented the misery of crushed and dominated people in the guise of an Irish beggar nursing her child on the bare ground. Courbet described this Irish Mother/Mother Ireland as representing and embodying both real and symbolic dimensions:

> The Irish woman is still an English product. I met this woman in a London street, she wore a black straw hat, a green veil with a hole in it, a frayed black shawl beneath which she held a naked child under her arm.[45]

NATIONALIST IRELAND AND THE FEBRUARY REVOLUTION

When the July Monarchy was overthrown in France in February 1848, the Irish population was preoccupied with survival, as the Great Famine killed over one

Correspondence of O'Connell, v, letter 1957; Daniel O'Connell to E. Dwyer, 14 Apr. 1829, in O'Connell (ed.), *Correspondence of O'Connell*, iv, letter 1551: 'It is one of the greatest triumphs recorded in history – a bloodless revolution more extensive in operation that any other political change that could have taken place. I say *political* to contrast it with *social* changes which might break to pieces the framework of society'. **42** Flora Tristan, *Promenades dans Londres* (Paris, 1840), pp 88–9; Flora Tristan, *Union ouvrière* (Paris, 1843); *L'Atelier* (Buchez's newspaper), 31 May 1843, pp 65–6; *L'Atelier*, Mar. 1844, p. 88; *L'Atelier*, Dec. 1843, p. 38. **43** *Le Populaire* (Cabet's newspaper), 13 Nov. 1841; *Le Populaire*, 3 Apr. 1844, *Le Populaire*, 28 Aug. 1846; Étienne Cabet, *État de la question sociale en Angleterre, en Écosse, en Irlande et en France* (Paris, 1843), chapter iv; Flora Tristan, 'Lettre aux bourgeois' in *Union ouvrière*, pp 267–8. **44** Grace Neville, 'Remembering and forgetting the Great Famine in France and Ireland', *New Hibernia Review*, 16:4 (2012), pp 80–94. **45** Courbet to Champfleury, November–December 1854, in Petra

million and scattered one-and-a-half million more to the United States. Yet the
events that shook Paris to its foundations at the time did not pass unnoticed in
Ireland. The Irish press reported that men and women celebrated the revolution
on the streets, to the ringing rhythm of *La Marseillaise* – translated by the poet
James Clarence Mangan – that trees of liberty were planted and that bonfires
blazed in the countryside[46]. Even in the hardest of hard times, the proclamation
of the French Republic was synonymous with hope, for the members of
Young Ireland.

This coterie of nationalist intellectuals, with Thomas Davis as their figure-
head, emerged within the Repeal Association from 1842. In their newspaper, *The
Nation*, Young Ireland supported O'Connell, promoted an inclusive vision of the
nation, called for the reconciliation of ancient religious antagonisms, and sought
rediscovery of and reconnection with the pre-colonial 'golden age' before the
English invasion.[47] However, the Young Irelanders gradually distanced themselves
from O'Connell's Old Ireland between 1844 and 1846. They disliked O'Connell's
promotion of an exclusive link between nationalism and Catholicism, his
strategic alliance with the British Liberals, and his peremptory refusal to even
consider the possibility of political violence as an ethical reponse to over-
whelming oppression. On 28 July 1846, after an umpteenth debate on these
bones of contention, the rupture opened.[48]

The members of Young Ireland (renamed the Irish Confederation in January
1847) were not the 'fanatical revolutionaries' that later historians imagined.[49]
With rare exceptions, notably John Mitchel, they did not advocate revolutionary
armed struggle or separatism, and Repeal remained the outer limit of their
political horizon. The negligence of the Irish by an uncaring British state in the
face of the Great Famine, allied to the galvanising announcement of the Paris
revolution, radically changed the situation. The Republican project, sidelined
during the entire O'Connellite period, suddenly re-entered the field of
political possibilities.

John Mitchel, from his first articles in *The Nation* in the mid-1840s,
reclaimed the Franco-Irish revolutionary legacy of the late eighteenth century.
On 12 February 1848, just a few days before the fall of Louis-Philippe, he
founded *The United Irishman*, whose title unambiguously sought affiliation with
the republicanism of Theobald Wolfe Tone. After 24 February, the revolution in

Ten-Doesschate Chu (ed.), *Correspondance de Courbet* (Paris, 1996), pp 121–2. Thanks to
Michèle Riot-Sarcey for this reference.   **46** Pierre Joannon, 'L'Irlande et la France en 1848',
Études Irlandaises, 12:2 (1987), pp 133–54.   **47** Richard Davis, *The Young Ireland movement*
(Dublin, 1987); Christine Kinealy, *Repeal and revolution: 1848 in Ireland* (Manchester, 2009).
48 Charles Gavan Duffy, *Four years of Irish history, 1845–1849* (London, Paris & New York,
1883), p. 239; Oliver MacDonagh, *The life of Daniel O'Connell, 1775–1847* (Dublin, 1991),
chapter 23.   **49** Kinealy, *Repeal and revolution*, p. 10.

Paris enthused and inspired the promoters of this weekly newspaper. As of 25 March, *The United Irishman* adopted on its masthead 'Liberty-Equality-Fraternity', the motto of the young Republic. On 4 March, Mitchel advocated, in the Parisian manner, the revolutionary potential of narrow streets, and explained how to rain down bricks, paving stones and vitriol on troops from high windows, how to build barricades, and how to make improvised bombs – a practical manual of urban guerrilla warfare *à la française*.[50] This article among others led to the banning of the newspaper, and Mitchel was sentenced to fourteen years of deportation, a brutal punishment which transformed him into a nationalist hero, all the more so when he produced his searing and brilliantly written indictment of British colonialism in his *Jail Journal*.

Galvanised by the events in Paris, the Irish Confederates quickly converted to Republicanism and democracy, despite the previous conservative profiles of leaders like William Smith O'Brien and Charles Gavan Duffy. *The Nation* saluted the courage of the Parisians. An 'Address of the Irish Confederation to the Citizens of the French Republic', dated 15 March, read: 'In imitation of your example we propose to exhaust all resources of constitutional action, before we resort to other efforts for redress'.[51] On 25 March, Thomas Francis Meagher explained his own evolution, in a starkly compelling aphorism: 'The revolution in France has made me a democrat'.[52]

Unexpectedly, John O'Connell, the new head of the Repeal Association, also welcomed the political upheavals unfolding before his eyes. At the outbreak of the revolution, he was still in Paris, having attended, a few days earlier, the reception organised by the French Catholics in homage to his father. While he noted that it might appear odd 'that a moral force man should appear glad of such a struggle', yet, he said, 'I can rejoice without abating one jot of my moral force principles'. He believed that the revolution gained its legitimacy from the corruption of the political system and the hostility of Louis-Philippe's regime towards freedom.[53] In the name of the Repeal movement, he presented Ledru-Rollin with money for the wounded and families of the victims, accompanied by compliments to the Parisians for their moderation.[54] However, O'Connell emphasised that Ireland was 'not yet brought to the point that France was

---

50 'The French fashion', *The United Irishman*, 4 Mar. 1848; James Quinn, *John Mitchel* (Dublin, 2008). **51** 'Address of the Irish Confederation to the Citizens of the French Republic' [15 March 1848], quoted by Michael Cavanagh, *Memoirs of Gen. Thomas Francis Meagher* (Worcester, MA, 1892), pp 102–4. **52** Quoted in Christine Kinealy, '"Brethren in bondage": Chartists, O'Connellites, Young Irelanders and the 1848 uprising' in F. Lane & D. Ó Drisceóil (eds), *Politics and the Irish working class, 1830–1945* (London, 2005), p. 100. **53** *Freeman's Journal*, 7 March 1848. A few days earlier, writing from Paris on 25 February, John O'Connell had regretted that 'Liberty has been baptised in blood': *Freeman's Journal*, 1 Mar. 1848. **54** John O'Connell (Paris) to Alexandre Ledru-Rollin 29 Feb. 1848, *Freeman's Journal*, 7 Mar. 1848. John O'Connell, 'Lettre à Andryane, 2 mars 1848' in *Les murailles révolutionnaires de 1848* (Paris, 1868), ii, p. 227.

brought to' and that strictly legal and constitutional agitation should remain the sole credo of the Repealers.[55]

In March, in the effervescence of the French revolutionary moment, reunification of the nationalist split in Ireland seemed a possibility. For a few weeks, discussions occurred, meetings were held, and the idea of sending a representative delegation of the various nationalist currents to Paris gained support. However, at the last moment, John O'Connell disassociated the Repeal Association from this initiative. The deputation left Dublin on 22 March 1848 composed solely of members of the Irish Confederation, notably Smith O'Brien and Meagher. Its mission was to congratulate the young Republic and, if possible, to obtain the support (even if only rhetorical) of the new regime for the Irish struggle.[56]

A few days earlier, on 17 March, a delegation of Irishmen from Paris, led by John Patrick Leonard, were received at the Hotel de Ville by Alphonse de Lamartine.[57] The reply of the minister for foreign affairs of the Provisional Government contained an astonishing passage: 'The great man whose name you have recalled, O'Connell, has taught the world what was the most energetic means, though wisest, for the people for the conquest of their rights'. He concluded that 'peaceful agitation' had made Ireland 'the admiration of the world'.[58] Coming from Lamartine (a Republican), this unexpected tribute to O'Connell's strict constitutionalism reassured London about the peaceful intentions of the young Republic, while he also clarified that the new regime would not support the Irish militarily.

Smith O'Brien's delegation obtained a hearing on 3 April, in an episode that is well documented.[59] During this meeting, Lamartine confirmed that the Second Republic, unlike the First Republic, intended to maintain peaceful relations with its neighbouring powers and that it had no desire to interfere in the internal affairs of Great Britain.[60] The disillusionment of the Irish representatives was great, all the more so as they had travelled buoyed up by such great expectations.

Lamartine's firm line, which undoubtedly prevailed on the diplomatic level, was not shared by all of the Parisian revolutionaries in 1848. Some of the new free press condemned the minister.[61] Several corroborating testimonies,

---

55 *Freeman's Journal*, 7 Mar. 1848.   **56** Kinealy, *Repeal and revolution*, pp 136–40.   **57** Janick Julienne, *Un Irlandais à Paris. John Patrick Leonard, au cœur des relations franco-irlandaises, 1814–1889* (Frankfurt, 2016).   **58** Lamartine's speech (17 March 1848), published in *Le Moniteur universel*, 18 Mar. 1848, p. 633.   **59** The Irish delegates' addresses and Lamartine's answer were published in *Le Moniteur universel*, 4 April 1848, pp 758–9; D.N. Petler, 'Ireland and France in 1848', *Irish Historical Studies*, 96 (1985), pp 493–505; Joannon, 'L'Irlande et la France en 1848'; Robert Sloan, *William Smith O'Brien and the Young Ireland rebellion of 1848* (Dublin, 2000), pp 218–21; Kinealy, *Repeal and revolution*, pp 140–7.   **60** *Le Moniteur universel*, 4 Apr. 1848, p. 759. Lamartine's answer was well-received in Britain where it was translated and circulated widely in England and Ireland. The text in English is reproduced in Jeremiah O'Donovan Rossa, *Rossa's recollection, 1838 to 1898* (New York, 1898), pp 136–9.   **61** *La Vraie République*, 8 Apr. 1848, a

including the hostile one by British Ambassador, the second marquess of Normanby, highlighted the extent to which the delegates had received an enthusiastic reception in the new revolutionary clubs founded in the aftermath of the revolution. According to Normanby, Lamartine was 'much abused last night at many of the violent clubs, and especially at Blanqui's, the reception of whose speech, in favour of these Irish traitors, was enthusiastic'.[62] Some comforting words, attentive to Irish claims, were pronounced in those clubs, as illustrated, for example, by the message of the poster 'To the people of Ireland', broadcast by the *Club de l'émancipation des peuples*:

> Liberty for Ireland. After six centuries of the most inhuman oppression, justice must be done. It must! For France has sounded the hour of the awakening of nationalities and the enfranchisement of peoples ... Prepare yourselves! [...]. Son of Gael! Forward for the country, forward! Soul, heart, arms and chest, the people of France will be with you to defend you and to avenge you![63]

Paris in 1848 and the following decades remained attractive to exiled Irish nationalists. The city became a refuge for many fleeing Irish revolutionaries. While the majority crossed the Atlantic, some settled in Paris, notably John O'Mahony and James Stephens, both young insurgents in 1848, later founders of the Fenian Brotherhood and the Irish Republican Brotherhood. For several years, they were active in the clandestine republican and revolutionary networks in Paris of the Second Empire, the European capital of political exile in the second half of the nineteenth century.

CONCLUSION

These Franco-Irish connections – the Irish model of the 1830s and 1840s, the French revolutionary example of 1848 – were part of a broader international dynamic, characterised by aspirations for freedom and emancipation of individuals and groups during this 'time of possibilities' in the first half of the nineteenth century in Europe. These aspirations confronted and were confronted everywhere by the existing powers, although they were sometimes carried forward by a powerful popular current, as in Ireland in the time of O'Connell or in France in 1848.

daily newspaper founded by Théophile Thoré, a member of Barbès's *Club de la Révolution*, who later achieved fame as the rediscover of Vermeer's paintings.   **62** [George Phipps], *A year of revolution, from a journal kept in Paris in 1848* (London, 1857), i, p. 294. Kevin B. Nowlan, *The politics of repeal: a study in the relations between Great Britain and Ireland, 1841– 1850* (London, 1965).   **63** *République française. Au peuple d'Irlande, le club de l'Émancipation des peuples, salut et fraternité, signé: le président, Suau* (Paris, [1848]).

The richness and complexity of this dialogue between France and Ireland, even at a distance, during this period speaks volumes about the density of Franco–Irish relations. But it also reveals that we must always have regard for the particularities of each country: every discourse on another country is also, consciously among political actors, a reflection of a nation's own preoccupations. This is particularly clear in France in the 1830s and 1840s, when political confrontation crystallised around the future of a dislocated society whose norms and values had to be rethought and recalibrated. In this context, what made Ireland a 'model' until 1848 was not the memory of 1798, but the successes and limits of constitutional agitation, and O'Connell's stirring mobilisation and adroit canalisation of the masses – political projects which echoed the contemporary concerns of France. Any analysis of the popularity of O'Connell in France must consider the specificity of this moment, as well as the protean career of the Liberator himself: first an admired legal advocate for the oppressed Catholics, then a popular hero and a living messiah for his compatriots, and finally an indispensable actor on the European main stage.

John Patrick Leonard and the Irish colony in Paris, 1848–89

JANICK JULIENNE

Paris in the latter part of the nineteenth century was a capital city remarkably open to Europe and the world. Under the Second Empire, it became an imperial showcase as Napoleon III sponsored Haussmann's major transformation of the urban landscape between 1853 and 1870, while the universal exhibitions established Paris firmly as a global destination. Paris claimed to be the beacon of 'high' European culture and civilisation, intensifying the renown of the 'city of light' as a centre of art, entertainment, cuisine and pleasure. But Paris remained capable of sudden political upheavals, emblematic of developments in wider French, European and imperial politics. Twice the Paris streets were barricaded by insurgents, and the city increasingly became the asylum of choice of innumerable political refugees drawn from across Europe.

After 1848, Irish activists – Young Irelanders, Fenians, Home Rulers, Land Leaguers – came in successive waves to rejuvenate the greying ranks of earlier Irish exiles. Over time, a small expatriate community formed and expanded, reflecting the various political currents arising out of Ireland's social and political agitation. The Irish colony depended on the logistical skill, networking and political support of John Patrick Leonard (1814–89), whose contribution to this pivotal phase of Irish nationalist agitation has been overlooked.[1] Irish nationalists, either settled in or passing through Paris, thrived in the atmosphere of the cafés, then regarded as the 'salons of democracy'.[2] There they socialised and developed their radical projects, remarkably free from the state surveillance and repression that followed their every move in Ireland. How did these Irish nationalists incorporate France into their political strategy with Leonard's support? To what extent did they absorb and emulate the political atmosphere which defined the café culture of Paris? These questions can be examined through the lens of the Irish community in Paris during the second half of the nineteenth century, especially from 1848 to 1890, highlighting the pivotal role played by Leonard in helping this colony to lay down meaningful roots, allowing the French capital to become an especially significant sphere in the strategy of Irish nationalist movements.

1 Janick Julienne, *Un Irlandais à Paris: John Patrick Leonard au coeur des relations franco-irlandaises, 1814–1889* (Oxford, 2016).   2 According to Hippolyte Castille, cited in A. Delvau,

LEONARD AT THE HEART OF THE IRISH COLONY IN PARIS

John Patrick Leonard settled in France in 1834, and after 1848 assumed the role
of intermediary between Irish nationalists and France. Though he became fully
assimilated into French society, he maintained close links to his native land,
assisting his compatriots and also promoting Irish independence. He was born
on 22 October 1814 on Spike Island, a small and sequestered military garrison
in Cork harbour. He grew up in modest circumstances with his parents, two
sisters and one brother; his father, William Leonard, died in 1818 while the
children were still young.[3] His uncles, John (1785–1858), and especially P.J.
Leonard (1782–1831), quickly took charge of the young John Patrick, the latter
playing a fatherly role until his own death in 1831.[4] The Leonard uncles were
both founding members of the Christian Brothers in Cork, based at the famous
'North Mon', and they were actively involved in educating the poorer Catholic
children of the city. They exerted a significant influence on their nephew who
remained a loyal Catholic throughout his life, deeply attached to Catholic
education. In 1829, aged 14, he was sent to boarding school in France, at
Boulogne-sur-Mer.[5] In 1830, he returned to Cork to be near his gravely ill uncle
Joseph, who died shortly afterwards in 1831. In 1834 John Patrick decided to
return to France and enroll in medical school; this brought him to the Hôpital
Beaujon in Clichy near Paris, where he gained medical skills which would later
prove highly useful during the Franco-Prussian War in 1870–1.[6]

He never completed his medical training, presumably due to the high costs,
and he had to content himself with a position as an English teacher in a
municipal junior college in Sens in Burgundy.[7] Though he was based in a small
provincial town, the young Corkman managed to lead a rambunctious personal
life and he was regarded by the more buttoned-down French as turbulent at
work; inspectors' reports deplored his 'morally-questionable behaviour',
describing him as a 'dissipated man and lover of his pleasures, lacking order,
inconsistent, and reckless with money'.[8] Nonetheless, he was well integrated into

Histoire anecdotique des cafés & cabarets de Paris (Paris, 1862), p. viii.   3 Cork City Ancestral
Project, Cork County Library: Baptism Record: register 2, pp 12, 28, 174, 186.   4 J.B.
McGovern, 'Two notable self-exiled Corkmen', William Anderson O'Conor and John P.
Leonard', *Journal of the Cork Historical and Archaeological Society*, 10 (1904), pp 162–70.
5 McGovern, 'Two notable self-exiled Corkmen, p. 167.   6 Janick Julienne, 'Les Irlandais
dans le conflit franco-prussien: vers une renaissance des brigades irlandaises?', *Revue
Historique des Armées*, 253 (2008), pp 66–73; J. Julienne, 'The Irish and the Franco-Prussian
War: hopes and disappointments' in N. Genet-Rouffiac & D. Murphy (eds), *Franco-Irish
military connections, 1590–1945* (Dublin, 2009), p. 229. Leonard was made a Knight of the
Légion d'Honneur 'for the commitment of his own person on several battlefields' on 20
January 1872.   7 Archives municipales de Sens (Yonne, France), municipal register:
'déclaration faite par M. John Léonard, à l'effet d'obtenir des lettres de naturalité et la
jouissance de la qualité et des droits de citoyen français', 4 December 1841. According to the
Gazette médicale de Paris, 1 June 1833, medical school cost at a minimum 12,000 francs.
8 Archives Nationales de France [AN], F/17/21154: file on 'John Patrick Leonard',

local society, and he was considered good company; this was certainly the image that he projected throughout his life. In 1846, he was posted to the Collège Chaptal in Paris, and he settled in the 'quartier de l'Europe' around the Gare St Lazare, the district where he would spend the rest of his life. As well as his formal teaching, and like many of his low-paid colleagues, he made ends meet by also teaching English in the main commercial college of Paris, and privately to wealthy individuals. Clearly this private tuition allowed him to develop a network of contacts within the upper echelons of Parisian high society, even among the nobility.

1848: EARLY NATIONALIST AGITATION BETWEEN FRANCE AND
IRELAND

Leonard moved from Sens to Paris in 1846, arriving just in time for momentous political evolution. When the 'springtime of the people' erupted in Paris in 1848, Leonard was already chairman of the United Irish Club of Paris, an association of Irish residents in France. On 17 March 1848, he headed one of several delegations that marched to the Hôtel de Ville, gathering in the vast square to salute Lamartine, head of the provisional government of France. On behalf of the Irish community in Paris, Leonard congratulated the newly installed government, and stressed his personal involvement in the overthrow of the monarchy. Then he presented Lamartine with 'the flag of Ireland' and expressed the wish that it would 'always fly alongside that of fraternal nations'.[9] That flag, often assumed to be the first known Irish tricolour, was not actually described.[10] Contemporary press accounts of Irish delegations marching in Paris in 1848 refer to a green flag with a gold harp. The flag presented by Leonard was then deposited on 'a glorious pyramid of tricolour flags' in a reception room of the Hôtel de Ville.[11]

This Paris-based Irish delegation was warmly received by Lamartine, but he was much frostier with a visiting Irish delegation on 3 April, led by William Smith O'Brien and Thomas Francis Meagher, and which included Martin McDermott, Edward Hollywood, Richard O'Gorman and Eugene O'Reilly. Leonard accompanied them to act as an interpreter. That night he also presided at a dinner held in honour of the Irish delegation in the Minaret, a restaurant on the boulevard Poissonnière.[12] Wearing his uniform of the Garde Nationale, Leonard closed his speech with the following words: 'We offer you, gentlemen,

---

Inspection reports for 7 May 1837, 1842–3 and 1844–5. **9** *Le Moniteur Universel*, 18 Mar. 1848. **10** J.M. Hearne, 'Meagher to Leonard July, 1849. Thomas Francis Meagher's last letter written in Ireland and some new information pertaining to the origins of the Irish Tricolour', *Decies: Journal of the Waterford Archaeological and Historical Society*, 65 (2009), pp 59–66. **11** *The Nation*, 8 Apr. 1848. **12** *Cork Examiner*, 4 Apr. 1848.

our hearts, ours hands, our lives, to assist you in this struggle', words which struck a particular chord with Smith O'Brien.

Smith O'Brien and his compatriots left France quickly, not having obtained the wished-for support, but Meagher, O'Gorman and O'Reilly stayed on longer in Paris, where Leonard looked after them. Thanks to him they were able to join the Garde Nationale, living at first hand this French experience while moving around the capital, soaking up the revolutionary atmosphere and frequenting political clubs.[13] After they left, Leonard stayed in touch with these Irish nationalists, writing assiduously to Smith O'Brien, Meagher and many more. From that point onwards, he relentlessly developed links with various Irish nationalist movements, revolutionaries and members of parliament. In France, Leonard carved a role out for himself in this nationalist struggle. He welcomed newly arrived compatriots to the French capital, helped them throughout short or long stays, found them lodgings, and even work. Behind the scenes, he was always supportive. He thus became the indispensable contact in Paris for a small, eclectic, rapidly shifting and at times very active Irish community.

PARIS, 'CABARET OF EUROPE' AND 'CAULDRON OF REVOLUTION'

During the Second Empire (1852–70), political activists proceeded with caution, especially teachers who were required to swear an oath to the emperor, and who were closely watched. Leonard, a known republican and an ardent supporter of Irish independence, acted cautiously. From the 1850s onwards, he kept his convictions to himself and led the discreet and respectable life of a family man and teacher in Paris. In 1849, he had married an Irishwoman, Barbara O'Kearney, with whom he had two children: a daughter Mary born in 1850, then a son Maurice in 1858.[14] Both children were born and christened in Paris and had Irish godparents; Mary's godfather was John O'Mahony (1816–77), a Young Irelander and later a Fenian.[15] O'Mahony, exiled in Paris, lived on the rue Royer Collard near the Luxembourg gardens and the Sorbonne. Now a teacher at the Chaptal municipal junior college, Leonard was guardedly discreet in his political activities because he was contributing more and more frequently to the Irish press, notably in the leading nationalist newspapers such as the *Nation* and the *Cork Examiner*. Teachers, especially those doubling as journalists, were more closely watched than ever during the Second Empire.[16]

13 Archives de Paris, D3R4/36: roll of members of the gardes nationaux, rue de la Chaussée-d'Antin, no 57.   14 No records have been found corroborating the Leonards' marriage, either in the departmental archives of Paris or Sens, or the British consulate in Paris.   15 Archives de Paris, D6J 1902, baptismal register, parish of Notre-Dame-de-Lorette (9th arrondissement), baptism of Mary Leonard on 20 August 1850; baptismal register, parish of Saint-Augustin (1st arrondissement), baptism of Maurice Leonard on 19 July 1858.   16 Paul Gerbod, *La vie quotidienne dans les lycées et collèges du XIXe siècle* (Paris, 1968), pp 60–2.

Leonard swiftly inserted himself into the Irish colony, which was establishing itself in Paris in 1848. After the failure of the Rising in Ireland that year, and despite the lack of support from the provisional government of the Second Republic, Irish nationalists continued to regard France as a safe haven which was easily accessible from their native land. Paris by then had become a cosmopolitan capital to which numerous foreigners flocked; these communities included tourists but also political exiles, notably Poles and Italians.[17] During the Second Empire and the early years of the Third Republic, Paris was fast becoming the European capital for the arts, culture, leisure and pleasure seeking. Tourism was on the rise, and the British middle class could enjoy Paris through travel arrangements facilitated by travel agencies like Thomas Cook's.[18]

From the Second Empire until the 1890s, the Irish joined these expatriate communities, because, as Patrick Egan, treasurer of the Land League, observed: 'France is closer to us and ... apart from this material consideration, we have grown used to counting on her sympathy, which we believe we are entitled to lay claim to, flowing out of the sympathy we have expressed towards France'.[19] Some Irish nationalists were forced into exile after the failure of the 1848 rising. John O'Leary was banished from the United Kingdom until the end of his sentence in 1871, and settled in Paris.[20] The Irish were lucky that the French authorities were either indifferent or well disposed towards them, at least until the 1880s. The French capital was more than just a place of refuge; it was also a gateway to military training until the end of the Second Empire, again thanks to Leonard's active support. Whether it was the Garde Nationale in 1848 or later the Foreign Legion, Young Irelanders and Fenians sought to enlist to gain valuable military experience. James Stephens, founder of the Fenians, tried (vainly) to enroll in the French army when he was exiled in France in 1848, invoking 'the privileges of the Irish brigades'.[21] With Leonard's help, the Fenians John Devoy and James O'Kelly succeeded in joining the Foreign Legion, where they trained for some years.[22]

From the outset, the Fenian movement founded in 1858–9 by O'Mahony and Stephens was active throughout Ireland, France and the United States, but the presence of Fenians in Paris was particularly notable during the Second Empire.

---

17 Janine Ponty, 'Visite du Paris des Polonais' in A. Kaspi & A. Mares (eds), *Le Paris des étrangers, depuis un siècle* (Paris, 1989), p. 45. Pierre Milza, 'L'émigration italienne à Paris jusqu'en 1945' in Kaspi & Mares (eds), *Le Paris des étrangers*, pp 57–59. **18** Robert Tombs & Isabelle Tombs, *La France et le Royaume-Uni, des ennemis intimes* (Paris, 2006), p. 78. **19** *L'Univers*, 21 Oct. 1881. **20** T.W. Moody, 'The new departure in Irish politics 1878–79' in H. Cronne, T.W. Moody & D. Quinn (eds), *Essays in British and Irish history* (London, 1949), p. 326. **21** Archives diplomatiques [AD] (La Courneuve, France): Correspondance politique des consuls, Angleterre, vol. 41, Letter by Livio, French consul in Dublin, 31 December 1866. **22** Service historique de la Défense/Armée (Vincennes, France) [SHD]: 34YC5305, John Devoy's enlistment in the 2nd Foreign regiment, 9 February 1861 to 27 February 1862 ('Registre matricule de la troupe, 2è régiment étranger'); 48YC92, Jacques [sic] O'Kelly's enlistment in the 1st Foreign regiment ('Registre du Ier Régiment étranger,

In March 1859, Stephens returned to Paris where he met Thomas Clarke Luby and John O'Leary, while John Mitchel joined them shortly after. The Fenian brotherhood was tightly structured into three self-contained levels, and it was in Paris that the movement's top-tier decision-makers met, Stephens included, before transmitting their orders downwards to the next two levels.[23] This top tier remained in contact with the brotherhood in the United States where funds were raised, which were then received and managed in Paris by Mitchel. He was assisted by various members, notably Leonard who was described in diplomatic correspondence as 'an English teacher whose name crops up as the head of Irish events'.[24] Mitchel was also tasked with approaching the French government and procuring arms for an Irish insurrection, again with Leonard's help.[25] To plan the raids attempted in Canada, England and Ireland in 1866–7, the Fenians met regularly in Paris and sometimes also in the seaport of Boulogne-sur-Mer. Their comings and goings did not go unnoticed, as diplomats, police and the French, British and Irish press were all looking for the Fenian leader James Stephens, whose presence in Paris was noted at the Universal Exhibition of 1867.[26]

Due to the Fenian influx, the Irish community expanded to include William and Edmond O'Donovan, David Bell, Arthur O'Leary, Joseph Denieffe, John Augustus O'Shea, and the four Casey brothers, Andrew, James, Joseph and Patrick, who were cousins of James Stephens.[27] The Irish community in Paris also included artists, journalists, students and clergy.[28] All of them marinated themselves in French culture, as the memoirs of the Fenians Joseph Clarke and John O'Leary demonstrate; both make innumerable references to France's history and literature, i.e., Montesquieu, Rousseau, Balzac, Michelet and Thierry. Like the Parisians themselves, tourists and other expatriate communities, the Irish enjoyed the gaiety of the capital, and mingling in the political circles that expanded around hotels, restaurants and bars. Princess Sophie of Metternich referred to Paris in 1870 as 'the cabaret of Europe'.[29]

PARIS, THE COSMOPOLITAN CAPITAL OF EUROPE

From the early nineteenth century onwards and increasingly during the Second Empire, hotels and restaurants were opening to serve the foreigners flocking to Paris. Charles-Augustin Meurice's prestigious Hotel Meurice at 228 rue de

matricule 76'). **23** R.V. Comerford, *The Fenians in context: Irish politics and society, 1848–1882* (Dublin, 1985), p. 54. **24** AD, Affaires diverses politiques, Angleterre n°39: 'Mitchell, Stephens, Fenians en France', Livio to Drouyn de Lhuys, minister for foreign affairs, 5 Dec. 1865; Correspondance politique des consuls, Angleterre, vol. 41, Letter from Livio, 19 Mar. 1866. **25** W. D'Arcy, *The Fenian movement in the United States, 1858–1886* (Washington, 1947), p. 83. **26** *Cork Examiner*, 4 May 1867. **27** Janick Julienne, 'La question irlandaise en France de 1860 à 1890: perceptions et réactions' (PhD, Université de Paris VII, 1997), volume I, pp 46–7. **28** Julienne, *Un Irlandais à Paris*, p. 49. **29** Cited in Henry-Melchior de Langle,

Rivoli became very popular among a British clientele but also with Irish visitors, namely Charles Stewart Parnell in 1881–3.[30] Other hotels in this area also catered specially for British tourists, including the Grand Hôtel d'Angleterre and the Grand Hôtel de Londres.[31] Like the locals, foreign visitors spent their evenings socialising in other parts of the city, on the boulevards or at Montmartre or Montparnasse. Bars sprouted up in these areas, providing an ever-wider range of services.[32] Whether resident or just passing through, the Irish, familiar from back home with how best to take advantage of pub life, immersed themselves in this sphere of leisure and conviviality. The Fenian John O'Leary was in the habit of breakfasting, writing letters and reading newspapers each day in his favourite café, the café de la Paix on the rue Corneille, near the Odéon.[33] For lunch and dinner he resorted to the café Voltaire, also frequented by Léon Gambetta (1838–82) and other leading lights of French Republicanism, or to any of the new Duval chain of budget restaurants.[34] Then he strolled along the quays among the stalls to indulge his passion for antiquarian books.

In the nineteenth century, cafés were still elitist meeting places where intellectuals and the bourgeoisie mingled to enjoy coffee or liqueurs, but also, as in the previous century, to read the press, play billiards or card games like poker, manille (a trick-taking card game) or bridge.[35] In the second half of the nineteenth century, the chic cafés were joined by their shabbier counterparts the 'estaminets' (which served beer rather than wine, and allowed smoking), and players of the various games met in these smoke-filled spheres of sociability.[36] Parisian cafés were also an influential sphere of political networking.[37] Under the Second Empire and the Third Republic, cafés increasingly became the place where one went to talk politics and current affairs or read newspapers, as the price of a subscription was still quite high. Many licensed premises provided a range of titles to attract an ever-growing number of clients whose profiles were diversifying too.[38] Travellers mingled with journalists, facilitating the circulation of news and ideas, and some venues became specifically political.[39]

Le petit monde des cafés et débits parisiens au XIXè siècle (Paris, 1990), p. 261.   **30** Initially located on rue Saint-Honoré, it then moved to 228 rue de Rivoli in 1835; Meurice had previously been a director of the Paris-Calais mail coach service.   **31** P-O. Lapie, *Les Anglais à Paris de la Renaissance à l'Entente cordiale* (Paris, 1976), p. 202.   **32** There were 349,000 premises licensed to sell drink in Paris in the 1870s, 372,000 in the early 1880s, then 418,000 a decade later, i.e., one bar per 92 inhabitants, whereas this ratio was in decline in the rest of Europe: Didier Nourrisson, *Le buveur du XIXè siècle* (Paris, 1990), p. 95.   **33** Marcus Bourke, *John O'Leary: a study in Irish separatism* (Athens, GA, 1967), p. 133.   **34** John Devoy, *Recollections of an Irish rebel* (New York, 1929), p. 282.   **35** Nourrisson, *Le buveur du XIXè siècle*, p. 103.   **36** Nourrisson, *Le buveur du XIXè siècle*, p. 105.   **37** Langle, *Le petit monde des cafés*, p. 251.   **38** Langle, *Le petit monde des cafés*, p. 253.   **39** Beatrice Malki-Thouvenel, *Cabarets, cafés et bistrots de Paris* (Paris, 1987), p. 94.

THE LATIN QUARTER, RENDEZ-VOUS OF FRENCH AND IRISH
REPUBLICANS

At this time, and until the end of the 1870s, the Irish mostly congregated in the cheaper Latin Quarter, famously populated by students, but also frequented by great literary figures like Baudelaire and Verlaine. Irish exiles of 1848 (John O'Mahony, John Martin) and later Fenians (James Stephens, John Mitchel, Edmund O'Donovan, John Augustus O'Shea) lived modestly in this area, many of them crowded into a small *pension* at 26 rue Lacépède, near the Panthéon.[40] The Fenian Denieffe recalled with nostalgia his long walks in the Latin Quarter.[41] His fellow Fenian Clarke described how the Irish haunted this area, and how he was generally fascinated by 'fine, Haussmanized Paris' with its 'splendid new boulevards', and all the pomp, 'dazzle' and joie de vivre of the Second Empire.[42] The Irish met in the cosmopolitan cafés and bars of the Latin Quarter, like the café Racine (near the Théâtre de l'Odéon), the Brasserie des Fleurs (rue d'Enfer), where Stephens then lived, where 'the quartier's artists came with their models', and also the café de l'Europe.[43]

Some cafés became designated meeting places of specific expatriate communities, like the café Anglais on the boulevard des Italiens, where English newspapers were available, or the café Américain at 2 boulevard des Capucines, or Harry's Bar at 5 rue Daunou.[44] The smaller and poorer Irish community did not have a dedicated haunt, but preferred the ambience of the Latin Quarter, at least until the 1880s. In 1865, some of these cafés and brasseries on the Left Bank became meeting places for the opposition and even revolutionaries, and some Irish activists sought to forge links with the French left-wing activists with whom they mixed in the Latin Quarter.[45] Thus O'Shea met Raoul Rigault, a future Communard, who was a regular at the cafés around the Fontaine Saint-Michel, like the café de la Renaissance or the café Serpente.[46] Clarke saw Gambetta and Henri Rochefort in a café in the Latin Quarter, probably the café Voltaire where Gambetta frequently dropped in, or the Procope or the Frontin, renowned republican haunts. He recalled the subversive atmosphere of these cafés of the Latin Quarter, where all 'sang in mad chorus behind closed shutters the *Marseillaise* which was then forbidden in public'.[47] His compatriot O'Shea also imbibed the heady atmosphere of the *quartier*: returning late one night from a republican meeting, he roared the *Marseillaise* with two Irish comrades near the Panthéon, when they were stopped by two *sergents de ville* and narrowly escaped

40 J.M. Lennon, 'Paris of the Irish', *Irish Ecclesiastical Record*, 83 (Jan. 1955), p. 260. 41 Joseph Denieffe, *A personal narrative of the Irish Revolutionary Brotherhood* (New York, 1906), p. 48.   42 Joseph Ignatius Constantine Clarke, *My life and memories* (New York, 1926), pp 33–4. 43 Alfred Delvau, *Histoire anecdotique des cafés* (Paris, 1862), pp 292–3.   44 Malki-Thouvenel, *Cabarets, cafés et bistrots de Paris*, p. 45.   45 François Fosca, *Histoire des cafés de Paris* (Paris, 1934), p. 180.   46 James Augustus O'Shea, *Leaves from the life of a special correspondent*, 2 vols (London, 1885), i, pp 35–6.   47 Clarke, *My life and memories*, p. 61.

7.1 Oscar Wilde in a cabaret, rue de Dunkerque, Paris. Drawing by Jean Matet (1870–1936).

imprisonment.[48] Though Irish nationalists preferred mixing with French republicans with whom they shared political affinities, some sought contacts with other French political movements, in the sphere of the salons. O'Shea gained access to the 'Royalist assemblies of the faubourg Saint-Germain'.[49] Stephens attended the salon of the marquis de Boissy du Coudray, a Legitimist senator and anglophobe, and also gained access to prominent Bonapartists.[50]

Separate from this community, Paris had another network – the so-called *Anciens Irlandais*, or Old Irish, made up of descendants of the Wild Geese or men who had served in the Irish Brigades under the Ancien Régime, as well as veterans of 1798 or Napoleon's Irish Legion like Arthur O'Connor, Major General William Corbet and Colonel Miles Byrne. From the 1850s onwards, these Ancient Irish formed a closed circle of 'gentlemen' elders, in which Leonard was an outsider, not sharing their background or their claim to a specific tradition.[51] But gradually Leonard infiltrated himself and he was soon organising their annual St Patrick's dinner at the prestigious Grand Véfour restaurant. Fully

48 *The Irishman*, 26 Jan. 1867.   **49** O'Shea, *Leaves from the life*, i, pp 35–6.   **50** Desmond Ryan, *The Fenian chief: a biography of James Stephens* (Dublin, 1967), p. 233, p. 313.   **51** *The Irishman*, 23 Mar. 1867, 20 Feb. 1869.

integrated into their tight-knit circle, he also became their chronicler, reporting their births, marriages, deaths, gatherings and celebrations.[52] Though they were an exclusive and elitist group, every now and again the Ancient Irish would welcome newcomers introduced by Leonard like John O'Leary, Charles Stewart Parnell and (much later) Maud Gonne.

During the Second Empire and at the beginning of the Third Republic, the French capital was easily accessible for Irish nationalists, as well as a safe place to meet, to network, to gain political experience, and to access military training. And as Home Rulers and Land Leaguers were gaining ground at home over the Fenian movement, Paris remained a neutral territory for them and ideal for discreet encounters.

THE CONVERGENCE OF IRISH NATIONALIST MOVEMENTS IN PARIS
(1870–90)

The maps of where Irish nationalists lived and socialised in Paris makes it clear that activists crossed each other's paths and congregated in specific *quartiers*, regardless of their political allegiances. Parisians cafés were semi-public, but neutral ground, and thus important political discussions could take place there with total discretion. Though they were heavily divided in the 1870s, French republicans gathered willingly in *estaminets* like the café Riche for heated exchanges or reconciliations, or to devise common strategies.[53] Irish nationalist movements also congregated in Paris, especially towards the end of the 1870s. It was in Paris in August 1877 that the Fenian James O'Kelly met Parnell, leader of the Home Rule party, in the utmost secrecy; O'Kelly's conversion to constitutional nationalism dated from this encounter.[54]

Over the next few months, leaders of the three main nationalist movements (Fenians, Home Rulers, Land Leaguers), met in the French capital. In December 1878, and again in January 1879, Michael Davitt, a prominent Fenian driving the land struggle, met Devoy at the Hôtel des Missions Étrangères on the rue du Bac; it was also here that the eleven members of the Supreme Council of the IRB met from 19 to 26 January 1879. This last meeting was noticed by the authorities, and a police report voiced suspicions about these secretive 'Englishmen' who kept to their rooms, even having their meals sent there, and who rarely ventured out. However, no action ensued from this report.[55] This IRB

---

52 Julienne, *Un Irlandais à Paris*, p. 65.   53 The café Riche was located at 16 boulevard des Italiens, on the corner of the rue Pelletier: Jérôme Grévy, 'Les cafés républicains de Paris au début de la Troisième république. Etude de sociabilité politique', *Revue d'histoire moderne et contemporaine*, 50–2 (2003), pp 60–1.   54 Moody, 'New Departure', p. 311.   55 Archives de la préfecture de police de Paris [APPP], Cabinet du Préfet de Police, sous-série BA [general intelligence reports], BA 338: 'Personnages notables de passage à Paris-1879', report by an 'officier de paix', 21 Jan. 1879.

council decided to clearly distance the Fenian movement both from the Home Rule party and the land agitators, soon to become the Irish National Land League. Discussions between the various strands of Irish activism continued and exchanges often took place in Paris, but also in French ports like Boulogne-sur-Mer, where Devoy met Parnell and Joseph Biggar in February 1879, and then again from 7 to 9 March when O'Leary joined them. During the 1880s, various Irish nationalist movements frequented the same venues, but shifts were occurring in terms of the sectors of Paris favoured by the Irish.

THE IRISH IN PARIS: SHIFTING TO THE RIGHT BANK, RUE DE RIVOLI AND THE PALAIS-ROYAL

During the 1880s, the small Irish colony in Paris continued to welcome revolutionaries, and was enriched by the comings and goings of Home Rulers and Land Leaguers, but also smaller cells of Irish revolutionaries. A shift then occurred from the Latin Quarter across the river, within a triangle formed by the Champs-Elysées and the area around the Opéra and the Palais-Royal, in a sector divided by the rue de Rivoli. It is striking that the same shift occurred within French republican circles, who had previously congregated in the Latin Quarter. They too now migrated towards the Saint Lazare train station, through which members of parliament passed, and near the head offices of the main republican newspapers like the *République française* or *Le Temps*.[56] The Irish also sought out busy and animated meeting places to blend into the crowd of passers-by or patrons of the cafés. The general sector around the rue de Rivoli, radiating out towards the Opéra and the Champs-Élysées, was especially lively, which provided welcome anonymity.

Here there was a dense concentration of hotels, restaurants and cafés where Irish nationalists of all strands met, whether Fenians, Land Leaguers or Home Rulers. Leonard remained in contact with all these movements and he remained the pivotal figure of the Irish colony in Paris. He was close to O'Leary but also Patrick Egan, treasurer of the Land League, and he knew members of the Home Rule party, including James J. O'Kelly and Patrick J. Smyth.

PARIS, CAULDRON OF IRISH REVOLUTIONARY AGITATION

Surveillance of cafés frequented by republicans relaxed at the end of the 1870s when the opportunist republicans came to power, but the more militant activists were still closely watched by the préfecture de police. An outbreak of revolutionary activity was feared, given the threats voiced through anarchist

56 Grévy, 'Les cafés républicains de Paris', p. 59.

propaganda, reviving the painful memories of the French Revolution and the Paris Commune of 1871, and anarchist activities were on the rise in the capital during the 1880s. Furthermore, especially between 1883 and 1885, the activity of Irish revolutionaries intensified, as some plotted dynamite campaigns in Britain, emulating anarchists and nihilists on the Continent. The Fenians and Irish secret societies like the Invincibles, who carried out the Phoenix Park murders in 1882, were thus kept under tight scrutiny by the authorities in Paris. The Invincibles, the Moonlighters and the Fenians continued to congregate, plot and approach other European movements.[57] If the Fenian leadership under Devoy was firmly rooted in the United States, part of the organisation remained in Paris, centred around O'Leary but with Leonard's constant support.[58]

Police reports suggest that there were regular comings and goings by the Irish in America, Britain and those based in Paris, especially by the Casey brothers and Eugene Davis, who were fascinated by dynamite, and who were devising a strategy based on targeted explosions and assassinations. During the Prince of Wales' visit to Paris in May 1884, these Irish revolutionaries even managed to penetrate the Hotel Bristol where he was staying.[59] This fevered agitation by Irish revolutionaries peaked in 1884, when Patrick Casey and Eugene Davis, closely watched by the French police, made numerous contacts with French and foreign anarchists and socialists, and took part in demonstrations. The exasperated police prefect of Paris finally requested the minister of the interior to deport them, stating that 'in no way should the presence of these two aliens be tolerated any longer on French soil, given they have shown how unworthy they are of the hospitality which had been afforded to them'.[60] Though no immediate action was taken, the police stepped up their surveillance of Irish revolutionaries in Paris, who met regularly in the cafés on the rue de Rivoli and a restaurant at 40, rue de Lille. In March 1885, Davis, Mortimer Leroy and the ageing Fenian leader James Stephens, though no longer active, were deported.

PARIS AT THE HEART OF LAND LEAGUE AND HOME RULE STRATEGY

Both the press and the French authorities distinguished Fenians from Land Leaguers and Home Rulers. Yet the three movements maintained links in Paris, as demonstrated by Devoy's correspondence and numerous exchanges between Egan and O'Leary. Parnell too was meeting Fenians in Paris, and in the utmost secrecy, although the French press certainly got wind of it.[61] On 18 February

---

57 K.R.M. Short, *The dynamite war: Irish–American bombers in Victorian Britain* (Dublin, 1979), p. 212.   58 Dr Carroll to Devoy, 11 May 1880 in W. O'Brien & D. Ryan (eds), *Devoy's post bag*, 2 vols (Dublin, 1948), ii, pp 528–9.   59 APPP, Rapports quotidiens du préfet: rapports en date du 15 février, des 3 et 4 mars, du 18 avril, du 17 mai 1884.   60 APPP/BA 921/'Eugène Davis': The préfet de police to the minister of the interior, Dec. 1884.   61 *Devoy's post bag*, ii, pp 107, 46,

1881, *Le Temps* reported a meeting between Parnell and Stephens in Paris. From 1881 to 1882, Frank Byrne, general secretary of the Land League in Britain, met revolutionaries in Paris, namely the Casey brothers and Davis, former Fenians.[62] In May 1882, Parnell, Davitt and Egan met in Paris.

The Home Rule party and the Land League reinforced their presence in Paris at the beginning of the 1880s. The Land League was suppressed in Ireland as a result of the raging land agitation, and it decided in 1881 to deposit its funds at the Paris bank of John Munroe & Co., located at 7 rue Scribe, near the Opéra. In 1882, the Land League shifted its newspaper, *United Ireland*, to Paris. According to Egan, Land League funds then amounted to one-and-a-half million francs.[63] Funds were raised in the United States in 1879 for distressed tenants in Ireland, and were then channelled through Paris to be redistributed by O'Leary.[64] Paris thus became a safe financial haven for Irish agitators. A second account was opened in the Munroe bank in 1886; this 'Paris Fund', to which American sympathisers contributed, financed the parliamentary activities of Irish nationalist elected representatives.[65]

In the early 1880s, in parallel to the successful fund-raising tours in the US influencing public opinion, the Home Rule Party launched a propaganda campaign to raise French awareness about Ireland. Against the backdrop of intense political agitation and social unrest at home, prominent Home Rulers, including Parnell himself, O'Kelly and Egan, increased their trips to Paris. Parnell arrived on 16 February 1881, returned briefly to Ireland two days later but was back in Paris the following week and stayed at the Hotel Brighton at 218 rue de Rivoli until 23 March. With the help of O'Kelly, who spoke French, Parnell met several French journalists, some in his hotel room; there he met Henri Rochefort from the *Intransigeant* and reporters from the *Figaro*, the *Événement*, the *Gaulois*, the *Citoyen*, the *Télégraphe*, and the *Triboulet*. Parnell also visited the offices of the ultramontane and pro-Irish *L'Univers*. Each morning, he had seventeen Parisian papers delivered to him, from which O'Kelly read him translated extracts.[66] The cafés and bars of Paris, where major politicians in republican circles but also part members and agitators mingled with journalists, were significant 'spheres for political propaganda', which Irish politicians and agitators learned to exploit.[67] When Parnell was not in town, Egan pursued his own proselytising; his contacts with the French press intensified, and numerous articles and pamphlets on Ireland appeared in France during the 1880s. In the following years, Irish leaders continued to visit Paris and always aroused the interest of the French press.[68]

39–40, 161.   **62** APPP/BA 924/'Frank Byrne, inculpé d'assassinat en Irlande' [charged with assassination in Ireland].   **63** *L'Univers*, 21 Oct. 1881.   **64** Dr Carroll to John O'Leary, 23 Apr. 1879 in *Devoy's post bag*, i, pp 429–30.   **65** F.S.L. Lyons, 'The fall of Parnell' in T.W. Moody, J.C. Beckett & T.D. Sullivan (eds), *Studies in Irish history* (London, 1960), p. 152. **66** APPP/BA 1214/'Parnell': police reports, 18 and 23 Mar. 1881.   **67** Grévy, 'Les cafés républicains de Paris', p. 60.   **68** Julienne, 'La question irlandaise en France', pp 399–402.

It was most certainly through Leonard that Parnell was invited to the prestigious annual St Patrick's Day banquet organised by *the Anciens Irlandais* at the Grand Véfour in 1881. The Irish 'elders' may even have asked Parnell to preside at the ceremony. Parnell was not in Paris that day and could not accept their invitation.[69] Leonard also introduced Parnell and O'Kelly to two major figures: Maréchal MacMahon received them in his *hôtel particulier* on the rue de Bellechasse, and Ferdinand de Lesseps invited them to dinner in February 1881.[70] At this time they also met Victor Hugo and Henri Rochefort, a former communard and editor of the *Intransigeant*[71] (neither personal acquaintances of Leonard), as well as George Clemenceau, then the leader of the French radicals, in March 1883.[72] Parnell did not succeed in arranging a private meeting with the French president, Jules Grévy.[73] Irish agitators in France had until then enjoyed total immunity as the French authorities were indifferent to them, but now revolutionaries and elected representatives alike were increasingly suspected by the French police who began tailing them. As of 1881, O'Kelly and Parnell were under constant surveillance by the Paris police, whenever they visited the capital: police reports confirmed that they monitored whether or not they were being followed, and responded by running or jumping into cabs and changing their destination several times to shake off anyone pursuing them.[74] This surveillance was aimed at maintaining law and order in Paris, and there was no formal sharing of information between the French and the British security services.

CONCLUSION: LEONARD'S PERSONAL AGENCY

Paris clearly played an important role in the strategy of Irish nationalists from 1848 to the 1880s. Thanks to John Patrick Leonard's unfailing political and logistical talents, Irish activists found places to meet, to live and to work. Some hoped for political and even military support from the French state, but most wanted to establish political connections with the French elites, frequenting republican cafés or the salons of the capital. This strategy peaked in the early 1880s with frequent trips by Parnell but also his 'lieutenants', when they arranged as many encounters as possible with key figures in French politics and journalism. But in the end, nothing concrete ever emerged out of this work: no French political party ever made any commitments towards Irish nationalists, and the French authorities targeted Irish agitators on their soil.

69 AD/Affaires diverses politiques, Angleterre, vol. 5: 'dossier Grande-Bretagne. Pièces et documents divers – 1881': telegram sent from Paris by the *Freeman's Journal*, 26 Feb. 1881. 70 APPP/BA 924, various press clippings, February 1881.   71 Julienne, 'La question irlandaise en France', pp 399–402.   72 *La Patrie*, 20 Mar. 1883.   73 *Le Moniteur Universel*, 26 Feb. 1881.   74 APPP/BA 924, several reports, especially from 1881 to 1882.

Leonard maintained his position at the heart of the Irish community in Paris, managing to sustain various networks between France and Ireland. Republican and conservative in France, but a nationalist seeking independence in Ireland, Leonard was convinced that external assistance was essential to achieve the independence of his native country. Relentlessly, he pleaded for a Franco-Irish rapprochement, recalling the deep historical ties between the two nations, and endeavoured to develop this Franco-Irish friendship through religious, economic and political links. With French support, Leonard hoped to consolidate Ireland's development as a pathway to freedom. He thus instigated various projects with the help of his French and Irish networks.[75]

Utilising these networks, Leonard sought access for Irish firms at the great universal exhibitions in Paris in 1866, 1878 and 1889. He translated Louise, comtesse d'Haussonville's *Robert Emmet* in 1858, Henri Martin's *The Irish question* in 1860 and Adolphe Perraud's *Ireland under English rule* in 1864. In 1879, he organised the removal of the remains of Pamela, wife of Lord Edward FitzGerald, from Montmartre to Thames Ditton in England. With Maréchal MacMahon's active patronage, he established an Irish settlement in Algeria in 1869. Of the 130 Irish who landed at Bône in Algeria on 6 November 1869, only half were still there in summer 1871, mainly at Aïn-Smara near Constantine.[76] During the Franco-Prussian War, he was appointed inspector of ambulances and took charge of the Irish field ambulance assigned to the battle zone.[77] His links with the Irish and French clergy, facilitated by the liberal Bishop of Orleans Félix Dupanloup, equally allowed him to develop networks among church groups. One outcome was the collection of funds for the Irish in distress, while the Irish reciprocated by raising funds at home to be distributed in France to the needy, to flood victims or to those affected by the Franco-Prussian War.

When the French state deported the veteran Fenian leader James Stephens in 1885, Paris ceased to be an asylum for the Irish. After John Patrick Leonard's death in 1889, the networks that he had so patiently constructed during his lifetime, both in France and Ireland, began to unravel, because they had been largely grounded in his personal agency.

---

75 Julienne, *Un Irlandais à Paris*.   76 'Marshal MacMahon, desirous of diverting some portion of the stream of emigration from the country of his forefathers to the rich and fertile fields of Algeria, despatched a confidential agent [Leonard] to Ireland in 1869, with the result that about 150 Irishmen of the farming class set sail for Algeria in the October of that year. The experiment, however, proved a failure owing to lack of capital and the inroads caused by fevers, and in a few years the Irish colony vanished from this historic part of Northern Africa' (*Irish Times*, 27 Dec. 1929).   77 Archives municipales de Sens (Yonne, France), municipal register: 'déclaration faite par M. John Léonard, à l'effet d'obtenir des lettres de naturalité et la jouissance de la qualité et des droits de citoyen français', 4 Dec. 1841.

Maud Gonne and Irish revolutionary agitation in Paris

ANNE MAGNY

To understand Maud Gonne's political activism, it is necessary to consider the many years that she spent in Parisian society from 1888 to 1917.[1] She was a striking public figure, an early celebrity, whose deeds and actions were recorded by the burgeoning French press. Her relations with the Boulangiste Lucien Millevoye (1850–1915) were well known, and she held a popular weekly salon, attended by writers, journalists, politicians and key figures within the emerging French nationalist movement. A telegram from Lucien Millevoye to Maurice Barrès on 1 January 1893 points to how he used her salons to expand his network: 'My dear friend, can you come Tuesday evening to Maud Gonne's residence? I hope that … will be there. I have important and urgent information to communicate to you both. Yours …'[2] Her salon was a place where sensitive political information was exchanged, in the clandestine atmosphere of intrigue that was typical of late nineteenth-century French nationalism.[3] The movement of thought of the 1890s was above all a movement of revolt whose aims included the overthrow of the government.[4] French history was punctuated by stirring episodes that conferred legitimacy on revolutionary violence, which was celebrated by writers, historians and politicians under the Third Republic.[5]

It is precisely within this context that Maud Gonne worked to establish links between French and Irish nationalism. Her speeches and articles frequently spoke of love of the motherland, the glory of its heroes, sacrifice, and unyielding hatred of the enemy.[6] She drew on French and Irish traditions that associated allegorical feminine heroines with the nation. French nationalists influenced her methods of popular agitation, especially in understanding how politics impacted upon the public sphere, the connection between the actor of a political event and the public, which merge drama, theatre and performance.[7] In Paris, Gonne learned at first hand the driving forces behind street demonstrations, and various

---

1 Adrian Frazier, *The adulterous muse: Maud Gonne, Lucien Millevoye and W.B. Yeats* (Dublin, 2016). 2 Forty letters of Lucien Millevoye, Maurice Barrès collection, NAF 28210. 3 Michel Winock, *Nationalisme, antisémitisme et fascisme en France* (Paris, 1982), p. 15. 4 Zeev Sternhell, *Maurice Barrès et le nationalisme français* (Paris, 1985), p. 8. 5 Robert Lynn Fuller, *The origins of the French nationalist movement, 1886–1914* (London, 2012), p. 247. 6 Anne Magny, 'Comment défendre la cause de l'Irlande en France. Maud Gonne et la propagande nationaliste, 1891–1900', *Étude Irlandaises*, 20:2 (automne 1995), pp 18–26. 7 Jenny Edkins & Adrian Kear (eds), *International politics and performance: critical aesthetics and creative practice* (New York, 2013).

8.1 'Miss Maud Gonne', *Figures contemporaines tirées de l'Album Mariani*, volume 2 (Paris 1896) (Collection Pierre Joannon).

ways of staging political protest. She could immerse herself in politics as played out in the street, in agitation, demonstrations, spectacular acts and impassioned public addresses. All these acts require physical staging, a creative performativity that was popular among French nationalists and which Gonne embraced enthusiastically. Gonne's involvement in an active, confrontational style of politics was influenced by the French nationalists that she met when she first became politically aware, and with whom she socialised during her decades spent in France.

How did this form of revolutionary nationalism influence Gonne's political activity in France and Ireland? What expression did it find, what strategies did Gonne employ, and what effect did it have on the nationalist rebellion in Ireland?

MAUD GONNE'S POLITICAL APPRENTICESHIP: HOW TO CREATE
EMOTION

Gonne took her first steps in the world of political agitation in Paris through the
manipulation of emotion, a preferred tactic of the nationalists. Protest groups
share, transmit and develop an energy that above all comes from a deeply felt
internal emotional drive that confronts and reveals the desires that animate the
state itself.[8] Freud pointed out during the First World War that 'nations still obey
their passions far more readily than their interests'.[9] This analysis is particularly
appropriate for Boulangisme, a surprisingly successful revolutionary movement
that was led by a charismatic mounted officer. It generated a popular form
of nationalism in which passion, rather than thought or reason, was the
driving force.

   W.B. Yeats ceaselessly wondered about the complexities of this enigmatic
woman with whom he fell in love at the age of twenty-two. In 1915, more than
three decades after their first encounter and having probed the source of her
violence through many poems, he spoke about his first impressions of Gonne's
personality. He saw from the beginning the influence that the French nationalists
wielded on the virulence of her nationalist feelings. 'Her two and twenty years
had taken some colour, I thought, from French Boulangist adventurers and
journalist arrivistes of whom she had seen too much'.[10] Yeats could not have
intuited this when he first met Gonne because he knew nothing then about her
life in Paris (he had no idea that she was already sexually experienced and a
mother, for example), but his later analysis was accurate. Gonne had literally
fallen into the arms of French nationalism at a young age. She was only twenty-
one when she met Lucien Millevoye, and then soon afterwards key nationalist
figures such as Déroulède, Rochefort, Drumont and Barrès. It is easy to imagine
the impression that such flamboyant characters must have had upon a young
woman taking her first steps in politics and who already felt that her political
engagement must involve action rather than age-old feminine passivity.

   As an actress, Gonne understood how to appeal to the emotions of her
audience. Her first published French article, 'Un peuple opprimé' (An
oppressed people) (1891), the starting point of her propaganda work in France,
is indicative of her emerging style. It is energetic and passionate, demagogic
towards France and aggressive towards England, and employs striking prose, and
heart-felt accounts of eviction scenes designed to arouse the reader's indignation:
'I saw what I describe: it made me cry. What woman would hold back her tears
at the sight of such suffering? It is time to be moved'. This article was likely
written with the help of Millevoye and it was perhaps even proofread by Paul

8 Diana Taylor, 'Animating politics' in Edkins & Kear (eds), *International politics and
performance*, p. 84.   9 Sigmund Freud, 'Thoughts for the times on war and death' (1915) in
Complete works, xiv, p. 288.   10 W.B. Yeats, *Memoirs* (London, 1972), p. 41.

Déroulède, president of the Ligue des Patriotes. She was with her lover in the south of France while she was writing the article, where she was joined by Déroulède (for whom she had little time, feeling that he was overly anglophile). In 1896, when she already had become an experienced journalist, she informed Yeats that all her 'French articles require considerable corrections'.[11]

From the beginning of her writing career, Gonne enjoyed the help of excellent manipulators of words. Millevoye, an orator and experienced journalist, was known for his passionate style, while Déroulède was a patriotic poet whose every 'public pronouncement gave rise to wild cheering'.[12] Boulangism and broader nationalism, with the participation of journalists like Édouard Drumont and Henri Rochefort, was characterised by propaganda techniques in which stark pronouncements and declarative statements communicated uncomplicated ideas that would be easily digested and remembered by ordinary people.[13]

Maud Gonne's powerfully polemical article did not go unnoticed.[14] It stimulated invitations to high-society gatherings and attracted the attention of the French and Irish press. Her career as a propagandist had started. She went on to make many speeches, participate in demonstrations, write articles and enjoy success in Parisian nationalist circles. Gonne learned that to have her voice heard, she must reach her audience through an emotional rhetoric based on affect.

REJECTION OF THOUGHT AND LOVE OF THE CROWD

This cult of emotion was accompanied by a rejection of intellectualism and by a search for communion with the instinctive crowd. In 1892, a police report recounted:

> There comes a moment when their imagination [Millevoye and le Marquis de Morès] goes wild, when they believe that all is near, that the time is right, that events are about to break forth. These are extremely dangerous minds, because they never listen to reason; the impressions left by their wildest and most unrealistic dreams take the upper hand, and these impressions become their guiding force. With such disturbed people, anything is possible.[15]

The end of the nineteenth century witnessed the resurgence of irrational values. People were passionate about the occult (as Gonne herself was), with an intense interest in feelings and the subconscious, and men like Barrès were caught up in

11 Anna MacBride White & A. Norman Jeffares (eds) *The Gonne–Yeats letters, 1893–1938* (London, 1992), p. 59. 12 Winock, *Nationalisme*, p. 365. 13 Winock, *Nationalisme*, p. 51. 14 Frazier, *Adulterous muse*, p. 90. 15 Archives de la préfecture de police de Paris [APPP],

'le culte de l'élan', the cult of impetus.[16] People had to act: Gonne wrote that 'she redoubled work to avoid thought'.[17] Later, after her messy and fraught divorce, when she distanced herself from French and Irish nationalism, she concluded that she had been wearing blinkers all along in order to keep only a single aim in sight.[18]

Through the cultivation of emotion and passion and by being determined (with the help of Millevoye) to so inflame French public opinion that it would hate England and love Ireland, Gonne sought to impress the Irish political struggle on the French public and to create a link with her audience. Her lectures became moments where her audience enjoyed a feeling of shared values. This desire to achieve a sense of communion with the public, and more generally with the crowd, is a characteristic of the nationalism that Gonne's circle of friends espoused. Barrès glorified the warm instincts of the 'humble', contrasted with the cold intellectualism of individual reason. This way of seeing things offered fresh thinking to the popular right, contrasting the common sense and honesty of the plain people with the corrupt and lazy political class.[19] Every possible means was used to arouse this 'desire of the masses', such as street posters, drawings (which Gonne included in her newspaper *l'Irlande Libre* (1897)), almanacs and songs.[20] Some French nationalists preferred to descend onto the street, exciting the crowd and becoming a part of it, making emotions the drivers of collective action.[21] There are numerous examples of people taking to the street, from the crowd accompanying General Boulanger to the Gare de Lyon when he was exiled to Clermont-Ferrand on 8 July 1887, to the coup attempt by Déroulède on 23 February 1899 at the Place de la Nation. The activity of the Ligue de la Patrie Française, whose members included Millevoye and François Coppée (an ardent admirer of Gonne), was regarded as violent and destructive. One of its preferred methods was to organise rowdy demonstrations in theatres and churches.[22]

It was during demonstrations in favour of the Boers that Gonne's activism became particularly violent through contact with French nationalists. She considered acts of terrorism and she did all that she could to bring France and Ireland closer together in their opposition to England.[23] The pro-Boer movement presented an opportunity to exhibit extreme anglophobia in France, and some demonstrations orchestrated by Millevoye bordered on rioting. A public meeting held at Tivoli Vaux-Hall descended into a brawl and Millevoye was forced to leave under police escort.[24] In April 1900, a demonstration led by Millevoye was

Cabinet du Préfet de Police, sous-série BA [general intelligence reports], 1193, dossier Morès, 13 April 1892.   **16** Sternhell, *Barrès*, p. 23.   **17** Maud Gonne MacBride, *A servant of the Queen* (Buckinghamshire, 1994), p. 287.   **18** *Gonne–Yeats letters*, p. 246.   **19** Winock, *Nationalisme*, p. 49.   **20** Winock, *Nationalisme*, p. 341.   **21** Taylor, 'Animating politics', p. 87. **22** Quoted Frazier, *Adulterous muse*, p. 190   **23** Pierre Ranger, *La France vue d'Irlande. L'histoire du mythe français de Parnell à l'État Libre* (Rennes, 2011).   **24** Fuller, *Origins of the French nationalist movement*, p. 172.

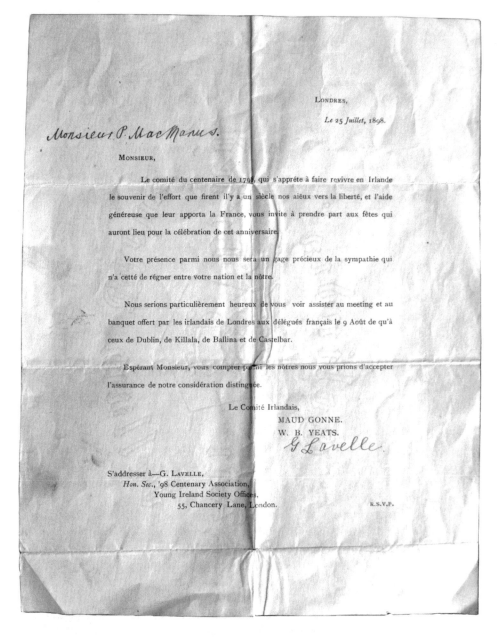

8.2 On 25 July 1898, Maud Gonne, W.B. Yeats and G. Lavelle issued an invitation from London on behalf of 'Le Comité Irlandais', in a printed circular in French, to join in the 1898 centenary. This letter was addressed to Patrick McManus (1864–1929), republican activist and journalist, then living in Buenos Aires. In 1897, he visited France and wrote two articles for Gonne's *L'Irlande libre*. In 1928 his three sons were at college in Paris and their parents came to visit them. An influenza epidemic was raging, and both Patrick McManus and his wife Elsa died in January 1929 (Collection Kevin Whelan).

organised in front of Notre-Dame in memory of Villebois-Mareuil (a veteran colonel who fought on the side of the Boers): it was dispersed by the police and he was arrested.[25]

Gonne was equally active in the pro-Boer movement in Paris, but it was in Ireland that she applied the revolutionary methods of her French friends and brought the struggle onto the streets. In Dublin, Gonne was a member of the Transvaal Committee, an association characterised by fiery anti-imperial rhetoric and confrontational tactics.[26] She campaigned against the recruitment of Irish soldiers for the war in South Africa and suggested organising pro-Boer gatherings around the country and in Dublin. In November 1899, she went to Cork with her friend Arthur Griffith, where they were welcomed by a tumultuous crowd that unharnessed their horses and pulled their carriage to their hotel. In Dublin in April 1900, she ignored the official ban on demonstrations against a visit by Joseph Chamberlain, secretary of state for the colonies. Seated with Arthur Griffith, James Connolly and others in a carriage and accompanied by a fired-up crowd, she was heading to the offices of her committee when the police encircled them. Connolly grabbed the reins and successfully broke through the cordon, leading the police on a frantic chase through the streets of Dublin. Gonne revelled in such dramatic situations. Sean O'Casey, who witnessed the incident, described her as a young woman 'smiling happily, like a child out on her first excursion'.[27] The demonstration culminated in a confrontation between the police and the activists, and that evening British flags and effigies of Chamberlain were burnt. The atmosphere is redolent of Barrès' recollection of Boulangisme: 'what fun I had! There was fantasy, freedom from all concern, youth, the idea of teasing the teacher, the philistine, the adults'.[28]

Gonne's message was successful due also to its entertaining theatricality, which was seductive and inclusive for the general public. Other examples illustrate her flair for agitation. On 18 May 1903, as the head of a delegation called the Citizens' Watch Committee, she triggered a massive brawl at the Rotunda, where the Parliamentary Party had gathered, presided over by Tim Harrington, the mayor of Dublin. Edward VII was due to make an official visit to the city and Gonne wanted to embarrass the mayor publicly about his intention to receive the king in his official capacity. After she had interrupted Harrington several times to pose her question, shouting and fighting erupted between rival supporters of Gonne and Harrington and chairs started to fly. To her disappointment, Gonne was pulled away from the stage by a friend who feared for her safety. The *Irish Times* concluded that the delegation had perpetrated 'one of the most sensational incidents in the recent history of Irish politics'.[29]

25 Fuller, *Origins of the French nationalist movement*, p. 174.   26 P.J. Mathews, 'Stirring up disloyalty: the Boer War, the Irish literary theatre and the emergence of a new separatism', *Irish University Review*, 33:1 (Spring 2003), pp 99–116.   27 Quoted by Margaret Ward in *Maud Gonne. Ireland's Joan of Arc* (London, 1990), p. 59.   28 Sternhell, *Barrès*, p. 108. 29 Quoted Ward, *Gonne*, p. 81.

The incident that best demonstrated the emotional connection between Gonne and the Dublin crowd occurred on 21 June 1897. To protest against the visit of Queen Victoria, Connolly organised a massive meeting and asked Gonne to make a speech. She roused the crowd using her sonorous deep voice to ask if 'the graves of our dead should go undecorated because Victoria has her jubilee', and then she led a procession with Yeats and Connolly by her side.[30] Seeing the numbers involved, the police tried to disperse it with a baton charge. Gonne heard of the death of an old woman and she wanted to leave the Contemporary Club, where she had gone to rest, to help the wounded. Yeats stopped her, fearful of the danger. A furious Gonne accused him of being responsible for the most cowardly moment of her life: 'Do you ask a soldier for explanations on the battlefield; of course it is only a very small thing a riot and a police charge but the same need for immediate action is there – there is no time to give explanations'. She stressed the differences between Yeats and her: 'I was born to be in the midst of a crowd'.[31] It is striking to note the parallel between Gonne's statement and that of Maurice Barrès who could feel 'deeply the instinctive pleasure of being among the herd'.[32]

Later, she would take this kinetic connection with the crowd even further, claiming to Yeats that she was 'the voice and the soul of the crowd'.[33] The high-minded poet wrote several poems about her love of the 'low' crowd and the poor. In 'The Praise', he predicted that the downcast would remember her name: 'if there be rags enough, he will know her name'. In 'The People', a poem inspired by one of her letters, he admires the fact that she never complained about the crowd, despite the gossip that she had to endure following her divorce. On the contrary, she regarded the people's reaction as healthy from a nationalist perspective: 'it would be a misfortune if the crowd began worrying over subtleties for it would be an end of action'.[34]

Gonne was not necessarily influenced by Barrès directly, although he did claim that rationality killed instinct and that 'it can only annihilate the driving forces of national activity'.[35] She was exposed in France to acts and thoughts that conferred legitimacy on her instincts. The populist nature of French nationalism suited her temperament.

STAGING A PERFORMANCE

To excite the crowd and establish a connection with it, more is required than just to deliver speeches and join in street protests. One must appeal to its emotions, but one must also devote one's heart and soul to reach it through symbolic

30 Quoted by Yeats, *Autobiographies*, p. 367.   31 *Gonne–Yeats letters*, p. 72.   32 Sternhell, *Barrès*, p. 279.   33 *Gonne–Yeats letters*, p. 166.   34 *Gonne–Yeats letters*, p. 241.   35 Sternhell, *Barrès*, p. 272.

language and, to that end, to be creative and engaged. To lead the crowd, one must deliver a physical performance. Political activists must be seen, and organise events in which the body performs: 'marches, rallies, amusing and disruptive acts, solidarity networks, cultural events and other embodied and virtual practices'. The streets manifests the connections among these various elements.[36]

Once again Gonne learnt much through her contacts with the French nationalists. Having herself exchanged the theatrical for the political stage even before meeting Millevoye, she was not surprised to see the nationalists mixing political action and theatre. Street performance was indeed an essential part of French nationalism. Boulanger understood how to perform the hero in this cult of personality, as he showed on 14 July 1886. During the troop review at Longchamp racetrack, he appeared in a feathered cocked hat, white breeches and black palfrey, and was greeted by audience acclaim. He became the focus of everyone's attention by standing completely still and erect in front of the presidential tribune. This gesture and his regal bearing completely eclipsed the dull and staid President and it inspired the songwriter Paulus to compose the catchy song 'En revenant de la revue' that cemented the general in the popular imagination – 'Moi, j'faisais qu'admirer notr' brav' général Boulanger'. The term Boulangisme quickly entered the political vocabulary.[37]

This example shows the essential role of creativity, and of the necessary transformation of reality that occurs in three identifiable phases. The first relates to Boulanger's clothes, which introduce a character that will perform someone who in reality he is not. The second phase is the artistic staging of the character, how the costumed body features within its public surroundings, while the third is the consecration, the appropriation of the character by the crowd via the rousing song that everyone can sing together.

Boulanger liked to preen and as Clemenceau said, he also liked the acclamation, but he was not alone in this. The Marquis de Morès, co-founder with Edouard Drumont of the Anti-Semitic League of France, encouraged popular agitation in the company of, among others, apprentice butchers recruited at the Villette, who marched in the streets wearing sombreros and red cowboy shirts. Jules Guérin, another notorious anti-Semite and friend of Millevoye at the Grand Occident de France, was called the 'fairground Hercules' by his opponents. To avoid arrest for his participation in the failed February 1899 coup d'état, he barricaded himself with his troops inside a house on the rue Chabrol for a 38-day siege, while Millevoye tried in vain to extricate him.[38] This theatrical episode, which came to be known as Fort Chabrol, evolved like a play in several acts and stimulated huge reaction. Henri Rochefort, a member of Millevoye's inner circle and a key figure in the nationalist movement, was a brilliant polemicist but he had to endure mocking nicknames, such as 'popular

36 Taylor, 'Animating politics', p. 85.   37 Winock, *Nationalisme*, p. 339.   38 Frazier,

buffoon', 'entertainer of the rabble', 'old jester' and 'old clown'.[39] Millevoye himself never hesitated to provide a show and to attract attention, and he had a particular fondness for duels and other provocations. His taste for agitation allied to his poor judgment surfaced during the Norton affair in June 1893, during which he became a laughing stock over his credulity in accepting that documents, forged by Norton, proved that Clemenceau was a traitor in the pay of the English. The satirical cartoonists had a field day.

Gonne shared with Millevoye and his friends a taste for ostentation, panache, exhibitionism and provocation. As a former actress with a commanding appearance, she was a stunning performer. Over six feet tall, she was perfectly aware of the seductive effect of her stunning beauty, figure, poise and sultry voice, taking lessons in diction from a Comédie Française actress for her public speeches.[40] Witnesses to her Paris speeches observed how she aroused enthusiasm, and poems compared her to a Celtic druidess. Every aspect of her public life became a staged performance. At the opening of a Parisian salon in 1895, she created a sensation by appearing dressed from head to toe in white, complete with an extravagant hat and boa around her neck. The bourgeois *Freeman's Journal* of 23 May considered that 'the effect was far too striking'.[41] Similarly, an extraordinary appearance at the Dublin Horse Show bemused an *Irish Times* journalist, who focused on her dress: 'the most bewildering arrangement of fancy blue and white silk and cream lace, which hung, *en désordre*, as if it had been flung on her, her hair which was done in a thousand curls all over her head, which made it appear a tremendous size' and a hat 'that baffles description'.[42] Gonne liked to make an appearance and Yeats at times squirmed at his friend's grandstanding, which he regarded as more vulgar than flamboyant.

THE PUBLIC ARENA BECOMES A STAGE

That Gonne liked extensive decoration and placed symbolic value in it can be seen in photographs of her Parisian interiors. A Saint Patrick's Day banquet at her home was attended by the mayor of Paris. Her apartment was festooned with green, silk flags and shamrocks. Likewise, the baptism of her son was staged to leave no room for doubt about parental intentions to make their son into a future revolutionary.

In addition to the importance assigned to one's appearance and one's body, symbolic actions theatricalise the public space, staging a performance that includes the audience. Kant had claimed that 'revolutions and transformations

Adulterous muse, p. 187.   **39** Winock, *Nationalisme*, p. 373.   **40** Anne Magny, 'Maud Gonne et la propagande nationaliste en France (1891–1901): image, pathos et liens' in C. Maignant (éd.), *La France et l'Irlande: destins croisés 16ème–21ème siècles* (Lille, 2013), pp 89–100.   **41** Frazier, *Adulterous muse*, p. 136.   **42** Frazier, *Adulterous muse*, p. 139.

succeed when bystanders join in'.[43] Gonne used various types of display to place herself, as a rebel, inside a theatrical decor, in the public arena. One of her preferred activities was to stage memory through a public homage to heroes of the past, Irish and French, who had fought for Ireland, for example the 1798 commemoration ceremony that she organised in Ballina.[44] Gonne was also an Irish pioneer of street protest. During the protest organised with Connolly in 1897, she obtained permission to use a window at the Contemporary Club, and on it she projected, on a big screen, images illustrating English atrocities: descriptions of massacres committed by Cromwell, photographs of evictions, tables enumerating the victims of the Great Famine, etc. She also made small black flags with white letters and numerals showing Irish deaths from famine, the number of demolished houses, and men imprisoned during Victoria's reign. These flags waved around a coffin, the symbol of the British Empire's destiny, in a procession led by Connolly. This coffin, thrown into the Liffey despite the efforts of the police (thereby delighting the crowd), featured on the cover of *le Journal des Voyages*, a magazine to which Gonne frequently contributed. Gonne and Connolly enjoyed a particular talent for sensational symbolic acts and Gonne exhibited a flair for street theatre.[45] Millevoye, delighted, reported the episode in *La Patrie*, his newspaper. Yeats was particularly aware of the dramatic and symbolic dimension that Gonne adopted during this protest. He described her emotional state on this occasion: 'Maud Gonne has a look of exultation as she walks with her laughing head thrown back'.[46] This image of the revolutionary so struck him that he used it in his 1904 play *On Baile's Strand*, in a description of his heroine, Aoife:

> You have never seen her. Ah! Conchubar, had you seen her
> With that high, laughing, turbulent head of hers
> Thrown backwards, and the bowstring at her ear.

Gonne showed an impressive and precocious command of modernity in her methods: the representation of England's depravity through props staged in the middle of the crowd; the projected images that she had initially used in her Paris performances; the elevated big screen, allowing the whole crowd's immersion; the flags with pithy inscriptions flying over the crowd. These were also the propaganda methods used by the French nationalists. They were among the first to understand the need for simplification and exaggeration to engage public attention. They also understood that the emotional content was at least as important as the rational content, and that the message needed to be dramatic, symbolic and mythical.[47]

---

43 Taylor, 'Animating politics', p. 93.   44 Emilie Pine, *The politics of Irish memory: performing remembrance in contemporary Irish culture* (London, 2011).   45 Frazier, *Adulterous muse*, p. 147. 46 W.B. Yeats, *Autobiography* (London, 1991), p. 368.   47 Winock, *Nationalisme*, pp 140–1.

Gonne demonstrated her audacity one day by hooking a petticoat of hers up in the air in a public space. The same visit by Edward VII in 1903 gave rise to a remarkable event called the 'Battle of Coulson Avenue'. The death of Pope Leo XIII coincided with the king's visit to Dublin. The Unionists hung union jacks in front of their houses, but Gonne, in a gesture of pure provocation, attached one half of a black petticoat to a broomstick at the front of her house as a sign of mourning. The next day, three detectives and a policeman removed it. Gonne immediately attached the second half of her petticoat, precipitating a brawl between the policemen, angry neighbours and nationalist friends who came to help her. The black petticoat (itself with the added *frisson* of exhibiting female underclothes in public) flying among the bourgeois union jacks had a much more striking impact than any speech. Her house, her garden, the pavement and the street all became a theatrical space in which a drama was played out, complete with pantomime villains and heroes.

The sexual connotation of the petticoat assumed a particular meaning in the nationalist context. If Gonne personified Ireland, then, the house from which the petticoat flew represented a pure Ireland threatened with rape by a masculine England. The Gaelic Leaguers who defended Maud personified the valiant nationalists willing to defend her and the national honour.[48] The image of the rape of a virtuous feminine Ireland by a vampiric England intent on sucking her lifeblood was a recurrent theme in the speeches and articles of Gonne, in particular while in France.[49] The trope enjoyed much success, as can be seen in the poems about her by François Coppée (1842–1908), 'le poète des humbles' (the poet of the poor), in which she is likened to Ireland and is compared to a weeping virgin. While this image could derive from the Irish literary tradition, we can also consider the role of Millevoye and the French nationalists in the systematic use of this same image. Jeanne d'Arc, as virgin but also as warrior, occupied a key symbolic role within the movement.

INGHINIDHE NA hÉIREANN AND MAUD GONNE

The links among nation, womanhood and theatrical expression would express themselves most spectacularly in Inghinidhe na hÉireann (Daughters of Ireland), the association created by Maud Gonne in 1900. From the beginning, its activists expressed nationalism as a performance. It was in this context that Gonne and her companions surpassed the French nationalists in their creativity.

Inghinidhe na hÉireann, to legitimise their presence on the political scene, embraced the traditional role of motherhood and launched an extensive

---

48 Sian Harwood, 'Performing Irish womanhood. Maud Gonne, the Daughters of Erin and early twentieth-century Irish nationalism' (PhD, New York University, 2001), p. 154. 49 L. Perry Curtis, *Images of Erin in the age of Parnell* (Dublin, 2000) shows how Irish cartoonists depicted

campaign aimed at the education of children. They sought to instill a sense of Gaelic culture, but what was novel was the revolutionary orientation that Gonne gave to her movement. In an article, 'Ireland and the children' published in the *United Irishman* in 1902, she advocated that children should be attached to their country by a mystical bond and that they must be made aware that one day a sacrifice might be demanded of them. We can again ponder the influence of French nationalism. Juliette Adam (1836–1936), Léon Gambetta's former mistress, helped Gonne to publish her first article, and she believed that children should be taught to be ready to die for France. Paul Déroulède made the education of children a priority for his League of Patriots. While Gonne disliked him, he influenced Millevoye who admired him greatly.[50] The education system advocated by Déroulède had two basic principles: patriotism is also a religion that has its own symbols and rites just as it has its apostles and martyrs. The educator's role is to incubate in children in every way possible a deep and rational love of their nation and their land, and to nourish their imaginations with the glory of France, its history and its landscape, through books, images and drawings, songs learned by heart, national feast days.

The effectiveness of such indoctrination depended on the careful selection of suitable stories and their effective dramatisation. The use of literature was a feature of Irish nationalism but let us again remember the link with French nationalism: Barrès, Déroulède, Rochefort, Coppée and others expressed, albeit with varying success, their nationalism through poetry, prose and drama. Although Gonne continued to project images and make speeches, she put as much effort into staging scenes drawn from mythology and from rural life in Ireland. Through readings and tableaux vivants, Inghinidhe na hÉireann presented their audience with an idealised vision of the past and of contemporary rural life in Ireland. In August 1901, Gonne gave a public reading of the legend of Red Hugh, carefully presented against a theatrical setting. The tableaux vivants presenting Irish country people inspired the stylised dramas set in rural Ireland later performed at the Abbey Theatre, where the west of Ireland folk were projected as the symbol of a pure Irish people, yearning for their lost liberty.

Gonne played her most celebrated role in 1902 in *Cathleen ni Houlihan*, the play written by Yeats and Lady Gregory, that can be regarded as a compelling modern version of classic tragedy.[51] Gonne's embodiment of Caitlín Ní hUallacháin inflamed the intimate nationalist audience, as if all their dreams had suddenly sprung into spectacular life in front of their yearning eyes.[52] In performative terms, Gonne had utilised a language that brings about the reality that it announces.[53] A theatre scenario that sheds light on a possible future

the female personification of Ireland.   **50** Quoted by Sternell, *Barrès*, p. 69.   **51** Declan Kiberd, *Inventing Ireland: the literature of the modern nation* (London, 1995), p. 200. **52** Harwood, 'Performing Irish womanhood', p. 78.   **53** Taylor, 'Animating politics', p. 86.

8.3 Maud Gonne, *c.* 1901 (Library of Congress).

confers an existence on futurity. This in turn releases frozen political desire into the living mainstream of history, and it is why Yeats was so focused on creating a national theatre at this time. By embodying a hitherto-inchoate desire, these plays enabled a demand for change, and created the possibility of a different future.[54] Rebels, artists and writers adopted a self-consciously literary approach, evident in their choices of deep symbolic meaning in their preferred dates, clothes and behavior.[55]

Cathleen ni Houlihan was the apotheosis of Gonne's dramatic work, obliterating the lines that had until now divided theatre and street propaganda. Critics noted that she was not so much acting her role as living it: 'she does not address the audience as an actor normally does but she speaks to it directly just as she would were she at Beresford Place' (near Liberty Hall).[56] In personifying the allegorical role of a Mother Ireland coming to claim the allegiance of her children, she was completely consistent with the role that she had personified from the start. This undoubtedly followed an Irish tradition, but it also reflected values and methods absorbed from French nationalism, including an appeal to intuitive feeling, an elevation of rural life, an emotional connection with the audience, self-dramatisation and a distinct whiff of violence and of sacrifice. The reference in the play to the arrival of French soldiers coming straight from their revolution is clearly not a coincidence. Would the play have existed without the French nationalists and would it have had the same impact? Besides the identification that occurred between her character and a romantic image of Ireland, her incarnation of Caitlín and of her message was all the more convincing because of her high reputation as a street activist. Gonne's French apprenticeship injected the confidence that she needed to stage her public performances, insofar as they inspired her, set an example to follow, and provided encouragement.[57]

---

54 Taylor, 'Animating politics', p. 92.   **55** Declan Kiberd, *The Irish writer and the world* (Cambridge, 2005), p. 200.   **56** Frazier, *Adulterous muse*, p. 208.   **57** I wish to thank Pierre Ranger for supplying me with helpful archival references.

'Shattered glass and toppling masonry': war damage in Paris and Dublin

JUSTIN DOLAN STOVER

INTRODUCTION

The German army shelled Rheims Cathedral in late September 1914, inflicting severe damage on its façade and igniting a fire that attacked its wooden roof. International opinion viewed its targeting as evidence of determined German savagery, despite their claims that the venerable church was being used by the French army for observation and was an established battery.[1] The damage extended beyond the erosion of a French cultural icon. Like the burning of Louvain a month earlier, Rheims elicited strong ethical condemnation and was quickly deployed to serve allied propaganda. The *Irish Independent* reprinted an eyewitness account:

> There is no crime in the history of civilisation comparable with the wanton destruction by the Germans of the Cathedral at Rheims – one of the great architectural treasures of the world. There was nothing in the world more beautiful than the western facade of this great edifice, and few who have seen it in the moonlight can ever forget the sublimely beautiful picture.[2]

Another witness half-admiringly recounted the Gothic Sublime of the destruction:

> What a spectacle it was! Under the cold, drifting grey rain clouds, one whole semi-circle of the horizon edged by the heights on which the German batteries were mounted three miles away, was nothing but an inferno of bursting shells.[3]

War damage to landscapes, villages, and religious sites produced a global echo. The atrocity continued to circulate in various mediums throughout the war, and for years after the Armistice. Collier's 1916 *Photographic history of the European war* informed the still-neutral United States of America that 'The wars of seven centuries had passed over Rheims, and still all armies spared the beautiful

---

1 Alan Kramer, *Dynamic of destruction: culture and mass killing in the First World War* (Oxford, 2007), pp 18–19. 2 *Irish Independent*, 21 Sept. 1914. 3 *Sunday Independent*, 20 Sept. 1914 [reproduced from the *Evening News* (London)].

cathedral. It is now a wonderful ruin'.[4] Memorial photographs, postcards, serialisations of 'les misères de la guerre',[5] and a range of other treatments sustained French national mourning, conveyed its suffering to the world, and stiffened public opinion against the Germans.

Irish public opinion was manipulated into how to understand the Great War through such depictions, and through the transnational Catholic context in which they were framed. Kevin O'Shiel recalled that it was the invasion of Belgium that inflamed Irish feelings:

> Worse of all, to the deep perfervid Catholic conscience that predominated in country districts and the small towns, came accounts of the burning of cathedrals and churches and the tragic destruction of the great University Library of Louvain and the beautiful cathedral of St Pierre.[6]

This imagery gradually manifested beyond the news page as soldiers on leave brought home the reality of the Continental struggle to Ireland, authenticating rumours as well as confirming the war's apocalyptic effects.

The 1916 Rising was a similarly transformative experience for individuals, as well as for Dublin's urban landscape. The suppression of the insurrection damaged or destroyed numerous commercial buildings, residences and public spaces. This destruction stemmed from rebels' use of civic and commercial buildings as defensive positions, and ruthless British efforts to dislodge them through artillery shelling and machine-gun fire. The rebels had assumed that the British would never destroy the commercial core of Dublin, as their thinking was that commercial self-interest would govern the British response. James Connolly, on classic Marxist grounds, assumed that the 'second city of the empire' would be spared but he also thought that 'if the British were ever compelled to use artillery, they were doomed'.[7] The main impact of the rebellion was concentrated on and adjacent to Dublin's main thoroughfare Sackville (now O'Connell) Street, and this intensified the Rising's material impact. Numerous properties were subjected to preparatory barricading by both Irish and British soldiers; insurgents tunnelled between buildings, looters ravaged shops, while artillery shelling and the inevitable subsequent fires eventually reduced several buildings to their foundations. Scarred edifices, collapsed structures, smoke-filled skies, and smouldering rubble repositioned the true extent of the Western Front. Mary

---

4 F. Reynolds & C. Taylor, *Collier's photographic history of the European war* (New York, 1916), pp 42–3; Cynthia Wachtell, 'Representations of German soldiers in American World War I literature' in T. Schneider (ed.), *'Huns' vs. 'corned beef': representations of the other in American and German literature and film on World War I* (Göttengen, 2007), p. 64.   **5** Compositions from J. Thil and Lucien Jonas illustrating *'Les misères de la guerre'* appeared in *La Guerre documentée* throughout the war.   **6** Kevin O'Shiel, Bureau of Military History, Witness Statement 1770, pp 472–3.   **7** Fearghal McGarry, *The Rising. Ireland: Easter 1916* (Oxford, 2011), pp 191–2, citing Bob de Coeur, who heard it from Liam Ó Briain.

458 — Nº 3819   L'ILLUSTRATION   13 MAI 1916

La proclamation du gouvernement provisoire
de la « République Irlandaise ».

Pendant la lutte contre l'émeute :
soldats guettant les rebelles.

Une fenêtre du Palais de Justice barricadée
avec les livres de la bibliothèque.

Le quartier qui a le plus souffert de l'incendie, à l'angle de Sackville Street et du quai de la Liffey. — Au premier plan, le pont O'Connell.

Liberty Hall, quartier général des insurgés, qui fut bombardé
par une canonnière.

Le porche du Post Office central, dans Sackville Street,
vu de la colonne de Nelson.

DUBLIN APRÈS L'ÉMEUTE

9.1 'Dublin apres l'émeute' ('Dublin after the riot'). These images of destruction in Dublin appeared two weeks after the Rising (here described under the favoured English term 'riot') in *L'Illustration*, 13 May 1916 (Collection Pierre Joannon).

Louisa Hamilton Norway, wife of a senior civil servant, witnessed 'such a sight as you will never see in your life unless you go to Belgium.'[8]

Like the war damage in north-western France and Belgium, the memory of the Rising was coloured by the scope and scale of destruction that it had produced. Moreover, insurrection recalibrated the political geography of the city. Humdrum commercial and legal buildings like the General Post Office, the Four Courts, and Jacob's biscuit factory became newly venerated as sites of nationalist defiance, heroism and sacrifice. T.W. Murphy's *Dublin after the six days' insurrection* and *'The 'Sinn Féin' revolt illustrated* featured post-rebellion ruins, provided visual keys to Dublin's fresh ruins.[9] By late August 1916, the *Sinn Fein rebellion handbook* – a cheap (six-pence) guide to the Rising – had sold out. Re-released in 1917, it featured expanded coverage of the damage that the suppression of the rebellion had inflicted, with notes on the progress of reconstruction and guidelines for filing property compensation claims.[10]

On the Continent, French and Belgian newspapers, whose columns regularly featured 'ruines et dévastation', reported the material damage caused by the Rising and speculated on its cost. To bolster the French war effort, the French press took up the 'German plot' line of their British allies while stressing staunch Irish loyalty to the allied cause. In early May, *Le Petit Journal* described Dublin as 'a city of death and desolation, where many streets are nothing but smoking ruins'; 'houses are gutted and materials of all kinds litter the ground'. Several days later, it reported that 'the destruction of half of the lower part of Sackville Street is complete'.[11] *Le Matin* also focused on physical damage and the disruption to trade: 'The destruction of built properties is enormous. At least twenty major trading houses, three bank branches, dozens of offices and smaller shops were burned to the ground'.[12] From Belgium, *Le Bruxellois* reported that in Sackville Street ('one of the most beautiful in the city'), 'all the buildings are destroyed' and that 'one sees only the smoking debris'.[13]

Initially the Rising's transformative influence was ignored. Slowly though the sombre mood changed as the execution of key leaders articulated the rebellion as tragedy. Unlike the devastation of Louvain or Rheims, treated only as negative, the British destruction of Dublin quickly developed a counter-narrative – that it signalled the resurrection of Ireland. Schooled in the Fenian myth of the Phoenix, Patrick Pearse associated ruin with rebirth in both cultural and physical terms. Contemplating the fires consuming rebel headquarters, he assured his former St Enda's pupil, Desmond Ryan, that the rubble would prove a nest for the risen Irish people. 'Dublin's name will be glorious forever. Men will speak of her as one of the splendid cities, as they speak now of Paris!'[14]

8 Mo Moulton, *Ireland and the Irish in interwar England* (Cambridge, 2014), p. 27.   9 *Dublin after the six days' insurrection: thirty-one pictures from the camera of Mr T.W. Murphy* (Dublin, 1916); *The 'Sinn Féin' revolt illustrated, April 1916* (Dublin, 1916).   10 *The Sinn Fein rebellion handbook. Easter 1916* [1917 issue], compiled by the *Weekly Irish Times* (Dublin, 1917).   11 *Le Petit Journal*, 2 May, 5 May 1916.   12 *Le Matin*, 4 May 1916.   13 *Le Bruxellois*, 3–4 May 1916.   14 McGarry,

Pearse's perception was accurate in political if not in architectural terms. Yeats' conception of the Easter Rising in the Gothic Sublime register of the rough birthing of a 'terrible beauty' echoed earlier European commentary on the 'wonderful ruin' of Rheims. The 'shattered glass and toppling masonry' that littered Dublin's streets in the aftermath of rebellion were recycled from 'the ruins of time' to 'build mansions in eternity'.[15] Damage and destruction presented a shared experience through which Ireland and France were forced to contextualize their varied war experiences. While the extent and cost of the damage remained greatly imbalanced between two disparate countries, the empathy was genuine. A common thread of victimhood and ruined spaces existed, helping to articulate separate national traumas in France and Ireland arising from the First World War and the 1916 Rising.[16]

WAR DAMAGE AND THE 1916 RISING

Contemporary observers noted several Franco-Irish parallels in the wake of the Easter Rising.[17] *The Liverpool Daily Post* deemed the rebellion 'a literary revolution' and 'a students' revolution'. It mused that something 'strangely Parisian' was afoot in Dublin. 'Has not this revolution in some sense a genesis in the Irish theatre?' it asked; 'Where out of Paris would you find the Countess Markievicz?' Dublin now exhibited 'the heady wine of the French Revolution in new bottles'. Despite the proximity of the First World War, in both time and space, more immediate comparisons did not initially develop, though not for want of coverage. Since August 1914, Irish newspapers featured a blend of military and civilian experiences, including the evacuation of Paris,[18] destruction visited on the city by bombs dropped from aeroplanes,[19] and how, after the great retreat from the Marne, 'Parisians spent their Sunday at leisure' cycling to adjacent battlefields to retrieve souvenirs.[20] The *Kerry News* reported in September 1914: 'the Gare de l'Est was crowded with returning trippers, mostly bringing back relics of the war, in the shape of German helmets, fragments of shells, cartridges, and weapons'.[21]

The Rising, p. 196.   **15** Apocalyptic visions visit Stephen Dedalus several times throughout James Joyce's *Ulysses*, which the character perceives as incorporating 'shattered glass and toppling masonry'. This is influenced by William Blake, who conceived of the world ending in flames; Joyce also incorporated concepts of rebirth, influenced by Blake's letter to William Hayley on the death of his son: 'Every mortal loss is an immortal gain. The ruins of time build mansions in eternity'. Yeats had popularised an 'Irish' Blake in his introduction to his 1893 and 1903 editions of his *Poems of William Blake*, where he claimed that Blake's grandparents had kept a shebeen in Rathmines.   **16** Justin Dolan Stover, 'Violence, trauma and memory in Ireland: the psychological impact of war and revolution on a liminal society, 1916–1923' in J. Crouthamel & P. Leese (eds), *Psychological trauma and the legacies of the First World War* (Switzerland, 2017), pp 117–40.   **17** *Connacht Tribune*, 6 May 1916.   **18** Niall Ferguson, *The pity of war* (New York, 1999), p. 186.   **19** *Irish Independent*, 31 Aug. 1914; *Kerry News*, 2 Sept. 1914.   **20** *Irish Independent*, 28 Sept. 1914, p. 3.   **21** *Kerry News*, 14 Sept. 1914.

The First World War and the Irish Revolution permitted civilians to penetrate normally sealed conflict boundaries in various ways, including civilian souvenir hunting and looting. A more considered view of the Easter Rising, however, might integrate what happened in the city as *preparation* for rebellion. In this regard, Dublin in 1916 resembled the Paris of 1870–1. Barricades and street fighting during the Paris Commune – particularly during the Bloody Week (21–28 May 1871) – foreshadowed Dublin's Easter Week experience. The construction of barricades throughout Dublin and the digging of trenches suggest that the military strategy of the rebel leaders harked back to France's revolutionary past, as much as towards the contemporary European conflict. Pearse, Connolly and Plunkett had all lectured on the principles of urban warfare prior to 1916; they were fascinated by the construction of barricades – a traditionally French urban form of republican revolt.[22] Robert Emmet, who had personal experience of revolutionary Paris, had also devoted considerable thought to the importance of barricades in his thinking on an urban insurrection in 1803. It was, after all, the very type of conflict that they had anticipated – frustrate the enemy's movement, incite large-scale communal resistance and inflict sufficient casualties to weaken Britain's resolve to stay in Ireland. By choosing to fortify locations in the heart of the city, the rebels banked on support and sympathy from their own people. They were also well aware that all the British barracks from which troops could be despatched to dislodge them were located outside the inner city perimeter that they sought to establish.

Early efforts to fortify positions and to erect barricades throughout the city and suburbs resulted in minor if widespread damage. After ejecting clerks and their customers from the General Post Office (GPO) on Easter Monday, Volunteers smashed its windows and barricaded them with mailbags filled with sand, coal and 'all the available books'.[23] On the roof, rebels bored through slate to establish communication with the floors below. They continued to burrow between buildings throughout the week, establishing communication lines and avoiding enemy fire. Such networks could connect entire building blocks. Arthur Agnew, Peadar Bracken and Joe Good dug through Kelly's gunsmiths at O'Connell Bridge toward Middle Abbey Street, emerging in Elvery's several buildings away.[24] Boring their way toward the Imperial Hotel, Kevin McCabe and his comrades found that some of the walls at Clery's department store were 'three feet thick'. This small-scale destruction was proleptic of the broader destruction that would be visited upon the Sackville Street area over the following week.[25]

---

22 Donal Fallon, 'While Dublin was reproducing its squalid version of the Paris Commune' in *Come Here to Me!: Dublin Life and Culture blog*, 13 Jan. 2016.   23 Bureau of Military History, James Kavanagh, Witness Statement 889; Michael O'Reilly, Witness Statement 886; Seán MacEntee, Witness Statement 1,052; *Kerry News*, 1 May 1916.   24 Arthur P. Agnew, Bureau of Military History, Witness Statement 152, p. 4; *Sinn Féin rebellion handbook*, p. 12. 25 Kevin McCabe, Bureau of Military History, Witness Statement 926, p. 8.

Confiscation of goods, explosives and munitions also preceded the rebellion. In an improvised initiative, Fianna Éireann boys and Irish Volunteers sought to ignite the British army high explosive and ammunition reserve in the Phoenix Park.[26] The manoeuvre failed because the high explosives had been previously transferred to England for the war effort.[27] Small fires did consume some small arms and ammunition, which produced a 'dull boom' as the saboteurs departed.[28] Soldiers and the fire brigade extinguished the fires the following day.[29]

Other preparations were made along the river Liffey to prevent movement and to secure retreat routes. The Four Courts provided a commanding view, and also acted as a bulwark against British reinforcements coming down the quays from the huge barracks and the railway termini on the western fringes of the city.[30] Its windows were smashed and barricades constructed from the weighty tomes of its Law Library (a practice that would be replicated during the Civil War).[31] It was the honeycomb of tightly packed streets and alleys behind the Four Courts that truly entrenched the rebels. Dublin Volunteers established various positions along Church Street and its maze of side streets, preparing barricades from local sources and smashing glass bottles on the road to impede cavalry movement.[32]

The composition of barricades in rebel strongholds reflected the rebels' unapologetic practicality. Paving stones, carts and other vehicles gave the impression that the street extended up into the barriers. Pubs were raided for furniture and barrels. Because pubs were often located on strategic corners, some were occupied, such as Reilly's pub on North King street; private homes, too, were stripped of furnishings that were piled up to congest the area.[33] Bicycles, cars, builder's rubbish all supplemented barriers throughout the city.[34] A useful function was found for the staunchly unionist *Irish Times*, as large drums of paper from its office formed a barricade in Lower Abbey Street. 'A young man of the student type' poured petrol on it and ignited it as troops advanced.[35] These practices were not unique to any one area, as the *Kerry Weekly Reporter* later onveyed:

> The rebels were not particular how they got barricades. At Sackville St. and East-street corner one is made of cushions, chairs, furniture, etc., seized from Tyler's shop nearby, which is a wreck. The barricade in

26 Charles Townshend, *Easter 1916: the Irish rebellion* (London, 2006), p. 155.   **27** Derek Molyneux & Darren Kelly, *When the clock struck in 1916: close-quarter combat in the Easter Rising* (Cork, 2015), pp 9–22; Eamon Murphy, 'The raid on the magazine fort, Phoenix Park, Easter Monday 1916' (www.fiannaeireannhistory.wordpress.com/).   **28** Molyneux & Kelly, *When the clock struck in 1916*, p. 21; McGarry, *The Rising*, p. 138.   **29** *Belfast Newsletter*, 4 May 1916; *Irish Examiner*, 3 May 1916.   **30** Molyneux & Kelly, *When the clock struck in 1916*, p. 171.   **31** *Leitrim Observer*, 13 May 1916.   **32** Francis X. Coghlan, Bureau of Military History, Witness Statement, 1760, p. 2. Molyneux & Kelly, *When the clock struck in 1916*, pp 169–70.   **33** Ignatius Callender, Bureau of Military History, Witness Statement 923, p. 8.   **34** Coghlan, Witness Statement 1760, p. 4.   **35** *Irish Independent*, 13 May 1916.

Sackville-place is made from old packing cases raided from White's shop. In Lower Abbey-street there is a barricade made of new bicycles, cycle accessories of all kinds, and barbed wire taken from neighbouring shops, and near Jacob's biscuit works there is a barricade of flour and sugar sacks.[36]

Raiding of retailers and traders to stock barricades and occupation of buildings extended the Rising's economic impact beyond interruption of operating hours. Compensation claims for property losses cited destruction of inventory and loss of revenue. Miss Kathleen Gregg, proprietor of the Antient Concert Rooms of Great Brunswick Street, claimed a loss of bookings as a result of the rebellion, while Devine & Sons, Fruit Sellers of Corporation Market, sought recompense for 358 cases of apples that went off while awaiting collection at the North Wall. Neither Gregg nor Devine were compensated.[37] By midweek, British soldiers had pivoted from frontal assaults to construct their own barricades on streets and within buildings. One such position, on Moore Street, comprised 'butchers' blocks, crates and barrels, as well as a pony van that was turned on its side'.[38] The Inniskilling Fusiliers prepared a barricade in Lower Gardiner Street from goods raided from Redmond's Pawnbroker & Jewellers, which included fifteen beds and three tables.[39] Purcell's tobacco shop, at 22 Westmoreland Street, was gutted to accommodate a machine-gun nest.[40]

South of the river, Volunteers also prepared defences to impede reinforcement by British troops. The Grand Canal and docklands provided natural barriers, but the bridges and rail lines linking Kingstown to the city required immediate attention. On Monday morning, Volunteers destroyed communication lines and began to occupy and barricade key positions along the canal, and on surrounding streets and buildings.[41] Bolted rail joints ('fish plates'), were lifted to disconnect rails while trenches were dug along the lines between Beggars Bush and Westland Row.[42] These preparations, which also included barricading railway workshops alongside the track, allowed Volunteers to control both the place and the pace of likely engagement. Uprooting and trenching the line would 'prevent an armoured train or the like from passing through'.[43] On Wednesday, Sean O'Keefe and his colleagues reinforced barricades at the railway timber yard, destroyed telephone installations, trenched rail lines, and erected barbed wire that was eventually extended nearly a mile to cover positions between Erne

---

36 *Kerry Weekly Reporter*, 6 May 1916.   37 Claim of Kathleen Gregg, Property Losses (Ireland) Committee, PLIC/1/0798 and D. Devine & Sons, PLIC/1/4763.   38 Barry Kennerk, 'Compensating for the Rising: the papers of the Property Losses (Ireland) Committee, 1916', *History Ireland*, 21:2 (2013), pp 31–4.   39 Claim of Laurence Redmond, 96 Lower Gardiner Street, National Archives of Ireland (NAI), Property Losses (Ireland) Committee (PLIC)/1/1304.   40 NAI, PLIC/1/0495; Eamonn Bulfin Bureau of Military History, Witness Statement 497, pp 8–9.   41 Seán O'Keefe, Bureau of Military History, Witness Statement 188, p. 6.   42 Joseph O'Connor, Bureau of Military History, Witness Statement 157, p. 27.   43 O'Connor, Witness Statement 157, p. 27.

Street and South Lotts Road.[44] Because they were such an obvious way to move large numbers of British troops quickly into the heart of the city, Dublin's railway and tram systems were explicitly targeted and they experienced the most significant material damage.[45] Occupation and destruction of Dublin and South-Eastern Railway property cost the company £2,000.[46]

Trenching was not confined to rail lines but also impacted some of Dublin's best-known public spaces, like Stephen's Green. An eye-witness told Irish readers:

> Immediately hostilities were opened, the rebels prepared to hold on to Stephen's Green at all costs. They copied the methods employed in the much greater conflict now being waged on the Continent, and hurried forward the work of digging trenches. Four lines of fairly deep entrenchments were dug, and the rebels, who were well supplied with ammunition, held themselves in readiness to meet an attack.[47]

Séamus Kavanagh arrived at Stephen's Green at one o'clock on Easter Monday and proceeded to organise its defence. He inspected the circumference of the Green, and ordered trenches to be dug at the different gate entrances, as well as barricades to be erected from commandeered bicycles, cars and cabs between Stephen's Green and the Russell Hotel.[48] James O'Shea and Jim Fox dug a trench facing down Dawson Street, 'putting some bushes around it as camouflage', while outfitting the trench with a shelf for bombs and shotguns by 'cutting into the earth'.[49]

The *Northampton Chronicle* reported that 'the rebels barricaded St Stephen's Green with motor-cars and tramcars, as in the French Revolution,' to which the *Donegal News* replied: 'The 1789 models of motor-cars and tramcars are of course out of date by now'.[50] *Le Figaro*'s description of the garrison drew on a familiar French analogy that described the insurgents in Stephen's Green as establishing 'un Fort Chabrol', aligning their fortification of the Dublin park with Jules Guérin's Parisian stronghold during the Dreyfus affair. 'They are now desperate and remain inaccessible to all means of conviction other than force'.[51] Guérin held out for twenty-three days, while the overlooked Stephen's Green capitulated after a week's bombardment by machine guns from the adjacent Shelbourne Hotel. A Kerry newspaper reported 'an appalling picture of litter and earth and holes and damaged property' in Stephen's Green.[52]

44 O'Keefe, Witness Statement 188, pp 7–8. Molyneux & Kelly, *When the clock struck in 1916*, p. 46.   45 *The Liberator* (Tralee), 2 May 1916; Townshend, *Easter 1916*, p. 178; Richard Hayes, Bureau of Military History, Witness Statement 97, pp 3–4.   46 'The railways during the Rising,' in *Sinn Féin rebellion handbook*, p. 31.   47 *Irish Examiner*, 4 May 1916; *Kerry Advocate*, 6 May 1916.   48 Séamus Kavanagh, Bureau of Military History, Witness Statement 1670.   49 James O'Shea, Bureau of Military History, Witness Statement 733.   50 *Donegal News*, 27 May 1916.   51 *Le Figaro*, 30 April 1916.   52 *Kerry Weekly Reporter*, 6

As the week progressed, established rebel bases and commandeered positions succumbed to fire from artillery shelling, or were intentionally burned. Irish Volunteers occupied Clanwilliam House in Ballsbridge due to its strategic position in the Mount Street Bridge area overlooking Northumberland Road. It eventually burned down to its braces, despite guarantees given to the owner that the structure would be evacuated unharmed. On Wednesday of Easter Week, the Linenhall Barracks on Coleraine Street, north of the Four Courts, was intentionally burned, as it was deemed to be too large to occupy. 'Cans of oil and flammable paint [were] poured throughout the building' to act as chemical kindling.[53] As it spread, fire engulfed the stores of oil, which exploded and filled the air with thick smoke. As it escalated, the fire claimed the adjacent Moore & Alexander's Chemists, producing a blaze that could be seen for miles.[54] Seán Prendergast described this fire as a 'new and perhaps extremely frightful feature in the long series of thrills', something 'awesome, fearsome and amazing', 'a spectacle beyond description and comprehension':

> It resembled a huge burning furnace, a veritable inferno. The belching flames that shot skyward lit up a wide area and transformed an otherwise dark night into uncommonly lurid brightness, brighter even than daylight.[55]

Because night fires and day plumes were visible all over the city, these conflagrations certainly amplified the Rising's emotional weight – suggesting a more significant overlap with war damage experienced on the Continent. Louisa Norway was 'spell-bound': 'the whole city was on fire, the glow extending right across the heavens, and the red glare hundreds of feet high, while above the roar of the fires the whole air seemed vibrating with the noise of the great guns and machine guns. It was an inferno!'[56] John MacDonagh, looking out from Jacob's factory, interpreted the flames positively: the fires 'heartened us, for it showed the magnitude of the Rising, which we knew would change the whole position of Ireland'.[57]

Dublin continued to smoulder for weeks after the Rising, as rebels and alleged collaborators were removed to jails and internment camps throughout Britain. 'The smell of smoke in the air and the spectacle of charred corpses' were, in the words of the *Evening Herald*, evidence that 'the nightmare has not yet passed'.[58] Inquiries into the origins of the rebellion, discussions of the government's failure

---

May 1916.   **53** Molyneux & Kelly, *When the clock struck in 1916*, pp 183–4.   **54** Molyneux & Kelly, *When the clock struck in 1916*, p. 184; *Sunday Independent*, 14 May 1916. Garry Holohan revisited Hugh More & Alexander, wholesale chemists in 1917, installing lighting to their new offices, on exactly the same site that he and his comrades had torched the previous year. Gary Holohan, Bureau of Military History, Witness Statement 336, pp 10–11.   **55** Seán Prendergast, Bureau of Military History, Witness Statement 755, pp 137–8.   **56** McGarry, *The Rising*, p. 194.   **57** John McDonagh, Bureau of Military History, Witness Statement 532, p. 13.   **58** *Evening Herald*, 4 May 1916.

to prevent it, debates about the clean-up, and strategies for compensation and rebuilding reverberated through the summer. Parisian parallels were again presented. The conservative tabloid, *Daily Sketch*, opined that just as Paris had suffered at the hands of the 1871 Communards so, too, 'does Dublin today, with its blazing buildings, shattered street-barricades, and piles of wreckage, present as tragic a spectacle as if the city had indeed been shelled by an invading foe'.[59]

WAR DAMAGE IN PARIS

The Rising occurred at the height of First World War, at a time when the vast scale of military attrition and the sieges of Paris in 1914 and 1918 hogged the media headlines. Concentrated bombings – particularly in 1918 – produced an immediate tension and acute fear, descriptions of which complement rebels' experiences during Easter Week.[60] The January 1919 edition of *Excelsior* comprehensively mapped the extent of bombings in Paris between 23 March and 8 August 1918. Its list of impact sites distinguished between aerial and artillery bombardment, and detailed the number killed and wounded at each location – numbers that exceeded Parisians' understanding of the sheer extent of the war damage inflicted on the capital.[61]

The impact of damage and destruction in Paris was experienced individually as well as collectively. Ruined urban landscapes prompted both anger and resolve, and helped to solidify communal strength. An intimate view of such damage can be seen in the records of the Centre Culturel Irlandais, the site of the former Irish College in Paris. The college suffered significant damage during the Franco-Prussian War, and then survived attempts at religious liquidation during the Commune, but it endured the First World War while situated right in the eye of the storm.[62] The Superior, Patrick Boyle, recalled not only the impact and proximity of bombardment within the fifth arrondissement, but the public response to it. His letters detail aerial bombing raids that destroyed portions of the nearby Boulevard St Germain and Boulevard St Michel, as well as a string of homes and businesses between the Jardin de Luxembourg and the Pantheon, right on the college's doorstep. Boyle explained that the approaching German airplanes were usually observed before they reached the city:

59 Fallon, 'While Dublin was reproducing its squalid version of the Paris Commune'. **60** Stéphane Audoin-Rouzeau, 'Paris bombardé, 1914–1918' in J.M. Largeaud & P. Chassaigne (eds), *Villes en guerre, 1914–1945* (Paris, 2004), pp 31–6. The Germans sought to elicit a bombardment psychosis in Paris to hasten a French surrender: Emmannuelle Danchin, *Le temps des ruines, 1914–1921* (Rennes, 2015), p. 43.   **61** Audoin-Rouzeau, 'Paris bombardé', p. 33.   **62** Justin Dolan Stover, 'Witness to war: Charles Ouin-la-Croix and the Irish College Paris, 1870–1921', *Études Irlandaises*, 36:2 (2011), pp 21–38.

> Immediately the alarm was given by the fire-brigade which drove through
> the streets at full speed, its trumpet emitting a most piercing sound. On
> hearing the signal of danger people rushed to the cellar for protection and
> on the porch of all houses and public buildings where there were cellars,
> notice was posted up with the words: *Abris pour 200 ou 1000*. [Shelters for
> 200 or 1000]

Paris fell within range of *la grosse Bertha* in late March 1918. Boyle recalled that
'a shell fell in the city every twenty minutes from 7am to 12.30'. Despite the
more frequent bombardment in April 1918, 'Parisians showed great coolness and
all business went on as usual'.

Assessment and remuneration for damage caused during the Easter Rising
was uneven. Insurance clauses, claims lodged collectively and strict reinstate-
ment requirements slowed Dublin's restoration. Style was also debated. In June
1916 the Royal Institute of Architects of Ireland urged the home secretary to
ensure that builders observe conformity, 'harmony and symmetry' when
undertaking reconstruction. In most instances, buildings were repaired on their
original lines, negating the potential for Pearse's Parisian parallel and denying
Dublin any Haussmannesque rebirth.

Other sites remained in ruins throughout the post-Rising and War of
Independence period, suggesting an Irish body politic ideologically transformed
but still physically wounded. Significant damage from the Easter Rising
remained unrepaired even after the formation of the Irish Free State in 1922. In
1924, Labour leader Thomas Johnson identified this enduring disrepair as an
impediment to national healing in the wake of civil war: 'There will be no real
revival of industry and trade until a determined effort is made to efface these
visual reminders of our recent agony'.[63] Wartime inflation, a shortage of builders
and material, and demobilisation contributed to reconstruction delays. By
comparison, Paris prioritised the clearing of barricades and urban restoration in
the wake of the Commune (except for the Tuileries Palace, which was not
demolished until 1883). The French conducted surveys of damaged and
destroyed villages, and had already planned for regeneration along the Western
Front years prior to the 1918 Armistice.[64]

CONCLUSION

Conflict nurtured the Franco-Irish relationship over centuries, drawing
specifically on religious connections and republican ideals to strengthen its bond.
The materially uneven though devastating experiences of modern war and

---

63 *Irish Times*, 26 April 1924.   **64** Danchin, 'Penser les ruines de l'apres-guerres' in *Le temps
des ruines, 1914–1921*, pp 95–122.

revolution further cemented this connection. While the devastated *departements* of northern France and Belgium were on an entirely different scale, the 1916 Easter Rising demonstrated a concentrated episode of similar devastation, and this was one of several significant spikes in urban destruction throughout the broader revolutionary period, which included the sack of Balbriggan, the burning of Cork, the destruction of Thurles, and further damage wrought on Dublin in 1922. France remained central to the narrative of Irish victimhood throughout this period, and anchored foreign recognition of the Irish independence movement. To many in France, the Great War reinforced a common bond of persecution and framed the chronology of the Irish question. In early 1920, George Gavan Duffy, Irish republican envoy to Paris, outlined the development of Irish nationalism from the French point of view: 'before the war … during the war [… and] after the war'.[65] Similarly, Denis Morgan, Chairman of the Thurles Urban Council, claimed that the destruction of his town in January 1920 by British auxiliary policemen rivaled the ruin of Flanders.[66]

For many others, the Rising exposed Britain's hypocrisy in claiming to be the defender of small nationalities, whose ideals were crushed by German atrocities in Belgium. The Dublin socialist and Irish Volunteer Seán Prendergast reflected on the Irish experience, underlining the relativist view toward war damage echoed by many during the Irish Revolution:

> With the blackened walls and tumbled ruins of Dublin echoing the volleys of firing squads, shooting down surrendered prisoners whose crime was to love their native land and to yearn for its independence and liberty, we hope, for decency's sake, we shall hear no more snivelling in America over broken stained-glass or shattered statues in Rheims or Louvain. With the blood of Irish prisoners and patriots reddening poor Ireland's soil in streams, we hope for decency's sake that we shall hear no more of England's passionate and heroic sympathy for the rights and liberties of small peoples.[67]

65 George Gavan Duffy, 'La Question Irlandaise: exposée par un Sinn-Feiner', *Les Cahiers*, 23 April 1920 (NLI, P. 2282). 66 Albert Coyle, *Evidence on conditions in Ireland comprising the complete testimony, affidavits and exhibits presented before the American Commission on Conditions in Ireland* (Washington, DC, 1921), pp 18–19. 67 Prendergast, Witness Statement 755, pp 192–3.

Paris, diplomatic capital of the world: Sinn Féin diplomatic initiatives, 1919–21

PIERRE RANGER

INTRODUCTION

From January to June 1919, the Versailles Peace Conference gathered in the Hall of Mirrors the most powerful men – and they were all men – in the world in Paris. From a teleological perspective, the event is now remembered for the stubborn failure of its participants to think through the strategic consequences of their decisions. Versailles had to handle the aftermath of the most catastrophic international conflict of modern times. The human destruction had been unprecedented, the future looked gloomy, Europe was awash in widows and wounded, some territories had been wiped out in the north of France, the political context was particularly unstable. The aftershocks of the Russian Revolution convulsed Europe after 1917, the Austro-Hungarian empire was disintegrating under the pressure of competing nationalist demands, the German Empire was finished, the Weimar Republic was wracked by conflicts that endangered its survival, even the British Empire had suffered a reverse in Dublin in 1916.[1]

Irish political life was far from immune to the general sense of European turbulence. 1919 signalled the start of the War of Independence that ended with the creation of an Irish Free State in January 1922. Two demoralising years of civil war followed. Sinn Féin, the political party that inherited the independence project after its resounding victory in the 1918 election, contemplated this agitated European context as it pondered how best to further its quest for internal and external legitimacy. Knowing that the European map was being redrawn in Paris inspired Irish advanced nationalists to anticipate solutions that dismantled or dramatically reconfigured the imperial framework.

Moreover, radical Irish nationalism enjoyed a long tradition of looking abroad, particularly to France, for concrete help and ideological inspiration. Any enemy of Great Britain was a potential ally. Diplomatic relations in the early twentieth century were becoming more complex, as newly-formed international organisations began to codify an emerging international law. If Sinn Féin craved

---

1 Introduction to Margaret MacMillan, *Peacemakers: six months that changed the world* (London, 2001).

international recognition and legitimacy for Ireland, it needed to stake its claim in this post-war world order.

The republican party included two novel elements in its new constitution of October 1917: Ireland's demands should be heard at the Peace Conference after the war, and Sinn Féin delegates would be sent abroad to promote Irish interests when the war ended. In February 1919, this diplomatic policy was implemented, with Paris as the chosen venue.

THE PEACE CONFERENCE: SINN FÉIN'S QUEST FOR RECOGNITION

In February 1919, Paris witnessed unprecedented media, political and diplomatic excitement. The salons and the cafés resounded with questions and speculations concerning the decisions to be taken by the victorious powers. The global gaze was focussed on Paris, as were many colonised people's hopes. Ho-Chi-Minh, a Chinese cook in the Ritz restaurant, petitioned for his small Asian homeland. Egyptian delegates, suffragettes, African-Americans seeking equality – all rubbed shoulders in Paris. Sinn Féin were also there. Sean T. O'Kelly, Dáil spokesman, and founder member of the second Sinn Féin party, was their first diplomat to arrive on 8 February 1919. He opened a bureau in the Grand Hotel, close to the Opera Garnier, a well-chosen location, as it was near the Crillon Hotel where the American delegation set up its office, close to Concorde Square and the French Foreign Office, where the initial tentative peace treaty meetings were taking place.

From his prison cell, Arthur Griffith, founder of Sinn Féin, journalist and propagandist, presented his recommendations a few days before O'Kelly's arrival in Paris. He encouraged fostering a French network of support for the Irish cause:

> As to French politicians, George Barry, and Denys Cochin more or less Royalists and Catholic leaders, are powerful, especially the latter, and the former is very sympathetic. Lucian Millevoye, the nationalist, is a fairly strong man and sympathetic.[2]

Cochin was a conservative Catholic who had rallied to the Republic during the war. Lucien Millevoye (Maud Gonne's lover during the 1890s) was an extremely anglophobic boulangiste. Within the diverse political and intellectual world of French nationalism, a Parisian network of support for Ireland had evolved that was well known to Griffith as he and Gonne had built it.[3]

---

2 O'Kelly to Cathal Brugha, the Dáil president, NAI, Gavan Duffy Papers, MS 1125, Files 1 to 5.   3 Pierre Ranger, *La France vue d'Irlande. Histoire du mythe français de Parnell à l'Etat Libre* (Rennes, 2011), pp 122–222.

O'Kelly rolled up his sleeves, setting aside temporarily the old guard of Franco-Irish friendships. He sought to impact French politics on a grander scale than mere political agitation. On 22 February 1919, he petitioned Georges Clémenceau, the French prime minister and Peace Conference president, seeking Irish credentials for the conference. By 7 March, he had delivered a petition to the 71 delegates staying in Paris.[4] These two initiatives fell on deaf ears.

O'Kelly soon realised that Irish access to the conference was being stonewalled. Sinn Féin lacked any credible support network to relay its demands, the British were adamantly opposed (Tardieu noted that 'every one gave way to the British objections') and Clemenceau himself was at very best lukewarm about Irish demands.[5] He wanted to placate Great Britain, his closest ally in negotiating the conditions to be imposed on Germany. There was also the 1916 Rising. Since then, French political circles, manipulated by the British press, nursed a persistent grudge against an Ireland that they regarded as pro-German.[6] André Tardieu, the Franco-American business commissioner, summed it up: 'During the war, Sinn Feiners harboured and supplied German submarines and took German gold to pay for Casement's treason'.[7]

Rebuffed by the French, O'Kelly approached the American delegation – his premier objective in Paris. Since Woodrow Wilson was on public record supporting the principle of self-determination, kindling great expectations in colonised peoples globally, Irish hopes were high that the president would support Irish independence.[8] These hopes were quickly dashed. O'Kelly wrote on 7 March 1919:

> I called at the Hotel [Crillon] and after some trouble saw [Herbert] Hoover who gave the published explanation in which he spoke of 'an unfortunate misunderstanding'. He promised faithfully to investigate the matter fully and to write me later. I have never had any communication from him since, though I called a few times at his hotel to remind him of his promise.[9]

Some days later Wilson returned to the United States. The 'unfortunate misunderstanding' concerned Ireland's possible seat at the conference. The American president wanted to avoid at all costs entanglement in British domestic policy. Bamboozled by Lloyd George, Wilson had quickly caved in to British demands that the principle of self-determination should apply only to the defeated countries. Wilson was persuaded by Lloyd George's argument that Irish national claims were illegitimate as Irish people already lived in a democratic British state. The American delegation was instructed to discourage any Irish

4 NAI, DFA, Early Series, Paris 1919. 5 André Tardieu, *The truth about the Treaty* (Indianapolis, 1921), p. 122. 6 Mervyn O'Driscoll, *Ireland, Germany and the Nazis* (Dublin, 2004), p. 25. 7 Tardieu, *The truth about the Treaty*. Clemenceau supplied the introduction. Originally published as La Paix. 8 Michael Hopkinson, *The Irish War of Independence* (Dublin, 2002), pp 20–1. 9 NAI, DFA, Early Series, Paris 1919.

hopes. This choice was reinforced when Irish initiatives clashed with Anglo-American relations. When an American delegation supporting the Irish claim for independence sought permission to enter Ireland, Wilson convinced Lloyd George to allow them in. O'Kelly noted the warm welcome received by the Americans: 'they were charmed beyond measure with their wonderful reception and with all they saw and heard while in Ireland'.[10]

However, the consequences proved disastrous. The American delegates in Ireland delivered passionate speeches against British domination and Lloyd George, a master manipulator, accused Wilson of fomenting Irish separatism. This alarmed the diplomatically naïve American president, who believed that he needed unconditional British support to implement his grand plan of a society of nations.[11] He immediately took American support for Irish independence off the table during the peace negotiations. Griffith engaged in damage limitation with Sinn Féin back home: 'If we don't get in – which I suspect is possible – we shall stand on the stairs and harangue the world outside'.[12]

In his view, it was more than ever necessary to convince the world of the legitimacy of Irish demands for independence and of Sinn Féin's ability to bear the responsibility that came with it. This was also politically prudent as the Parliamentary Party, trounced in 1918, berated inexperienced Sinn Féin as lacking the maturity to safeguard Ireland's interest.

1919–21: PERSEVERANCE

O'Kelly, fighting an uphill battle, could not contemplate coming back to Ireland empty-handed as it was in Europe that Sinn Féin needed to make its mark in the quest for recognition. France, its newspapers and its public opinion remained prime targets, all the more so because the idea of unwavering French sympathy for Ireland from the Wild Geese onwards was so strongly ingrained in the Irish nationalist psyche. Moreover, Paris was the ideal location from which to organise diplomacy on a European scale. A Dáil report from August 1919 explained: 'In view of the international importance of Paris, it was essential that the services of Ó Ceallaigh [O'Kelly] should be retained there for the time being'.[13]

A year later, George Gavan Duffy, the second Sinn Féin envoy in Paris, justified keeping a Paris bureau:

> It is the most important international meeting ground. There is there no censorship and comparative liberty of speech and growing hostility to

10 NAI, DFA, Early Series, Paris 1919. 11 Gerard Keown, *First of the small nations, the beginnings of Irish foreign policy in inter-war Europe, 1919–1932* (Oxford, 2016), pp 40–1. 12 Michael Laffan, *The resurrection of Ireland. The Sinn Féin Party, 1916–1923* (Cambridge, 1999), p. 251. 13 *Documents on Irish foreign policy*, vol. 1, 1919, 19 Aug. 1919.

England and a genuine traditional sympathy for Ireland; immense facilities for communications.[14]

Free from British censorship, Paris became a focal point for Sinn Féin political communication as the War of Independence peaked. In February 1921, de Valera suggested to Robert Brennan, the Sinn Féin delegate in the United States, that he should direct his letters to O'Kelly in Paris.[15]

The other major player in Sinn Féin's diplomatic offensive during 1920–1 was George Gavan Duffy (1882–1951), son of Charles Gavan Duffy, the Young Ireland leader. A true Francophile, he moved comfortably in the sophisticated and class-conscious milieu of diplomatic meetings. His knowledge of French was a valuable asset in achieving through propaganda what Sinn Féin could not obtain through direct political activities. On his arrival in Paris in Easter 1919, Gavan Duffy noted:

> The French side of the work here has been most disappointing; the French press and politicians are very anxious to keep on good terms with England and they are so afraid of the Germans that I think this policy will be kept up ... The only way to effective propaganda is to get personal introductions to well-known and influential people and to get French writers interested in this way.[16]

However, he observed a thaw in Parisian journalistic and editing circles early in 1920. On 1 March 1920 he received a proposal from Frédéric Causse-Maël (1892–1951), a much-in-demand literary agent, who had introduced himself to the Sinn Féin envoy as the co-director of the Agence Littéraire Française.[17] Causse-Maël advanced proposals as to how the Irish cause could achieve recognition from the French press. He offered a 'sustained effort in society' that 'would soon garner interest for your cause from politicians and intellectuals whose influence is real'. He suggested co-operating with an information agency, which 'would slip into the sheets sent to the newspapers the telegrams most likely to reverse or eradicate the influence of the English press'.[18] Their strategy should be to infiltrate Parisian intellectual and cultural circles as a means of first influencing public opinion and then political circles.

To ascertain Causse-Maël's reliability, Gavan Duffy consulted the literary critic Maurice Bourgeois, a long-time friend of the Irish cause, a specialist on the Irish Literary Revival, the author of a 1913 work in English on John Millington

---

14 *Documents on Irish foreign policy*, vol. 1, 1920, 1 Aug. 1920.   **15** Eamon de Valera to Robert Brennan, 28 Feb. 1921, NAI, D.É.   **16** Gavan Duffy Papers, NAI, MS 1125, Files 1 to 5. **17** Causse-Maël was the nom de plume of Jean d'Agraives. He published children's books and translated Robert Louis Stevenson's *Island nights' entertainment* for *La Nouvelle Revue Française*.   **18** Gavan Duffy Papers, NAI, 1125, File 9.

Synge and the translator of several of his plays.[19] Bourgeois reassured Gavan Duffy that Causse-Maël did indeed have 'the machinery to help you'.[20]

At the same time, propaganda work was underway via several Parisian newspapers. In May 1920, Gavan Duffy noted: 'All the French correspondents were quite friendly – except perhaps for the *Temps*.'[21] This task was carried out simultaneously with propaganda from Ireland itself. The republican Desmond FitzGerald (1888–1947), chief of publicity, was responsible for maintaining good relations with foreign correspondents in London. He made progress and explained to Gavan Duffy the necessity of 'educating' European journalists about Irish realities.[22] On the same day, Gavan Duffy celebrated his progress with the French press, a consequence of Causse-Maël's connections:

> The French campaign is so much bigger ... I felt sure that it would not be long before the French press generally opened its columns wide to us, in self-defence against England ... we were beyond the pale; but opinion is moving. *L'Eclair* also wants to send a correspondent of its own at our expense to Dublin.[23]

L'Eclair was a virulently anglophobic periodical that had developed significant relations with the Vatican after 1914. Gavan Duffy chose not to work further with this niche newspaper because he was more interested in reaching moderate respected newspapers that were closer to the centre of French political stage, such as *Le Temps* or *Le Journal des Débats*. Above all, Gavan Duffy sought respectability.

He was on the verge of attaining this, so he thought, as a newly anglophobic atmosphere permeated French public opinion in the 1920s. Several issues strained the bond between the war allies, such as the intractable questions of the reparations owed by Germany and the balkanisation of the Ottoman Empire. The spirit in Ireland was becoming friendlier towards France, thus assisting Gavan Duffy's and O'Kelly's propaganda work. This evolution is obvious in the *Freeman's Journal* and the *Independent*, two newspapers well known previously for both their hostility to Sinn Féin and to France's stance towards the Catholic

---

19 Maurice Bourgeois, *John Millington Synge and the Irish theatre* (London, 1913). Bourgeois's close connections with Ireland continued after the Anglo-Irish treaty, as he rendered his services as a translator for the Irish diplomatic delegates on several occasions in 1923. NAI, DFA, Early Series, Paris, 1923. A report of 23 January 1923 also mentioned an article for the *Revue de Genève* that the Irish authorities commissioned from Bourgeois. **20** Gavan Duffy Papers, NAI, 1125. *Le Temps*, 'the most influential paper in France', was careful to guard its privileged access to the French Foreign Office, and dutifully toed the official French line on Ireland. Gavan Duffy was keen to have 'a correspondent from *Le Temps* in Dublin'. **21** Gavan Duffy Papers, NAI, MS 1125. **22** 'The least we can do is in my opinion to educate the correspondents as we have tried to, provide them proved facts, show them how badly they have been informed by the official reports': Gavan Duffy Papers, NAI, MS 1125. **23** Gavan Duffy Papers, NAI, MS 1125.

church, especially after the separation of church and state in 1905. On 7 July 1920, the *Freeman* published a positive report of a public meeting organised by the Catholic MP Marc Sangnier, an old ally of Ireland in France.[24] The *Independent* drew attention to the publicity work done in France by Gavan Duffy and O'Kelly:

> French sympathy with Ireland is centuries old, but it is only quite recently that Frenchmen began to understand the Irish question … numerous French writers have somehow obtained first-hand information as to the position in Ireland.[25]

Nothing concrete actually happened. As Gavan Duffy explained in October 1920, he only managed to solicit support from people already friendly to the Irish cause: some on the left, but mostly extreme right-wing, Catholic and conservative men who had already been convinced by Gonne's and Griffith's earlier endeavours:

> Catholics generally are friendly. The Socialists support Ireland on principle, but nearly all hate the hold of religion in Ireland. The other third broadly constitutes the Bloc National, the inert and selfish mass without ideals. On its left wing are the Radicals who are fiercely anti-clerical, dominated by the Masonic interests. The Bloc National is no lover of England, but it is too wise to antagonise a friend it expects to need.[26]

On 5 October 1921, Pierre Benoit (writer and future member of the *Académie Française*) contacted O'Kelly about his most recent novel, *La chaussée des géants* [The Giant's Causeway].[27] Benoit was then only starting his career, but his reputation rapidly soared as an intellectual close to Maurras and his mouthpiece *Action Française*. Benoit's novel was published serially by the *Revue Universelle* (founded in April 1920 by Jacques Bainville and Henri Massis and one of Maurras' publications).

In the end, the only tangible reaction to Sinn Féin's activities in France was inglorious: Gavan Duffy was expelled from the country in September 1920. Duffy declared:

---

24 Marc Sangnier (1873–1950), a Christian Democrat, was founder of the Sillon movement that sought to align Catholicism with French Republican and socialist ideals, to provide a moderate alternative to anticlerical labour movements. This doctrine had been condemned by Pope Pius X in 1912. He wanted to establish a democratic republic between the traditional left and right. In his opinion, Christianity was the moral foundation of democracy. In 1905, he launched the *Eveil démocratique* and in 1912 he created the League of the Young Republic that drew on Sillonist thinking.   25 *Irish Independent*, 3 January 1920.   26 Memorandum of France toward Ireland, 10 Oct. 1920, NAI, Gavan Duffy Papers, MS 1125.   27 He was reported to have told him 'I am more of a Sinn Féiner than you': NAI, DFA, Early Series, 1921.

The French Govt. is very sorry it took the step, which diplomats blame as a blunder because it may not only offend Ireland but also alienate American opinion; therefore, if I return for 3 days, it is likely I may be told I may return 10 days later and that if I then stay and don't make a noise, nothing more will be said.[28]

This optimistic view overestimated French sensitivity to Irish nationalist feelings, as their main concern remained to protect British interests. Political and social unrest in the Arabian peninsula, the danger of a war with Turkish nationalists, the threat of Bolshevik Russia, these fears created tensions in Franco-British relations, but they mostly exposed the French government's vulnerability when confronted with these alarming events. The French were obsessed with curbing Germany, and squeezing it financially to make it pay for war damages. As Clemenceau observed, post-war Germany 'was beaten but not crushed, ready by a rare blending of shameless trickery and pugnacity to aspire to hegemony'.[29] Accordingly the French conviction was that to discipline Germany and manage global turmoil, it must maintain a solid alliance with Great Britain[30] Although tolerated during the Peace Conference, the Sinn Féin delegates became an increasing irritant in 1920 as violence intensified in Ireland. Gavan Duffy paid the price. The French sent him packing, first to Belgium, and then to Rome.

His deportation did not terminate Irish diplomatic efforts throughout Europe. From 1921 onward in Paris, O'Kelly was involved in diplomatic contacts with Vatican representatives and met Mussolini. Gavan Duffy went to Spain in 1921 to carry on his propaganda work. In 1922, while Ireland descended into civil war, he remembered this time with nostalgia and buoyant optimism: 'After the war, no country than ours started its international career with a better potential'.[31]

Sinn Féin suffered from basic limitations in its relations with the European powers between 1919 and 1921. Establishing an alternative administration was a central aspect of Sinn Féin's strategy to attain power in Ireland.[32] It was essential to demonstrate to foreign countries, and the Irish people, that the party had the capacity to govern an independent Ireland. Sinn Féin won the 1918 general election, but this did not end initiatives from more moderate nationalists. Stephen Gwynn, an Irish Parliamentary Party MP until 1918, and Horace Plunkett, founder of the Irish Dominion League, promoted Irish autonomy within the British Empire.[33] In this internal battle, Sinn Féin had to demonstrate the legitimacy of its political and military campaign.

28 NAI, Gavan Duffy Papers, MS 1125. 29 Introduction to Tardieu, *The truth about the Treaty*. 30 Keown, *First of the small nations*, p. 51. 31 Dermot Keogh, 'The origins of the Irish Foreign Service in Europe', *Études Irlandaises*, 7 (1982), pp 145–64. 32 Hopkinson, *Irish War of Independence*, p. 44. 33 Keown, *First of the small nations*, p. 44.

However, the party's human resources were limited and strategically sensitive postings were assigned to young and inexperienced men. Members who had been civil servants at a relatively high level in the British administration were promoted to be Sinn Féin ministers or heads of a governmental department. This situation was exacerbated by lack of money. The Dáil, prohibited by the British, met only eight times between September 1919 and July 1921, and Sinn Féin had real difficulties in raising funds, despite its many branches.[34] The Dáil was never a governing body in actuality and functioned primarily as a propaganda bureau, supporting the actions of its representatives.[35] Diplomacy was one field above all where inexperience and lack of financial means was particularly consequential. O'Kelly often complained in Paris that he was overworked:

> The work I have in hands is I would like to remind you of the highest importance at the moment and it cannot possibly be done to best advantage if I don't get help. It is inhuman to ask one man to carry it on all alone.[36]

This difficulty was not solved in 1919, as shown by a letter O'Kelly received from Dublin the same year on 25 June:

> The distinction between consular work and political activities is clearly realised, and it is our idea that one man shall not hold the dual position if possible. In any event the consular system is only in its infancy, and we are quite alive to the difficulties of getting suitable men.[37]

Sinn Féin's representatives abroad were left free to act upon their own discretion. On 30 January 1920, Gavan Duffy complained that he had not received any formal instructions since October 1919.[38] This situation gave Irish diplomacy a strongly decentralised aspect, involving personal, disjointed and sometimes clashing initiatives.[39] Patrick McCartan, the Sinn Féin envoy in Moscow, who was also in regular contact with Mexican revolutionaries, exhibited strong radical and socialist sympathies, while Gavan Duffy possessed much more cautious and diplomatically acceptable instincts. This dearth of human and material resources prevented the establishment of operations with a larger scope. In June 1920, Gavan Duffy's hopes of creating a news agency in Paris were squashed by a Dáil report which described it as impossible because of cost considerations.[40]

34 Arthur Mitchell, 'Alternative government: exit Britannia – the formation of the Irish National State, 1918–1921' in J. Augusteijn (ed.), *The Irish Revolution, 1913–1923* (New York, 2002), p. 75.   35 Keiko Inoue, 'Propaganda II: Propaganda of Dáil Éireann, 1919–1921' in Augusteijn (ed.), *The Irish Revolution*, pp 87–102.   36 NAI, DFA, Early Series, Paris, 1919. 37 Dáil Eireann, Report of the Propaganda Department, NAI, D.É.   38 NAI, DFA, Early Series, Paris, 1920.   39 Keown, *First of the small nations*, p. 66.   40 Dáil Éireann, Report of the Propaganda Department, NAI, D.É.

DEFINING IRELAND

These meagre results would have been all the more disappointing if a deeper logic did not underlay them, a logic which can best be understood through a more elongated, larger time-frame than the few months of the Peace Conference itself. Did men like Gavan Duffy and O'Kelly, who later proved to be pragmatic in the exercise of power, truly believe that international recognition of an Irish republic was possible? Did they genuinely believe that newly independent Ireland could influence such giant states as France, Great Britain and the United States, and fracture their alliances?

In spite of these odds, they made exceptional efforts, because their objective was not only immediate but also embraced the broader task of drawing the contours of a viable diplomatic service for an independent Ireland. They were imagining and defining a suitable role for this new state in the wider context of bilateral and multilateral diplomacy. This new role had to be conceived in the context of a radically transformed context which saw the establishment of an international community organised around new laws implemented through organisations such as the League of Nations.

Some radical Irish nationalists, firmly influenced by Fenian traditions, maintained the old shibboleth of English difficulties and Irish opportunities during the war. This negative and opportunistic definition of Ireland's place in the world was rendered obsolete in the new diplomatic context after 1919. The war was also a time when these same nationalists sought to link their political destiny to continental Europe. Indeed, the pursuit of these formal alliances, or at least of mutual understanding, preoccupied many soon-to-be Sinn Féiners during the conflict.

In this swirling diplomatic context, Gavan Duffy and O'Kelly rethought the project initiated during the war years. Both overestimated the strategic, economic and geopolitical weight of Ireland. This is illustrated by a memorandum about the attitude of France towards Ireland by Gavan Duffy:

> The French Government is in a critical position internationally and very uncertain of itself. It is living under very abnormal conditions and is nervous. It has not yet realised what the Republic of Ireland may mean for France.[41]

Because of these unrealistic expectations, Gavan Duffy spent his time in Paris vigorously seeking to establish a network of alliances to aid Ireland. A note of 1 August 1920 explained:

41 Memorandum of France toward Ireland, 10 Oct. 1920, NAI, Gavan Duffy Papers, MS 1125.

Latin Europe is the Europe that matters most today; Central Europe is too unsettled and desperate to trouble much about remote affairs, while the tendencies in Germany are now in general quite openly pro-English; Paris is the best centre to combine work in France, Spain, Portugal, Italy, Rumania, Switzerland, the Rhenish Provinces and Belgium.[42]

The possibility of building an informal alliance between Catholic and/or Latin countries that Ireland could join was abandoned when Gavan Duffy was expelled from France in September 1920. By 1921, writing from his new base in Rome, he had profoundly altered his position with regard to the geography of Irish links with the world:

France is a decadent and a decreasing country, Italy is in low water, Spain belongs to other days. There is here no vitalising element to give life and strength to the combination. What a contrast to the Teutons, to say nothing of the Slavs or even the Saxons. I think we should back a totally different combination ... the economic alliance of U.S. and Germany to exploit Russia with German brains and American dollars.[43]

These plans never materialised. Nevertheless, they afforded an opportunity to neophyte Sinn Féin leaders to ponder the interests that an official Irish diplomacy should promote. The implausibility of their most idealistic ambitions should, moreover, be balanced against their urgent search for the appropriate stance that Ireland should adopt in the international world of diplomacy. This position eventually solidified as that of an independent nation serving the preservation of the common good and world peace.[44] Arthur Griffith, Éamon de Valera and Count George Plunkett declared this officially in a letter to George Clemenceau on 26 May 1919: 'The declared object of the Conference is to establish a lasting peace, which is admittedly impossible if the legitimate claims to self-determination of nations such as Ireland be denied'.[45]

Across the nineteenth century, advanced Irish nationalist propaganda returned again and again to celebrating Ireland's distinguished military past, from the Irish brigade at Fontenoy to the United Irishmen's rebellion. In 1919, this attitude somersaulted in a transformed international context where the main objective was securing and maintaining peace. The new message from Dublin was that Ireland had no prejudice towards any State whatsoever, apart from England. As a consequence, Ireland could become a guarantor for safeguarding peace, as Sinn Féin's *Nationality* explained: 'There are no skeletons in our cupboards, no bloodstains on our hands: no mark of hypocrisy on our face. We are Irish'.[46]

42 Memorandum of France toward Ireland, 10 Oct. 1920, NAI, Gavan Duffy Papers, MS 1125.   **43** NAI, DFA, Early Series, Box 33, File 232.   **44** Keown, *First of the small nations*, pp 87–90.   **45** NAI, DFA, Early Series, Paris, 1919.   **46** *Nationality*, 8 Feb. 1919.

The link between popular self-determination and lasting peace remained a concept with strong geographical variables for many Sinn Féin leaders. Only a handful of them, like Liam Mellowes and Frederick Ryan, thought that it should include other populations from the British Empire or even other smaller European nations.[47]

In a booklet published in 1920, entitled *The first of the small nations*, Ireland was compared with eleven other European countries. Ireland could lay claim to an economic superiority that qualified her, more than any other nations, to become independent. The thought was not entertained that the Irish case was comparable to the Romanian or Serbian ones, for example. Only Catholic Poland, associated so often with Ireland since the crushing of its 1830 rising, had the right to be regarded as a proper parallel to Ireland. This argument proposed that Ireland in a European context was historically, culturally and economically unique. It also placed it in a republican tradition, reinforced by the rise of cultural nationalism at the end of the nineteenth century, which established Ireland's trajectory as clearly distinct from the wider international community. This exceptionality came into sharper focus when the claims of other nationalities from the Empire, notably Indian and Egyptian, had to be addressed.

Contacts were entertained with Egyptian nationalists in Paris, and Indians in New York. But Sinn Féin never supported the idea of an effective alliance or of a 'general uprising' of the kind that Harry Boland had briefly contemplated. One of the main reasons for this isolationist thinking is expressed in an appeal sent to Pope Benedict XV by O'Kelly in May 1920:

> The Irish National Movement (now commonly known as Sinn Féin) aims simply and solely at the achievement of the sovereign independence of Ireland – in other words, our aim is to obtain that independence which every other white race in the world has already won. We claim merely the same sovereign independence that Poland has won after one hundred and fifty years of slavery and struggle.[48]

Once more, this briefing document stressed the comparison with Catholic Poland. Its main message was to assert that Ireland belonged to the white race. When Egyptian nationalists offered to establish an '*entente cordiale* with Ireland against England', their 'foolish and oriental' offer was immediately rebuffed by Gavan Duffy. He opposed co-operation with the Egyptians who were described as 'not quite white'.[49] In a world where colonialism was still regarded as a positive force by many Western powers, the recurrence of the description of Ireland as white raises many questions.

---

47 Bruce Nelson, *Irish nationalists and the making of the Irish race* (Princeton, 2012).   **48** NAI, DFA, Early Series, Paris, 1920.   **49** Keown, *First of the small nations*, pp 82–3.

In fact, this was not a novel position for Irish nationalist leaders. In the 1880s, Parnell claimed that his project to disengage Ireland from the British Empire would not help other populations under British rule to obtain their freedom. Griffith classified Irish identity as white European: 'white men, master of Europe and dominator of the world'. Sinn Féin did not escape the gravitational forcefield of contemporary racial prejudices, and they also felt the pressure of counteracting an English satirical press which depicted the Irish as a racially inferior Celtic people. It was a fatally attractive argument to assert that Ireland was a white civilisation that should occupy the same privileged place at the apex of the world racial hierarchy as Great Britain or France. This distanced Ireland from association with non-white populations under British colonial rule, an association that damaged Irish claims to legitimacy.[50]

This particular rhetoric and its evolution illustrated the deep scission that had fractured Irish nationalism following the Parnell split. Radical anti-Parnellites such as T.M. Healy deployed clericalist, conservative, anti-modernist and racial rhetoric which was quickly reinterpreted by advanced nationalists such as Griffith. A similar ideological drift to the right happened in France after the demoralising military defeat against Prussia in 1870, when a nationalist movement obsessed with national degradation, enhanced militarism and redemption surged, that also opposed liberal democracy and cosmopolitanism as a limp alternative to national self-confidence and assertiveness. Other strains of Irish nationalism, including the socialism of James Connolly, pulled in a more intenationalist direction but ultimately the conservative stance of Healy won out, especially as the Free State (of which Healy became Governor General in 1922) moved in a socially conservative direction.[51] Political activists were trying to become pragmatic statesmen, and the strains showed.

CONCLUSION

Following Sinn Féin's victory in 1918 and the establishment of Dáil Éireann, Sinn Féin delegates posted abroad looked for international recognition to justify their demands for an emerging Irish independence, and to encourage Euopean powers, notably France, to move beyond outmoded British perspectives. Between 1919 and 1921, a novel Irish diplomatic mission was launched, with Europe and the United States as its main targets. France, the country that hosted the Peace Conference, the country that won the war but that thought itself treated unfairly by Great Britain, remained the main focus of attention. The

---

50 Ranger, *La France vue d'Irlande*, pp 92–3. 51 Pierre Ranger, 'Le péril français, affirmation de foi et anticléricalisme français dans l'Irlande nationaliste 1890–1900' in R. Fabre & M. Rapoport (eds), *Affirmations de foi* (Bordeaux, 2012), pp 93–103 and Ranger, *La France vue d'Irlande*, pp 118–49.

realities of international power relations quickly dawned on men from a fledgling independence movement, who lacked the bargaining chips and diplomatic gravitas that would broker a fair balance of power with British and French diplomacy. In a narrow reckoning, Sinn Féiners in France did not achieve much, but what they did achieve is best understood in a wider context.

Irish historiography insists on the triviality of Irish diplomacy during the War of Independence. Sinn Féiners themselves undermined their foreign initiatives. Griffith warned the delegates abroad that they should never lose sight of the priority of the military and political campaign at home. However, this fledgling diplomacy influenced the development and the choices made by official Irish diplomacy after 1922, when it could rely on the authority of a state. Sinn Féiners, far from withdrawing into a purely Irish and Anglo-Irish cocoon, followed Griffith's lead in looking to continental Europe and particularly to France for identification and inspiration as they inserted an Irish seat at the global table.

Ludovic Naudeau and the Irish War of Independence

PIERRE JOANNON

Between 1919 and 1921, many distinguished French journalists including Henri
Béraud,[1] Joseph Kessel[2] and Simone Téry[3] visited Ireland to cover the guerrilla
war that pitted British forces against the Irish Republican Army. Their reports
for the major Paris newspapers fuelled a keen sympathy with oppressed Ireland
in French public opinion, sufficient to dissolve the feelings of solidarity with
their British allies dating from the shared dark days of the First World War.

While the Irish reports of Béraud, Kessel and Téry have received recent
scholarly attention, those by Ludovic Naudeau have been neglected. Naudeau,
a highly respected journalist, developed a fascination with 'the Irish Question'
at the turn of the century. Born in Boulogne sur Mer in 1872, he embarked early
on a journalistic career. A hands-on man of action, he was eager to experience the
unprecedented events that were then shaping the course of history, regardless of
personal safety in strife-torn zones.

In 1904, *Le Journal*, a Paris daily paper to which he was a regular contributor,
despatched him to Asia to cover the Russo-Japanese war.[4] In March 1905, he was
captured by Japanese troops, escaped, was recaptured, shipped to Japan on a
steamer crammed with Russian prisoners, freed in Japan but trapped there for
another eighteen months. During his enforced exile, he produced two works, one
of which, *Le Japon moderne, son évolution* (The evolution of modern Japan), won
an Académie Française award in 1910. His novel *Plaisir du Japon* (Joy of Japan)
appeared in 1922. Some years later, Naudeau plunged into the cauldron of the
Russian Revolution. He interviewed Lenin in Petrograd but was once again

---

1 Henri Béraud, *Le flâneur salarié* (Paris, 1927), pp 115–50; Henri Béraud, *Les derniers beaux jours* (Paris, 1953), pp 57–70; Thierry Arminjon, 'Henri Béraud, Joseph Kessel, L'Irlande', *Cahier de l'Association Rétaise des Amis d'Henri Béraud*, 37 (2015); Thierry Arminjon, 'Henri Béraud et l'Irlande', *Cahier de l'Association Rétaise des Amis d'Henri Béraud*, 38 (2015). 2 Joseph Kessel, *Mary de Cork* (Paris, 1925) (dedicated 'A mon cher Henri Béraud, en souvenir de Dublin et de Cork, cette histoire irlandaise'); Joseph Kessel, *Le temps de l'espérance* (Paris, 1968); Yves Courrière, 'Joseph Kessel, témoin de l'insurrection irlandaise', *Études Irlandaises*, 10 (1985), pp 167–80. 3 Simone Téry, *En Irlande, de la guerre d'indépendance à la guerre civile (1914–1923)* (Paris, 1923); Simone Téry, *L'île des Bardes. Notes sur la littérature irlandaise contemporaine* (Paris, 1925); Oliver O'Hanlon, 'Simone Téry: une Française en Irlande' in C. Maignant (ed.), *La France et l'Irlande: destins croisés 16ème–21ème siècles* (Villeneuve d'Ascq, 2013), pp 133–45. 4 *Le Journal*, founded in 1892 by Fernand Xau, was one of the most important daily papers in France in the first half of the twentieth century. In 1900, its circulation was 450,000. It ceased publication in 1944.

arrested and jailed by the Bolsheviks. His prison experiences inspired two more books, both published by Hachette in 1920: *En prison sous la terreur russe* (In prison under the Russian terror), another Académie Française prize-winner; and *Les dessous du chaos russe* (Secrets of the Russian chaos).

In subsequent years, Naudeau took his pen and notebook to global trouble spots, not just Ireland but also Manchuria, Morocco, Germany, Asia and neighbouring fascist Italy. His reports were respected by a wide audience because, in the words of Albéric Cahuet, they evidenced a quality journalist 'in their precision and timeliness, their historian's concern to extrapolate an overall view from particular incidents, and the characteristic attention of the novelist to setting the scene in all its colour, while adding a picturesque element to truthful realism, thereby making the narrative come to life'.[5]

Naudeau's first article on Ireland appeared on the front page of *Le Journal* on 23 November 1901. It was devoted to the election of an exotic character, Arthur Lynch, a new Home Rule member of parliament for County Galway. Lynch was born in Australia to Irish parents, studied in Melbourne, Berlin and Paris, taught mathematics and published several literary and pedagogical works. He was a military correspondent during the war against the Ashantis and lived for a while in the United States. At the beginning of the Boer War, he went to the Transvaal as correspondent for *Le Journal*, the same daily paper that congratulated him after his election to the House of Commons. It was not in Lynch's nature to remain a by-stander. Exchanging his pen for the sword, he became a colonel in the Second Irish Brigade on the side of the Boers. He stayed for seven months in southern Africa, was reportedly killed, but got back to Europe after the fall of Pretoria.

Meeting Lynch at the offices of *Paris-Nouvelle*, Naudeau was impressed by his military bearing:

> Arthur Lynch is a name which bears a proud connotation. A quint-essentially Irish name, it gained much honour from the many valiant warriors who composed the Irish Legion in our own army in former times, men who shed their blood in twenty battles and launched the decisive charge against the English at Fontenoy.[6]

Reporting on Lynch's election campaign in Galway, Naudeau got a sober statement from the former colonel:

> I am not a revolutionary. I am not contemplating an overthrow of the monarchy, neither am I demanding any separation of Ireland and England. I ask only that England would grant Home Rule to Ireland, that is,

5 *L'Illustration*, 18 Feb. 1922.   6 Ludovic Naudeau, 'L'élection d'Arthur Lynch', *Le Journal*, 23 Nov. 1901.

complete autonomy. Don't Canada and Australia have their own Home Rule?[7]

Naudeau's Irish empathy and familiarity with the 'Irish Question' made him the obvious person to cover the Irish War of Independence, which broke out in the wake of the First World War. On behalf of *L'Illustration*, Naudeau spent six weeks in Ireland in January and February 1921.[8] The Paris magazine published four reports, each of three to five pages long, and with copious illustrations. An editorial note introduced the first article:

> It is difficult to talk about Ireland, especially in a French publication which cannot forget that the Sinn Féin revolt is directed against the unity of the British empire, and that we French remain bound to that empire on account of assistance rendered, and because of our shared battle. The English are sensitive. They are irritated by any interference in their internal affairs. However, the Irish cause is noble and gallant, it has its martyrs who touch humanity's heart. In sending a past master of major reportage to Ireland, *l'Illustration* has considered all these difficulties but when choosing a witness, who could be more scrupulous or more impartial than Ludovic Naudeau? Everyone remembers his remarkable series of studies and articles on the Russo-Japanese war. More recently, in two other works, M. Naudeau has described the Bolshevik régime with an often prophetic depth of perception ... nothing could be more appropriate than that he should go to Ireland to observe what is happening and to report it honestly.[9]

In Ireland, the journalist was astonished at the initial absence of checks and administrative formalities. Dublin seemed peaceful and quiet. The streets were brightly lit, the most desirable products were displayed in the windows of luxury shops, crowds swarmed cinema doors, unarmed soldiers strolled with lady friends, the pubs were overflowing. The enthusiast for tumult shared his disappointment: 'In the damp white mist of a mild winter, the atmosphere was one of boring and slightly dull calm'.[10]

However, as dusk descended, the hotel porter warned him about the curfew and the danger of risky encounters in the dark. At one in the morning, a dull explosion, followed by gunshot, woke him up. Suddenly alert, *L'Illustration*'s correspondent made quick notes:

---

7 Naudeau, 'L'élection d'Arthur Lynch'.   8 Modelling itself on the *Illustrated London News*, the Paris weekly *L'Illustration. Journal Universel* first appeared in 1843. After 1905, it became the leading French magazine and it rapidly eclipsed its English competitors. In 1929, its circulation reached 650,000. *L'Illustration* ceased publication in 1944.   9 Editorial introduction for the series by Ludovic Naudeau, 'Six semaines en Irlande (Janvier-Février 1921)', *L'Illustration*, 26 Feb. 1921, p. 189.   10 *L'Illustration*, 26 Feb. 1921, p. 189.

There is shooting over there in the fog, about five or six metres from the hotel. Are people fighting in the streets of Dublin at night? A second bomb explodes, five or six gunshots go off, then the city quietened once more and I fell back asleep, nonetheless thinking that something is obviously going on.[11]

Naudeau set out to explore the Irish capital, admiring its orderly eighteenth-century facades, its quays, its many statues and its broad streets. An elegant city but just a little too English:

The shops are British shops; the signs, the advertising, the shop fronts, the bookshops, the style of house – all are typically and uniformly English. On every gable end, just as in London, big painted murals extol the praises of Bovril, Lipton's tea, Fry's cocoa or Bryant and May matches.[12]

Over the shops, there were indeed some names beginning with O or Mac:

But on going into the shops bearing these old Irish names, you won't find anyone remotely like a long-haired and colourful Gael voicing pain romantically in harp lament; in the shop you will speak to men who, at first glance, are indistinguishable from the English of London or Liverpool.[13]

Beneath this anglicised veneer, a deeper Ireland was still visible to the eye of a careful observer: it was recognisable in the women wrapped in traditional shawls (reminding Naudeau of the Arab *burnous*), in the gangs of barefoot urchins traipsing through the mud, and by the distinctive jaunting cars carrying passengers who sat back to back. Ireland was also identifiable by the statues bearing irreconcilable aspirations: Nelson's Pillar in Sackville Street, George II in St Stephen's Green, William III in Dame Street, the Wellington obelisk in the Phoenix Park, the Fusiliers' Arch in memory of Dublin soldiers killed in the Boer War, 'so many symbols commemorating the glory of empire and asserting its splendour and indestructible unity'.[14] Confronting them in silent reproach were statues of Irish nationalist heroes: Grattan, the father of parliamentary independence, O'Connell, Liberator of the Catholics, Parnell, the uncrowned king of Ireland, William Smith O'Brien, the romantic rebel of 1848, Thomas Moore, the bard of Erin, 'all these Irish leaders who suffered for insisting that their country was a nation and not a colony'.[15] Fixed in stone, these conflicting symbols memorialised a centuries-old war, sometimes latent, sometimes overt. That same contrast festooned city walls where, side by side, were recruitment

11 *L'Illustration*, 26 Feb. 1921, p. 189.   12 *L'Illustration*, 26 Feb. 1921, p. 189.   13 *L'Illustration*, 26 Feb. 1921, p. 190.   14 *L'Illustration*, 26 Feb. 1921, p. 190.   15 *L'Illustration*, 26 Feb. 1921, p. 190.

notices enticing the youth of Ireland to enlist in the army of his gracious Majesty and posters putting a price on IRA and Sinn Féin leaders, and on deputies elected to the 'illegal' Dáil.

War was also apparent in the noise of armoured cars trundling through the streets with machine gunners up top, in lorries filled with tin-hatted soldiers, their guns pointed at the crowds, the powerful vehicles of the Black and Tans, those sinister police auxiliaries easily recognisable by their tam o'shanters (the big black pompon beret of the Scots). Soldiers and policemen were wary and watchful:

> Twenty four hours don't go by in Dublin, or elsewhere in the land, without two or three of these vehicles being unexpectedly hit by an exploding bomb or attacked by rifle fire This is guerrilla warfare – distressing, sporadic, dispersed, almost invisible and made more insidious by the jumpiness it generates than by the relatively tiny losses inflicted. The traps are everywhere but nowhere visible.[16]

This shadowy, treacherous and unpredictable war posed a moral dilemma for the reporter from *L'Illustration*. He could not forget that the Lord Lieutenant French (first earl of Ypres) was respected by all French patriots, that French's staff had covered themselves in glory in Flanders and Picardy, that the Black and Tans and the Auxiliaries had spilt their blood in the trenches resisting the Prussian invader. But then, how could a Frenchman forget the Irish Brigade that served under the banners of Louis XIV and Louis XV, or that ancient alliance that had left in French hearts a 'sympathetic compassion' where the Irish were concerned? In addition, how could a moral person not be nauseated by oppressive methods strongly reminiscent of the brutal subjugation of indigenous peoples who resisted the colonial yoke?

> Is it expedient, is it prudent when repressing the strong momentum of a small western community towards independence, to use similar suppression tactics that every European nation inflicts pitilessly on coloured people in its colonies if they attempt to achieve any relief at all? Can one treat a white population, a people who are intellectually the equal of the most civilised people and who have provided famous men for several nations, as one would punish a Berber tribe, controlling them by wiping out their native villages? In twentieth-century Europe, can one of the most distinguished white nations continue to dominate another white nation that is physically less strong but is morally its equal?[17]

---

16 *L'Illustration*, 26 Feb. 1921, p. 191.   17 *L'Illustration*, 26 Feb. 1921, p. 191.

In the impenetrable Irish countryside, which resembles 'the Vendée, the Bocage, a Marais, a Brittany divided by innumerable bushy and tangled hedges', there were natural limits to what could be achieved by repression.[18] The army and police patrolled the main routes but once their armoured cars and lorries had passed by, the roads and paths were once again under the control of the insurgents:

> To all intents and purposes, the area belongs to the small mobile military detachments of insurgents [Flying Columns]; there, they are invisible and cannot be discovered; their small numbers constitute their main strength and it is enough for Sinn Féin to have two to three thousand men deployed at a time over the whole island for them to inflict the jitteriness of an interminable guerrilla war on the British troops.[19]

For the benefit of *L'Illustration*'s readers, Naudeau outlined the origins of the conflict. He noted the hesitations, prevarications and procrastinations on the draft Home Rule bill that eventually exasperated Irish public opinion and had finally humiliated the nationalist party whose leader, John Redmond, sought his country's salvation through parliamentary and peaceful means within a strictly constitutional framework. Naudeau emphasised that the First World War had changed the fundamental rules of the old imperial game because the right of peoples to self-determination lay at the heart of the victorious Allies' war aims: 'The total emancipation of the Poles, the Finns, the Czechs, and of many other small and previously subject peoples inflames the Irish imagination'.[20]

For Naudeau, it was incomprehensible that England should seek to employ in Ireland the same terror tactics inflicted by the Germans on Belgium. Crisscrossing the country by car, Naudeau surveyed the scars inflicted by that blindly repressive policy. There was the sack of Balbriggan in north Dublin, which the *Manchester Guardian* deemed an Irish Louvain. There was the burning of Cork city centre, 'an act of furious madness' by the Black and Tans and the police on 12 December 1920. There was the systematic destruction of creameries belonging to rural cooperative societies, punitive reprisals aimed at communities accused of supporting the IRA and Sinn Féin. Naudeau personally visited several ruined creameries and he reported that at Bridgetown, in County Clare, 'I saw the burst boilers, the shattered cogs, the pipework twisted by flames, the blackened walls, and I shuddered to think that this appalling devastation had been carried out in defense of law and order'.[21]

He noted that 'unofficial reprisals' usually involved violence and looting, and that they were quickly followed by 'official' reprisals under martial law. He experienced an overpowering sense of déjà-vu:

18 Ludovic Naudeau, 'Six semaines en Irlande (Janvier-Février 1921)', *L'Illustration*, 5 Mar. 1921, p. 221.   19 *L'Illustration*, 5 Mar. 1921, p. 221.   20 *L'Illustration*, 5 Mar. 1921, p. 222. 21 *L'Illustration*, 5 Mar. 1921, p. 223.

In Ireland today a whole series of occurrences is taking place that I have already written about eighteen years ago when I reported on the cruelty suffered by the Macedonian population then quaking before the scimitar of the cruel Turk. When the Ottomans burned the villages where Bulgarian *comitadjis* [guerillas] had been seen, there was no limit to our indignation. In a country ruled by our illustrious ally, under the rule of a noble country like England which has set a democratic example for all peoples, how is it possible that the traveller cannot escape witnessing such tragedy?[22]

Naudeau declined to adjudicate 'whether Ireland is or is not a nation' but on the basis of his journalistic investigations he noted:

The traveller who goes from south to north in Ireland will discover – except in the exceptional and important Belfast enclave – that everything is vibrant, radiant and aquiver with this irrepressible attitude, this involvement of hearts which George Russell defined precisely for me: the national spirit.[23]

As he travelled in the West of Ireland, Ludovic Naudeau was seduced by the magnificent Atlantic landscapes, which almost made him forget the IRA ambushes, the violent attacks, the police brutality. He was brought rudely back to earth in the lounge of a little old-fashioned Galway hotel where he was engaged in conversation by a British officer. This man was irked at being an easy target for these Irish who were no doubt very likable but who possessed 'an exceptionally restless unruly disposition, are impractical and full of contradictions'.[24] All in all, the Irish were just another set of colonial natives who could not be entrusted with self-government since they were so obviously incapable. An Irishman, a war-wounded former soldier, butted into the conversation, accusing England of decimating the Irish population, inflicting the scourge of emigration and suffocating the smaller island economically. Regarding the hit-and-run tactics of the IRA, he argued that the French would have enthusiastically embraced the same tactics if the Germans had proved victorious:

If France were to be occupied, oppressed, exploited and fleeced by the Germans, wouldn't there always be patriots who would risk all to hurt the enemy? Would the Germans have the right to expect willy-nilly the loyalty of conquered France? Would they have ever thought of branding as traitors the people who were the champions and the martyrs of French nationalism?[25]

---

22 *L'Illustration*, 5 Mar. 1921, p. 224.   23 *L'Illustration*, 5 Mar. 1921, p. 224.   24 Ludovic Naudeau, 'Six semaines en Irlande (Janvier–Février 1921)', *L'Illustration*, 19 Mar. 1921, p. 263.   25 *L'Illustration*, 19 Mar. 1921, p. 264.

As he concluded his journey in Munster, Naudeau displayed prescience concerning the hidden divisions in nationalist Irish opinion with regard to the future status of the sister island. He distinguished three strands within nationalism: first, IRA volunteers and Sinn Féin militants, who would never lay down their arms before achieving their objective; second, intellectuals and Catholic church leaders, no less national than the first group, but reluctant to embrace violence, and from whose ranks the treaty compromise would have to come; and finally, country people, workers and small shopkeepers, all in favour of freedom but longing for a return to normal life even if it meant resiling from some principles. For the time being, the second and third strands were subordinated to the first group, but would that state of affairs last? Naudeau's report was proleptic of civil war and fratricidal confrontations.

Naudeau reported his conversation with a reputedly moderate Irish notable to whom he posed the question of whether he would accept dominion Home Rule status on the model of Canada and Australia. The reply was: 'we could be happy with it today but without committing to it for the future because it would be for future generations to decide if they wished to retain or break the final link tying them to the British empire'. For Naudeau, this equivocal response revealed 'the deeper thought that is hidden beneath the benign words, the restrained words of these moderates whose total ambition now seems to be achievement of dominion Home Rule. Yes, that very system would only be considered as a staging post on the route towards total achievement of Irish aspirations'.[26]

Irish constitutional development since 1921 followed Naudeau's predicted trajectory: from the acceptance of dominion status as 'the freedom to achieve freedom' up to Éamon de Valera's dismantling of Commonwealth trappings, to the passing of the Executive Authority External Relations Act (1936), which abrogated the last Commonwealth links, and finally the proclamation of the Republic in front of the General Post Office on Easter Sunday 1949.

Naudeau's Irish journey ended in Ulster. The contrast struck him forcibly: 'We have suddenly passed from a primitive, insular Vendée [quintessentially rural and Catholic] into a pulsating Creusot [a region noted for its heavy industry]'.[27] In Belfast, resounding with the din of hammers, the roar of machine tools, the wailing of sirens and the operations of enormous cranes, the journalist took the pulse of an industrial society working at full pelt. The naval shipyards of Harland & Wolff boasted of being the biggest in the world, and launched transatlantic liners by the dozen. The steam textile looms were reeling off the famous Irish linen. The York Street Mill alone produced enough yarn in one day to go three times around the world. The biggest rope factory in the world was converting fifteen thousand tons of hemp into mooring lines, ropes and nets. Belfast unleashed an avalanche of economic superlatives, a dizzying deluge of statistics.

26 *L'Illustration*, 19 Mar. 1921, p. 265.   **27** Ludovic Naudeau, 'Six semaines en Irlande (Janvier–Février 1921)', *L'Illustration*, 2 Apr. 1921, p. 298.

The economic supremacy of the northern province was simply over-whelming: Belfast the most populous of the Irish cities, paid half the tax revenue and three-fifths of the customs duties of the whole island, and single-handedly it was responsible for seventy per cent of the island's exports. It was a Manchester grafted on to a foreign country. The names over its shops were overwhelmingly Scottish and English. 'Everything tells us that Ireland is no longer Ireland here but rather a settlement of people from the neighbouring island'.[28] This population was so integrated with London and the Empire – supplier of its raw materials and market for its exports – that it was the exact antithesis of a nationalist and agricultural Ireland in thrall to the mirage of economic and intellectual self-sufficiency.

Superimposed over that conflict of economic interest was the denominational conflict that fostered an irreconcilable split. While the Protestants (mostly Anglican) were hardly visible or audible elsewhere in Ireland, a colony 'planted' in Ulster from the seventeenth century formed a homogenous 'Protestant block'. This group was largely composed of Scottish Presbyterians, whose sensibility was predisposed to regard themselves to be a besieged minority surrounded by a 'Papist' majority, and accordingly suitably suspicious of their Catholic neighbours. They banded together in the Orange Order, a 'traditionalist and authoritarian confraternity' whose name was taken from the Battle of the Boyne in 1690, celebrated by the Orangemen every year 'as though it had just taken place'.[29]

This double antagonism, economic and sectarian, conceivably justified the Partition Act passed by the Westminster parliament in 1920.[30] However, in fragmenting the historic province of Ulster by excluding the three counties of Cavan, Donegal and Monaghan, the British legislators had exacerbated the situation by setting up a miniature 'Orange Ireland'.

> If the population of that Northern Ireland had been totally Protestant, or had a huge majority of Protestants, that solution would have been sensible. But the 820,370 Protestants had 400,000 Catholics alongside them. Consequently, the Catholics of the three other big provinces demanded to know by what right 400,000 of their co-religionists were being cut off in order to set up, for the benefit of a Protestant minority, a small artificial state that had never previously existed.[31]

Naudeau explained to his French readers that the Catholics unanimously proclaimed that Ireland must remain indivisible. He acknowledged that the exceptional industrial structure of Belfast and its own distinctive economic requirements were an argument in favour of Partition Home Rule. But Naudeau noted that what was true of Belfast did not apply to the totality of 'Northern

28 *L'Illustration*, 2 Apr. 1921, p. 298.   29 *L'Illustration*, 2 Apr. 1921, p. 299.   30 *L'Illustration*, 2 Apr. 1921, p. 299.   31 *L'Illustration*, 2 Apr. 1921, p. 299.

Ireland'. He then minutely detailed the stages of the Ulster revolt and its consequences – the Covenant in 1912, the Ulster Volunteer Force, the purchase of German arms and ammunition and their landing in Larne, the refusal of British officers to quell the '*Orange revolt*', the quasi-certainty of separate treatment for Ulster in the Home Rule Bill, the acceleration of the First World War, Easter 1916, and the breakdown of the Irish Convention. Then there was the 'Khaki elections' in 1918 that further polarised the two parts of the island, followed by 'Sinn Féin terrorism' and the bloody reaction of the Ulster Orangemen.[32] Naudeau supplied detail:

> In Londonderry in May and June 1920, twenty were killed and eighty wounded in skirmishes. In Belfast in August, Catholics, outnumbered three to one by their attackers, were driven out of the shipyards by the mob of Protestant workers, their houses were burnt, they were tracked and hunted down, it was a manhunt! By the beginning of September, fifty-eight had already been killed, more than six hundred wounded, and the cost of the damage amounted to one million, five hundred pounds. Seven thousand workers (a thousand of whom had taken part in the Great War) were left unemployed.[33]

Naudeau reviewed the arguments of nationalists and unionists, of Catholics and Protestants, of Northern industrialists and Southern farmers. He described the mutual resentments and recriminations, without seeking to arbitrate between these angry arguments: 'In the absence of a United Nations which could bring reason to bear, and without a European consciousness sufficiently powerful to nullify the poison of hereditary hatreds, only force can separate the opponents'.[34]

He sensed that 'ineluctable circumstances', notably international opinion, would curtail the use of unbridled force. 'In the USA, sixteen million Irish are following the Irish question with passionate sympathy, and watchful eyes in India, Egypt and in far away South Africa, are observing the bloody events'.[35] Only a presumptuous person would suggest a solution to the Anglo–Irish crisis. But if Naudeau's opinion were solicited, he would tell 'our English friends' that 'the solution advocated by Mr Asquith – implementation of as wide-ranging a form of Home Rule as was granted to Canada and Australia – would be the most effective measure for disarming Sinn Féin immediately'.[36] As a realist, he knew that such a solution would never pacify a 'suspicious Orangeman'.

Naudeau's six weeks in Ireland in January and February 1921 affected him every bit as much as his enforced stay in Japan at the turn of the century. In the 1920s, he produced two works of fiction, one set in Japan and the other in

32 *L'Illustration*, 2 Apr. 1921, p. 300. 33 *L'Illustration*, 2 Apr. 1921, p. 300. 34 *L'Illustration*, 2 Apr. 1921, p. 301. 35 *L'Illustration*, 2 Apr. 1921, p. 301. 36 *L'Illustration*, 2 Apr. 1921, p. 301.

Ireland – the only novels by this great journalist who published more than twenty-five books dealing with the most incendiary of global conflicts. His Irish novel, *La jolie fille de Dublin*, appeared in 1923 in the famous literary monthly collection *Les Œuvres Libres*, published by Arthème Fayard, the Parisian publishers (and republished by Ernest Flammarion in 1928). This novel, dealing with the Irish War of Independence, does not reach the level of other French novels on Ireland – for example, Pierre Benoit's *La Chaussée des Géants* or Joseph Kessel's novella *Mary de Cork*. The plot is anorexic, the characters are stereotypes and the dialogue is bombastic. But the work does provide a snapshot of contemporary French public opinion on the Irish problem.

The novel's three main characters are Florence Brehan, daughter of a prominent Dublin doctor, and a supporter of Sinn Féin; O'Carrol, the elusive and legendary leader of the guerillas against the British forces; and George Mac Namara, Dr Brehan's top intern and favourite student, a cold and calculating individual who intends to stay well out of the fray. Both male protagonists love Florence Brehan, and she is aware of the quiet passion of her father's student but also of the romantic love of the on-the-run revolutionary. O'Carrol, a blend of Pearse and Collins, is 'the Irish hero and martyr':

> His soul is pure, lofty like the early Christians, and like them, he is always ready to offer himself up in sacrifice … This leader of uprisings has a saint's innocence, the warlike faith of a crusader, and an ascetic life … Firing squad, gallows or stake do not frighten him, his aim is self-sacrifice, and he is seen to die with deep serenity.[37]

Florence regards him as a 'reincarnation of Christ, a redeemer always ready to shed his blood for the salvation of his brothers'.[38]

Accustomed to caring for bodies, whether he is tending to a Sinn Féiner or a Black and Tan, George MacNamara diagnoses fanaticism as a sickness of the soul: 'In the east of Europe, by their frenzied efforts, some monomaniacs have brought about the destruction of Russia, and at the same time in the west, other monomaniacs fail to recoil from spilling blood to resuscitate Ireland'.[39] Confronting O'Carrol, whom he has just saved from certain death, he admonishes him to turn his back on the toxic past:

> You believe that Ireland's destiny should be resolved only by continually harping on about its bloody stories. You rummage around desperately in history, trying to discover motives for hatred. It's obvious that it just takes a look into the past of any people to discover reasons for hating all their neighbours and to plot the most savage reprisals against them.[40]

37 Ludovic Naudeau, *La jolie fille de Dublin* (Paris, 1928), pp 19–21.   **38** Naudeau, *La jolie fille de Dublin*, p. 29.   **39** Naudeau, *La jolie fille de Dublin*, p. 36.   **40** Naudeau, *La jolie fille*

Mac Namara believes that ordinary people everywhere prefer peace, happiness and work to war, upheaval and rancour. He holds a mirror up to this revolutionary with his unstable mixture of enlightenment and demagoguery:

> Atavistic individuals who think themselves avatars of glory, they identify their country's future with their own need for fame; they think they are heroes but they build their fame on a pedestal of human flesh. Most people hate these fanatical minorities, these purveyors of public calamity who periodically in every country supply the killing squads.[41]

He senses that Florence is moving away from him, and warns her:

> If Europe wants to stay alive, she must forget all hereditary bitterness. It is vital that it pursues unity; the perpetuation of century-old vendettas threatens civilisation, a threat escalating every day by the ominous advances in destructive methods. The more Europe fragments into innumerable petty antagonistic factions, the more enmities multiply, the more there is decadence.[42]

The heroes of the novel meet their bloody fates: O'Carrol is gunned down by the police in Tipperary; Florence dies, gun in hand, attacking a detachment of Auxiliaries in the Phoenix Park; MacNamara is killed, to the shouts of 'Ireland Forever' [Éireann Go Brách], firing at the Auxies. Among his notes was found this disillusioned reflection:

> Some English soldiers are immediately and directly descended from Irish forebears. On the other hand, many Irish fighters have Anglo-Saxon heredity. The former fight with conviction in the service of England; the latter consider it praiseworthy to be mangled for the salvation of Ireland. More than once, a supposed Englishman kills a make-believe Irishman in the name of England, or a phony Irishman, eager to save Ireland, disembowels a partly English man.[43]

Naudeau, in his journalism and his novel, remained puzzled by the complexity of Irish affairs, but the Irish case always fascinated him. In summer 1922, Seán Murphy, second secretary at the Free State diplomatic mission (and future Irish minister plenipotentiary in France from 1938 to 1950), stated: 'Naudeau gave six lectures last year in Northern France and was converted himself after the third lecture by the enthusiasm of his audience'.[44]

de Dublin, pp 107–8.   **41** Naudeau, *La jolie fille de Dublin*, p. 108.   **42** Naudeau, *La jolie fille de Dublin*, p. 191.   **43** Naudeau, *La jolie fille de Dublin*, pp 245–6.   **44** Ronan Fanning, Michael Kennedy, Dermot Keogh & Eunan O'Halpin (eds), *Documents on Irish foreign policy,*

Actually, Ludovic Naudeau had been a convert for more than two decades to the idea that Ireland deserved to be a sovereign nation, and through his nuanced, perceptive stances, he had appreciably strengthened the current of sympathy for Ireland in French public opinion.

volume I, 1919–1922 (Dublin, 1998), p. 487. This undated letter was despatched between 12 April 1922 and 9 September 1922. The lectures by Naudeau would therefore have been delivered in 1921, the same year as his reports for *L'Illustration*.

Roger Chauviré's perspective on 1916 and its aftermath

PHYLLIS GAFFNEY

Roger Chauviré (1880–1957) presents a striking case of hibernophilia. A French academic and man of letters, who initially moved to Ireland in 1919 intending to stay for a short period, he settled in Dublin for his working life, becoming a respected commentator on Irish history and current affairs during the opening decades of Irish independence. He grew passionately interested in Ireland, finding there an enchanting 'other world' where the unexpected tended to happen, and where imagination was more influential than reason.

Born in Algeria in 1880, Chauviré was educated in Lille and Lyon, and graduated in 1898. *Agrégé* in 1902, he secured a teaching post in 1905 in a leading military academy, the Prytanée National at La Flèche, where he taught Latin, Greek and French literature to final-year students preparing for entry to the *grandes écoles*. He was awarded a doctorate by the Sorbonne in 1914 for his thesis on Jean Bodin, the sixteenth-century founder of French political philosophy. His active engagement in the First World War was short-lived: wounded in the trenches, he was demobilised before the end of 1914, and returned to his job at La Flèche.[1]

Chauviré's career took a surprising turn in 1918, when he was encouraged to apply for the vacant Chair of French at University College Dublin, part of the recently established National University of Ireland.[2] He was offered the post and he moved to University College Dublin in February 1919, where he worked until his retirement. Returning to live in his family home in Anjou, he died in Paris on 14 March 1957. Apart from being an academic specialist on Jean Bodin, Chauviré was also a poet, a historian, a translator, a journalist, and a creative

1 He lost a younger brother at the front in 1915. Biographical sources include: Ministère des Affaires Étrangères, Centre des Archives Diplomatiques de Nantes, Dublin (Consulat-Légation), article 102: Professeurs (dossiers individuels), dossier Roger Chauviré [hereafter CADN]: brief *curriculum vitae*; UCD, French Department files, correspondence, 1982–1983, between Professor Caldicott and Professor Chauviré's daughter, Madame A. Blondeau; UCD Archives (Michael Hayes Papers); author's correspondence, 2003, with the Prytanée National Militaire, La Flèche, and with the Direction des Archives Départementales de Maine-et-Loire; Bibliothèque nationale de France, Recherche bibliographique: Chauviré, Paul Roger, FOL LN1 232 (5297), Dossier de coupures de presse; Seán T. Ó Ceallaigh (Additional Papers), NLI, Collection List 160; correspondence (2009 et ss) with Madame Antoinette Johanet-Blondeau, Chauviré's grand-daughter. 2 There had been a vacancy since the death

writer of some distinction. One of his novels was awarded the Grand Prix du Roman de l'Académie Française and there is a rue Roger Chauviré in his home town of Angers.

Nothing in this biographical summary suggests that Chauviré's career would take the course it did. Having come to Ireland on secondment for five years, with a rudimentary reading knowledge of English, a poor command of spoken English,[3] and little sense of the differences between Ireland and England, he chose Ireland as his home for over thirty years. More unexpectedly, a significant proportion of his published work is about Ireland's heritage, history and troubled present.[4] Two of his six novels are set in Ireland; a dozen of his short stories have Irish subjects; he produced a study of the Irish Rebellion, a guide to Ireland and a history of Ireland; he translated ancient legends from the Ulster Cycle and the Cycle of Fionn Mac Cumhaill into French. He was also an occasional correspondent on Ireland and Irish affairs for French journals, for over four decades.[5] These writings testify to an unusually detailed knowledge and understanding of Ireland, as well as an enduring admiration for Irish culture.

The specific interest of his writings on 1916 and its aftermath is twofold. In the first place, they differ from comparable sources because of their sheer duration. Chauviré was by no means the only French commentator on Ireland, in prose and fiction, during this turbulent period but he was the most sustained[6]. Moreover, living and working in the country for over three decades, while forming close friendships with Irish people,[7] gave him time to develop his acquaintance and refine his understanding, particularly of the complexities of Anglo-Irish relations. His output on 1916 and its aftermath reflected the evolving historical realities of the period in which they were written.

Second, he interpreted Ireland's changing times in different ways, expressing his views not only through political commentary and history, but also through

---

of Professor Édouard Cadic, early in 1914. Filling the chair with a well-qualified French academic was high on the agenda for Alfred Blanche, French Consul in Dublin (since 1917). Phyllis Gaffney, 'Une certaine idée de l'Irlande, or the professor as propagandist: Roger Chauviré's Irish fictions' in P. Gaffney, M. Brophy & M. Gallagher (eds), *Reverberations: staging relations in French since 1500: a festschrift in honour of C.E.J. Caldicott* (Dublin, 2008), pp 390–403. **3** Chauviré was worried about his insufficient competence in English to accept the job. These scruples were assuaged by Blanche. CADN correspondence, 2 and 7 Sept. 2018. **4** If one excludes his two books on Jean Bodin based on his doctoral research, half of his published writings concern Ireland. **5** The following Chauviré publications are Irish-related: [pseud. Sylvain Briollay], *L'Irlande insurgée* (Paris, 1921); *La Geste de la Branche Rouge ou l'Iliade irlandaise* (Paris, 1926); *L'Incantation* (Paris, 1929); *L'Irlande* (Paris, 1935); *Contes d'un autre monde* (Paris, 1947); *Greg le Libérateur* (Paris, 1949); *Les Contes Ossianiques* (Paris, 1949); *Histoire de l'Irlande* (Paris, 1949). Journals where he corresponded on Irish subjects include the *Revue des Deux Mondes, Affaires étrangères, L'Illustration,* and the *Bulletin de l'Association Guillaume Budé.* **6** Kathleen O'Flaherty, 'Regards français sur l'Irlande', *Études Irlandaises*, 13 (1988), pp 31–43; Phyllis Gaffney, 'Une terrible beauté or 1916 and all that: French fictional representations of modern Irish history' in A. Pearson-Evans & A. Leahy (eds), *Intercultural spaces: language, culture, identity* (Bern, 2007), pp 137–48. **7** For example,

fiction and occasional opinion pieces for French journals. This diverse response to 'contradictory, enigmatic, unfathomable' Ireland allows the reader to gauge the extent to which his fiction and non-fiction complement and illuminate each other.[8] This chapter concentrates on Chauviré's writings on 1916 and its aftermath that move beyond the brief factual summaries in his two monographs, *L'Irlande* (1935)[9] and *Histoire de l'Irlande* (1949).[10]

POLITICAL COMMENTARY

When Chauviré landed in Ireland, the Sinn Féin landslide election of December 1918 and the historic meeting of Dáil Éireann in January 1919 were headline news. This was surely exciting for an academic interested in theories of political power and how republics operate.[11] Ireland's independence was shortly to be won, the island was to be partitioned and the fledgling state plunged into bitter civil war.

Chauviré observed these critical events unfolding and, in a remarkably short time, mastered enough facts about Irish history, and the tangle of Anglo-Irish relations, to write a book on current affairs in Ireland, *L'Irlande insurgée* (Plon, 1921). Published under the pseudonym Sylvain Briollay, it was commissioned by Plon for their 'Contemporary problems' series.[12] This series covered topical issues, in an accessible format, for the French reading public whose knowledge of foreign politics had been found wanting during the First World War. As described on a preliminary page of *L'Irlande insurgée*, the collection published works that were short, factually reliable, readable, objective and informative, and that would offer solutions to the issues discussed:

> In a set of short, highly accurate and readable texts, aimed at decision-makers, and offering definite solutions, this series will tackle all the large current questions likely to interest public opinion, and will deal with them in an impeccably objective manner, thereby seeking only to serve the national interest.[13]

Chauviré met his publisher's criteria perfectly. Succinct (132 pages) and readable, his book was considered sufficiently well-informed to be translated into English, and published by the Talbot Press in Dublin and Fisher Unwin in London as *Ireland in rebellion* in 1922. Explaining how and why the 1916

---

his friendship with Seán T. O'Kelly and his wife, Mary Kate, and subsequently his second wife, Phyllis, lasted till the end of his life.   8 Chauviré, *L'Incantation*, p. 18.   9 Roger Chauviré, *L'Irlande* (Paris, 1935), pp 16–20.   10 Roger Chauviré, *Histoire de l'Irlande* (Paris, 1949), pp 115–19.   11 Chauviré's work on Jean Bodin is still relevant. https://fr.wikipedia.org/wiki/Jean_Bodin.   12 Briollay was the name of a village outside Angers where the Chauviré family home was situated.   13 Sylvain Briollay, *L'Irlande insurgée* (Paris, 1921), p. ii.

Rebellion had originated, Chauviré offered a lucid summary of the Irish Question, from the rejection of Home Rule to the impasse at the time of writing. On the basis of newspaper reports and his conversations with leading personalities, he produced a balanced, coherent account of the state of play in Anglo-Irish relations. Unsurprisingly, given that he finished the book *before* the Truce of July 1921, and that he discussed several possible scenarios for emerging out of the current bloodbath, he ends with a question mark.

What we see, then, is an efficient researcher and an effective communicator seeking to remain as objective as possible in his appraisal of Irish affairs. Apart from the book's structure – the material is laid out in true *dissertation* style, with every chapter subdivided neatly into a pleasing array of topics – there is very little in the substance of *L'Irlande insurgée* that betrays the author's nationality.

Only in one or two specific places does the author speak directly as a Frenchman. He is not impressed by how the Crown allowed politics to drift in Ireland since 1919, which gifted a resurgent Sinn Féin the upper hand. He was astonished that Irish Volunteers were allowed to drill in the streets, and that tricolours were permitted to fly from houses on St Patrick's Day: 'Is it not inconceivable that a Government in France would tolerate comparable manifestations?'

The Frenchman criticised the brutal British counter-offensive, and commented negatively on Britain's negligence in these terms:

> This is the perennial British wait-and-see policy, that celebrated empiricism so much admired by Taine: in short, it is the same lack of constructive imagination which makes the English take things as they happen, from day to day, without foresight or precaution; which makes them fight the symptoms without investigating the causes, which makes them, to put it frankly, reluctant to understand. This lack of curiosity produces a certain mental lethargy.[14]

At the same time, while deploring British muddle-through and lack of understanding of the Irish Question, he was sympathetic to London's need to balance conflicting interests, and understood that Britain had just emerged from a costly and protracted war. He is more critical of Carson and the Orangemen.

The author devotes an entire chapter to parsing and analysing Sinn Féin, the organisation requiring most explanation for the perplexed outsider: 'What a strange thing is Sinn Féin, a mixture of bluff, self-suggestion and faith, almost unanalysable, and so very Irish!'[15] Through his academic colleagues, Chauviré was on good terms with many Sinn Féiners, and accordingly had ample opportunity to understand them himself.[16] Presenting the party's leaders as

---

14 *L'Irlande insurgée*, p. 68.   15 *L'Irlande insurgée*, p. 30.   16 His colleagues in French, also close personal friends, included Michael Hayes and Mary Kate Ryan, later wife of Seán T.

idealists, poets and dreamers, he compares their youthful intransigence to that of Saint-Just, the revolutionary follower of Robespierre, guillotined in his mid-twenties. Their millenarian faith is portrayed as utterly alien to the sense of realism and spirit of compromise, perceived as typically English. Imbued with an indomitable belief in their cause, they disregarded inconvenient realities, such as asymmetric power relations (Ireland versus Empire). French idealists, the author asserts, at least knew enough to know that 'might without right' is futile.

The Irish had an inflated sense of the importance of their cause: 'They see nothing but their village. They would set fire to all Europe to boil their Irish egg ... for men of this stamp, Ireland is the centre of the world'.[17] Above all, Irish nationalists were driven more by sentiment and poetry than by logic:

> Here people are of a different cast. Their belief is an intuitive and direct act of the will, of the imagination, of love; it is one of those mental forms that they produce quite naturally, more akin to feelings than to ideas, to poetry than to logic; in which a thought is all the more powerful in proportion to its lack of clarity, and easily stirs up the unconscious powers of the soul; fundamentally it is a religious state.[18]

Echoing a long-standing trope, he is struck by the Irish love for the loser and predilection for disaster:

> The Irish soul does not so much sing of might or triumph in its poetry, even in its remote epics, as it loves to celebrate, to pity and to lament the outcasts and the losers in a just cause; its heroes are Deirdre and Naoise, the Sean-Bhean Bhocht, Lord Edward and Robert Emmet. Ireland has a despairing affection for misfortune. And even if the sacrifice of these young men was doomed to futility, this was merely an additional reason why they should offer that sacrifice.[19]

FICTION

Chauviré's awareness that nationalist Ireland thrived on sentiment and myth and cherished its martyrs encouraged his turn to fiction. Indeed, in an article on Irish neutrality in 1940, he highlighted the permanent *poétique* orchestrating all political thinking in Ireland.[20] For this commentator, there was an enduring

O'Kelly. Chauviré's letters to Michael Hayes, internee, 1921 (UCD Archives, P53/89 and P53/96). The Chauvirés' flat at 46 Lower Leeson Street was searched by British forces on the night of 18–19 November 1920.　**17** *L'Irlande insurgée*, p. 28.　**18** *L'Irlande insurgée*, pp 22–3.　**19** *L'Irlande insurgée*, p. 33.　**20** Roger Chauviré, 'Que pense l'Irlande?', *Revue des Deux Mondes* (mars 1940), pp 151–9 (pp 153–4): 'there is a kind of "poetics" – I can think of no other word to describe it – which lends its unending harmony to underpin and orchestrate all

dimension to Irish politics that resisted discursive prose, calling for further exposition in imaginative writing. So Briollay the commentator became Chauviré the novelist. He published several novels and novellas over his career, many of them historical and not all based on Irish subjects. Two novels are set precisely in the period under consideration.[21] *L'Incantation* was his first publication in the genre. *L'Incantation* and *Greg le Libérateur* together form a diptych portraying current affairs in Ireland between the First World War and the Civil War. Swiftly paced, written in classically cadenced prose, with a good balance of dialogue, description and action, both fictions are closely based on historical events. Each reflected the mood of the time in which it is set: *L'Incantation*, redolent of romantic nationalism, relies on myth and melodrama to weave its highly dramatic tale around the heady days of the 1916 Rising; *Greg le Libérateur* is decidedly more prosaic, focusing on the need for a workable interpretation of freedom, as Ireland's 1920s politicians undertake the task of building a stable state in the aftermath of the War of Independence, only to collapse, willy-nilly, into civil war. The use of fictional narratives gave Chauviré a freedom that he could not indulge as commentator or journalist: to compress and re-shape real events the better to convey psychological truths and to present the dilemmas faced by the major players, staging political dramas that represented diverse strands of opinion concerning the Rising and the flawed independence that followed in its troubled wake.

L'Incantation, written while *L'Irlande insurgée* was being published, appeared in print at the end of the 1920s. In this vivid story, Chauviré fictionalised the 1916 rebellion and the peculiar stresses bearing on Irish people's reactions to the Great War. Partly inspired by the career of Robert Barton – a case actually highlighted in *L'Irlande insurgée*[22] – the hero, Sir Francis Hackville, is a County Wicklow Protestant landowner who served with the Leinster Fusiliers in Flanders. On returning home with an injured jaw in early summer 1916, he discovers a changed Ireland: his Catholic small-farming neighbours have all been won over to the separatist side. The hero gradually moves to embrace the same cause, culminating in a rousing call to resist violence with violence, in his native Wicklow village. As he throws in his lot with his farming neighbours, Hackville loses the hand of his beloved fiancée, Beatrice Austin; the novel closes with his meditations in Portland prison, where he has been sentenced by court martial to ten years' hard labour for incitement to sedition.

Irish political thinking'.   **21** *L'Incantation* (Paris, 1929), written in 1921–2, and *Greg le Libérateur* (Paris, 1949), written in 1931–2. Several shorter pieces by Chauviré from the 1920s and 1930s are also set in Ireland, and treat both historical and contemporary subjects: *Contes d'un autre monde* (Paris, 1947).   **22** *L'Irlande insurgée*, p. 27.   **23** A dénouement the author once described as 'cornélien': E. Prisset, 'Un entretien, à Briollay, avec M. Roger Chauviré, professeur et écrivain', *L'Ouest (d'Angers)*, [c.1933?]. [BnF, Recherche bibliographique Chauviré, Paul Roger: FOL LN1 232 (5297), *Dossier de coupures de presse.*]

In an effort to make this dénouement plausible, Sir Francis Hackville's political U-turn is strewn with apparently casual references[23]. He drinks with the local farmers, socialises with the parish priest and takes Irish-language classes with the Gaelic League. Every chapter specifically alludes to an Irish nationalist perspective, and to the hero's sympathy with it: a potted history of the oppressed hill people of Wicklow; an appreciation of the patriotic treasures of seventeenth-century bardic poetry; a tour of the museum of Lord Edward FitzGerald, where Hackville is able to handle the patriot's sword; a visit to the nationalist shrine of St Enda's ... There is a wedding between a condemned prisoner and his fiancée on the eve of his execution (recalling Grace Gifford and Joseph Plunkett's tragic marriage). Above all, a performance of Yeats and Lady Gregory's *Cathleen Ní Houlihan* moves the hero.[24] This drama is consciously woven into the plot: both the play and the novel use the myth of the Sean-Bhean Bhocht to relate a conversion story. Like the Yeatsian hero, the novel's central character is also a man torn between the comforts of domesticity (marrying his fiancée) and the pursuit of an elusive ideal (joining an ill-starred struggle for independence).

These nationalist allusions clothe the novel in an unambiguously green local colour. Indeed, Chauviré seemed so tuned in to Irish cultural realities that his work was translated into English by Ernest Boyd, and published for the American market by Longmans in 1929 with a preface by James Stephens (*The sword in the soul*). Yet, *L'Incantation* cannot simply be dismissed as partisan. To quote Boyd's Foreword to his English translation, 'Chauviré has no thesis to sustain; he takes no sides'. While sympathetic and sensitive, he writes 'with the detachment of a foreigner'.[25] He empathised with all the characters and with their opposing dilemmas. The novel's title, a comment on the hero's irrational change of side, refers to the enchantment to which Sir Francis Hackville gradually succumbs: the hero is portrayed as increasingly spellbound, almost hypnotised, by a romantic and futile call to arms, as he sleepwalks his way into the nationalist struggle despite his own rational judgment and the pleas of his fiancée.

L'Incantation's dreamers enacted rebellion and took arms against the ancient oppressor. Chauviré's second Irish novel, *Greg le Libérateur*, concerns rebellion's aftermath: waking up the morning after in the cold prosaic light of day. This highly political narrative opens with the silencing of the guns for the Truce on 11 July 1921, before moving to the Treaty debates and the slide into civil war in the 1920s. Four freedom fighters, representing different modes of interpreting

---

24 Phyllis Gaffney, 'Dramatising the myth and mythologising the drama: *Cathleen Ní Houlihan* and Roger Chauviré's *L'Incantation*' in M.-C. Considère-Charon, P. Laplace & M. Savaric (eds), *The Irish celebrating: festive and tragic overtones* (Newcastle, 2008), pp 86–95; Phyllis Gaffney, 'Revolutionary voices from the West: Yeatsian Hiberno-English migrates into French' in N. Armstrong & F. Federici (eds), *Translating voices, translating regions* (Rome, 2006), pp 379–91. **25** Chauviré, *Sword in the soul*, Foreword, p. vii.

the meaning of an independent Ireland, follow separate paths and meet separate fates.

The novel's eponymous main protagonist, Greg Molony, chairman of the new post-Treaty Irish parliament, emerges as the hero because he holds firm to the routine values of law, order and economic prosperity in a shaky Free State, against the forces of anarchy personified by anti-Treaty gunmen, his erstwhile comrades-in-arms. Once again, recognisable historical events and characters are woven into the fiction, including the murder of a British field marshal, the storming of the Four Courts, chases in the woods of Tipperary and Cork, and summary executions without trial. Greg's friend and Government minister, Alec Lynch (a conflation of Michael Collins and Kevin O'Higgins), is assassinated on his way to Mass and the culprits remain at large. In the final chapter, Greg is hailed as a 'Liberator' (Greg le Libérateur), at a ceremony in Dublin's Mansion House, for his steadfast determination to steer the ship of state despite the turbulence around and against him.

In calling his novel *Greg le Libérateur*, the author had in mind Daniel O'Connell, 'the Liberator', the illustrious predecessor of his staid, balding, protagonist, Greg Molony. Like many French observers of Ireland, Chauviré admired this nineteenth-century exemplar of non-violence. In *L'Irlande insurgée*, he castigated members of Sinn Féin who despised the great parliamentarian: 'They despised O'Connell's respect for legal forms. Judgments both hasty and unjust!'[26]

However, the novel is by no means an apologia for the Irish Free State. For all its celebration of a politician's efforts to impose the rule of law in a state where government has traditionally favoured the oppressor, antagonisms among the characters in *Greg le Libérateur* are portrayed with empathy, even humour. Chauviré is careful to represent all positions even-handedly.

Refusing to take sides, Chauviré understood the motivation of the various players, during these years of conflict. Both of his Irish novels are strikingly authentic. The reader is plunged into the realities of life and living, *à l'irlandaise*, with few concessions to a French readership.[27] The novels do not employ, as the author often does in his novellas treating Irish subjects, the distancing effect of introducing a French outsider's point of view.[28] Nor do French characters appear

---

26 *L'Irlande insurgée*, p. 34.   27 There are some concessions: Gaffney, 'Une certaine idée de l'Irlande, or the professor as propagandist'.   28 Chauviré mixes French and Irish characters in some of his *Contes d'un autre monde* (Paris, 1947). For example, the opening tale ('Histoire instructive et singulière du Mac Carthy Mór, tirée du livre de raison', pp 5–30) concerns an encounter at sea between a Breton naval officer and some Irish exiles from the Siege of Limerick, who have embraced a life of piracy. Another concerns a French Huguenot exile working in Marsh's Library who exults in the street when news of King William's victory at the Boyne comes to Dublin ('Super flumina Babylonis', pp 329–42). A French linguist's six-month stay on the Inishowen peninsula to study Donegal Irish is related in 'La fin d'un roi' (pp 195–220); 'La passion et la mort du Professeur Owen O'Dea, D. Litt., MRIA' (pp 167–93) contrasts Irish and French chauvinism when a visitor from the Collège de France,

in two novellas set during the Troubles, concerning political betrayal.[29] When fictionalising current political events in Ireland, Chauviré preferred to stick as close to the ground as possible.

OPINION PIECES

Greg le Libérateur, the novel depicting the Irish at war with one another, ends on an upbeat note. Greg Molony is putting on weight and taking up golf, and the country's economy is on an even keel. The Free State Government has apparently gained the upper hand over the diehard republicans.

Yet ominous notes still sound, because the author is well aware that in Ireland things are never simply black and white, and nothing can be taken for granted. His article on the Civil War, 'La Guerre civile en Irlande: l'énigme d'un peuple', was published during the conflict, a decade before writing *Greg*.[30] It seeks to explain the enigmatic plunge into civil strife of a people who had just gained their independence. Chauviré analyses, for French readers, the controversial Treaty conditions and the anarchic attitude to law and order prevalent in Ireland, a country where all true heroes are rebels. Because of the country's intimate scale, Irish wars are different from elsewhere; there is a cheerfulness about Ireland's divisions because Irish heroism is mingled with an irrepressible sense of fun, an innate good humour and an ironic habit of self-mockery.[31]

As to the rights and wrongs of the conflict, although he admitted that the Free State is logically and morally superior to the gunmen, Chauviré was slow to condemn the latter outright because of the exceptional conditions in Ireland:

> Steeped as we are in Roman law, enamoured of logic and common sense, we French are certainly inclined to ascribe blame to the republican rebels: their illegal action, causing bloodshed and financial loss with no obvious prospect of success, as far as human sight can tell, is to us manifestly outrageous, senseless and therefore criminal. However, on the other hand, the conditions of life in that country are so abnormal as to make one refrain from passing cut and dried judgments or even taking definitive positions.[32]

---

lecturing at the Royal Irish Academy, sows doubt in a clerical Professor of Old Irish on the reliability of Irish manuscript interpretation. A later novella, 'La Croix de Cong' (in *Les œuvres libres. Recueil littéraire ne publiant que de l'inédit*, 41 (Paris, 1949), pp 185–212), features Irish clerics, and introduces the Collège des Irlandais into its dénouement.   **29** *Contes d'un autre monde*, pp 285–327 ('Drogues'), written in 1933, and pp 31–76 ('Histoire d'amour'), written in 1928.   **30** *L'Illustration*, 4144, 1922, pp 110–11.   **31** This peculiarly Irish approach to war is portrayed in *Greg le Libérateur*: a ludic mood animates the storming of the Four Courts, the event that triggered the Civil War (*Greg le Libérateur*, pp 91–8).   **32** 'La Guerre civile en Irlande', p. 111.

Presciently pointing out the Free State Government's unpopularity among an
electorate that tended to side with losers, as well as the Government's collusion
with London and the danger of spawning fresh martyrs by precipitate actions,
Chauviré left the outcome of the Civil War open:

> The ricochets of Irish popular feeling are the most disconcerting in the
> world: that is what makes the country so difficult to govern, so fascinating
> to observe, and so risky to predict.[33]

Who in 1922 could foretell how the Irish Civil War might end or predict what
was in store a decade later? With the general election of 1932 came the de Valera
phenomenon. In February 1933, Chauviré gave the Fianna Fáil leader credit for
a certain pragmatism, despite his trenchant position on Irish unity.[34] A lengthier,
more nuanced, appraisal of de Valera was published later in 1933 in the *Revue des
Deux Mondes*.[35] Portraying the politician in a satiric vein, as a romantic hero with
iconic status, Chauviré conveyed to French readers his charisma and the extent
of his cult in a country where, unlike in France, no clear lines were drawn
between public and private spheres, or between nationality and religion. Nobody
can understand Ireland if they fail to grasp the country's clan mentality that
demanded a chief, supported out of fervent personal loyalty, rather than a
democratic leader. Hence, the Irish electorate voted for the leader, not for his
party. Treating de Valera as a more complex figure than usually believed, he
painted him as solemn, morally pure, a woeful orator, but a wily politician and
spokesman for the plain people of Ireland, commanding universal respect.

The article evokes the intimacy of the Irish experience, which distorted
perspectives:

> In their rebellion against England, they suffered a thousand casualties in
> the space of two years. These people have no idea what a real war is like.
> For them, an ambush is a battle, the kidnapping of a few policemen is an
> Austerlitz. But by the same token, precisely on account of this absence of
> scale, on account of this weakness, they can confer a quasi-poetic idealism
> on the idea of a futile rebellion, that rebellion so defiantly aware of its own
> hopelessness.[36]

In the Irish political psyche, where poetry and imagination still lord it over
logic and reason, de Valera is idolised and mythified, having fanned the flames of
'fanaticisms where pure reason is helpless'.[37]

33 'La Guerre civile en Irlande', p. 111.   34 'Réactions extérieures des élections irlandaises',
Affaires étrangères: revue mensuelle de documentation internationale et diplomatique, 3 (février
1933), pp 80–90.   35 Roger Chauviré, 'M. de Valera', 1er août 1933, *Revue des Deux Mondes*,
16, 8e période, pp 534–50.   36 Chauviré, 'M. de Valera', p. 539.   37 Chauviré, 'M. de
Valera', p. 542.

In spring 1940, Chauviré commented on Irish neutrality for the *Revue des Deux Mondes*.[38] De Valera's policy of neutrality was not in Ireland's best interests and he dismissed as unfounded the fear of a Republican–German alliance. Irish neutrality was not at all straightforward. His Irish acquaintances hoped for an Allied victory, but they were afraid to assert this too loudly in public since, in Ireland, to be patriotic meant to be anti-British: 'Nothing Irish is simple, not even neutrality'.[39]

In this 1940 article, the author returns once more to the myth of 1916, which he blames for skewing Ireland's self-image. He disputes the claim, widespread in Ireland, that the Rising *alone* had forced London to concede independence, and argued that, if only Ireland aligned with the Allies, a thirty-two county Republic could become a pragmatic possibility. However, faced with the tenacious impact that the Rising had exerted on the Irish popular imagination, he realised the limitations of his powers to persuade. 'It is hard to imagine the magic that the undreamed-of success of the 1916 insurrection – against all the odds – has worked on Irish minds'.[40]

In 1993, Danielle Jacquin noted changes in the French historiography of Ireland as relayed in successive volumes of *Que sais-je?*, a series published by the Presses Universitaires de France.[41] The first *Que sais-je?* volume to treat the topic, Chauviré's *Histoire de l'Irlande* (1949), was revised in 1970 by René Fréchet, who updated his own text in a sixth edition published shortly before his death in 1992. Chauviré gave pride of place to Gaelic Ireland and wrote with passion in a somewhat outmoded romantic style whereas Fréchet sought a more neutral voice, and the contemporary issue of Northern Ireland loomed sufficiently large to blot out any concern for Gaelic culture.

To every age its historian. Chauviré regarded Irish history through the lens of a scholar steeped in the Classics, who had become familiar with early Irish history and translated old Irish legends. For him, Ireland's pre-Norman roots represented *l'Irlande profonde* and he retained a special admiration for the fading Celtic culture of Ireland's western seaboard, an 'other world' that was worth preserving as a unique vestige of Europe's heritage.[42] In his Epilogue to *Histoire de l'Irlande*, he acknowledges his bias towards Gaelic Ireland: 'Perhaps excessively, perhaps abusively, my book emphasises the Gaelic dimension'. However he justifies this imbalance: 'because it was in that Gaelic dimension, those ways of life, of thought, of art, that Ireland presented a unique profile, without peer or parallel in the contemporary world, because this loss can never

38 Roger Chauviré, 'Que pense l'Irlande?', *Revue des Deux Mondes* (mars 1940), pp 151–9. 39 Chauviré, 'Que pense l'Irlande?', p. 151.   40 Chauviré, 'Que pense l'Irlande?', p. 155. 41 Danielle Jacquin, 'Note de lecture. *Histoire de l'Irlande*, PUF, collection *Que sais-je?* de 1949 à 1992, de Roger Chauviré à René Fréchet', *Études Irlandaises*, 18 (1993), pp 168–70.   42 This world is sympathetically evoked in the elegiac essay 'Un monde qui meurt', *Contes d'un autre monde* (pp 221–42) and in Roger Chauviré, 'Le génie celte', *Bulletin de l'Association Guillaume Budé*, 1 (1955), pp 86–110.

again be made whole. Once that is destroyed, Ireland becomes only another outcrop of Europe'.[43]

However, Roger Chauviré knew that fiction could achieve effects that academic history cannot. In interpreting the phenomenon of 1916 and what followed in its wake for his compatriots, he was well aware of the complexities, uniqueness and volatility of Irish affairs. Vividly and sympathetically evoking current events in his fiction, he could be sharply critical in his non-fiction of misguided policies, and he cast a cool rational French eye on the Rising, and more especially its hotly mythologised aftermath.

These views were based on years of close observation and study, by an outsider unusually in tune with his host country, in all its dimensions, whether unsettled present or distant past. If 1916 cast a continuing spell, as Chauviré claimed, over the Irish, perennial Ireland worked its own enchantment on the man himself.[44]

---

43 Chauviré, *Histoire de l'Irlande*, p. 120. **44** This was paradoxical in that his quasi-diplomatic mission, when he took up the Chair of French in UCD in 1919, required that he represent and spread French language and culture in Ireland, instead of enlightening the French about his host country. Gaffney, 'Une certaine idée de l'Irlande or the professor as propagandist'.

Dublin, Paris, and the world republic of letters

BARRY McCREA

TWO PARISES

The relationship between real places and their fictional versions is complicated: even in the most realist of novels, physical places are also landscapes of the imagination. In *La république mondiale des lettres*, Pascale Casanova uses an analogous idea to argue that the creation of a national literary space requires a disconnection from the national territory.[1] Casanova argues that this separation is often achieved via Paris, or rather 'Paris', a concept which is linked to but not wholly identical with the actual city: the capital of France and the capital of the world republic of letters are related but distinct spaces.

How are these places connected? What does it mean for a literary work to inhabit one or both of these Parises? Irish modernism is one of Casanova's key examples, and one way to approach this question is to take an Irish modernist in Paris – Joyce – and a Parisian modernist in Paris – Proust – and compare how they shared, exploited, and struggled with Paris both as a physical place to live in and as the capital of the World Republic of Letters.

Joyce moved to Paris only in 1920. He was planning to stay for a week, but ended up staying for twenty years. Much of *Ulysses* had already been written in Zurich and Trieste, but it was in some respects a Parisian work already. In the novel, Stephen Dedalus is back in Dublin (as Joyce was in 1904) in the wake of a sojourn studying medicine at the Sorbonne. For Stephen, as it had been for Joyce, it was a short and in many ways fruitless trip, but Paris serves a crucial symbolic function in *Ulysses* as *the* place of exile, *the* artistic alternative to Dublin – the capital, indeed, of a longed-for republic of letters. This symbolic Paris and the real one overlap in Stephen's mind. His stay there, cut short by news of his mother's impending death, seems to have been in many ways a failure, but it has become a crucial part of his identity. In the first chapter, when they find that they have run out of milk, Stephen suggests to Buck Mulligan that they can drink their breakfast tea with lemon instead. Mulligan retorts: 'Damn you and your Paris fads! I want Sandycove milk'.[2] There is a typical Joycean hint here to the future of the novel: the 'maternal' nutrition of Ireland will be replaced by Mediterranean citrus, a harbinger of the Jewish Bloom.

---

1 Pascale Casanova, *La République mondiale des Lettres* (Paris, 1999).   2 James Joyce, *Ulysses*, ed. Hans Walter Gabler (New York: 1986 [1922]), p. 10 (*U* 1.342–3).

In the third chapter, 'Proteus', Stephen's meditations on himself and on the more general question of identity are woven through with memories of and reflections upon his time in Paris:

> My Latin quarter hat … Eating your groatsworth of *mou en civet*, fleshpots of Egypt, elbowed by belching cabmen. Just say in the most natural tone: when I was in Paris, *boul'Mich'*, I used to. Yes, used to carry punched tickets to prove an alibi if they arrested you for murder somewhere. Justice. On the night of the seventeenth of February 1904 the prisoner was seen by two witnesses. Other fellow did it: other me. Hat, tie, overcoat, nose. *Lui, c'est moi.*[3]

Stephen's rambling thoughts suggest that paranoia and free-floating guilt are part of the way certain young people construct their identity – the confused, anxious answers that at a difficult stage of life come tumbling out in response to the question 'who am I like?' But Stephen is also thinking of another possible, Parisian mirror-version of himself. In fact, he conjures up a Parisian counterpart to Ireland – he recalls in some detail a meeting with a French-speaking Patrice Egan, the son of an exiled Fenian.

Ulysses was finished and first published in Paris, as seems in retrospect to have been its destiny. *Finnegans wake*, however, was largely written in Paris and it is the product of Joyce's Parisian years. It is his true Paris novel. French and Italian are, after English, the second languages of the *Wake*. The first word of the *Wake*, 'rivverun', contains a French meaning. As an imperative in English, it is an invocation to the muse, a command to the river of thought and language to run, as in a dream. As a noun, the word flows on from – as we learn when we read the *Wake* for the second time – the last word of the novel, 'the': we are going along the course of a river, following the water-cycle, and in this spirit, riverrun explicitly echoes the Italian *riverranno*, 'they will return'. There is also a ghost of Irish in the word, in the word *rún* which means 'secret' and is also an endearment. But the most phonetically suggestive counterpart to the word is the French *riverain*. This word originally meant someone living on the banks (*rives*) of a river. This opening word suggests up front that the river in question is both the Liffey and the Seine, a Dublin–Paris amalgam. The *Wake* indeed deals extensively with people living beside the Liffey, from HCE, ALP and their children in Chapelizod to the famous chattering washerwomen who gradually lose each other's voices across the widening river, but it is a novel written by an Irishman living by another river, the Seine; Paris, in both its literal and symbolic forms, is the other city of the *Wake*.

The word *riverain* in French was extended from this riverside etymology to mean more generally 'residents', the local inhabitants of a place or a street. The

---

3 Joyce, *Ulysses*, p. 35 (*U* 3.174–83).

13.1 Joyce in Zurich 1918 by Carl Ruf. Ruf opened commercial photographic studios in Mannheim, Freiburg, Basel, Darmstadt, Heidelberg, Karlsruhe, Basle and Zurich (Collection Kevin Whelan).

French equivalent of a 'Residents Only' parking sign is *Sauf riverains*. A *riverain* is someone with the privileges and insights of a local, so its place at the beginning of *Finnegans wake* is complex. Joyce adopts an infamously local perspective, indeed he imposes a local perspective on his reader; the implied reader of the

Wake is expected to have an encyclopaedic knowledge of Dublin. This is one of the many modernist provocations of *Finnegans wake*: the implication is that you will only understand it if you are from Dublin. But it is equally true that the implied readers of the *Wake* will only follow the novel if they are also from 'Paris' – in Casanova's sense: you have to be a citizen of world literature to inhabit this novel. Moreover, in a novel as dense and allusive as *Finnegans wake* who, in the real world could possibly be imagined as the intended reader? Who is the novel's insider, its *riverain*, its 'local' with all the insider knowledge of literally scores of languages, military and imperial history, American geography, Norse mythology, ancient and modern Ireland, ballads, obscure nineteenth-century opera, and so on?

The narrator of *Finnegans wake* is announced in the first word of the novel as a local of two places, a resident of two imaginary riverside cities. The other *riverain* referred to in the word is Joyce himself, a local of Dublin but now a resident of Paris, the place where the novel was written. The twenty years in Paris is the period of Joyce's life about which we know the least. We know a good deal about his life in Dublin, Zurich and Trieste, but his two decades as a Parisian *riverain* are still obscure (in part because of destroyed or suppressed correspondence). He seems not to have been especially attached to it (in the 1930s he contemplated a move to London) as a place. But Paris became his home both literally and in Casanova's sense of the clearinghouse for world literature.

For his first two years there, Joyce shared the physical city with Marcel Proust. In terms of literary history, the two writers also uneasily share an iconic status: along with a handful of other novelists and poets, they epitomise difficult high modernism, and tackling their work requires a similar leap of faith on the part of the reader. But their two 'worlds' were almost wholly separate. 1922, the iconic year of modernism, was the year when *Ulysses* was published and when Proust died.

Physically the two writers largely stuck to opposite sides of the Seine – indeed, they were attached respectively to the city's two different *rives*. Proust was right bank – *rive droite* – and Joyce *rive gauche*. These geographical sides of the city (like uptown/downtown in New York) also corresponded to two different social spheres, the old Parisian upper classes on the right bank – with its banks, opera houses etc. – while workers, students, artists, and expatriates were on the left. Joyce and Proust also inhabited the city in radically different *ways*. Proust lived his entire life in the same neighbourhood and the same family apartments; moving to the Left Bank would have been like going abroad. Joyce lived at a total of eighteen addresses, and while most of them were physically on the Left Bank, the geographical distinctions hardly meant that much to him – his *rive* was really that of the World Republic of Letters.

Joyce attended Proust's funeral; a rare sign that they inhabited the same city, in which they circulated – as immigrants and natives often do – in thoroughly different spheres. They met only once, an infamous moment in literary history. Their encounter has attracted much fanciful retrospective embellishment, the eyewitness accounts differing on all details of the conversation, except for the fact that it was a failure. Nonetheless, it is still possible to infer some details from the story about the different ways in which the two men inhabited Paris. The meeting – a late-night supper at the Hotel Majestic following the première of Stravinsky's *Renard* – was arranged by the Schiffs – Sydney, a wealthy English novelist and publicist, and Violet. The well-connected couple were determined to bring together the great modernists of Paris at the same party – Diaghilev, Stravinsky, Picasso, Proust, Joyce. The real social cachet was to get the two novelists – both, perhaps Proust especially, notoriously difficult to pin down – under the same roof. The invitation to Proust, who was in poor health, was deliberately misleading, omitting Joyce's name from the list of guests.[4]

Joyce arrived before Proust, drunk and apologising for not having 'changed' for dinner. Joyce did not possess any formal evening wear at a time when clothes were a crucial marker of status and social identity, as well as being a significant expense in a way hard to imagine nowadays (in his correspondence with Ezra Pound, planning a trip to see him, Joyce returns again and again to the fact that he lacks appropriate clothes and the funds to buy them; via T.S. Eliot, Pound dispatched a parcel of second-hand clothing and shoes to Joyce in Paris). Proust arrived at 2.30a.m. wearing a fur coat. The accounts agree that Joyce was keen to speak to Proust but that the interest was not reciprocated; Joyce inveigled his way into the taxi that was taking Proust and the Schiffs back to Proust's apartment, hoping for a nightcap and more conversation, but Proust, with the help of the Schiffs, got rid of him.

Since Joyce read French easily but Proust could not read English, it is not overly surprising that the interest was so one-sided (despite some dismissive comments in his letters, Arthur Power and Joyce himself attest that in later life Joyce read and admired parts of the *Recherche*, which appears frequently in *Finnegans wake*). But the literary side of it is only part of the story. For all of the differing details of what the two novelists allegedly discussed – truffles, ailments, their ignorance of each other's work – what really stands out is the barrier of social class dividing them. It was for reasons of class that Woolf, too, found Proust's work easier to relate to than Joyce's. In the end, the conclusion we can draw from this famously flopped meeting is that, even though they epitomise modernist Paris, Joyce and Proust lived in different Parises, Proust the *riverain*, Joyce the outsider. From the Schiffs' perspective, the meeting would bring together social and literary, lived and fictional, real and imaginary worlds. In fact, Joyce and Proust could not share the social space of Paris, in the way that they did share its notional literary space.

4 William Carter, *Marcel Proust: a life* (New Haven: 2000), pp 777–8: Richard Ellmann, *James Joyce* (Oxford, 1982 [1959]), pp 508–9.

THE LITERAL CITY AND THE LITERARY CITY

Their different ways of inhabiting the geographical Paris also correspond to different ways of finding the imaginary, extra-territorial space of the World Republic of Letters within the real-life city. Differences between *Ulysses* and the *Recherche*, two great embodiments of high modernism, can be accounted for by their authors' vastly different experiences of Paris – both the literal city and the literary city.

Joyce left Dublin at 22, and lived the rest of his life in exile in continental Europe. He set foot in Ireland again on only a handful of occasions, for a couple of brief and disengaged visits. Proust, the *riverain*, was born, lived and died in the city where he was born. Indeed, with the exception of a few short trips, Proust barely left France in his whole lifetime.

Ulysses and the *Recherche* share the same twin aims, and both books struggle with reconciling these aims: on the one hand, the examination and accurate representation of individual human consciousness and psychology, and on the other, the portrayal of a specific social, historical and cultural context, a community anchored in a specific place and time. Both novels are dedicated equally to these two goals, the depiction of the inner world of the individual and of collective realities at a particular historical moment. The individual is examined in *Ulysses* mostly through the workings of the mind of Leopold Bloom, but also others, especially Stephen Dedalus and Molly Bloom, as well as more peripheral figures such as Gerty McDowell. The collective culture plumbed by *Ulysses* is that of middle-class Dublin in 1904 (in *Finnegans wake* the range of consciousnesses depicted expands, and the novel's scope ranges much further in history and geography, but it is nonetheless still defined by the dynamic between these two aims). For Proust, the individual consciousness is chiefly that of his self-analytic first-person narrator, as well as this narrator's analysis of the motivations and psychologies of the people who cross his path. The collective, socio-historical reality that Proust wishes to depict is high Parisian society from the Belle Époque to the First World War.

In both cases, while the two aims are linked, they pull the novels in opposed directions. While the two tendencies are characteristic of all novels in some way, the tension between the two in *Ulysses* and *Recherche* is not merely present but formally *constitutive* of both novels. The class and national differences between the two writers determine to a considerable extent how this tension plays out: Joyce came from a poor, peripheral, colonised country and from a social class where economic deprivation and emigration were the norm; Proust came from a background where such things were unheard of.

The two very different modes of approaching the same subject in Joyce and Proust are inextricably linked to the broad shape of the ways in which they lived out their lives – being a local and being a foreigner. Joyce's fictional homeland –

the Dublin of *Ulysses* and *Finnegans wake* – had to be conjured up from the imagination and memory of an ever-receding past, magically constructed and reconstructed at a distance in faraway cities. Proust's Paris was also the site of his own daily life, just outside his window, in the shops, streets, language and friends of his own life experience.

The most important effect that exile or migration exerts on the imagination is not so much the experience of place but the experience of time. For Proust, the home bird, the *riverain*, living his whole life out in the society in which he was born, the lovers, friends and playmates of his childhood were always liable to show up again, older, fatter, greyer, kinder. This experience was entirely alien to Joyce, whose life was shaped by a constantly shifting constellation of multinational individuals, while the personalities of his youth, the flowering boys and girls of *A portrait of the artist as a young man*, faded out of lived reality and into the realm of art and eternal youth (and sometimes the focus of intense fantasies).

The snapshot method of *Ulysses* paints, like a census, an instantaneous, frozen reality of a community at a single but irretrievably past moment. Stephen Dedalus is a Peter Pan: it is not just that he happens to be young but that he incarnates the *idea* of inexperience, promise and youth. Dublin remains solid and real in Joyce's imagination, but also ageless and immobile, and its inhabitants, petrified like the inhabitants of Pompeii, must bear the heavy weight of allegorical and symbolic meaning: the Invalid, the Poet, the Adulterer, the Wife. In exile, temporary characteristics freeze as innate qualities, and the *routine* of everyday life, as we see so clearly in *Ulysses*, becomes sacralised and solidified as *ritual*.

No friendship, even that with his brother Stanislaus, lasted throughout Joyce's lifetime, with only a handful of exceptions, such as the Colums. Only his co-exile Nora stayed constant, for Joyce a treasury of cultural and linguistic artifacts. Otherwise, in middle age Joyce saw few people whom he had known when they were young; people younger than himself, like Beckett or James Stephens, he would not know when they grew older, and in any case he invariably broke friendships due to one or another imagined offence or jealousy. Characters passed through his experience fixed and unchanging in age and circumstance; people in Joyce's life must have been in some respects as characters are in *Ulysses*, pre-formed, immediately symbolic of some fixed idea, caught forever as they were when Joyce left Ireland, like a game of musical statues.

A life like Proust's, however, lived in or around one fixed place, offers space for reversals, returns and development, and unlike *Ulysses*, few characters in the *Recherche* turn out as they first seem. No one ends the novel as they began. The rich become poor, the cowardly become brave, the heartless adulterer becomes a devoted and caring husband, the most avid heterosexual turns out to have been gay. Proust's own quotidian world always held out the possibilities of long-lost individuals showing up again, living proof of the passage of time and the constant work of change. *Ulysses* is a portrait of given immanent realities in the rigidly restricted temporal zone of a single day. We do not know what the future may hold for the Blooms' marriage, or even where Stephen spends the night after leaving Eccles Street, let alone if he will become an artist or be transformed by his encounter with Bloom.

The *Recherche* on the other hand is a novel of *change*, of temporal and psychological development. Where *Ulysses* spans a day, the *Recherche* spans a lifetime – more, a lifetime and a half – and in it, individual identities that in youth seem fixed turn out to be contingent, subject to time and change. This is the obvious reality of the *Recherche*: the allegorical forms and moulds that we find in *Ulysses* are there, but individuals pass through them, rather than embodying them permanently.

The narrative desire to see mythic identities embodied by real people is not a struggle for Joyce, who lived far away from his family and from the companions of his youth. This is however precisely the challenge for Proust's novel: how to identify and situate a stable individual consciousness or moment outside of all this change, something fixed within all that ceaseless flux and flow. How could Proust find Joyce's 'Paris', Casanova's transnational literary space, while growing up and continuing to live in the real Paris? How could he become a citizen of the deterritorialised world republic of letters while remaining a consummate *riverain* of the literal *rive droite*?

Written from the insider's perspective of the writer at home, the *Recherche* struggles to escape the flow of time and change, to find an internal exile of its own with which to catch the irreducible singularity of individuals, so clear to the allegorising, symbolising eye of Joyce.

Both Proust's life and work show constant attempts to get 'outside', seeking an exilic space within Paris, a way to evolve from a *riverain* into an exile at home. We can understand the famous ecstatic spasms of involuntary memory as one attempted solution to this problem – they freeze time, place and persons just as Joyce's imagination does, decades and hundreds of miles away, to Dublin on 16 June 1904. The many times in *Recherche* in which the narrator goes to extraordinary, sometimes comical lengths to position himself as an outside looking in – clambering up ladders, hiding in bushes beside windows, standing on stools to look through peep-holes, etc. – might be read as inscriptions of the struggle to acquire an outsider's perspective, the need to find an exile within.

Moreover, the *Recherche* emphasises hidden civilisations – Jews, gays, lesbians, freemasons – hiding in plain sight beneath the surface of city, realities not immediately legible in the busy daily life of the city. To these aspects of his novel we might relate Proust's obsessive anxiety about his physical working space, and his extreme, eccentric writing habits. *Ulysses* is a book of the light, written during the daytime, whereas the *Recherche*, which seeks out so many dark places, was written at night. When Joyce was offered an apartment with a dedicated study, he found that he could not write there, as he needed to be surrounded by the sounds of daily life. Conversely, Proust went to extraordinary lengths to keep out precisely those sounds. In his notorious cork-lined room, we can see a precise, material expression of the different consequences of living in Paris as an outsider or as a *riverain*.

THE DRIFT OF LANGUAGE

This experience of time has an analogous counterpart in the experience of language. Joyce exiled himself not only from Ireland, but also from the English language. The vernacular of the streets, the speech of the *riverains* of Dublin, mattered hugely to Joyce, and his mastery of it was a source of great pride. But the languages he heard spoken around him for his whole creative life were Italian, the Triestine dialect, and later in his life, Swiss-German and especially French. For Joyce in Paris, speaking Italian at home, his Dublin English was sealed off from vernacular change, preserved in the deep freeze of his mind, fresh and unchanged since 1904. Like its portraits of Bloom or Molly, or its thumbnail sketches of everyone else who passes through his imaginary Dublin on that day, the Dublin dialect is recorded in *Ulysses* in once-off detail and accuracy. For Joyce, finishing *Ulysses* in Paris, the city of light, Dublin and its language lay in the darkness. Thus in *Ulysses*, the life and speech of one day come fully formed into the daylight, from the darkness of Joyce's exiled mind, emerging like a Neolithic body recovered from a bog, fully preserved, formed, complex and unique, preserved with magical accuracy – a miracle enabled by Paris, a place in which to find a space in world republic of letters.

This linguistic distance was impossible to reproduce for Proust, who never successfully mastered any language except French. Whereas Joyce used his own memory and Nora's voice to conjure up – like a medium – his lost mother tongue, Proust employed for his novel the same language that he used in all his daily interactions with his friends, and with his faithful maid. Living in Paris, Proust witnessed his language changing with the times, assuming Americanisms, minting new words, developing modish fads in syntax and style. Watching his own language evolve was a source of both great interest and sadness for Proust, as he saw sounds and words die out or be superseded. Linguistic fads – such as a fashionable vogue for English words[5] – attain a great symbolic freight of meaning in the *Recherche*, for they highlight the essential alienation of the individual from the language. We ground our identities and sense of self in language, but, the *Recherche* suggests, something so unreliably subject to change

5 For an analysis of this aspect of Proust, see Daniel Karlin, *Proust's English* (New York, 2005).

can hardly provide a solid basis for it. The changeability of language – something so constitutive of the self – becomes one of the existential panics of Proust's novel.

At the same time, there is a powerful desire in the *Recherche* to show, as *Ulysses* does, that individuals are constituted not only in their singularity, but as unconscious vessels of collective realities, as repositories of communal cultural material. In *À l'ombre des jeunes filles en fleurs* [*In the shadow of young girls in flower* – formerly translated as *Within a budding grove*] when the narrator is listing the individual traits of the girls, he reflects that 'L'individu baigne dans quelque-chose de plus général que lui' ('The individual is steeped in something more general than himself'). Writing from the vantage point of exile, Joyce is certain of himself, and of his characters, as both belonging to and representing a culture. This is the condition, willed or not, of the expatriate, after all. For the *riverain* Proust, surrounded by changing and differentiated vernacular French, this question about what an individual might be steeped in that is more general than she is – a given in *Ulysses* – is the problem of his novel. Situated in the middle of the world that he wishes to describe, Proust must seek out dark spaces within, enduring realities outside of the heedless flow of days, just as the narrator has ecstatic experiences when moments of involuntary memory connect one time to another, proving the existence of a reality impervious to the erosion of time.

In Proust, individuals are often described in linguistic terms – idiosyncrasies of pronunciation, fondness for English words, solecisms, pretensions, archaisms, fastidiousness, rare words, vulgarities and so on. The character whose manner of speaking is most carefully interrogated is Françoise, the individual with whom the narrator has the most sustained intimacy. She is tasked by the novel with embodying the history of France. Only in moments of inadvertent 'darkness' does she reveal the immense cultural legacy that flows through her:

> On sentait que les notions que l'artiste médiéval et la paysanne médiévale (survivant au XIXe siècle) avaient de l'histoire ancienne ou chrétienne … ils les tenaient non des livres, mais d'une tradition à la fois antique et directe, ininterrompue, orale, déformée, méconnaissable et vivante.

> One could see that the ideas which the medieval artist and the medieval peasant (still surviving in the nineteenth century) had of classical and of early Christian history … were derived not from books, but from a tradition at once ancient and direct, unbroken, oral, distorted, unrecognisable and alive.[6]

6 Marcel Proust, *À la recherche du temps perdu*, 7 vols (Paris, [1913–27]), i, p. 149; Marcel Proust, *In search of lost time*, translated by C.K. Scott Moncrieff & Terence Gilmartin, 6 vols (New York, 1993), i, p. 212 (translation modified).

Again and again, in these moments of darkness, Françoise reveals that her own individual speech accidentally incarnates 'the language of Saint Simon', or the 'spirit of medieval France', the vocabulary of Mme de Sévigné or of La Bruyère, the great seventeenth-century French prose stylist.

Joyce, in exile from Ireland and from the characters who populated his youth, is, in a crucial sense, in exile from time. By contrast, Proust inhabits it. These moments of privileged darkness, conduits through which accumulated cultural history reaches into the light, like Freud's unconscious revealed through a slip of the tongue, these moments of darkness when communal culture and language surface from the depths, are threatened by the passage of time.

Only in these moments of exile from the self, when the collective experience from which language derives makes itself visible, are people connected to one another and to a common, mystical cultural reservoir. Living through years, and contaminated by long-term interactions with others, Françoise is a mortal, changeable fictional individual in a way that Molly Bloom, eternally 27, eternally in 1904, can never be. Towards the end of Françoise's life, the narrator remarks:

> Car dans son humilité, dans sa tendre admiration pour des êtres qui lui étaient infiniment inférieurs, elle adoptait leur vilain tour de langage. Sa fille s'étant plainte d'elle à moi et m'ayant dit (je ne sais de qui elle l'avait reçu): 'Elle a toujours quelque chose à dire, que je ferme mal les portes, et patatipatali et patatapatala'. Françoise crut sans doute que son incomplète éducation seule l'avait jusqu'ici privée de ce bel usage. Et sur ses lèvres où j'avais vu fleurir jadis le français le plus pur j'entendis plusieurs fois par jour: Et patatipatali et patatapatala.

> For in her humility, in her affectionate admiration for people infinitely inferior to herself, she had come to adopt their ugly habits of speech. Her daughter having complained to me about her and having used the words (I do not know where she had heard them): 'She's always finding fault with me because I don't close the doors properly and <u>patatipatali</u> and <u>patatapatala</u>'. Françoise doubtless thought only her insufficient education that had deprived her until now of this beautiful idiom. And from those lips which I had once seen bloom with the purest French I heard several times a day, *Et patatipatali patata patala*.[7]

The imagined linguistic purity whose loss the narrator is regretting here expresses the general longing in Proust for a spontaneous dimension of experience which is not worked on, not shaped, wrought or eroded by reflection or by time. The quasi-mystical linguistic inheritance and continuity that the narrator hears in Françoise and the Duchesse is part of the longing for a reality

---

7 Proust, *À la recherche du temps perdu*, vii, pp 56–7; Proust, *In search of lost time*, vi, p. 86.

that is immune to the bourgeois realm of change and development. The contamination of Françoise's language by social aspiration, by the middle-class fads of her daughter and niece, represent the impossibility of this ideal.

The dream of a language untouched by time and change, and the projection by the middle class onto the speech of the peasantry as a living example of this idealised language is represented in Joyce's 'The Dead' by the Irish language (the language which people at home, Dublin *riverains*, were seeking to adopt as a barrier to the reality of change around them). The yearnings projected onto the Irish language can be regarded as a dream of a stable form of language itself, as a response to the relentless march of change. In Trieste, Zurich, and Paris, Joyce had no need of Irish as an object of longing, because his own Dublin English already functioned for him as a lost language, itself now a language of a distant western periphery.

In Casanova's view, Paris allowed Joyce to avoid the choice between English and Irish, which paralysed writers who stayed at home in Ireland, and thus freed him to build an Irish national space in the world republic of letters. The distance of Paris allowed Joyce in *Finnegans Wake* to turn Dublin into 'Dublin', with Annalivia Plurabelle as the Liffey and so on. French is one of the many linguistic ghosts that haunt the *Wake*, appearing in some form or other behind practically every sentence. But the fundamental language of the novel is Hiberno-English, whose rhymes, rhythms, and expressions confer a distinctive shape and structure to the prose of the *Wake*. Irish-English is the linguistic river which flows through the novel. Thanks to its transformation in Paris, capital of the World Republic of Letters, however, the form of Hiberno-English in the *Wake* is internationalised, the local vernacular of the *riverains* of Dublin transformed into a cosmopolitan world language.

The last line of *Ulysses*, is not 'yes I said yes I will Yes', but rather 'Trieste-Zurich-Paris 1914–1921'. Joyce's last word is a reminder of his own exclusion from the place and the time of his fictional world. These words seem at first glance to be extraneous to the chapter preceding them, just as the author was to Dublin. But these names and dates are of a piece both with the 'Penelope' chapter and with the question of the World Republic of Letters. In this final chapter, the novel's world, in which we have been so long immersed, is revisited and redescribed. Molly's monologue offers a bird's-eye, external view of this world, as she lies in bed thinking about it, evoking its characters and their histories from her memory: a situation analogous to the novel's author, recalling the Dublin of his youth from faraway continental cities. We the readers have spent the day with men in the public spaces of the city: streets, pubs, cafés, beaches. Molly has spent her whole day, as far as we can gather, at home in Eccles Street.

As a woman, the life of the offices, brothels, and taverns of turn-of-the-century Dublin, transformed into sites of epic adventure by *Ulysses*, are not as open to Molly as they are to Bloom or Stephen. She does not circulate in the streets and spaces of the city where the novel takes place. Physically, she is not part of the community that we are exposed to in the novel, but she is often thought and talked about there. Like the emigrant Joyce, she is present in minds and gossip but not in body. She is not a *riveraine*. Through Molly's mind, we are given an overview of the novel's Dublin and its population, not experienced directly, but at one remove, reconstructed in her imagination, at a spatial and temporal distance. We might read here a secret fellowship between Joyce and Molly; we might even read her as a counterpart for Proust, awake when everyone else is asleep, shut up at home in bed in Dublin, but active in the exile of her imagination, in the dark 'Paris' of her mind.

Postscript

PIERRE JOANNON & KEVIN WHELAN

> Here in Ireland,
> Am I, my brother,
> And you far from me
> In gallant Paris.[1]
>
> P.H. Pearse

In 1922, the novelist James Stephens, who moved constantly between Dublin and Paris, summarised the challenges facing an independent Ireland:

> In my own country of Ireland, man is now in the making, and in a very few years our national action will tell us what it is we may hope for culturally, or what it is that we may be tempted to emigrate from. But Irish national action and culture can no longer be regarded as a thing growing cleanly from its own root. We have entered the world. More, the world has entered us, and a double, an internal and an external, evolution is our destiny, as it is the destiny of every race in the world.[2]

BRITAIN, IRELAND AND THE EUROPEAN UNION

Since the Reformation, Britain's relationship with the European continent has been at best uneasy, at worst queasy. At the end of the Second World War, British leaders still regarded themselves both as the leaders of a great empire and as the superior European civilisation. The British view of its place within Europe evolved within the context of decolonisation, the Cold War, and the American relationship. With the decline of the British Empire, the rise of America and the formation of the European Economic Community, however, British post-imperial melancholy hardened into Euroscepticism, as Britain retreated from imperialism to huddle under the comfort blanket of nationalism.[3]

By contrast, Mary Robinson while President of Ireland concluded that 'Europe has enhanced the national identity of Irish people'. Entry into the

---

1 P.H. Pearse, *Collected works of Padraic H. Pearse. Plays, stories, poems* (Dublin, 1922), p. 330.
2 James Stephens, 'The outlook for literature' in *The uncollected prose of James Stephens*, ed. P. McFate (New York, 1983), pp 187–8.   3 Benjamin Grob-Fitzgibbon, *Continental drift: Britain and Europe from the end of Empire to the rise of Euroscepticism* (Cambridge, 2016).

14.1 John O'Leary (1830–1907), the veteran Fenian, spent a long period in Paris, where he absorbed secularism. His gravestone at Glasnevin shows an incongrous combination of the Phrygian cap and shamrock. The rhetoric of freeman and slave permeated republicanism, to the extent that the French revolutionaries reinstated the red Phrygian cap – worn by freed slaves in republican Rome – as fashionable head wear. Yeats made O'Leary famous with two stirring lines from his poetry: 'Romantic Ireland's dead and gone; it's with O'Leary in the grave' and 'Beautiful lofty things: O'Leary's noble head' (Photograph by Laura Conlon).

European project offered Ireland an escape hatch out of a stifling confinement within a British sphere, opening the handcuffs of history. Since independence, the drive to embed Irish sovereignty by achieving economic independence from the UK became the key national interest. Ireland had been excluded from earlier engagement with globalisation given its lack of autonomy. Access to and embrace of first a European and then a globalisation project offered an enchancement rather than an erosion of Irish national identity. The EU encouraged the Republic of Ireland to emerge fully from under the long imperial and economic shadow cast by Britain.

The infantile mortality rate of new states is remarkably high and post-colonial states struggle to avoid nativism and economic introversion: crucially, the EU offered Ireland an externally oriented economic and political trajectory that avoided those pitfalls. The EU rebalanced the hitherto asymmetric relationship

between the European powers and the Irish state, as the EU at its best
functioned as a partnership of equals. France and Ireland saw eye to eye in the
EU: France was considered to be broadly sympathetic to Ireland, if only because
of a long-standing shared anglophobia (de Gaulle had commented on Churchill:
'always remember that within him breathes the soul of Pitt').[4]

EU participation released Ireland from its crippling dependency on sterling.
In 1973, the Irish economy was manacled to the pound and locked into a
depressing economic geography as a cheap food supplier for industrial Britain:
90 per cent of its exports (mostly agricultural) then went to the UK. Openness
to and engagement with Europe accelerated the maturation of the Irish state
since 1973, as well as kick-starting the Irish economy by allowing Ireland to pivot
towards being a launch pad for global investment into the EU. The Republic of
Ireland's status within the EU and its integration into the global economy as the
centre for EMEA (Europe, Middle East and Africa) allowed it to exit the
gravitational political and economic force field of Great Britain. The UK state
currently faces more constitutional and even existential threats – Brexit, the
Scottish crisis, the recrudescence of English nationalism – than the Republic of
Ireland, which has shown remarkable resilience in weathering a catastrophic
financial crisis, and enjoying a much more assured relationship with the EU.

In the Brexit crisis, the Irish state has unambiguously aligned with the EU 27
rather than Britain. Sovereignty and national democracy – the key themes of the
Irish national independence movement, but often considered to be at worst
atavistic and destabilising, at best antiquated and irrelevant – have re-emerged
as necessary democratic and centrist bulwarks against a heartless globalisation or
the siren rants of the rancid right and left.

This in turn has ensured that the Republic of Ireland remains among the
most Europhile of European countries. Whereas on entry into the EU in 1973,
the UK received 90 per cent of Irish exports, that figure has now shrunk to 17
per cent. The national population has soared since entry to the EU from 2.9m in
1970 to 4.8 m in 2017. A revitalised Dublin has asserted itself as a significant
player in the global economy. The Republic has now higher living standards than
the UK, and it has become a self-confident and mature state. All these changes
have also encouraged a psychic thaw that facilitated a much softer relationship
with the UK, underpinning a remarkably successful Peace Process that has
transformed the dreary steeples of Northern Ireland – long regarded as a
Jurassic Park of politics.

---

4 Pierre Joannon, *L'hiver du connétable. Charles de Gaulle et l'Irlande* (La Gacilly, 1991): Pierre
Joannon (ed.), *De Gaulle and Ireland* (Dublin, 1991).

CONCLUSION

The long-standing but dormant French connection was reanimated with Ireland's entry into the European project in 1973. 16,000 Irish people currently live in France and the two countries maintain cordial connections. The marvellously restored Irish Embassy, the successful reimagining of the Irish College as a cultural centre, the existence of An Ghaeltacht-sur-Seine all reflect the vibrant contemporary Irish scene in Paris. The ebullient behaviour of the Irish soccer fans in Euro 2016 charmed France.

The French novelist Michel Déon, long domiciled in Ireland, expressed this heartfelt appreciation of Ireland:

> For me, to live in Ireland had been a long-term objective delayed only by circumstances and the places where newspapers or chance were kind enough to despatch me. As a teenager and, then as a young journalist and author, I was enthused by Irish playwrights, poets, essayists and novelists. What magic had conjured up such a flowering of genius on that impoverished island in the few decades before and after it gained its independence? If I had finally managed to finish the novel that I had been struggling with for so many years, it was partly due to the culture and the people that I had met. The only problem left then was to understand why most of the Irish authors that I so much admired fled their country and lived elsewhere in the world, and mainly in France. Wilde and Yeats died there and for two decades, Joyce had his table reserved at Fouquet's on the Champs Elysée. But wherever they ended up, their main and only subject was Ireland. Was it not high time to reverse that flow and have foreign authors test a country that so greatly stirred the imagination? So we remained in Ireland, captivated by its 'terrible beauty', becoming more Irish than the Irish themselves. Ireland seeped into my novels, in one entirely, in others occasionally, as a reminder of what I saw through my window or encountered in east Galway.[5]

President Michael D. Higgins, in an address at the Sorbonne in 2013, set out the reasons why so many Irish sought answers to their perplexing questions on the banks of the Seine:

> Described by James Joyce as 'the last of the human cities', Paris was, at the beginning of the twentieth century, one of the most appropriate locations for seeing one's own people through the lens of exile, and mould-breaking writers were not alone in utilising the experience of exile, or the freedom and the stimulating company of fellow exiles in Paris. The city's diverse

---

5 Michel Déon's script in possession of Pierre Joannon.

community of dissidents was far from limited to literature. Paris was frequently both a source and inspiration of the radical ideas and deeds that led the Irish on their slow road to independence. The talk among the exiles in the cafés and in the bars sought to define the meaning of a genuine Republic, to discuss how it might be achieved, and what independence might bring with its promises of freedom, of dignity, of creativity, of solidarity, of a more complete humanity.[6]

Paris – and France – occupy a mythic role in the Irish national narrative – one definition of myth is history plus imagination.[7] Even the very possibility of Paris offered a distinct perspective and consolation: as Henry James noted, 'You may find a room very comfortable to sit in with the window open and not like it at all when the window has been shut'.[8] Paris and its vista on France has for centuries offered Irish people that open window. The pendulum of Paris/France oscillated for the Irish between the poles of myth and reality, between home and away, between an open and a closed society. Paris/Dublin, France/Ireland – the connections are long-standing, the weight of a shared history binds us together as does the buoyancy of our imaginations: long may they flourish.

6 Michael D. Higgins, *When ideas matter: speeches for an ethical republic* (London, 2016), p. 236.   7 An aphorism by John Kelly at the 1916 Conference in Monaco.   8 Henry James, *The art of travel: scenes and journeys in America, England, France and Italy*, ed. M.D. Zabel (New York, 1958), p. 215. The observation was made in Paris in 1878.

Contributors

THOMAS BARTLETT holds the Chair in Irish History at the University of Aberdeen. He was previously professor of history at University College Dublin and University College Galway. He was elected to the Royal Irish Academy in 1995 and has held visiting professorships in the US and Britain, including at Notre Dame and Cambridge. Among his books are *The fall and rise of the Irish nation: the Catholic question, 1690–1830* (1992), *A military history of Ireland* (1996) and *Ireland: a history* (2010).

LAURENT COLANTONIO is professor of British and Irish history at the Université du Québec à Montréal. His PhD was dedicated to French political uses of O'Connell. His work focuses on nineteenth-century Irish national movements. His research interests include memory issues. He recently co-authored, *La Grande Famine en Irlande* (2014). He is about to publish the first volume of his biography of Daniel O'Connell.

SEAMUS DEANE is the Donald and Marilyn Keough Professor of Irish Studies Emeritus at the University of Notre Dame. A distinguished poet, critic, novelist and public intellectual, he is a founding director of Field Day Theatre Company, the author of *A short history of Irish literature* (1986); *Celtic revivals* (1985); *The French Revolution and Enlightenment in England, 1789–1832* (1988), and *Strange country* (1997), and the editor of the *Field Day anthology*. His novel, *Reading in the dark* (1997), has been translated into more than twenty languages.

PHYLLIS GAFFNEY studied in Dublin, Strasbourg, Cambridge and Florence, and her Cambridge PhD is on medieval French. A *chevalier dans l'ordre des palmes académiques*, she lectured in French for four decades, retiring from UCD in 2015. Her research interests include French literature, translation, and Franco-Irish relations. Among her books are *Healing amid the ruins: the Irish Hospital at Saint-Lô, 1945–6* (1999) and *Constructions of childhood and youth in Old French narrative* (2011).

PIERRE JOANNON, historian, and one of the foremost French specialists on Ireland, is author of *Histoire de l'Irlande et des Irlandais* (2009), *Il était une fois Dublin* (2013) and French biographies of Michael Collins and John Hume. He is founder of the Ireland Fund of France, Honorary Consul General of Ireland in the South of France from 1973 and was awarded honorary doctorates by the National University of Ireland and the University of Ulster. In 2012, he was among the inaugural recipients of the Presidential Distinguished Service Award for his sustained promotion of Franco-Irish relations.

JANICK JULIENNE obtained her PhD from University of Paris VII (1997). She has studied the connections between France and Ireland in the nineteenth century. Her work has been published in France and Ireland, in the *Irish Sword*, *Études Irlandaises*, *La Revue française des armées*, in *Franco-Irish military connections, 1590–1945* (2009) and *Un Irlandais à Paris: John Patrick Leonard au cœur des relations franco-irlandaises, 1814–1889* (2016).

SYLVIE KLEINMAN studied history and translation in Paris and specialised in Franco-Irish links during the Revolutionary and Napoleonic wars after moving to Ireland. She was an Irish Research Council Postdoctoral Fellow at Trinity College (2007–9), and has lectured and published widely on Theobald Wolfe Tone's military career and adventures in Europe (1796–1798), and on cultural nationalism. A member of the Trinity College Centre for War Studies, she currently works in Dublin Castle.

ANNE MAGNY wrote her doctoral dissertation on Maud Gonne. Titled, 'Maud Gonne: réalité et mythe, analyse d'une présence historique et littéraire', it was defended in 1995 at the University of Caen. She has since published widely on Gonne and the links between French and Irish nationalists.

BARRY McCREA is a Professor of English, Irish and Romance Languages at the University of Notre Dame. His *Languages of the night* (2015) won the American Comparative Literature Association's award for best book of that year. He is the author of a novel, *The first verse*, and of *In the company of strangers* (2011). He holds a PhD from Princeton and was formerly a Professor of Comparative Literature at Yale University.

PIERRE RANGER completed his PhD on the history of Irish nationalism and of its links with France at the turn of the nineteenth and twentieth centuries. He published a book on the topic *La France vue d'Irlande. L'histoire du mythe français de Parnell à l'État Libre* (2011) and several articles. He has taught at Queen's University Belfast and Paris-Diderot University.

JUSTIN DOLAN STOVER is Assistant Professor of History at Idaho State University. Among his research and publication interests are the transnational history of nationalism, war and violence; First World War and interwar period; modern France; the French Revolution and its legacy; modern Ireland and the Irish Revolution and the environmental history of war.

KEVIN WHELAN is Director of the University of Notre Dame Global Gateway in Dublin since 1998. He has lectured in almost twenty countries and he has written or edited twenty books and over one hundred articles. These include *The tree of liberty* (1996), *Fellowship of freedom* (1998), and the best selling *Atlas of the Irish rural landscape* (2011).

Index

Page references in **bold** refer to images